Praise for *The New Confessions of*

"When I read *Confessions of an Economic Hit Man* I could not have known that, some years later, I would be on the receiving end of the type of 'economic hit' that Perkins so vividly narrated. This book reso-nates with my experiences of the brutish methods and gross economic irrationality guiding powerful institutions in their bid to undermine dem-ocratic control over economic power. Perkins has, once again, made a substantial contribution to a world that needs whistle-blowers to open its eyes to the true sources of political, social, and economic power."
—**Yanis Varoufakis, former Minister of Finance, Greece**

"I loved *Confessions of an Economic Hit Man*. Ten years ago it exposed the real story. *The New Confessions* tells the rest of that story—the terrible things that have happened since and what we all can do to turn a death economy into a life economy."
—**Yoko Ono**

"*The New Confessions* offers deep insights into the nefarious ways economic hit men and jackals have expanded their powers. It shows how they came home to roost in the United States—as well as the rest of the world. It is a brilliant and bold book that illuminates the crises we now face and offers a road map to stop them."
—**John Gray, PhD, author of the *New York Times* #1 bestseller *Men Are from Mars, Women Are from Venus***

"John Perkins probed the dark depths of global oligarchy and emerged into the light of hope. This true story that reads like a page-turning novel is great for all of us who want the better world that we know is possible for ourselves, future generations, and the planet."
—**Marci Shimoff, #1 *New York Times* bestselling author of *Happy for No Reason* and *Chicken Soup for the Woman's Soul***

"Perkins provides a profound analysis of two forces vying to define the future. One is intent on preserving systems that serve the few at the expense of the many, while the other promotes a new consciousness of what it means to be human on this beautiful, fragile planet. This powerful book inspires and empowers actions that manifest an awak-ening to our collective ecosystem and the rebirth of humanity—an ECOrenaissance."
—**Marci Zaroff, ECOlifestyle pioneer/serial entrepreneur and founder of ECOfashion brands Under the Canopy and Metawear**

"*The New Confessions* is an amazing guide to co-creating a human presence on our planet that honors all life as sacred. It exposes our past mistakes; offers a vision for a compassionate, sustainable future; and provides practical approaches for making the transition between the two. A must-read for anyone who loves our beautiful home, Earth."

—**Barbara Marx Hubbard, bestselling author and President, Foundation for Conscious Evolution**

"As one who has helped thousands of people grow their businesses, I've learned firsthand the importance of facing the crises old economic models created and acting positively to develop new approaches. Perkins's experiences, his exposé of the failures, his clear vision of what needs to be done, his call to action, and the sense of joy he feels for being part of this consciousness revolution are deeply inspiring."

—**Sage Lavine, women's business mentor; CEO, Conscious Women Entrepreneurs; and founder of the Entrepreneurial Leadership Academy**

Samples of What the Media Said about *Confessions of an Economic Hit Man*

"[This] book seems to have tapped into a larger vein of discontent and mistrust that Americans feel toward the ties that bind together corporations, large lending institutions and the government—a nexus that Mr. Perkins and others call the 'corporatocracy.'"

—*New York Times*

"This riveting look at a world of intrigue reads like a spy novel...Highly recommended."

—*Library Journal*

"[A] parable for all Americans who try to deny the heartbreaking fact that our society's affluence often comes at the wider world's expense."

—*Utne Reader*

"Imagine the conceptual love child of James Bond and Milton Friedman."

—*Boston Herald*

"Perkins claims may seem unthinkable to most Americans. But the evidence, looking at the world economy, is damning...the citizens of this country need to be willing to examine the actions of our political and corporate leaders and demand that they stop the destruction that is making the world an increasingly dangerous place to live."

—*Charlotte Observer*

THE NEW CONFESSIONS OF AN ECONOMIC HIT MAN

THE **NEW CONFESSIONS** OF AN **ECONOMIC HIT MAN**

JOHN PERKINS

BK

Berrett-Koehler Publishers, Inc.
a BK Currents book

BERRETT-KOEHLER PUBLISHERS, INC.
1333 Broadway, Suite 1000, Oakland, CA 94612-1921
Tel: (510) 817-2277   Fax: (510) 817-2278   www.bkconnection.com

ORDERING INFORMATION
QUANTITY SALES. Special discounts are available on quantity purchases by corporations, associations, and others. For details, contact the "Special Sales Department" at the Berrett-Koehler address above.
INDIVIDUAL SALES. Berrett-Koehler publications are available through most bookstores. They can also be ordered directly from Berrett-Koehler: Tel: (800) 929-2929; Fax: (802) 864-7626; www.bkconnection.com
ORDERS FOR COLLEGE TEXTBOOK/COURSE ADOPTION USE. Please contact Berrett-Koehler: Tel: (800) 929-2929; Fax: (802) 864-7626.
ORDERS BY U.S. TRADE BOOKSTORES AND WHOLESALERS. Please contact Ingram Publisher Services, Tel: (800) 509-4887; Fax: (800) 838-1149; E-mail: customer.service@ ingrampublisherservices.com; or visit www.ingrampublisherservices.com/Ordering for details about electronic ordering.

Berrett-Koehler and the BK logo are registered trademarks of Berrett-Koehler Publishers, Inc.

Printed in the United States of America

Berrett-Koehler books are printed on long-lasting acid-free paper. When it is available, we choose paper that has been manufactured by environmentally responsible processes. These may include using trees grown in sustainable forests, incorporating recycled paper, minimizing chlorine in bleaching, or recycling the energy produced at the paper mill.

LIBRARY OF CONGRESS CATALOGING-IN-PUBLICATION DATA
Names: Perkins, John, 1945–
Title: The new confessions of an economic hit man / John Perkins.
Other titles: Confessions of an economic hit man
Description: Oakland, CA : Berrett-Koehler Publishers, Inc., 2015. | Includes
    bibliographical references and index.
Identifiers: LCCN 2015036436 | ISBN 9781626566743 (paperback : acid-free paper)
Subjects: LCSH: Perkins, John, 1945– | Intelligence officers — United States — Biography. |
    United States. National Security Agency — Biography. Economists — United States —
    Biography. | Energy consultants — United States — Biography. | Chas. T. Main, Inc. |
    World Bank — Developing countries. | Corporations, American — Corrupt practices. |
    Imperialism — History — 20th century. | Imperialism — History — 21st century.
Classification: LCC UB271.U52 P47 2015 | DDC 332/.042092 — dc23
LC record available at http://lccn.loc.gov/2015036436

FIRST EDITION
20 19 18 17 16   10 9 8 7 6 5 4 3 2 1

Cover design: Wes Youssi, M.80 Design. Interior production and design: VJB/Scribe. Proofreader: Elissa Rabellino. Index: George Draffan. Author photo: Connie Ekelund.

To my grandmother, Lula Brisbin Moody, who taught me the power of truth, love, and imagination, and to my grandson, Grant Ethan Miller, who inspires me to do whatever it takes to create a world he and his brothers and sisters across the planet will want to inherit.

CONTENTS

John Perkins Personal History   339

Economic hit men (EHMs) are highly paid professionals who cheat countries around the globe out of trillions of dollars. They funnel money from the World Bank, the US Agency for International Development (USAID), and other foreign "aid" organizations into the coffers of huge corporations and the pockets of a few wealthy families who control the planet's natural resources. Their tools include fraudulent financial reports, rigged elections, payoffs, extortion, sex, and murder. They play a game as old as empire, but one that has taken on new and terrifying dimensions during this time of globalization.

I should know; I was an EHM.

I wrote that in 1982, as the beginning of a book with the working title *Conscience of an Economic Hit Man*. The book was dedicated to the heads of state of two countries, men who had been my clients, whom I respected and thought of as kindred spirits — Jaime Roldós of Ecuador and Omar Torrijos of Panama. Both had just died in fiery crashes. Their deaths were not accidental. They were assassinated because they opposed that fraternity of corporate, government, and banking heads whose goal is global empire. We EHMs failed to bring Roldós and Torrijos around, and the other type of hit men, the CIA-sanctioned jackals who were always right behind us, stepped in.

I was persuaded to stop writing that book. I started it four more times during the next twenty years. On each occasion, my decision to begin again was influenced by current world events: the US invasion of Panama in 1989, the first Gulf War, Somalia, the rise of Osama bin Laden. However, threats or bribes always convinced me to stop.

In 2003, the president of a major publishing house that is owned by a powerful international corporation read a draft of what had now become *Confessions of an Economic Hit Man*. He described it as "a riveting story that needs to be told." Then he smiled sadly, shook his head, and told me that since the executives at world headquarters might object, he could not afford to risk publishing it. He advised me to fictionalize it. "We could market you in the mold of a novelist like John le Carré or Graham Greene."

But this is not fiction. It is the true story of my life. It is the story of the creation of a system that has failed us. A more courageous publisher, one not owned by an international corporation, agreed to help me tell it.

What finally convinced me to ignore the threats and bribes?

The short answer is that my only child, Jessica, graduated from college and went out into the world on her own. When I told her that I was considering publishing this book and shared my fears with her, she said, "Don't worry, Dad. If they get you, I'll take over where you left off. We need to do this for the grandchildren I hope to give you someday!" That is the short answer.

The longer version relates to my dedication to the country where I was raised; to my love of the ideals expressed by our Founding Fathers; to my deep commitment to the American republic that today promises "life, liberty, and the pursuit of happiness" for all people, everywhere; and to my determination after 9/11 not to sit idly by any longer while EHMs turn that republic into a global empire. That is the skeleton version of the long answer; the flesh and blood are added in the chapters that follow.

Why was I not killed for telling this story? As I will explain in more detail in the pages of *The New Confessions of an Economic Hit Man*, the book itself became my insurance policy.

This is a true story. I lived every minute of it. The sights, the people, the conversations, and the feelings I describe were all a part of my life. It is my personal story, and yet it happened within the larger context of world events that have shaped our history, have brought us to where we are today, and form the foundation of our children's futures. I have made every effort to present these experiences, people, and conversations accurately. Whenever I discuss historical events or re-create conversations with other people, I do so with the help of several tools: published documents; personal records and notes; recollections — my own and those of others who participated; the five manuscripts I began previously; and historical accounts by other authors — most notably, recently published ones that disclose information that formerly was classified or otherwise unavailable. References are provided in the endnotes, to allow interested readers to pursue these subjects in more depth. In some cases, I combine several dialogues I had with a person into one conversation to facilitate the flow of the narrative.

My publisher asked whether we actually referred to ourselves as economic hit men. I assured him that we did, although usually only by the initials. In fact, on the day in 1971 when I began working with my teacher, Claudine, she informed me, "My assignment is to mold you into an economic hit man. No one can know about your involvement — not even your wife." Then she turned serious. "Once you're in, you're in for life."

Claudine pulled no punches when describing what I would be called upon to do. My job, she said, was "to encourage world leaders to become part of a vast network that promotes US commercial interests. In the end, those leaders become ensnared in a web of debt that ensures their loyalty. We can draw on them whenever we desire — to satisfy our political, economic, or military needs. In turn, they bolster their political positions by bringing industrial parks, power plants, and airports to their people. The owners of US engineering/construction companies become fabulously wealthy."

If we faltered, a more malicious form of hit man, the jackal, would step to the plate. And if the jackals failed, then the job fell to the military.

))

Now, nearly twelve years after *Confessions of an Economic Hit Man* was first published, that original publisher and I know that it is time for a new edition. Readers of the 2004 book sent thousands of e-mails asking how its publication impacted my life, what I am doing to redeem myself and change the EHM system, and what actions they can take to turn things around. This new book is my answer to those questions.

It is also time for a new edition because the world has changed radically. The EHM system — based primarily on debt and fear — is even more treacherous now than it was in 2004. The EHMs have radically expanded their ranks and have adopted new disguises and tools. And we in the United States have been "hit" — badly. The entire world has been hit. We know that we teeter on the edge of disaster — economic, political, social, and environmental disaster. We must change.

This story *must* be told. We live in a time of terrible crisis — and tremendous opportunity. The story of this particular economic hit man is the story of how we got to where we are and why we currently face crises that often seem insurmountable.

This book is the confession of a man who, back when I was an EHM, was part of a relatively small group. People who play similar roles are much more abundant now. They have euphemistic titles; they walk the corridors of Fortune 500 companies like Exxon, Walmart, General Motors, and Monsanto; they use the EHM system to promote their private interests.

In a very real sense, *The New Confessions of an Economic Hit Man* is the story of this new EHM breed.

It is your story, too, the story of your world and mine. We are all complicit. We must take responsibility for our world. The EHMs succeed because we collaborate with them. They seduce, cajole, and threaten us, but they win only when we look the other way or simply give in to their tactics.

By the time you read these words, events will have happened that I cannot imagine as I write them. Please see this book as offering new perspectives for understanding those events and future ones.

Admitting to a problem is the first step toward finding a solution. Confessing a sin is the beginning of redemption. Let this book, then, be the start of our salvation. Let it inspire us to new levels of dedication and drive us to realize our dream of balanced and honorable societies.

John Perkins
October 2015

The New Confessions

I'm haunted every day by what I did as an economic hit man (EHM). I'm haunted by the lies I told back then about the World Bank. I'm haunted by the ways in which that bank, its sister organizations, and I empowered US corporations to spread their cancerous tentacles across the planet. I'm haunted by the payoffs to the leaders of poor countries, the blackmail, and the threats that if they resisted, if they refused to accept loans that would enslave their countries in debt, the CIA's jackals would overthrow or assassinate them.

I wake up sometimes to the horrifying images of heads of state, friends of mine, who died violent deaths because they refused to betray their people. Like Shakespeare's Lady Macbeth, I try to scrub the blood from my hands.

But the blood is merely a symptom.

The treacherous cancer beneath the surface, which was revealed in the original *Confessions of an Economic Hit Man*, has metastasized. It has spread from the economically developing countries to the United States and the rest of the world; it attacks the very foundations of democracy and the planet's life-support systems.

All the EHM and jackal tools — false economics, false promises, threats, bribes, extortion, debt, deception, coups, assassinations, unbridled military power — are used around the world today, even more than during the era I exposed more than a decade ago. Although this cancer has spread widely and deeply, most people still aren't aware of it; yet all of us are impacted by the collapse it has caused. It has become the dominant system of economics, government, and society today.

Fear and debt drive this system. We are hammered with messages that terrify us into believing that we must pay any price, assume any debt, to stop the enemies who, we are told, lurk at our doorsteps. The problem comes from somewhere else. Insurgents.

1

Terrorists. "Them." And its solution requires spending massive amounts of money on goods and services produced by what I call the corporatocracy — vast networks of corporations, banks, colluding governments, and the rich and powerful people tied to them. We go deeply into debt; our country and its financial henchmen at the World Bank and its sister institutions coerce other countries to go deeply into debt; debt enslaves us and it enslaves those countries.

These strategies have created a "death economy" — one based on wars or the threat of war, debt, and the rape of the earth's resources. It is an unsustainable economy that depletes at ever-increasing rates the very resources upon which it depends and at the same time poisons the air we breathe, the water we drink, and the foods we eat. Although the death economy is built on a form of capitalism, it is important to note that the word *capitalism* refers to an economic and political system in which trade and industry are controlled by private owners rather than the state. It includes local farmers' markets as well as this very dangerous form of global corporate capitalism, controlled by the corporatocracy, which is predatory by nature, has created a death economy, and ultimately is self-destructive.

I decided to write *The New Confessions of an Economic Hit Man* because things have changed so much during this past decade. The cancer has spread throughout the United States as well as the rest of the world. The rich have gotten richer and everyone else has gotten poorer in real terms.

A powerful propaganda machine owned or controlled by the corporatocracy has spun its stories to convince us to accept a dogma that serves its interests, not ours. These stories contrive to convince us that we must embrace a system based on fear and debt, accumulating stuff, and dividing and conquering everyone who isn't "us." The stories have sold us the lie that the EHM system will provide security and make us happy.

Some would blame our current problems on an organized global conspiracy. I wish it were so simple. Although, as I point out later, there are hundreds of conspiracies — not just one grand conspiracy — that affect all of us, this EHM system is fueled by something far more dangerous than a global conspiracy. It is driven by concepts that have become accepted as gospel. We believe that all economic growth benefits humankind and that the greater the growth, the more widespread the benefits. Similarly, we believe that those people who excel at stoking the fires of economic growth should be exalted and rewarded, while those born at the fringes are available for exploitation. And we believe that any means — including those used by today's EHMs and jackals — are justified to promote economic growth; preserve our comfortable, affluent Western way of life; and wage war against anyone (such as Islamic terrorists) who might threaten our economic well-being, comfort, and security.

In response to readers' requests, I have added many new details and accounts of how we did our work during my time as an EHM, and I have clarified some points in the previously published chapters. More importantly, I have added an entirely new part 5, which explains how the EHM game is played today — who today's economic hit men are, who today's jackals are, and how their deceptions and tools are more far-reaching and enslaving now than ever.

Also in response to readers' requests, part 5 includes new chapters that reveal what it will take to overthrow the EHM system, and specific tactics for doing so.

The book ends with a section titled "Documentation of EHM Activity, 2004–2015," which complements my personal story by offering detailed information for readers who want further proof of the issues covered in this book or who want to pursue these subjects in more depth.

Despite all the bad news and the attempts of modern-day robber barons to steal our democracy and our planet, I am filled with hope. I know that when enough of us perceive the true workings of this EHM system, we will take the individual and collective actions necessary to control the cancer and restore our health. *The New Confessions of an Economic Hit Man* reveals how the system works today and what you and I — all of us — can do to change it.

Tom Paine inspired American revolutionaries when he wrote, "If there must be trouble, let it be in my day, that my child may have peace." Those words are as important today as they were in 1776. My goal in this new book is nothing less than Paine's: to inspire and empower us all to do whatever it takes to lead the way to peace for our children.

PART I: 1963–1971

CHAPTER 1

Dirty Business

When I graduated from business school in 1968, I was determined not to participate in the Vietnam War. I had recently married Ann. She too opposed the war and was adventurous enough to agree to join the Peace Corps with me.

We first arrived in Quito, Ecuador, in 1968. I was a twenty-three-year-old volunteer assigned to develop credit and savings cooperatives in communities deep in the Amazon rain forest. Ann's job was to teach hygiene and child care to indigenous women.

Ann had been to Europe, but it was my first trip away from North America. I knew we'd fly into Quito, one of the highest capitals in the world – and one of the poorest. I expected it to be different from anything I'd ever seen, but I was totally unprepared for the reality.

As our plane from Miami descended toward the airport, I was shocked by the hovels along the runway. I leaned across Ann in the middle seat and, pointing through my window, asked the Ecuadorian businessman in the aisle seat next to her, "Do people actually live there?"

"We are a poor country," he replied, nodding solemnly.

The scenes that greeted us on the bus ride into town were even worse – tattered beggars hobbling on homemade crutches along garbage-infested streets, children with horribly distended bellies, skeletal dogs, and shantytowns of cardboard boxes that passed as homes.

The bus delivered us to Quito's five-star hotel, the InterContinental. It was an island of luxury in that sea of poverty, and the place where I and about thirty other Peace Corps volunteers would attend several days of in-country briefings.

During the first of many lectures, we were informed that Ecuador was a combination of feudal Europe and the American Wild West. Our teachers prepped us about all the dangers: venomous

snakes, malaria, anacondas, killer parasites, and hostile head-
hunting warriors. Then the good news: Texaco had discovered vast
oil deposits, not far from where we'd be stationed in the rain forest. We were assured that oil would transform Ecuador from one
of the poorest countries in the hemisphere to one of the richest.

One afternoon, while waiting for a hotel elevator, I struck up
a conversation with a tall blond man who had a Texas drawl. He
was a seismologist, a Texaco consultant. When he learned that
Ann and I were poor Peace Corps volunteers who'd be working
in the rain forest, he invited us to dinner in the elegant restaurant
on the top floor of the hotel. I couldn't believe my good fortune. I'd
seen the menu and knew that our meal would cost more than our
monthly living allowance.

That night, as I looked through the restaurant's windows out
at Pichincha, the mammoth volcano that hovers over Ecuador's
capital, and sipped a margarita, I became infatuated with this man
and the life he lived.

He told us that sometimes he flew in a corporate jet directly
from Houston to an airstrip hacked out of the jungle. "We don't
have to endure immigration or customs," he bragged. "The Ecuadorian government gives us special permission." His rain forest
experience included air-conditioned trailers and champagne and
filet mignon dinners served on fine china. "Not quite what you'll
be getting, I assume," he said with a laugh.

He then talked about the report he was writing that described
"a vast sea of oil beneath the jungle." This report, he said, would
be used to justify huge World Bank loans to the country and to
persuade Wall Street to invest in Texaco and other businesses that
would benefit from the oil boom. When I expressed amazement
that progress could happen so rapidly, he gave me an odd look.
"What did they teach you in business school, anyway?" he asked.

I didn't know how to respond.

"Look," he said. "It's an old game. I've seen it in Asia, the Middle
East, and Africa. Now here. Seismology reports, combined with
one good oil well, a gusher like the one we just hit..." He smiled.
"Boomtown!"

Ann mentioned all the excitement around how oil would bring
prosperity to Ecuadorians.

"Only those smart enough to play the game," he said.

I'd grown up in a New Hampshire town named after a man who'd built a mansion on a hill, overlooking everyone else, using the fortune he'd amassed by selling shovels and blankets to the California gold miners in 1849. "The merchants," I said. "The businessmen and bankers."

"You bet. And today, the big corporations." He tilted back in his chair. "We own this country. We get a lot more than permission to land planes without customs formalities."

"Like what?"

"Oh my God, you do have a lot to learn, don't you?" He raised his martini toward the city. "To begin with, we control the military. We pay their salaries and buy them their equipment. They protect us from the Indians who don't want oil rigs on their lands. In Latin America, he who controls the army controls the president and the courts. We get to write the laws — set fines for oil spills, labor rates, all the laws that matter to us."

"Texaco pays for all that?" Ann asked.

"Well, not exactly…" He reached across the table and patted her arm. "You do. Or your daddy does. The American taxpayer. The money flows through USAID, the World Bank, CIA, and the Pentagon, but everyone here" — he swept his arm toward the window and the city below — "knows it's all about Texaco. Remember, countries like this have long histories of coups. If you take a good look, you'll see that most of them happen when the leaders of the country don't play our game."[1]

"Are you saying Texaco overthrows governments?" I asked.

He laughed. "Let's just say that governments that don't cooperate are seen as Soviet puppets. They threaten American interests and democracy. The CIA doesn't like that."

That night was the beginning of my education in what I've come to think of as the EHM system.

Ann and I spent the next months stationed in the Amazon rain forest. Then we were transferred to the high Andes, where I was assigned to help a group of campesino brick makers. Ann trained handicapped people for jobs in local businesses.

I was told that the brick makers needed to improve the efficiency of the archaic ovens in which their bricks were baked.

However, one after another they came to me complaining about the men who owned the trucks and the warehouses down in the city.

Ecuador was a country with little social mobility. A few wealthy families, the *ricos*, ran just about everything, including local businesses and politics. Their agents bought the bricks from the brick makers at extremely low prices and sold them at roughly ten times that amount. One brick maker went to the city mayor and complained. Several days later he was struck by a truck and killed.

Terror swept the community. People assured me that he'd been murdered. My suspicions that it was true were reinforced when the police chief announced that the dead man was part of a Cuban plot to turn Ecuador Communist (Che Guevara had been executed by a CIA operation in Bolivia less than three years earlier). He insinuated that any brick maker who caused trouble would be arrested as an insurgent.

The brick makers begged me to go to the ricos and set things right. They were willing to do anything to appease those they feared, including convincing themselves that, if they gave in, the ricos would protect them.

I didn't know what to do. I had no leverage with the mayor and figured that the intervention of a twenty-five-year-old foreigner would only make matters worse. I merely listened and sympathized.

Eventually I realized that the ricos were part of a strategy, a system that had subjugated Andean peoples through fear since the Spanish conquest. I saw that by commiserating, I was enabling the community to do nothing. They needed to learn to face their fears; they needed to admit to the anger they had suppressed; they needed to take offense at the injustices they had suffered; they needed to stop looking to me to set things right. They needed to stand up to the ricos.

Late one afternoon I spoke to the community. I told them that they had to take action. They had to do whatever it would take — including taking the risk of being killed — so that their children could prosper and live in peace.

My realization about enabling that community was a great lesson for me. I understood that the people themselves were collaborators in this conspiracy and that convincing them to take action offered the only solution. And it worked.

The brick makers formed a co-op. Each family donated bricks, and the co-op used the income from those bricks to rent a truck and warehouse in the city. The ricos boycotted the co-op, until a Lutheran mission from Norway contracted with the co-op for all the bricks for a school it was building, at about five times the amount the ricos had paid the brick makers but half the price the ricos were charging the Lutherans — a win-win situation for everyone except the ricos. The co-op flourished after that.

Less than a year later, Ann and I completed our Peace Corps assignment. I was twenty-six and no longer subject to the draft. I became an EHM.

When I first entered those ranks, I convinced myself that I was doing the right thing. South Vietnam had fallen to the Communist north, and now the world was threatened by the Soviet Union and China. My business school professors had taught that financing infrastructure projects through mountains of World Bank debt would pull economically developing nations out of poverty and save them from the clutches of communism. Experts at the World Bank and USAID reinforced this mind-set.

By the time I discovered the falsehoods in that story, I felt trapped by the system. I had grown up feeling poor in my New Hampshire boarding school, but suddenly I was making a great deal of money, traveling first class to countries I'd dreamed about all my life, staying in the best hotels, eating in the finest restaurants, and meeting with heads of state. I had it made. How could I even consider getting out?

Then the nightmares began.

I woke in dark hotel rooms sweating, haunted by images of sights I had actually seen: legless lepers strapped into wooden boxes on wheels, rolling along the streets of Jakarta; men and women bathing in slime-green canals while, next to them, others defecated; a human cadaver abandoned on a garbage heap, swarming with maggots and flies; and children who slept in cardboard boxes, vying with roaming packs of dogs for scraps of rubbish. I realized that I'd distanced myself emotionally from these things.

Like other Americans, I'd seen these people as less than human; they were "beggars," "misfits" — "them."

One day my Indonesian government limo stopped at a traffic light. A leper thrust the gory remnants of a hand through my window. My driver yelled at him. The leper grinned, a lopsided toothless smile, and withdrew. We drove on, but his spirit remained with me. It was as though he had sought me out; his bloody stump was a warning, his smile a message. "Reform," he seemed to say. "Repent."

I began to look more closely at the world around me. And at myself. I came to understand that although I had all the trappings of success, I was miserable. I'd been popping Valium every night and drinking lots of alcohol. I'd get up in the morning, force coffee and pep pills into my system, and stagger off to negotiate contracts worth hundreds of millions of dollars.

That life had come to seem normal to me. I had bought into the stories. I was taking on debt to support my lifestyle. I was operating out of fear — the fear of communism, losing my job, failure, and not having the material things everyone told me I needed.

One night I woke up with the memory of a different type of dream.

I had walked into the office of a leader in a country that had just discovered it had lots of oil. "Our construction companies," I told him, "will rent equipment from your brother's John Deere franchise. We'll pay twice the going rate; your brother can share his profits with you." In the dream I went on to explain that we'd make similar deals with friends of his who owned Coca-Cola bottling plants, other food and beverage suppliers, and labor contractors. All he had to do was sign off on a World Bank loan that would hire US corporations to build infrastructure projects in his country.

Then I casually mentioned that a refusal would bring in the jackals. "Remember," I said, "what happened to . . ." I rattled off a list of names like Mossedegh of Iran, Arbenz of Guatemala, Allende of Chile, Lumumba of the Congo, Diem of Vietnam. "All of them," I said, "were overthrown or . . ." — I ran a finger across my throat — "because they didn't play our game."

I lay there in bed, once again in a cold sweat, realizing that this dream described my reality. I had done all that.

It had been easy for me to provide government officials like the one in my dream with impressive materials that they could use to justify the loans to their people. My staff of economists, financial experts, statisticians, and mathematicians was skilled at developing sophisticated econometric models that proved that such investments — in electric power systems, highways, ports, airports, and industrial parks — would spur economic growth.

For years I also had relied on those models to convince myself that my actions were beneficial. I had justified my job by the fact that gross domestic product did increase after the infrastructure was built. Now I came to face the facts of the story behind the mathematics. The statistics were highly biased; they were skewed to the fortunes of the families that owned the industries, banks, shopping malls, supermarkets, hotels, and a variety of other businesses that prospered from the infrastructure we built.

They prospered.

Everyone else suffered.

Money that had been budgeted for health care, education, and other social services was diverted to pay interest on the loans. In the end, the principal was never paid down; the country was shackled by debt. Then International Monetary Fund (IMF) hit men arrived and demanded that the government offer its oil or other resources to our corporations at cut-rate prices, and that the country privatize its electric, water, sewer, and other public sector institutions and sell them to the corporatocracy. Big business was the big winner.

In every case, a key condition of such loans was that the projects would be built by our engineering and construction companies. Most of the money never left the United States; it simply was transferred from banking offices in Washington to engineering offices in New York, Houston, or San Francisco. We EHMs also made sure that the recipient country agreed to buy airplanes, medicines, tractors, computer technologies, and other goods and services from our corporations.

Despite the fact that the money was returned almost immediately to the corporate members of the corporatocracy, the recipient country (the debtor) was required to pay it all back, principal plus interest. If an EHM was completely successful, the loans were so large that the debtor was forced to default on its payments after a few years. When this happened, we EHMs, like the Mafia, demanded our pound of flesh. This often included one or more of the following: control over United Nations votes, the installation of military bases, or access to precious resources such as oil. Of course, the debtor still owed us the money — and another country was added to our global empire.

Those nightmares helped me see that my life was not the life I wanted. I began to realize that, like the Andean brick makers, I had to take responsibility for my life, for what I was doing to myself and to those people and their countries. But before I could grasp the deeper significance of this understanding that had begun to stir within me, I had to answer a crucial question: How did a nice kid from rural New Hampshire ever get into such a dirty business?

CHAPTER 2

An Economic Hit Man Is Born

It began innocently enough.

I was an only child, born into the middle class in 1945. Both my parents came from three centuries of New England Yankee stock; their strict, moralistic, staunchly Republican attitudes reflected generations of puritanical ancestors. They were the first in their families to attend college — on scholarships. My mother became a high school Latin teacher. My father joined World War II as a Navy lieutenant and was in charge of the armed guard gun crew on a highly flammable merchant marine tanker in the Atlantic. When I was born, in Hanover, New Hampshire, he was recuperating from a broken hip in a Texas hospital. I did not see him until I was a year old.

He took a job teaching languages at Tilton School, a boys' boarding school in rural New Hampshire. The campus stood high on a hill, proudly — some would say arrogantly — towering over the town of the same name. This exclusive institution limited its enrollment to about fifty students in each grade level, nine through twelve. The students were mostly the scions of wealthy families from Buenos Aires, Caracas, Boston, and New York.

My family was cash starved; however, we most certainly did not see ourselves as poor. Although the school's teachers received very little salary, all our needs were met at no charge: food, housing, heat, water, and the workers who mowed our lawn and shoveled our snow. Beginning on my fourth birthday, I ate in the prep school dining room, shagged balls for the soccer teams my dad coached, and handed out towels in the locker room.

It is an understatement to say that the teachers and their spouses felt superior to the locals. I used to hear my parents joking about being the lords of the manor, ruling over the lowly peasants — the townies. I knew it was more than a joke.

My elementary and middle school friends belonged to that peasant class; they were very poor. Their parents were farmers, lumberjacks, and mill workers. They resented the "preppies on the hill," and in turn, my father and mother discouraged me from socializing with the townie girls, whom my dad sometimes referred to as "sluts." I had shared schoolbooks and crayons with these girls since first grade, and over the years, I fell in love with three of them: Ann, Priscilla, and Judy. I had a hard time understanding my parents' perspective; however, I deferred to their wishes.

Every year we spent the three months of my dad's summer vacation at a lake cottage built by my grandfather in 1921. It was surrounded by forests, and at night we could hear owls and mountain lions. We had no neighbors; I was the only child within walking distance. In the early years, I passed the days by pretending that the trees were knights of the Round Table and damsels in distress named Ann, Priscilla, or Judy (depending on the year). My passion was, I had no doubt, as strong as that of Lancelot for Guinevere — and just as secretive.

At fourteen, I received free tuition to Tilton School. With my parents' prodding, I rejected everything to do with the town and never saw my old friends again. When my new classmates went home to their mansions and penthouses for vacation, I remained alone on the hill. Their girlfriends were debutantes; I had no girlfriends. All the girls I knew were "sluts"; I had cast them off, and they had forgotten me. I was alone — and terribly frustrated.

My parents were masters at manipulation. They assured me that I was privileged to have such an opportunity and that someday I would be grateful. I would find the perfect wife, one suited to our high moral standards. Inside, though, I seethed. I craved female companionship — the idea of sex was most alluring.

However, rather than rebelling, I repressed my rage and expressed my frustration by excelling. I was an honors student, captain of two varsity teams, editor of the school newspaper. I was determined to show up my rich classmates and to leave Tilton behind forever. During my senior year, I was awarded a full scholarship to Brown. Although Ivy League schools did not officially grant athletic scholarships, this one came with a clear understanding that I would commit to playing soccer. I also was awarded a purely academic scholarship to Middlebury. I chose Brown, mainly because I preferred being an athlete – and because it was located in a city. My mother had graduated from Middlebury and my father had received his master's degree there, so even though Brown was in the Ivy League, they preferred Middlebury.

"What if you break your leg?" my father asked. "Better to take the academic scholarship." I buckled.

Middlebury was, in my perception, merely an inflated version of Tilton – albeit in rural Vermont instead of rural New Hampshire. True, it was coed, but I was poor in comparison to most everyone else in that school, and I had not attended school with a female in four years. I lacked confidence, felt outclassed, was miserable. I pleaded with my dad to let me drop out or take a year off. I wanted to move to Boston and learn about life and women. He would not hear of it. "How can I pretend to prepare other parents' kids for college if my own won't stay in one?" he asked.

I have come to understand that life is composed of a series of coincidences. How we react to these – how we exercise what some refer to as free will – is everything; the choices we make within the boundaries of the twists of fate determine who we are. Two major coincidences that shaped my life occurred at Middlebury. One came in the form of an Iranian, the son of a general who was a personal adviser to the shah; the other was a young woman named Ann, just like my childhood sweetheart.

The first, whom I will call Farhad, had played professional soccer in Rome. He was endowed with an athletic physique, curly black hair, soft walnut eyes, and a background and charisma that made him irresistible to women. He was my opposite in many ways. I worked hard to win his friendship, and he taught me many things that would serve me well in the years to come. I also met Ann. Although she was seriously dating a young man who attended another college, she took me under her wing. Our platonic relationship was the first truly loving one I had ever experienced.

Farhad encouraged me to drink, party, and ignore my parents. I consciously chose to stop studying. I decided I would break my academic leg to get even with my father. My grades plummeted; I lost my scholarship. The college gave me a loan. It was my first introduction to debt. It felt dirty to me, this idea that I would be shackled to paying off the principal – plus interest – after I graduated.

Halfway through my sophomore year, I elected to drop out. My father threatened to disown me; Farhad egged me on. I stormed into the dean's office and quit school. It was a pivotal moment in my life.

Farhad and I celebrated my last night in town together at a local bar. A drunken farmer, a giant of a man, accused me of flirting with his wife, picked me up off my feet, and hurled me against a wall. Farhad stepped between us, drew a knife, and slashed the farmer open at the cheek. Then he dragged me across the room and shoved me through a window, out onto a ledge high above Otter Creek. We jumped and made our way along the river and back to our dorm.

The next morning, when interrogated by the campus police, I lied and refused to admit any knowledge of the incident. Nevertheless, Farhad was expelled. We both moved to Boston and shared an apartment there. I landed a job at Hearst's *Record American/Sunday Advertiser* newspapers, as a personal assistant to the editor in chief of the *Sunday Advertiser*.

Later that year, 1965, several of my friends at the newspaper were drafted. To avoid a similar fate, I entered Boston University's College of Business Administration. By then, Ann had broken up with her old boyfriend, and she often traveled down from Middlebury to visit. I welcomed her attention. She was very funny and playful, and she helped soften the anger I felt over the Vietnam War. She had been an English major and inspired me to write short stories. She graduated in 1967, while I still had another year to complete at BU. She adamantly refused to move in with me until we were married. Although I joked about being blackmailed, and in fact did resent what I saw as a continuation of my parents' archaic and prudish set of moral standards, I enjoyed our times together and I wanted more. We married.

Ann's father, a brilliant engineer, had masterminded the navigational system for an important class of missile and was rewarded with a high-level position in the Department of the Navy. His best friend, a man that Ann called Uncle Frank (not his real name), was employed as an executive at the highest echelons of the National Security Agency (NSA), the country's least-known – and by most accounts largest – spy organization.

Shortly after our marriage, the military summoned me for my physical. I passed and therefore faced the prospect of Vietnam upon graduation. The idea of fighting in Southeast Asia tore me apart emotionally, though war has always fascinated me. I was raised on tales about my colonial ancestors — who include Thomas Paine and Ethan Allen — and I had visited all the New England and upstate New York battle sites of both the French and Indian and the Revolutionary wars. I read every historical novel I could find. In fact, when Army Special Forces units first entered Southeast Asia, I was eager to sign up. But as the media exposed the atrocities and the inconsistencies of US policy, I experienced a change of heart. I found myself wondering whose side Paine would have taken. I was sure he would have joined our Vietcong enemies.

Uncle Frank came to my rescue. He informed me that an NSA job made one eligible for draft deferment, and he arranged for a series of meetings at his agency, including a day of grueling polygraph-monitored interviews. I was told that these tests would determine whether I was suitable material for NSA recruitment and training, and if I was, they would provide a profile of my strengths and weaknesses, which would be used to map out my career. Given my attitude toward the Vietnam War, I was convinced I would fail the tests.

Under examination I admitted that, as a loyal American, I opposed the war, and I was surprised when the interviewers did not pursue this subject. Instead, they focused on my upbringing, my attitudes toward my parents, the emotions generated by the fact that I grew up feeling like a poor puritan among so many wealthy, hedonistic preppies. They also explored my frustration about the lack of women, sex, and money in my life, and the fantasy world that had evolved as a result. I was amazed by the attention they gave to my relationship with Farhad and their interest in my willingness to lie to the campus police to protect him.

At first I assumed that all these things that seemed so negative to me marked me as an NSA reject, but the interviews continued, suggesting otherwise. It was not until several years later that I realized that, from an NSA viewpoint, these negatives actually were positive. Their assessment had less to do with issues of loyalty to my country than with the frustrations of my life. Anger at my parents, an obsession with women, and my ambition to live the good life gave them a hook; I was seducible. My determination to excel in school and in sports, my ultimate rebellion against my father, my ability to get along with foreigners, and my willingness to lie to the police were exactly the types of attributes they sought. I also discovered, later, that Farhad's father worked for the US intelligence community in Iran; my friendship with Farhad was therefore a definite plus.

A few weeks after the NSA testing, I was offered a job to start training in the art of spying, to begin after I received my degree from BU several months later. However, before I had officially accepted this offer, I impulsively attended a seminar given at BU by a Peace Corps recruiter. A major selling point was that, like the NSA's, Peace Corps jobs made one eligible for draft deferments.

The decision to sit in on that seminar was one of those coincidences that seemed insignificant at the time but turned out to have life-changing implications. The recruiter described several places in the world that especially needed volunteers. One of these was the Amazon rain forest, where, he pointed out, indigenous people lived very much as natives of North America had until the arrival of Europeans.

I had always dreamed of living like the Abenaki who inhabited New Hampshire when my ancestors first settled there. I knew I had Abenaki blood in my veins, and I wanted to learn the type of forest lore they understood so well. I approached the recruiter after his talk and asked about the possibility of being assigned to the Amazon. He assured me there was a great need for volunteers in that region and that my chances would be excellent. I called Uncle Frank.

To my surprise, Uncle Frank encouraged me to consider the Peace Corps. He confided that after the fall of Hanoi — which in those days was deemed a certainty by men in his position — the Amazon would become a hot spot.

"Loaded with oil," he said. "We'll need good agents there — people who understand the natives." He assured me that the Peace Corps would be an excellent training ground, and he urged me to become proficient in Spanish as well as in local indigenous dialects. "You might," he chuckled, "end up working for a private company instead of the government."

I did not understand what he meant by that at the time. I was being upgraded from spy to EHM, although I had never heard the term and would not for a few more years. I had no idea that there were hundreds of men and women scattered around the world, working for consulting firms and other private companies, people who never received a penny of salary from any government agency and yet were serving the interests of empire. Nor could I have guessed that a new type, with more euphemistic titles, would number in the thousands by the end of the millennium, and that I would play a significant role in shaping this growing army.

Ann and I applied to the Peace Corps and requested an assignment in the Amazon. When our acceptance notification arrived, my first reaction was one of extreme disappointment. The letter stated that we would be sent to Ecuador.

Oh no, I thought. *I requested the Amazon, not Africa.*

I went to an atlas and looked up Ecuador. I was dismayed when I could not find it anywhere on the African continent. In the index, though, I discovered that it is indeed located in Latin America, and I saw on the map that the river systems flowing off its Andean glaciers form the headwaters to the mighty Amazon. Further reading assured me that Ecuador's jungles were some of the world's most diverse and formidable, and that the indigenous people still lived much as they had for millennia. We accepted.

Ann and I completed Peace Corps training in Southern California and headed for Ecuador in September 1968. We lived in the Amazon in the territory of the Shuar, whose lifestyle did indeed resemble that of precolonial North Americans. Then we moved to the Andes, where I worked with the brick makers, descendants of the Incas. It was a side of the world I never dreamed still existed. Until then, the only Latin Americans I had met were the wealthy preppies at the school where my father taught. I found myself sympathizing with these indigenous people who subsisted on hunting, farming, and molding bricks from local clay and baking them in primitive ovens. I felt an odd sort of kinship with them. Somehow, they reminded me of the townies I had left behind.

One day a man in a business suit, Einar Greve, landed at the airstrip in our community. He was a vice president at Chas. T. Main,

Inc. (MAIN), an international consulting firm that kept a very
low profile and was in charge of studies to determine whether the
World Bank should lend Ecuador and its neighboring countries
billions of dollars to build hydroelectric dams and other infrastructure projects. Einar also was a colonel in the US Army Reserve.

He started talking with me about the benefits of working for a
company like MAIN. When I mentioned that I had been accepted
by the NSA before joining the Peace Corps, and that I was considering going back to them, he informed me that he sometimes
acted as an NSA liaison; he gave me a look that made me suspect
that part of his assignment was to evaluate my capabilities. I now
believe that he was updating my profile, and especially sizing up
my abilities to survive in environments most North Americans
would find hostile.

We spent a couple of days together in Ecuador and afterward
communicated by mail. He asked me to send him reports assess-
ing Ecuador's economic prospects. I had a small portable type-
writer, loved to write, and was quite happy to comply with this
request. Over a period of about a year, I sent Einar at least fifteen
long letters. In these letters, I speculated on Ecuador's economic
and political future and appraised the growing frustration among
the indigenous communities as they struggled to confront oil companies, international development agencies, and other attempts to
draw them into the modern world.

When my Peace Corps tour was over, Einar invited me to a job
interview at MAIN headquarters in Boston. During our private
meeting, he emphasized that MAIN's primary business was engineering but that his biggest client, the World Bank, recently had
begun insisting that he keep economists on staff to produce the
critical economic forecasts used to determine the feasibility and
magnitude of engineering projects. He confided that he had previously hired three highly qualified economists with impeccable
credentials — two with master's degrees and one with a PhD. They
had failed miserably.

"None of them," Einar said, "can handle the idea of producing
economic forecasts in countries where reliable statistics aren't
available." He went on to tell me that, in addition, all of them had
found it impossible to fulfill the terms of their contracts, which

required them to travel to remote places in countries such as Ecuador, Indonesia, Iran, and Egypt, to interview local leaders, and to provide personal assessments about the prospects for economic development in those regions. One had suffered a nervous breakdown in an isolated Panamanian village; he was escorted by Panamanian police to the airport and put on a plane back to the United States.

"The letters you sent me indicate that you don't mind sticking your neck out, even when hard data isn't available. And given your living conditions in Ecuador, I'm confident you can survive almost anywhere." He told me that he already had fired one of those economists and was prepared to do the same with the other two, if I accepted the job.

So it was that in January 1971 I was offered a position as an economist with MAIN. I had turned twenty-six — the magical age when the draft board no longer wanted me. I consulted with Ann's family; they encouraged me to take the job, and I assumed this reflected Uncle Frank's attitude as well. I recalled him mentioning the possibility that I would end up working for a private firm. Nothing was ever stated openly, but I had no doubt that my employment at MAIN was a consequence of the arrangements Uncle Frank had made three years earlier, in addition to my experiences in Ecuador and my willingness to write about that country's economic and political situation.

My head reeled for several weeks, and I had a very swollen ego. I had earned only a bachelor's degree from BU, which did not seem to warrant a position as an economist with such a lofty consulting company. I knew that many of my BU classmates who had been rejected by the draft and had gone on to earn MBAs and other graduate degrees would be overcome with jealousy. I visualized myself as a dashing secret agent, heading off to exotic lands, lounging beside hotel swimming pools, surrounded by gorgeous bikini-clad women, martini in hand.

Although this was merely fantasy, I would discover that it held elements of truth. Einar had hired me as an economist, but I was soon to learn that my real job went far beyond that, and that it was in fact closer to James Bond's than I ever could have guessed.

CHAPTER 3

"In for Life"

In legal parlance, MAIN would be called a closely held corporation; roughly 5 percent of its two thousand employees owned the company. These were referred to as partners or associates, and their position was coveted. Not only did the partners have power over everyone else, but also they made the big bucks. Discretion was their hallmark; they dealt with heads of state and other chief executive officers who expected their consultants, like their attorneys and psychotherapists, to honor a strict code of absolute confidentiality. Talking with the press was taboo. It simply was not tolerated. As a consequence, hardly anyone outside MAIN had ever heard of us, although many were familiar with our competitors, such as Arthur D. Little, Stone & Webster, Brown & Root, Halliburton, and Bechtel.

I use the term *competitors* loosely, because in fact MAIN was in a league by itself. The majority of our professional staff was engineers, yet we owned no equipment and never constructed so much as a storage shed. Many MAINers were ex-military; however, we did not contract with the Department of Defense or with any of the military services. Our stock-in-trade was something so different from the norm that during my first months there even I could not figure out what we did. I knew only that my first real assignment would be in Indonesia, and that I would be part of an eleven-man team sent to create a master energy plan for the island of Java.

I also knew that Einar and others who discussed the job with me were eager to convince me that Java's economy would boom, and that if I wanted to distinguish myself as a good forecaster (and to therefore be offered promotions), I would produce projections that demonstrated as much.

"Right off the chart," Einar liked to say. He would glide his fingers through the air and up over his head. "An economy that will soar like a bird!"

Einar took frequent trips that usually lasted only two to three days. No one talked much about them or seemed to know where he had gone. When he was in the office, he often invited me to sit with him for a few minutes over coffee. He asked about Ann, our new apartment, and the cat we had brought with us from Ecuador. I grew bolder as I came to know him better, and I tried to learn more about him and what I would be expected to do in my job. But I never received answers that satisfied me; he was a master at turning conversations around. On one such occasion, he gave me a peculiar look.

"You needn't worry," he said. "We have high expectations for you. I was in Washington recently . . ." His voice trailed off and he smiled inscrutably. "In any case, you know we have a big project in Kuwait. It'll be a while before you leave for Indonesia. I think you should use some of your time to read up on Kuwait. The Boston Public Library is a great resource, and we can get you passes to the MIT and Harvard libraries."

After that, I spent many hours in those libraries, especially in the BPL, which was located a few blocks away from the office and very close to my Back Bay apartment. I became familiar with Kuwait as well as with many books on economic statistics, published by the United Nations, the International Monetary Fund, and the World Bank. I knew that I would be expected to produce econometric models for Indonesia and Java, and I decided that I might as well get started by doing one for Kuwait.

However, my BS in business administration had not prepared me as an econometrician, so I spent a lot of time trying to figure out how to go about it. I went so far as to enroll in a couple of courses on the subject. In the process, I discovered that statistics can be manipulated to produce a large array of conclusions, including those substantiating the predilections of the analyst.

MAIN was a macho corporation; only four women held professional positions in 1971. However, there were perhaps two hundred women divided between the cadres of personal secretaries — every vice president and department manager had one — and the steno pool, which served the rest of us. I had become accustomed to this gender bias, and I was therefore especially astounded by what happened one day in the BPL's reference section.

A self-assured businesswoman strode over to me and sat in a chair across the table. In her dark-green business suit, she looked very sophisticated. I judged her to be several years my senior, but I tried to focus on not noticing her, on acting indifferent. After a few minutes, without a word, she slid an open book in my direction. It contained a table with information I had been searching for about Kuwait — and a card with her name, Claudine Martin, and her title, Special Consultant to Chas. T. Main, Inc. I looked up into her soft green eyes, and she extended her hand.

"I've been asked to help in your training," she said. I could not believe this was happening to me.

Beginning the next day, we met in Claudine's Beacon Street apartment, a few blocks from MAIN's Prudential Center headquarters. During our first hour together, she explained that my position was an unusual one and that we needed to keep everything highly confidential. Then she laughed self-consciously and informed me that her assignment was to mold me into an economic hit man.

The very name awakened old cloak-and-dagger dreams. I was embarrassed by my own nervous laughter. She smiled and assured me that humor was one of the reasons they used the term. "Who would take it seriously?" she asked.

I confessed ignorance about the role of economic hit men.

"You're not alone," she said, and for a moment I thought I caught a glimpse of a crack in her self-confidence. "We're a rare breed, in a dirty business. No one can know about your involvement — not even your wife." Then she turned serious. "I'll be very frank with you, teach you all I can during the next weeks. Then you'll have to choose. Your decision is final. Once you're in, you're in for life." After that, she seldom used the full name; we were simply EHMs.

I know now what I did not then — that Claudine took full advantage of the personality weaknesses the NSA profile had disclosed about me. I do not know who supplied her with the information — Einar, the NSA, MAIN's personnel department, or someone else — only that she used it masterfully. Her approach, a combination of physical seduction and verbal manipulation, was tailored specifically for me, and yet it fit within the standard operating procedures I have since seen used by a variety of businesses when the stakes are high and the pressure to close lucrative deals is great. Claudine and her superiors knew from the start that I would not jeopardize my marriage by disclosing our clandestine activities. And she was brutally frank when it came to describing the shadowy side of things that would be expected of me.

I have no idea who paid her salary, although I have no reason to suspect that it was not, as her business card implied, MAIN. At the time, I was too naive, intimidated, and bedazzled to ask the questions that today seem so obvious.

Claudine told me that there were two primary objectives of my work. First, I was to justify huge international loans that would funnel money back to MAIN and other US companies (such as Bechtel, Halliburton, Stone & Webster, and Brown & Root) through massive engineering and construction projects. Second, I would work to bankrupt the countries that received those loans (after they had paid MAIN and the other US contractors, of course), so that they would be forever beholden to their creditors and would present easy targets when we needed favors, such as military bases, UN votes, or access to oil and other natural resources.

My job, she said, was to forecast the effects of investing billions of dollars in a country. Specifically, I would produce studies that projected economic growth twenty to twenty-five years into the future and that evaluated the impacts of a variety of projects. For example, if a decision was made to lend a country $1 billion to persuade its leaders not to align with the Soviet Union, I would compare the benefits of investing that money in power plants with the benefits of investing in a new national railroad network or a telecommunications system. Or I might be told that the country was being offered the opportunity to receive a modern electric utility system, and it would be up to me to demonstrate that such a system would result in sufficient economic growth to justify the loan. The critical factor, in every case, was gross national product. The project that resulted in the highest average annual growth of GNP won. If only one project was under consideration, I would need to demonstrate that developing it would bring superior benefits to the GNP.

The unspoken aspect of every one of these projects was that

they were intended to create large profits for the contractors, and to make a handful of wealthy and influential families in the receiving countries very happy, while assuring the long-term financial dependence and therefore the political loyalty of governments around the world. The larger the loan, the better. The fact that the debt burden placed on a country would deprive its poorest citizens of health care, education, and other social services for decades to come was not taken into consideration.

Claudine and I openly discussed the deceptive nature of GNP. For instance, GNP may show growth even when it profits only one person, such as an individual who owns a utility company, and even if the majority of the population is burdened with debt. The rich get richer and the poor grow poorer. Yet, from a statistical standpoint, this is recorded as economic progress.

Like US citizens in general, most MAIN employees believed we were doing countries favors when we built power plants, highways, and ports. Our schools and our press have taught us to perceive all of our actions as altruistic. Over the years, I've repeatedly heard comments like, "If they're going to burn the US flag and demonstrate against our embassy, why don't we just get out of their damn country and let them wallow in their own poverty?"

I now know that people who say such things often hold diplomas certifying that they are well educated. However, these people have no clue that the main reason we establish embassies around the world is to serve our own interests, which during the last half of the twentieth century meant creating history's first truly global empire — a corporate empire supported and driven by the US government. Despite their credentials, such people are as uneducated as those eighteenth-century colonists who believed that the Indians fighting to defend their lands were servants of the devil.

Within several months, I would leave for the island of Java in the country of Indonesia, described at that time as the most heavily populated piece of real estate on the planet. Indonesia also happened to be an oil-rich Muslim nation and a hotbed of Communist activity.

"It's the next domino after Vietnam," is the way Claudine put it. "We must win the Indonesians over. If they join the Communist bloc, well..." She drew a finger across her throat and then smiled sweetly. "Let's just say you need to come up with a very optimistic forecast of the economy, how it will mushroom after all the new power plants and distribution lines are built. That will allow USAID and the international banks to justify the loans. You'll be well rewarded, of course, and can move on to other projects in exotic places. The world is your shopping cart." She went on to warn me that my role would be tough. "Experts at the banks will come after you. It's their job to punch holes in your forecasts — that's what they're paid to do. Making you look bad makes them look good."

One day I reminded Claudine that the MAIN team being sent to Java included ten other men. I asked if they all were receiving the same type of training as me. She assured me they were not.

"They're engineers," she said. "They design power plants, transmission and distribution lines, and seaports and roads to bring in the fuel. You're the one who predicts the future. Your forecasts determine the magnitude of the systems they design — and the size of the loans. You see, you're the key."

Every time I walked away from Claudine's apartment, I wondered whether I was doing the wrong thing. Somewhere in my heart, I suspected I was. But the frustrations of my past lingered. MAIN seemed to offer everything my life had lacked. In the end, I convinced myself that by learning more, by experiencing it, I could better expose it later — the old "working from the inside" justification.

When I shared this idea with Claudine, she gave me a perplexed look. "Don't be ridiculous. Once you're in, you can never get out. You must decide for yourself, before you get in any deeper." I understood her, and what she said frightened me. After I left, I strolled down Commonwealth Avenue, turned onto Dartmouth Street, and assured myself that I was the exception.

One afternoon some months later, Claudine and I sat on a window settee watching the snow fall on Beacon Street. "We're a small, exclusive club," she said. "We're paid — well paid — to cheat countries around the globe out of billions of dollars. A large part of your job is to encourage world leaders to become part of a vast network that promotes US commercial interests. In the end, those leaders become ensnared in a web of debt that ensures their loyalty. We can draw on them whenever we desire—to satisfy our political, economic, or military needs. In turn, these leaders bolster their political positions by bringing industrial parks, power plants, and airports to their people. Meanwhile, the owners of US engineering and construction companies become very wealthy."

That afternoon, in the idyllic setting of Claudine's apartment, relaxing in the window while snow swirled around outside, I learned the history of the profession I was about to enter. Claudine described how, throughout most of history, empires were built largely through military force or the threat of it. But with the end of World War II, the emergence of the Soviet Union, and the specter of nuclear holocaust, the military solution became just too risky.

The decisive moment occurred in 1951, when Iran rebelled against a British oil company that was exploiting Iran's natural resources and its people. The company was the forerunner of British Petroleum, today's BP. In response, the highly popular, democratically elected Iranian prime minister (and *Time* magazine's Man of the Year in 1951), Mohammad Mossadegh, nationalized all Iranian petroleum assets. An outraged England sought the help of her World War II ally, the United States. However, both countries feared that military retaliation would provoke the Soviet Union into taking action on behalf of Iran.

Instead of sending in the Marines, therefore, Washington dispatched CIA agent Kermit Roosevelt (Theodore's grandson). He performed brilliantly, winning people over through payoffs and threats. He then enlisted them to organize a series of street riots and violent demonstrations, which created the impression that Mossadegh was both unpopular and inept. In the end, Mossadegh went down, and he spent the rest of his life under house arrest. The pro-American Mohammad Reza Shah Pahlavi became the unchallenged dictator. Kermit Roosevelt had set the stage for a new profession, the ranks of which I was joining.[1]

Roosevelt's gambit reshaped Middle Eastern history even as it rendered obsolete all the old strategies for empire building. It also coincided with the beginning of experiments in "limited nonnuclear military actions," which ultimately resulted in US humiliations in Korea and Vietnam. By 1968, the year I interviewed with the NSA, it had become clear that if the United States wanted to realize its dream of global empire (as envisioned by men like presidents Johnson and Nixon), it would have to employ strategies modeled on Roosevelt's Iranian example. This was the only way to beat the Soviets without the threat of nuclear war.

There was one problem, however. Kermit Roosevelt was a CIA employee. Had he been caught, the consequences would have been dire. He had orchestrated the first US operation to overthrow a foreign government, and it was likely that many more would follow, but it was important to find an approach that would not directly implicate Washington.

Fortunately for the strategists, the 1960s also witnessed another type of revolution: the empowerment of international corporations and of multinational organizations such as the World Bank and the IMF. The latter were financed primarily by the United States and our sister empire builders in Europe. A symbiotic relationship developed between governments, corporations, and multinational organizations.

By the time I enrolled in Boston University's business school, a solution to the Roosevelt-as-CIA-agent problem had already been worked out. US intelligence agencies — including the NSA — would identify prospective EHMs, who could then be hired by international corporations. These EHMs would never be paid by the government; instead, they would draw their salaries from the private sector. As a result, their dirty work, if exposed, would be chalked up to corporate greed rather than to government policy. In addition, the corporations that hired them, although paid by government agencies and their multinational banking counterparts (with taxpayer money), would be insulated from congressional oversight and public scrutiny, shielded by a growing body of legal initiatives, including trademark, international trade, and Freedom of Information laws.[2]

"So you see," Claudine concluded, "we are just the next generation in a proud tradition that began back when you were in first grade."

CHAPTER 4

Indonesia: Lessons for an EHM

In addition to learning about my new career, I spent time reading books about Indonesia. "The more you know about a country before you get there, the easier your job will be," Claudine had advised. I took her words to heart.

When Columbus set sail in 1492, he was trying to reach Indonesia, known at the time as the Spice Islands. Throughout the colonial era, it was considered a treasure worth far more than the Americas. Java, with its rich fabrics, fabled spices, and opulent kingdoms, was both the crown jewel and the scene of violent clashes among Spanish, Dutch, Portuguese, and British adventurers. The Netherlands emerged triumphant in 1750, but even though the Dutch controlled Java, it took them more than 150 years to subdue the outer islands.

When the Japanese invaded Indonesia during World War II, Dutch forces offered little resistance. As a result, Indonesians, especially the Javanese, suffered terribly. Following the Japanese surrender, a charismatic leader named Sukarno emerged to declare independence. Four years of fighting finally ended on December 27, 1949, when the Netherlands lowered its flag and returned sovereignty to a people who had known nothing but struggle and domination for more than three centuries. Sukarno became the new republic's first president.

Ruling Indonesia, however, proved to be a greater challenge than defeating the Dutch. Far from homogeneous, the archipelago of about 17,500 islands was a boiling pot of tribalism, divergent cultures, dozens of languages and dialects, and ethnic groups that nursed centuries-old animosities. Conflicts were frequent and brutal, and Sukarno clamped down. He suspended parliament in 1960 and was named president for life in 1963. He formed close alliances with Communist governments around the world in exchange for military equipment and training. He sent

Russian-armed Indonesian troops into neighboring Malaysia in an attempt to spread communism throughout Southeast Asia and win the approval of the world's Socialist leaders.

Opposition built, and a coup was launched in 1965. Sukarno escaped assassination only through the quick wits of his mistress. Many of his top military officers and his closest associates were less lucky. The events were reminiscent of those in Iran in 1953. In the end, the Communist Party was held responsible — especially those factions aligned with China. In the army-initiated massacres that followed, an estimated three hundred thousand to five hundred thousand people were killed. The head of the military, General Suharto, took over as president in 1968.[1]

By 1971, US determination to seduce Indonesia away from communism was heightened because the outcome of the Vietnam War was looking very uncertain. President Nixon had begun a series of troop withdrawals in the summer of 1969, and US strategy was taking on a more global perspective. The strategy focused on preventing a domino effect of one country after another falling under Communist rule, and it focused on a couple of countries; Indonesia was the key. MAIN's electrification project was part of a comprehensive plan to ensure American dominance in Southeast Asia.

The premise of US foreign policy was that Suharto would serve Washington in a manner similar to the shah of Iran. The United States also hoped the nation would serve as a model for other countries in the region. Washington based part of its strategy on the assumption that gains made in Indonesia might have positive repercussions throughout the Islamic world, particularly in the explosive Middle East. And if that was not incentive enough, Indonesia had oil. No one was certain about the magnitude or quality of its reserves, but oil company seismologists were exuberant over the possibilities.

As I pored over the books at the Boston Public Library, my excitement grew. I began to imagine the adventures ahead. In working for MAIN I would be trading the rugged Peace Corps lifestyle for a much more luxurious and glamorous one. My time with Claudine already represented the realization of one of my fantasies; it seemed too good to be true. I felt at least partially vindicated for serving the sentence at that all-boys' prep school.

Something else was also happening in my life: Ann and I were not getting along. We quarreled a great deal. She complained that I had changed, that I was not the man she'd married or with whom she had shared those years in the Peace Corps. Looking back, I can see that she must have sensed that I was leading two lives.

I justified my behavior as the logical result of the resentment I felt toward her for forcing me to get married in the first place. Never mind that she had nurtured and supported me through the challenges of Ecuador; I still saw her as a continuation of my pattern of giving in to my parents' whims. I have no doubt now that, on some level, Ann knew that there was another woman in my life. In any case, we decided to move into separate apartments.

One day in 1971, about a week before my scheduled departure for Indonesia, I arrived at Claudine's place to find the small dining room table set with an assortment of cheeses and breads, and there was a fine bottle of Beaujolais. She toasted me.

"You've made it." She smiled, but somehow it seemed less than sincere. "You're now one of us."

We chatted casually for half an hour or so. Then, as we were finishing off the wine, she gave me a look unlike any I had seen before. "Never admit to anyone about our meetings," she said in a stern voice. "I won't forgive you if you do, ever, and I'll deny I ever met you." She glared at me — perhaps the only time I felt threatened by her — and then gave a cold laugh. "Talking about us would make life dangerous for you."

I was stunned. I felt terrible. But later, as I walked alone back to the Prudential Center, I had to admit to the cleverness of the scheme. The fact was that all of our time together had been spent in her apartment. There was not a trace of evidence about our relationship, and no one at MAIN was implicated in any way. A part of me also appreciated her honesty; she had not deceived me the way my parents had about Tilton and Middlebury.

CHAPTER 5

Saving a Country from Communism

I had a romantic vision of Indonesia, the country where I was to live for the next three months. Some of the books I read featured photographs of women in brightly colored sarongs, Balinese dancers, shamans blowing fire, and warriors paddling long dugout canoes in emerald waters at the foot of smoking volcanoes. Particularly striking was a series on the magnificent black-sailed galleons of the infamous Bugi pirates, who still sailed the seas of the archipelago, and who had so terrorized early European sailors that they returned home to warn their children, "Behave yourselves, or the Bugimen will get you." Oh, how those pictures stirred my soul.

The history and legends of that country represent a cornucopia of larger-than-life figures: wrathful gods, Komodo dragons, tribal sultans, and ancient tales that, long before the birth of Christ, had traveled across Asian mountains, through Persian deserts, and over the Mediterranean to embed themselves in the deepest realms of our collective psyche. The very names of its fabled islands — Java, Sumatra, Borneo, Sulawesi — seduced the mind. Here was a land of mysticism, myth, and erotic beauty; an elusive treasure sought but never found by Columbus; a princess wooed yet never possessed by Spain, by Holland, by Portugal, by Japan; a fantasy and a dream.

My expectations were high, and I suppose they mirrored those of the great explorers. Like Columbus, though, I should have known to temper my fantasies. Perhaps I could have guessed that the beacon shines on a destiny that is not always the one we envision. Indonesia offered treasures, but it was not the chest of panaceas I had come to expect. In fact, my first days in Indonesia's steamy capital, Jakarta, in the summer of 1971, were shocking.

The beauty was certainly present. Men and women in brightly colored batik clothing. Lush gardens ablaze with tropical flowers. Bicycle cabs with fanciful, rainbow-colored scenes painted on the

sides of the high seats, where passengers reclined in front of the
pedaling drivers. Dutch Colonial mansions and turreted mosques.
But there was also an ugly, tragic side to the city. Lepers holding
out bloodied stumps instead of hands. Young girls offering their
bodies for a few coins. Once-splendid Dutch canals turned into
cesspools. Cardboard hovels where entire families lived along
the trash-lined banks of black rivers. Blaring horns and choking
fumes. The beautiful and the ugly, the elegant and the vulgar, the
spiritual and the profane. This was Jakarta, where the enticing
scent of cloves and orchid blossoms battled the miasma of open
sewers for dominance.

I had seen poverty before. Some of my New Hampshire classmates lived in cold-water tar paper shacks and arrived at school
wearing thin jackets and frayed tennis shoes on subzero winter
days, their unwashed bodies reeking of old sweat and manure. I
had lived in mud shacks with Andean peasants whose diet con-
sisted almost entirely of dried corn and potatoes, and where it
sometimes seemed that a newborn was as likely to die as to experience a birthday. I had seen poverty, but nothing to prepare me
for Jakarta.

Our team, of course, was quartered in the country's fanciest
hotel, the Hotel InterContinental Indonesia. Owned by Pan American Airways, like the rest of the InterContinental chain scattered
around the globe, it catered to the whims of wealthy foreigners,
especially oil executives and their families. On the evening of our
first day, our project manager, Charlie Illingworth, hosted a dinner for us in the elegant restaurant on the top floor.

Charlie was a connoisseur of war; he devoted most of his free
time to reading history books and historical novels about great military leaders and battles. He was the epitome of the pro–Vietnam
War armchair soldier. As usual, this night he was wearing khaki
slacks and a short-sleeved khaki shirt with military-style epaulets.

After welcoming us, he lit up a cigar. "To the good life," he
sighed, raising a glass of champagne.

We joined him. "To the good life." Our glasses clinked.

Cigar smoke swirling around him, Charlie glanced about the
room. "We will be well pampered here," he said, nodding his head
appreciatively. "The Indonesians will take very good care of us. As

will the US Embassy people. But let's not forget that we have a mission to accomplish." He looked down at a handful of note cards. "Yes, we're here to develop a master plan for the electrification of Java — the most populated land in the world. But that's just the tip of the iceberg."

His expression turned serious; he reminded me of George C. Scott playing General Patton, one of Charlie's heroes. "We are here to accomplish nothing short of saving this country from the clutches of communism. As you know, Indonesia has a long and tragic history. Now, at a time when it is poised to launch itself into the twentieth century, it is tested once again. Our responsibility is to make sure that Indonesia doesn't follow in the footsteps of its northern neighbors, Vietnam, Cambodia, and Laos. An integrated electrical system is a key element. That, more than any other single factor (with the possible exception of oil), will assure that capitalism and democracy rule.

"Speaking of oil," he said. He took another puff on his cigar and flipped past a couple of the note cards. "We all know how dependent our own country is on oil. Indonesia can be a powerful ally to us in that regard. So, as you develop this master plan, please do everything you can to make sure that the oil industry and all the others that serve it — ports, pipelines, construction companies — get whatever they are likely to need in the way of electricity for the entire duration of this twenty-five-year plan."

He raised his eyes from his note cards and looked directly at me. "Better to err on the high side than to underestimate. You don't want the blood of Indonesian children — or our own — on your hands. You don't want them to live under the hammer and sickle or the Red flag of China!"

As I lay in my bed that night, high above the city, secure in the luxury of a first-class suite, an image of Claudine came to me. Her discourses on foreign debt haunted me. I tried to comfort myself by recalling lessons learned in my macroeconomics courses at business school. After all, I told myself, I am here to help Indonesia rise out of a medieval economy and take its place in the modern industrial world. But I knew that in the morning I would look out my window, across the opulence of the hotel's gardens and swimming pools, and see the hovels that fanned out for miles beyond. I would know that babies were dying out there for lack of food and potable water, that infants and adults alike were suffering from horrible diseases and living in terrible conditions.

Tossing and turning in my bed, I found it impossible to deny that Charlie and everyone else on our team were here for self-ish reasons. We were promoting US foreign policy and corporate interests. We were driven by greed rather than by any desire to make life better for the vast majority of Indonesians. A word came to mind: *corporatocracy*. I was not sure whether I had heard it before or had just invented it, but it seemed to describe perfectly the new elite who had made up their minds to attempt to rule the planet.

This was a close-knit fraternity of a few men with shared goals, and the fraternity's members moved easily and often between corporate boards and government positions. It struck me that the current president of the World Bank, Robert McNamara, was a perfect example. He had moved from a position as president of Ford Motor Company to secretary of defense under presidents Kennedy and Johnson, and now occupied the top post at the world's most powerful financial institution.[1]

I also realized that my college professors had not understood the true nature of macroeconomics: that in many cases helping an economy grow only makes those few people who sit atop the pyramid even richer, while it does nothing for those at the bottom except to push them even lower. Indeed, promoting capitalism often results in a system that resembles medieval feudal societies. If any of my professors knew this, they had not admitted it — probably because big corporations, and the men who run them, fund colleges. Exposing the truth would undoubtedly cost those professors their jobs — just as such revelations could cost me mine.

These thoughts continued to disturb my sleep every night that I spent at the InterContinental. In the end, my primary defense was a highly personal one: I had fought my way out of that New Hampshire town, the prep school, and the draft. Through a combination of coincidences and hard work, I had earned a place in the good life. I also took comfort in the fact that I was doing the right thing in the eyes of my culture. I was on my way to becoming a successful and respected economist. I was doing what business school had prepared me for. I was helping to implement a development model that was sanctioned by the best minds at the world's top think tanks.

Nonetheless, in the middle of the night I often had to console myself with a promise that someday I would expose the truth. Then I would read myself to sleep with Louis L'Amour novels about gunfighters in the Old West.

CHAPTER 6

Selling My Soul

Our eleven-man team spent six days in Jakarta registering at the US Embassy, meeting various officials, organizing ourselves, and relaxing around the pool. The number of Americans who lived at the Hotel InterContinental amazed me. I took great pleasure in watching the beautiful young women — wives of US oil and construction company executives — who passed their days at the pool and their evenings in the half dozen posh restaurants in and around the hotel.

Then Charlie moved our team to the mountain city of Bandung. The climate was milder, the poverty less obvious, and the distractions fewer. We were given a government guesthouse known as the Wisma, complete with a manager, a cook, a gardener, and a staff of servants. Built during the Dutch colonial period, the Wisma was a haven. Its spacious veranda faced tea plantations that flowed across rolling hills and up the slopes of Java's volcanic mountains. In addition to housing, we were provided with eleven Toyota off-road vehicles, each with a driver and translator. Finally, we were presented with memberships to the exclusive Bandung Golf and Racquet Club, and we were housed in a suite of offices at the local headquarters of Perusahaan Umum Listrik Negara, the government-owned electric utility company.

For me, the first several days in Bandung involved a series of meetings with Charlie and Howard Parker. Howard was in his seventies and was the retired chief load forecaster for the New England Electric System. Now he was responsible for forecasting the amount of energy and generating capacity (the load) the island of Java would need over the next twenty-five years, breaking this down into city and regional forecasts. Because electricity demand is highly correlated with economic growth, his forecasts depended on my economic projections. The rest of our team would develop the master plan around these forecasts, locating and designing power plants, transmission and distribution lines, and fuel transportation systems in a manner that would satisfy our projections as efficiently as possible. During our meetings, Charlie continually emphasized the importance of my job, and he badgered me about the need to be very optimistic in my forecasts. Claudine had been right; I was the key to the entire master plan.

"The first few weeks here," Charlie explained, "are about data collection."

He, Howard, and I were seated in big rattan chairs in Charlie's plush private office. The walls were decorated with batik tapestries depicting epic tales from the ancient Hindu texts of the Ramayana. Charlie puffed on a fat cigar.

"The engineers will put together a detailed picture of the current electric system, port capacities, roads, railroads, all those sorts of things." He pointed his cigar at me. "You gotta act fast. By the end of month one, Howard'll need to get a pretty good idea about the full extent of the economic miracles that'll happen when we get the new grid on line. By the end of the second month, he'll need more details — broken down into regions. The last month will be about filling in the gaps. That'll be critical. All of us will put our heads together then. So, before we leave we gotta be absolutely certain we have all the information we'll need. 'Home for Thanksgiving,' that's my motto. There's no coming back."

Howard appeared to be an amiable, grandfatherly type, but he was actually a bitter old man who felt cheated by life. He had never reached the pinnacle of the New England Electric System, and he deeply resented it. "Passed over," he told me repeatedly, "because I refused to buy the company line." He had been forced into retirement and then, unable to tolerate staying at home with his wife, had accepted a consulting job with MAIN. This was his second assignment, and I had been warned by both Einar and Charlie to watch out for him. They described him with words like *stubborn*, *mean*, and *vindictive*.

As it turned out, Howard was one of my wisest teachers, although not one I was ready to accept at the time. He had never received the type of training Claudine had given me. I suppose they considered him too old, or perhaps too stubborn. Or maybe they figured he was only in it for the short run, until they could lure in a more pliable full-timer like me. In any case, from their standpoint, he turned out to be a problem. Howard clearly saw the situation and the role they wanted him to play, and he was determined not to be a pawn. All the adjectives Einar and Charlie had used to describe him were appropriate, but at least some of his stubbornness grew out of his personal commitment not to be their servant. I doubt he had ever heard the term "economic hit man," but he knew they intended to use him to promote a form of imperialism he could not accept.

He took me aside after one of our meetings with Charlie. He wore a hearing aid, and he fiddled with the little box under his shirt that controlled its volume.

"This is between you and me," Howard said in a hushed voice. We were standing at the window in the office we shared, looking out at the stagnant canal that wound past the Perusahaan Umum Listrik Negara building. A young woman was bathing in its foul waters. "They'll try to convince you that this economy is going to skyrocket," he said. "Charlie's ruthless. Don't let him get to you."

His words gave me a sinking feeling, but also a desire to convince him that Charlie was right; after all, my career depended on pleasing my MAIN bosses.

"Surely this economy will boom," I said, my eyes drawn to the woman in the canal. "Just look at what's happening."

"So there you are," he muttered, apparently unaware of the scene in front of us. "You've already bought their line, have you?"

A movement up the canal caught my attention. An elderly man had descended the bank, dropped his pants, and squatted at the edge of the water to answer nature's call. The bathing woman saw him but was undeterred; she continued washing herself. I turned away from the window and looked directly at Howard.

"I've been around," I said. "I may be young, but I just got back from three years in South America. I've seen what can happen when oil is discovered. Things change fast."

"Oh, I've been around too," he said mockingly. "A great many years. I'll tell you something, young man. I don't give a damn for your oil discoveries and all that. I forecasted electric loads all my life — during the Depression, World War II, times of bust and boom. And I can say for sure that no electric load ever grew by more than 7 to 9 percent a year for any sustained period. And that's in the best of times. Six percent is more reasonable."[1]

I stared at him. Part of me suspected he was right, but I felt defensive. I knew I had to convince him, because my own conscience cried out for justification.

"Howard, this isn't the United States. This is a country where, until now, no one could even get electricity. Things are different here."

He turned on his heel and waved his hand as though he could brush me away.

"Go ahead," he snarled. "Sell out. I don't give a damn what you come up with." He jerked his chair from behind his desk and fell into it. "I'll make my electricity forecast based on what I believe, not some pie-in-the-sky economic study." He picked up his pencil and started to scribble on a pad of paper.

It was a challenge I could not ignore. I went and stood in front of his desk.

"You'll look pretty stupid if I come up with what everyone expects — a boom to rival the California gold rush — and you forecast electricity growth at a rate comparable to Boston in the 1960s."

He slammed the pencil down and glared at me. "Unconscionable! That's what it is. You — all of you..," He waved his arms at the offices beyond his walls. "You've sold your souls to the devil. You're in it for the money. Now," he feigned a smile and reached under his shirt, "I'm turning off my hearing aid and going back to work."

It shook me to the core. I stomped out of the room and headed for Charlie's office. Halfway there I stopped, uncertain about what I intended to accomplish. Instead, I turned and walked down the stairs, out the door, into the afternoon sunlight. The young woman was climbing out of the canal, her sarong wrapped tightly about her body. The elderly man had disappeared. Several boys played in the canal, splashing and shouting at one another. An older woman was standing knee-deep in the water, brushing her teeth; another was scrubbing clothes.

A huge lump grew in my throat. I sat down on a slab of broken concrete, trying to disregard the pungent odor from the canal. I fought hard to hold back the tears; I needed to figure out why I felt so miserable.

You're in it for the money. I heard Howard's words, over and over. He had struck a raw nerve.

The little boys continued to splash one another, their gleeful voices filling the air. I wondered what I could do. What would it take to make me carefree like them? The question tormented me as I sat there watching them cavort in their blissful innocence, apparently unaware of the risk they took by playing in that fetid water. An elderly, hunchbacked man with a gnarled cane hobbled along the bank above the canal. He stopped and watched the boys, and his face broke into a toothless grin.

Perhaps I could confide in Howard; maybe together we would arrive at a solution. I immediately felt a sense of relief. I picked up a little stone and threw it into the canal. As the ripples faded, however, so did my euphoria. I knew I could do no such thing. Howard was old and bitter. He had already passed up opportunities to advance his own career. Surely, he would not buckle now. I was young, just starting out, and certainly did not want to end up like him.

Staring into the water of that putrid canal, I once again saw images of the New Hampshire prep school on the hill, where I had spent vacations alone while the other boys went off to their debutante balls. Slowly the sorry fact settled in. Once again, there was no one I could talk to.

That night I lay in bed, thinking for a long time about the people in my life – Howard, Charlie, Claudine, Ann, Einar, Uncle Frank – wondering what my life would be like if I had never met them. Where would I be living? Not Indonesia, that was for sure. I wondered also about my future, about where I was headed. I pondered the decision confronting me. Charlie had made it clear that he expected Howard and me to come up with growth rates of at least 17 percent per annum. What kind of forecast would I produce?

Suddenly a thought came to me that soothed my soul. Why had it not occurred to me before? The decision was not mine at all. Howard had said that he would do what he considered right, regardless of my conclusions. I could please my bosses with a high economic forecast and he would make his own decision; my work would have no effect on the master plan. People kept emphasizing the importance of my role, but they were wrong. A great burden had been lifted. I fell into a deep sleep.

A few days later, Howard was taken ill with a severe amoebic attack. We rushed him to a Catholic missionary hospital. The doctors prescribed medication and strongly recommended that he return immediately to the United States. Howard assured us that he already had all the data he needed and could easily complete the load forecast from Boston. His parting words to me were a reiteration of his earlier warning.

"No need to cook the numbers," he said. "I'll not be part of that scam, no matter what you say about the miracles of economic growth!"

PART II: 1971–1975

⊕ CHAPTER 7

My Role as Inquisitor

Our contracts with the Indonesian government, the Asian Development Bank, and USAID required that someone on our team visit all the major population centers in the area covered by the master plan. I was designated to fulfill this condition. As Charlie put it, "You survived the Amazon; you know how to handle bugs, snakes, and bad water."

Along with a driver and translator, I visited many beautiful places and stayed in some pretty dismal lodgings. I met with local business and political leaders and listened to their opinions about the prospects for economic growth. However, I found most of them reluctant to share information with me. They seemed intimidated by my presence. Typically, they told me that I would have to check with their bosses, with government agencies, or with corporate headquarters in Jakarta. I sometimes suspected that some sort of conspiracy was directed at me.

These trips were usually short, not more than two or three days. In between, I returned to the Wisma in Bandung. The woman who managed it had a son a few years younger than me. His name was Rasmon, but to everyone except his mother he was Rasy. A student of economics at a local university, he immediately took an interest in my work. In fact, I suspected that at some point he would approach me for a job. He also began to teach me Bahasa Indonesia.

Creating an easy-to-learn language had been President Sukarno's highest priority after Indonesia won its independence from the Netherlands. More than 350 languages and dialects are spoken throughout the archipelago, and Sukarno realized that his country needed a common vocabulary in order to unite people from the many islands and cultures. He recruited an international team of linguists, and Bahasa Indonesia was the highly successful result. Based on Malay, it avoids many of the tense changes, irregular verbs, and other complications that characterize most languages.

49

By the early 1970s, the majority of Indonesians spoke it, although they continued to rely on Javanese and other local dialects within their own communities.[1] Rasy was a great teacher with a wonderful sense of humor, and compared with learning Shuar or even Spanish, Bahasa was easy.

Rasy owned a motor scooter and took it upon himself to introduce me to his city and people. "I'll show you a side of Indonesia you haven't seen," he promised one evening, and urged me to hop on behind him.

We passed shadow-puppet shows, musicians playing traditional instruments, fire blowers, jugglers, and street vendors selling every imaginable ware, from contraband American cassettes to rare indigenous artifacts. Finally, we ended up at a tiny coffeehouse populated by young men and women whose clothes, hats, and hairstyles would have been right in fashion at a Beatles concert in the late 1960s; however, everyone was distinctly Indonesian. Rasy introduced me to a group seated around a table and we sat down.

They all spoke English, with varying degrees of fluency, but they appreciated and encouraged my attempts at Bahasa. They talked about this openly and asked me why Americans never learned their language. I had no answer. Nor could I explain why I was the only American or European in this part of the city, even though you could always find plenty of us at the Golf and Racquet Club, the posh restaurants, the movie theaters, and the upscale supermarkets.

It was a night I shall always remember. Rasy and his friends treated me as one of their own. I enjoyed a sense of euphoria from being there, sharing their city, food, and music, smelling the clove cigarettes and other aromas that were part of their lives, joking and laughing with them. It was like the Peace Corps all over again, and I found myself wondering why I had thought that I wanted to travel first class and separate myself from people like this. As the night wore on, they became increasingly interested in learning my thoughts about their country and about the war my country was fighting in Vietnam. Every one of them was horrified by what they referred to as the "illegal invasion," and they were relieved to discover I shared their feelings.

By the time Rasy and I returned to the guesthouse, it was late and the place was dark. I thanked him profusely for inviting me into his world; he thanked me for opening up to his friends. We promised to do it again, hugged, and headed off to our respective rooms.

That experience with Rasy whetted my appetite for spending more time away from the MAIN team. The next morning, I had a meeting with Charlie and told him I was becoming frustrated trying to obtain information from local people. In addition, most of the statistics I needed for developing economic forecasts could be found only at government offices in Jakarta. Charlie and I agreed that I would need to spend one to two weeks in Jakarta.

He expressed sympathy for me, having to abandon Bandung for the steaming metropolis, and I professed to detest the idea. Secretly, however, I was excited by the opportunity to have some time to myself, to explore Jakarta, and to live at the elegant Hotel InterContinental Indonesia. Once in Jakarta, however, I discovered that I now viewed life from a different perspective. The night spent with Rasy and the young Indonesians, as well as my travels around the country, had changed me. I found that I saw my fellow Americans in a different light. The young wives seemed not quite so beautiful. The chain-link fence around the pool and the steel bars outside the windows on the lower floors, which I had barely noticed before, now took on an ominous appearance. The food in the hotel's posh restaurants seemed insipid.

I noticed something else, too. During my meetings with political and business leaders, I became aware of subtleties in the way they treated me. I had not perceived it before, but now I saw that many of them resented my presence. For example, when they introduced me to each other, they often used Bahasa terms that according to my dictionary translated to *inquisitor* and *interrogator*. I purposely neglected disclosing my knowledge of their language — even my translator knew only that I could recite a few stock phrases — and I purchased a good Bahasa/English dictionary, which I often used after leaving them.

Were these addresses just coincidences of language? Mistranslations in my dictionary? I tried to convince myself that they were. Yet, the more time I spent with these men, the more convinced I became that I was an intruder, that an order to cooperate had come down from someone, and that they had little choice but to comply.

I had no idea whether a government official, a banker, a general, or the US Embassy had sent the order. All I knew was that, although they invited me into their offices, offered me tea, politely answered my questions, and in every overt manner seemed to welcome my presence, beneath the surface there was a shadow of resignation and rancor.

It made me wonder, too, about their answers to my questions and about the validity of their data. For instance, I could never just walk into an office with my translator and meet with someone; we first had to set up an appointment. In itself, this would not have seemed so strange, except that doing so was outrageously time consuming. Since the phones seldom worked, we had to drive through the traffic-choked streets, which were laid out in such a contorted manner that it could take an hour to reach a building only blocks away. Once there, we were asked to fill out several forms. Eventually, a male secretary would appear. Politely — always with the courteous smile for which the Javanese are famous — he would question me about the types of information I desired, and then he would establish a time for the meeting.

Without exception, the scheduled appointment was at least several days away, and when the meeting finally occurred, I was handed a folder of prepared materials. The industry owners gave me five- and ten-year plans, the bankers had charts and graphs, and the government officials provided lists of projects that were in the process of leaving the drawing boards to become engines of economic growth. Everything these captains of commerce and government provided, and all they said during the interviews, indicated that Java was poised for perhaps the biggest boom any economy had ever enjoyed. No one — not a single person — ever questioned this premise or gave me any negative information.

As I headed back to Bandung, though, I found myself wondering about all these experiences; something was deeply disturbing. It occurred to me that everything I was doing in Indonesia was more like a game than reality. It was as though we were playing a game of poker. We kept our cards hidden. We could not trust each other or count on the reliability of the information we shared. Yet this game was deadly serious, and its outcome would affect millions of lives for decades to come.

CHAPTER 8

Civilization on Trial

"I'm taking you to a *dalang*," Rasy beamed. "You know, the famous Indonesian puppet masters." He was obviously pleased to have me back in Bandung. "There's a very important one in town tonight."

He drove me on his scooter through parts of his city I did not know existed, through sections filled with traditional Javanese kampong houses, which looked like a poor person's version of tiny tile-roofed temples. Gone were the stately Dutch Colonial mansions and office buildings I had grown to expect. The people were obviously poor, yet they bore themselves with great pride. They wore threadbare but clean batik sarongs, brightly colored blouses, and wide-brimmed straw hats. Everywhere we went we were greeted with smiles and laughter. When we stopped, children rushed up to touch me and feel the fabric of my jeans. One little girl stuck a fragrant frangipani blossom in my hair.

We parked the scooter near a sidewalk theater where several hundred people were gathered, some standing, others sitting in portable chairs. The night was clear and beautiful. Although we were in the heart of the oldest section of Bandung, there were no streetlights, so the stars sparkled over our heads. The air was filled with the aromas of wood fires, peanuts, and cloves.

Rasy disappeared into the crowd and soon returned with many of the young people I had met at the coffeehouse. They offered me hot tea, little cakes, and satay, tiny bits of meat cooked in peanut oil. I must have hesitated before accepting the latter, because one of the women pointed at a small fire. "Very fresh meat," she laughed. "Just cooked."

Then the music started — the hauntingly magical sounds of the *gamalong*, an instrument that conjures images of temple bells.

"The dalang plays all the music by himself," Rasy whispered. "He also works all the puppets and speaks their voices, several languages. We'll translate for you."

It was a remarkable performance, combining traditional legends with current events. I would later learn that the dalang is a shaman who does his work in trance. He had more than a hundred puppets and spoke for each in a different voice. It was a night I will never forget, and one that has influenced the rest of my life.

After completing a classic selection from the ancient texts of the Ramayana, the dalang produced a puppet of Richard Nixon, complete with the distinctive long nose and sagging jowls. The US president was dressed like Uncle Sam, in a stars-and-stripes top hat and tails. He was accompanied by another puppet, which wore a three-piece pin-striped suit. The second puppet carried in one hand a bucket decorated with dollar signs. He used his free hand to wave an American flag over Nixon's head in the manner of a slave fanning a master.

A map of the Middle and Far East appeared behind the two, the various countries hanging from hooks in their respective positions. Nixon immediately approached the map, lifted Vietnam off its hook, and thrust it to his mouth. He shouted something that was translated as "Bitter! Rubbish. We don't need any more of this!" Then he tossed it into the bucket and proceeded to do the same with other countries.

I was surprised, however, to see that his next selections did not include the domino nations of Southeast Asia. Rather, they were all Middle Eastern countries — Palestine, Kuwait, Saudi Arabia, Iraq, Syria, and Iran. After that, he turned to Pakistan and Afghanistan. Each time, the Nixon doll screamed out some epithet before dropping the country into his bucket, and in every instance, his vituperative words were anti-Islamic: "Muslim dogs," "Mohammad's monsters," and "Islamic devils."

The crowd became very excited, the tension mounting with each new addition to the bucket. They seemed torn between fits of laughter, shock, and rage. At times, I sensed they took offense at the puppeteer's language. I also felt intimidated; I stood out in this crowd, taller than the rest, and I worried that they might direct their anger at me. Then Nixon said something that made my scalp tingle when Rasy translated it.

"Give this one to the World Bank. See what it can do to make us some money off Indonesia." He lifted Indonesia from the map and moved to drop it into the bucket, but just at that moment another puppet leaped out of the shadows. This puppet represented an Indonesian man, dressed in batik shirt and khaki slacks, and he wore a sign with his name clearly printed on it.

"A popular Bandung politician," Rasy explained.

This puppet literally flew between Nixon and Bucket Man and held up his hand.

"Stop!" he shouted. "Indonesia is sovereign."

The crowd burst into applause. Then Bucket Man lifted his flag and thrust it like a spear into the Indonesian, who staggered and died a most dramatic death. The audience members booed, hooted, screamed, and shook their fists. Nixon and Bucket Man stood there, looking out at us. They bowed and left the stage.

"I think I should go," I said to Rasy.

He placed a hand protectively around my shoulder. "It's okay," he said. "They have nothing against you personally." I wasn't so sure.

Later we all retired to the coffeehouse. Rasy and the others assured me that they had not been informed ahead of time about the Nixon–World Bank skit. "You never know what to expect from that puppeteer," one of the young men observed.

I wondered aloud whether this had been staged in my honor. Someone laughed and said I had a very big ego. "Typical of Americans," he added, patting my back congenially.

"Indonesians are very conscious of politics," the man in the chair beside me said. "Don't Americans go to shows like this?"

A sharp university student, an English major, sat across the table from me. "But you do work for the World Bank, don't you?" she asked.

I told her that my current assignment was for the Asian Development Bank and the United States Agency for International Development.

"Aren't they really all the same?" She didn't wait for an answer. "Isn't it like the play tonight showed? Doesn't your government look at Indonesia and other countries as though we are just a bunch of..." She searched for the word.

"Grapes," one of her friends coached.

"Exactly. A bunch of grapes. You can pick and choose. Keep England. Eat China. And throw away Indonesia."

"After you've taken all our oil," another woman added.

I tried to defend myself but was not at all up to the task. I wanted to take pride in the fact that I had come to this part of town and had stayed to watch the entire anti-US performance, which I might have construed as a personal assault. I wanted them to see the courage of what I had done, wanted them to know that I was the only member of my team who had bothered to learn Bahasa or had any desire to take in their culture, and wanted to point out that I was the sole foreigner attending this production. But I decided it would be more prudent not to mention any of this. Instead, I tried to refocus the conversation. I asked them why they thought the dalang had singled out Muslim countries, except for Vietnam.

The English student laughed at this. "Because that's the plan."

"Vietnam is just a holding action," one of the men interjected, "like Holland was for the Nazis. A stepping-stone."

"The real target," the woman continued, "is the Muslim world."

I could not let this go unanswered. "Surely," I protested, "you can't believe that the United States is anti-Islamic."

"Oh no?" she asked. "Since when? You need to read one of your own historians — a Brit named Toynbee. Back in the fifties he predicted that the real war in the next century would not be between Communists and capitalists, but between Christians and Muslims."[1]

"Arnold Toynbee said that?" I was stunned.

"Yes. Read *Civilization on Trial* and *The World and the West.*"

"But why should there be such animosity between Muslims and Christians?" I asked.

Looks were exchanged around the table. They appeared to find it hard to believe that I could ask such a foolish question.

"Because," she said slowly, as though addressing someone slow-witted or hard of hearing, "the West — especially its leader, the US — is determined to take control of all the world, to become the greatest empire in history. It has already gotten very close to succeeding. The Soviet Union currently stands in its way, but the Soviets will not endure. Toynbee could see that. They have no

religion, no faith, no substance behind their ideology. History demonstrates that faith — soul, a belief in higher powers — is essential.
We Muslims have it. We have it more than anyone else in the world,
even more than the Christians. So we wait. We grow strong."

"We will take our time," one of the men chimed in, "and then
like a snake we will strike."

"What a horrible thought!" I could barely contain myself. "What
can we do to change this?"

The English major looked me directly in the eyes. "Stop being so
greedy," she said, "and so selfish. Realize that there is more to the
world than your big houses and fancy stores. People are starving
and you worry about oil for your cars. Babies are dying of thirst
and you search the fashion magazines for the latest styles. Nations
like ours are drowning in poverty, but your people don't even hear
our cries for help. You shut your ears to the voices of those who try
to tell you these things. You label them radicals or Communists.
You must open your hearts to the poor and downtrodden, instead
of driving them further into poverty and servitude. There's not
much time left. If you don't change, you're doomed."

Several days later the popular Bandung politician, whose puppet stood up to Nixon and was impaled by Bucket Man, was struck
and killed by a hit-and-run driver.

Soon after that, I headed home.

Ann and I met in Paris to attempt a reconciliation. However, we
continued to quarrel. On our next to last day, she asked if I'd had
an affair. When I confessed, she said she had suspected it all along.
We spent many hours sitting on a bench, looking at the Seine and
talking. By the time we boarded our flight we had come to the conclusion that our long history of anger and resentment was too large
an obstacle and that we should live apart.

CHAPTER 9

Opportunity of a Lifetime

Indonesia was a test for me in so many ways, and still more tests awaited me in Boston.

I went to the Prudential Center headquarters first thing in the morning, and while I was standing with dozens of other employees at the elevator, I learned that Mac Hall, MAIN's enigmatic, octogenarian chairman and CEO, had promoted Einar to president of the Portland, Oregon, office. As a result, I now officially reported to Bruno Zambotti.

Nicknamed "the silver fox" because of the color of his hair and his uncanny ability to outmaneuver everyone who challenged him, Bruno had the dapper good looks of Cary Grant. He was eloquent and he held both an engineering degree and an MBA. He understood econometrics and was vice president in charge of MAIN's electrical power division and most of our international projects. He also was the obvious choice to take over as president of the corporation when his mentor, the aging Jake Dauber, retired. Like most MAIN employees, I was awed and terrified by Bruno Zambotti.

Just before lunch, I was summoned to Bruno's office. Following a cordial discussion about Indonesia, he said something that made me jump to the edge of my seat.

"I'm firing Howard Parker. We don't need to go into the details, except to say that he's lost touch with reality." His smile was disconcertingly pleasant as he tapped his finger against a sheaf of papers on his desk. "Eight percent a year. That's his load forecast. Can you believe it? In a country with the potential of Indonesia!"

His smile faded and he looked me squarely in the eye. "Charlie Illingworth tells me that your economic forecast is right on target and will justify load growth of between seventeen and twenty percent. Is that right?"

I assured him it was.

He stood up and offered me his hand. "Congratulations. You've just been promoted."

Perhaps I should have gone out and celebrated at a fancy restaurant with other MAIN employees — or even by myself. However, my mind was on Claudine. I was dying to tell her about my promotion, all my experiences in Indonesia, and my time with Ann.

She had warned me not to call her from abroad, and I had not. Now I was dismayed to find that her phone was disconnected, with no forwarding number. I went looking for her.

A young couple had moved into her apartment. It was lunchtime but I believe I roused them from their bed; obviously annoyed, they professed to know nothing about Claudine. I paid a visit to the real estate agency, pretending to be a cousin. Their files indicated they had never rented to anyone with her name; the previous lease had been issued to a man who would remain anonymous by his request. Back at the Prudential Center, MAIN's employment office also claimed to have no record of Claudine. They admitted only to a "special consultants" file that was not available for my scrutiny.

By late afternoon I was exhausted and emotionally drained. On top of everything else, a bad case of jet lag had set in. Returning to my empty apartment, I felt desperately lonely and abandoned. My promotion seemed meaningless or, even worse, a badge of my willingness to sell out. I threw myself onto the bed, overwhelmed with despair. I had been used by Claudine and then discarded. Determined not to give in to my anguish, I shut down my emotions. I lay there on my bed, staring at the bare walls for what seemed like hours.

Finally I managed to pull myself together. I got up, swallowed a beer, and smashed the empty bottle against a table. Then I stared out the window. Looking down a distant street, I thought I saw Claudine walking toward me. I started for the door and then returned to the window for another look.

The woman had come closer. I could see that she was dressed in that same sophisticated style and that her confident walk was reminiscent of Claudine's, but it was not Claudine. My heart sank, and my feelings changed from anger and loathing to fear. I wondered if she had died — or been killed. I took a couple Valium and drank myself to sleep.

The next morning, a call from MAIN's personnel department

woke me from my stupor. Its chief, Paul Mormino, assured me that he understood my need for rest, but he urged me to come in that afternoon.

"Good news," he said. "The best thing for catching up with yourself."

I obeyed the summons and learned that Bruno had been more than true to his word. I not only had been promoted to Howard's old job; I also had been given the title of Chief Economist and a raise. It did cheer me up a bit.

I took the afternoon off and wandered down along the Charles River with a quart of beer. As I sat there, watching the sailboats and nursing combined jet lag and vicious hangover, I convinced myself that Claudine had done her job and had moved on to her next assignment. She had always emphasized the need for secrecy. She would call me. Mormino had been right. My jet lag — and my anxiety — dissipated.

During the next weeks, I tried to put all thoughts of Claudine aside. I focused on writing my report on the Indonesian economy and on revising Howard's load forecasts. I came up with the type of study my bosses wanted to see: a growth in electric demand averaging 19 percent per annum for twelve years after the new system was completed, tapering down to 17 percent for eight more years, and then holding at 15 percent for the remainder of the twenty-five-year projection.

I presented my conclusions at formal meetings with the international lending agencies. Their teams of experts questioned me extensively and mercilessly. By then, my emotions had turned into a sort of grim determination, not unlike those that had driven me to excel rather than to rebel during my prep school days. Nonetheless, Claudine's memory always hovered close. When a sassy young economist out to make a name for himself at the Asian Development Bank grilled me relentlessly for an entire afternoon, I recalled the advice Claudine had given me as we sat in her Beacon Street apartment those many months before.

"Who can see twenty-five years into the future?" she had asked. "Your guess is as good as theirs. Confidence is everything."

I convinced myself I was an expert, reminding myself that I had experienced more of life in economically developing countries than many of the men — some of them twice my age — who now sat in judgment of my work. I had lived in the Amazon and had traveled to parts of Java no one else wanted to visit. I had taken a couple of intensive courses aimed at teaching executives the finer points of econometrics, and I told myself that I was part of the new breed of statistically oriented, econometric-worshipping whiz kids that appealed to Robert McNamara, the buttoned-down president of the World Bank, former president of Ford Motor Company, and John Kennedy's secretary of defense. Here was a man who had built his reputation on numbers, on probability theory, on mathematical models, and — I suspected — on the bravado of a very large ego.

I tried to emulate both McNamara and my boss, Bruno. I adopted manners of speech that imitated the former, and I took to walking with the swagger of the latter, attaché case swinging at my side. Looking back, I have to wonder at my gall. In truth, my expertise was extremely limited, but what I lacked in training and knowledge I made up for in audacity.

And it worked. Eventually the team of experts stamped my reports with their seals of approval.

During the ensuing months, I attended meetings in Tehran, Caracas, Guatemala City, London, Vienna, and Washington, DC. I met famous personalities, including the shah of Iran, the former presidents of several countries, and Robert McNamara himself. Like prep school, it was a world of men. I was amazed at how my new title and the accounts of my recent successes before the international lending agencies affected other people's attitudes toward me.

At first, all the attention went to my head. I began to think of myself as a Merlin who could wave his wand over a country, causing it suddenly to light up, industries sprouting like flowers. Then I became disillusioned. I questioned my own motives and those of all the people I worked with. It seemed that a glorified title or a PhD did little to help a person understand the plight of a leper living beside a cesspool in Jakarta, and I doubted that a knack for manipulating statistics enabled a person to see into the future. The better I came to know those who made the decisions that shape the world, the more skeptical I became about their abilities and their goals.

I doubted whether limited resources would allow the whole world to live the opulent life of the United States, when even the United States had millions of citizens living in poverty. In addition, it wasn't entirely clear to me that people in other nations actually wanted to live like us. Our own statistics about violence, depression, drug abuse, divorce, and crime indicated that although ours was one of the wealthiest societies in history, it might also be one of the least happy societies. Why would we want others to emulate us? Looking at the faces in the meetings I attended, my skepticism often turned to silent anger at the hypocrisy.

Eventually, however, this also changed. I came to understand that most of those men believed they were doing the right thing. Like Charlie, they were convinced that communism and terrorism were evil forces — rather than the predictable reactions to decisions they and their predecessors had made — and that they had a duty to their country, to their offspring, and to God to convert the world to capitalism. They also clung to the principle of survival of the fittest; if they happened to enjoy the good fortune to have been born into a privileged class instead of inside a cardboard shack, then they saw it as an obligation to pass this heritage on to their progeny.

I vacillated between viewing such people as an actual conspiracy and simply seeing them as a tight-knit fraternity bent on dominating the world. Nonetheless, over time I began to liken them to the plantation owners of the pre–Civil War South. They were men drawn together in a loose association by common beliefs and shared self-interest, rather than an exclusive group meeting in clandestine hideaways with focused and sinister intent. The plantation autocrats had grown up with servants and slaves, and had been educated to believe that it was their right and even their duty to take care of the "heathens" and to convert them to the owners' religion and way of life. Even if slavery repulsed them philosophically, they could, like Thomas Jefferson, justify it as a necessity, the collapse of which would result in social and economic chaos. The leaders of the modern oligarchies, what I now thought of as the corporatocracy, seemed to fit the same mold.

I also began to wonder who benefits from war and the mass production of weapons, from the damming of rivers and the destruction of indigenous environments and cultures. I began to look at who benefits when hundreds of thousands of people die from insufficient food, polluted water, or curable diseases. Slowly, I came to realize that in the long run no one benefits, but in the short term those at the top of the pyramid — my bosses and me — appear to benefit, at least materially.

This raised several other questions: Why does this situation persist? Why has it endured for so long? Does the answer lie simply in the old adage that "might makes right," that those with the power perpetuate the system?

It seemed insufficient to say that power alone allows this situation to persist. Although the proposition that might makes right explained a great deal, I felt there must be a more compelling force at work here. I recalled an economics professor from my business school days, a man from northern India, who lectured about limited resources, about man's need to grow continually, and about the principle of slave labor. According to this professor, all successful capitalist systems involve hierarchies with rigid chains of command, including a handful at the very top who control descending orders of subordinates, and a massive army of workers at the bottom, who in relative economic terms truly can be classified as slaves. Ultimately, then, I became convinced that we encourage this system because the corporatocracy has convinced us that God has given us the right to place a few of our people at the very top of this capitalist pyramid and to export our system to the entire world.

Of course, we are not the first to do this. The list of practitioners stretches back to the ancient empires of North Africa, the Middle East, and Asia, and works its way up through Persia, Greece, Rome, the Christian Crusades, and all the European empire builders of the post-Columbian era. This imperialist drive has been and continues to be the cause of most wars, pollution, starvation, species extinctions, and genocides. And it has always taken a serious toll on the conscience and well-being of the citizens of those empires, contributing to social malaise and resulting in a situation where the wealthiest cultures in human history are plagued with the highest rates of suicide, drug abuse, and violence.

I thought extensively on these questions, but I avoided considering the nature of my own role in all of this. I tried to think of myself not as an EHM but as a chief economist. It sounded so very legitimate, and if I needed any confirmation, I could look at my pay stubs: all were from MAIN, a private corporation. I didn't earn a penny from the NSA or any government agency. And so I became convinced. Almost.

One afternoon Bruno called me into his office. He walked behind my chair and patted me on the shoulder. "You've done an excellent job," he purred. "To show our appreciation, we're giving you the opportunity of a lifetime, something few men ever receive, even at twice your age."

CHAPTER 10

Panama's President and Hero

I landed at Panama's Tocumen International Airport late one night in April 1972, during a tropical deluge. As was common in those days, I shared a taxi with several other executives, and because I spoke Spanish, I ended up in the front seat beside the driver. I stared blankly out the taxi's windshield. Through the rain, the headlights illuminated a billboard portrait of a handsome man with a prominent brow and flashing eyes. One side of his wide-brimmed hat was hooked rakishly up. I recognized him as the hero of modern Panama, Omar Torrijos.

I had prepared for this trip in my customary fashion, by visiting the reference section of the Boston Public Library. I knew that one of the reasons for Torrijos's popularity among his people was that he was a firm defender of both Panama's right of self-rule and its claims to sovereignty over the Panama Canal. He was determined that the country under his leadership would avoid the pitfalls of its ignominious history.

Panama was part of Colombia when the French engineer Ferdinand de Lesseps, who had directed construction of the Suez Canal, decided to build a canal through the Central American isthmus, to connect the Atlantic and Pacific oceans. Beginning in 1881, the French undertook a mammoth effort that met with one catastrophe after another. Finally, in 1889, the project ended in financial disaster — but it had inspired a dream in Theodore Roosevelt. During the first years of the twentieth century, the United States demanded that Colombia sign a treaty turning the isthmus over to a North American consortium. Colombia refused.

In 1903, President Roosevelt sent in the US warship *Nashville*. US soldiers landed, seized and killed a popular local militia commander, and declared Panama an independent nation. A puppet government was installed and the first Canal treaty was signed; it

established an American zone on both sides of the future waterway, legalized US military intervention, and gave Washington virtual control over this newly formed "independent" nation.

Interestingly, the treaty was signed by US Secretary of State
John Hay and a French engineer, Philippe Bunau-Varilla, who had
been part of the original team, but it was not signed by a single
Panamanian. In essence, Panama was forced to leave Colombia in
order to serve the United States, in a deal struck by an American
and a Frenchman — in retrospect, a prophetic beginning.[1]

For more than half a century, Panama was ruled by an oligarchy of wealthy families with strong connections to Washington.
They were right-wing dictators who took whatever measures they
deemed necessary to ensure that their country promoted US interests. In the manner of most of the Latin American dictators who
allied themselves with Washington, Panama's rulers interpreted
US interests to mean putting down any populist movement that
smacked of socialism. They also supported the CIA and NSA in
anti-Communist activities throughout the hemisphere, and they
helped big American businesses like Rockefeller's Standard Oil
and United Fruit Company. These governments apparently did
not feel that US interests were promoted by improving the lives of
people who lived in dire poverty or served as virtual slaves to the
big plantations and corporations.

Panama's ruling families were well rewarded for their support; US military forces intervened on their behalf a dozen times
between the declaration of Panamanian independence and 1968.
However, that year, while I was still a Peace Corps volunteer in
Ecuador, the course of Panamanian history suddenly changed. A
coup overthrew Arnulfo Arias, the latest in the parade of dictators,
and Omar Torrijos emerged as the head of state, although he had
not actively participated in the coup.[2]

Torrijos was highly regarded by the Panamanian middle and
lower classes. He had grown up in the rural city of Santiago,
where his parents taught school. He had risen quickly through
the ranks of the National Guard, Panama's primary military unit
and an institution that during the 1960s gained increasing support among the poor. Torrijos earned a reputation for listening to
the dispossessed. He walked the streets of their shantytowns, held

meetings in slums that politicians didn't dare to enter, helped the unemployed find jobs, and often donated his own limited financial resources to families stricken by illness or tragedy.[3]

His love of life and his compassion for people reached even beyond Panama's borders. Torrijos was committed to turning his nation into a haven for fugitives from persecution, a place that would offer asylum to refugees from both sides of the political fence, from leftist opponents of Chile's Pinochet to right-wing anti-Castro guerrillas. Many people saw him as an agent of peace, a perception that earned him praise throughout the hemisphere. He also developed a reputation as a leader who was dedicated to resolving differences among the various factions that were tearing apart so many Latin American countries: Honduras, Guatemala, El Salvador, Nicaragua, Cuba, Colombia, Peru, Argentina, Chile, and Paraguay. His small nation of two million people served as a model of social reform and an inspiration for world leaders as diverse as the labor organizers who plotted the dismemberment of the Soviet Union and Islamic militants like Muammar Gadhafi of Libya.[4]

My first night in Panama, stopped at the traffic light, peering past the noisy windshield wipers, I was moved by this man smiling down at me from the billboard — handsome, charismatic, and courageous. I knew from my hours at the BPL that he stood behind his beliefs. For the first time in its history, Panama was not a puppet of Washington or of anyone else. Torrijos never succumbed to the temptations offered by Moscow or Beijing; he believed in social reform and in helping those born into poverty, but he did not advocate communism. Unlike Castro, Torrijos was determined to win freedom from the United States without forging alliances with the United States' enemies.

I had stumbled across an article in some obscure journal in the BPL racks that praised Torrijos as a man who would alter the history of the Americas, reversing a long-term trend toward US domination. The author cited as his starting point Manifest Destiny — the doctrine, popular with many Americans during the 1840s, that the conquest of North America was divinely ordained; that God, not men, had ordered the genocide of native North Americans, the destruction of forests, the near-extinction of buffalo, the draining of swamps, the rechanneling of rivers, and the development of an economy that depends on the continuing exploitation of labor and natural resources.

The article got me to thinking about my country's attitude toward the world. The Monroe Doctrine, originally enunciated by President James Monroe in 1823, was used to take Manifest Destiny a step further when, in the 1850s and 1860s, it was used to assert that the United States had special rights all over the hemisphere, including the right to invade any nation in Central or South America that refused to back US policies. Teddy Roosevelt invoked the Monroe Doctrine to justify US intervention in the Dominican Republic, in Venezuela, and during the "liberation" of Panama from Colombia. A string of subsequent US presidents — most notably Taft, Wilson, and Franklin Roosevelt — relied on it to expand Washington's Pan-American activities through the end of World War II. Finally, during the latter half of the twentieth century, the United States used the Communist threat to justify expansion of this concept to countries around the globe, including Vietnam and Indonesia.[5]

Now, it seemed, one man was standing in Washington's way. I knew that he was not the first — leaders like Castro and Allende had gone before him — but Torrijos alone was doing it outside the realm of Communist ideology and without claiming that his movement was a revolution. He was simply saying that Panama had its own rights — to sovereignty over its people, its lands, and a waterway that bisected it — and that these rights were as valid and as divinely bestowed as any enjoyed by the United States.

Torrijos also objected to the School of the Americas (renamed the Western Hemisphere Institute for Security Cooperation, in 2001) and to the US Southern Command's tropical warfare training center, both located in the Canal Zone. For years, the United States armed forces had invited Latin American dictators and presidents to send their sons and military leaders to these facilities — the largest and best equipped outside North America. There they learned interrogation and covert operational skills as well as military tactics that they would use to fight communism and to protect their own assets and those of the oil companies and other private corporations. They also had opportunities to bond with the United States' top brass.

These facilities were hated by Latin Americans — except for the few wealthy ones who benefited from them. They were known to provide schooling for right-wing death squads and the torturers who had turned so many nations into totalitarian regimes. Torrijos made it clear that he did not want training centers located in Panama — and that he considered the Canal Zone to be included within his borders.[6]

Seeing the handsome general on the billboard, and reading the caption beneath his face — "Omar's ideal is freedom; the missile is not invented that can kill an ideal!" — I felt a shiver run down my spine. I had a premonition that the story of Panama in the twentieth century was far from over, and that Torrijos was in for a difficult and perhaps even tragic time.

The tropical storm battered the windshield, the traffic light turned green, and the driver honked his horn at the car ahead of us. I thought about my own position. I had been sent to Panama to close the deal on what would become MAIN's first truly comprehensive master development plan. This plan would create a justification for World Bank, Inter-American Development Bank, and USAID investment of billions of dollars in the energy, transportation, and agriculture sectors of this tiny and very crucial country. It was, of course, a subterfuge, a means of making Panama forever indebted and thereby returning it to its puppet status.

As the taxi started to move through the night, a paroxysm of guilt flashed through me, but I suppressed it. What did I care? I had taken the plunge in Java, sold my soul, and now I could create my opportunity of a lifetime. I could become rich, famous, and powerful in one blow.

CHAPTER 11

Pirates in the Canal Zone

The next day, the Panamanian government sent a man to show me around. His name was Fidel, and I was immediately drawn to him. He was tall and slim and took an obvious pride in his country. His great-great-grandfather had fought beside Bolívar to win independence from Spain. I told him I was related to Tom Paine, and I was thrilled to learn that Fidel had read *Common Sense* in Spanish. He spoke English, but when he discovered I was fluent in the language of his country, he was overcome with emotion.

"Many of your people live here for years and never bother to learn it," he said.

Fidel took me on a drive through an impressively prosperous sector of his city, which he called the New Panama. As we passed modern glass-and-steel skyscrapers, he explained that Panama had more international banks than any other country south of the Rio Grande.

"We're often called the Switzerland of the Americas," he said. "We ask very few questions of our clients."

Late in the afternoon, with the sun sliding toward the Pacific, we headed out on an avenue that followed the contours of the bay. A long line of ships was anchored there. I asked Fidel whether there was a problem with the canal.

"It's always like this," he replied with a laugh. "Lines of them, waiting their turn. Half the traffic is coming from or going to Japan. More even than the United States."

I confessed that this was news to me.

"I'm not surprised," he said. "North Americans don't know much about the rest of the world."

We stopped at a beautiful park in which bougainvillea crept over ancient ruins. A sign proclaimed that this was a fort built to protect the city against marauding English pirates. A family was setting up for an evening picnic: a father, mother, son and daughter, and an elderly man who I assumed was the children's grandfather. I felt a sudden longing for the tranquility that seemed to embrace these five people. As we passed them, the couple smiled, waved, and greeted us in English. I asked if they were tourists, and they laughed. The man came over to us.

"I'm third generation in the Canal Zone," he explained proudly. "My granddad came three years after it was created. He drove one of the mules, the tractors that hauled ships through the locks." He pointed at the elderly man, who was preoccupied helping the children set the picnic table. "My dad was an engineer, and I've followed in his footsteps."

The woman had returned to helping her father-in-law and children. Beyond them, the sun dipped into the blue water. It was a scene of idyllic beauty, reminiscent of a Monet painting. I asked the man if they were US citizens.

He looked at me incredulously. "Of course. The Canal Zone is US territory." The boy ran up to tell his father that dinner was ready.

"Will your son be the fourth generation?"

The man brought his hands together in a sign of prayer and raised them toward the sky.

"I pray to the good Lord every day that he may have that opportunity. Living in the Zone is a wonderful life." Then he lowered his hands and stared directly at Fidel. "I just hope we can hold on to her for another fifty years. That despot Torrijos is making a lot of waves. A dangerous man."

A sudden urge gripped me, and I said to him, in Spanish, "Adios. I hope you and your family have a good time here, and learn lots about Panama's culture."

He gave me a disgusted look. "I don't speak their language," he said. Then he turned abruptly and headed toward his family and the picnic.

Fidel stepped close to me, placed an arm around my shoulders, and squeezed tightly. "Thank you," he said.

Back in the city, Fidel drove us through an area he described as a slum.

"Not our worst," he said. "But you'll get the flavor."

Wooden shacks and ditches filled with standing water lined the street, the frail homes suggesting dilapidated boats scuttled in a cesspool. The smell of rot and sewage filled our car as children with distended bellies ran alongside. When we slowed, they congregated at my side, calling me *Uncle* and begging for money. It reminded me of Jakarta.

Graffiti covered many of the walls. There were a few of the usual hearts with couples' names scrawled inside, but most of the graffiti comprised slogans expressing hatred of the United States: "Go home, gringo," "Stop shitting in our canal," "Uncle Sam, slave master," and "Tell Nixon that Panama is not Vietnam." The one that chilled my heart the most, however, read, "Death for freedom is the way to Christ." Scattered among these were posters of Omar Torrijos.

"Now the other side," Fidel said. "I've got official papers and you're a US citizen, so we can go." Beneath a magenta sky, he drove us into the Canal Zone. As prepared as I thought I was, it was not enough. I could hardly believe the opulence of the place — huge white buildings, manicured lawns, plush homes, golf courses, stores, and theaters.

"The facts," he said. "Everything in here is US property. All the businesses — the supermarkets, barbershops, beauty salons, restaurants, all of them — are exempt from Panamanian laws and taxes. There are seven 18-hole golf courses, US post offices scattered conveniently around, US courts of law and schools. It truly is a country within a country." Fidel peered at me. "Over there," he pointed back toward the city, "income per capita is less than one thousand dollars a year, and unemployment rates are 30 percent. Of course, in the little shantytown we just visited, no one makes close to one thousand dollars, and hardly anyone has a job."

"What's being done?"

He turned and gave me a look that seemed to change from anger to sadness.

"What *can* we do?" He shook his head. "I don't know, but I'll say this: Torrijos is trying. I think it may be the death of him, but he sure as hell is giving it all he's got. He's a man who'll go down fighting for his people."

As we headed out of the Canal Zone, Fidel smiled. "You like to dance?" Without waiting for me to reply, he said, "Let's get some dinner, and then I'll show you yet another side of Panama."[1]

CHAPTER 12

Soldiers and Prostitutes

After a juicy steak and a cold beer, we left the restaurant and drove down a dark street. Fidel advised me never to walk in this area. "When you come here, take a cab right to the front door." He pointed. "Just there, beyond the fence, is the Canal Zone."

He drove on until we arrived at a vacant lot filled with cars. He found an empty spot and parked. An old man hobbled up to us. Fidel got out and patted him on the back. Then he ran his hand lovingly across the fender of his car.

"Take good care of her. She's my lady." He handed the man a bill.

We took a short footpath out of the parking lot and suddenly found ourselves on a street flooded with flashing neon lights. Two boys raced past. The one behind, the larger of the two, was pointing a stick at the other and making the sounds of a man shooting a gun. The smaller one slammed into Fidel's legs, his head reaching barely as high as Fidel's thigh. He stepped back.

"I'm sorry, sir," he gasped in Spanish.

Fidel placed both his hands on the boy's shoulders. "No harm done, my man," he said. "But tell me, why was your friend shooting at you?"

The other boy came up to us. He placed his arm protectively around the first. "My brother," he explained. "We're sorry."

"It's okay," Fidel chuckled gently. "He didn't hurt me. I just asked him why you were shooting at him."

The brothers glanced at each other. The older one smiled. "He's the gringo general at the Canal Zone. He tried to rape our mother and I'm sending him packing, back to where he belongs."

Fidel stole a look at me. "Where does he belong?"

"At home, in the United States."

"Does your mother work here?"

"Over there." Both boys pointed proudly at a neon light down the street. "Bartender."

"Go on then." Fidel handed them each a coin. "But be careful. Stay in the lights."

"Oh yes, sir. Thank you." They raced off.

As we walked on, Fidel explained that Panamanian women were prohibited by law from prostitution. "They can tend bar and dance, but they cannot sell their bodies. That's left to the imports."

We stepped inside the bar and were blasted with a popular American song. My eyes and ears took a moment to adjust. A couple of burly US soldiers stood near the door; bands around their uniformed arms identified them as military police.

Fidel led me along a bar, and then I saw the stage. Three young women were dancing there, entirely naked except for their heads. One wore a sailor's cap, another a green beret, and the third a cowboy hat. They were laughing. They seemed to be playing a game with one another, as though dancing in a competition. The music, the way they danced, the stage — it could have been a disco in Boston, except that they were naked.

We pushed our way through a group of young English-speaking men. Although they wore T-shirts and blue jeans, their crew cuts gave them away as soldiers from the Canal Zone's military base. Fidel tapped a waitress on the shoulder. She turned, let out a scream of delight, and threw her arms around him. The group of young men watched this intently, glancing at one another with disapproval. I wondered if they thought Manifest Destiny included this Panamanian woman. The waitress led us to a corner. From somewhere, she produced a small table and two chairs.

As we settled in, Fidel exchanged greetings in Spanish with two men at a table beside ours. Unlike the soldiers, they wore printed short-sleeved shirts and creased slacks. The waitress returned with a couple of Balboa beers, and Fidel patted her on the rump as she turned to leave. She smiled and threw him a kiss. I glanced around and was relieved to discover that the young men at the bar were no longer watching us; they were focused on the dancers.

The majority of the patrons were English-speaking soldiers, but there were others, like the two beside us, who obviously were Panamanians. They stood out because their hair would not have passed inspection, and because they did not wear T-shirts and jeans. A few of them sat at tables; others leaned against the walls.

They seemed to be highly alert, like border collies guarding flocks of sheep.

Women roamed the tables. They moved constantly, sitting on laps, shouting to the waitresses, dancing, swirling, singing, taking turns on the stage. They wore tight skirts, T-shirts, jeans, clinging dresses, high heels. One was dressed in a Victorian gown and veil. Another wore only a bikini. It was obvious that they had to rely on their beauty to survive here. I marveled at the numbers of displaced women who made their way to Panama, and wondered at the desperation that had driven them to this.

"All from other countries?" I shouted to Fidel above the music.

He nodded. "Except..." He pointed at the waitresses. "They're Panamanian."

"What countries are the others from?"

"Honduras, El Salvador, Nicaragua, and Guatemala."

"Neighbors."

"Not entirely. Costa Rica and Colombia are our closest neighbors."

The waitress who had led us to the table came and sat on Fidel's knee. He gently rubbed her back.

"Clarissa," he said, "please tell my North American friend why they left their countries." He nodded his head in the direction of the stage. Three new girls were accepting the hats from the others, who jumped down and started dressing. The music switched to salsa, and as the newcomers danced, they shed their clothes to the rhythm.

Clarissa held out her right hand. "I'm pleased to meet you," she said. Then she stood up and reached for our empty bottles. "In answer to Fidel's question, these girls come here to escape even worse brutality. I'll bring a couple more Balboas."

After she left, I turned to Fidel. "Come on," I said. "They're here for US dollars."

"True. But why so many from the countries where fascist dictators rule?"

I glanced back at the stage. The three of them were giggling and throwing the sailor's cap around like a ball. I looked Fidel in the eye. "You're not kidding, are you?"

"No," he said seriously, "I wish I were. Most of these girls have lost their families—fathers, brothers, husbands, boyfriends. They grew up with torture and death. Most of them are single mothers. Dancing and prostitution seem their only options. They can make a lot of money here, then start fresh somewhere, buy a little shop, open a cafe —"

He was interrupted by a commotion near the bar. I saw a waitress swing her fist at one of the soldiers, who caught her hand and began to twist her wrist. She screamed and fell to her knee. He laughed and shouted to his buddies. They all laughed. She tried to hit him with her free hand. He twisted harder. Her face contorted with pain.

The MPs remained by the door, watching calmly. Fidel jumped to his feet and started toward the bar. One of the men at the table next to ours held out a hand to stop him. "Tranquillo, hermano," he said. "Be calm, brother. Enrique has control."

A tall, slim Panamanian came out of the shadows near the stage. He moved like a cat and was upon the soldier in an instant. One hand encircled the soldier's throat while the other doused him in the face with a glass of water. The waitress slipped away. Several of the Panamanians who had been lounging against the walls formed a protective semicircle around the tall bouncer. He lifted the soldier against the bar and said something I couldn't hear. Then he raised his voice and spoke slowly in English, loudly enough for everyone in the still room to hear over the music.

"The waitresses are off-limits to you guys, and you don't touch the others until after you pay them."

The two MPs finally swung into action. They approached the cluster of Panamanians. "We'll take it from here, Enrique," they said.

The bouncer lowered the soldier to the floor and gave his neck a final squeeze, forcing the other's head back and eliciting a cry of pain.

"Do you understand me?" There was a feeble groan. "Good." He pushed the soldier at the two MPs. "Get him out of here."

Conversations with the General

The invitation was completely unexpected. One morning during that same 1972 visit, I was sitting in an office I had been given at the Instituto de Recursos Hidráulicos y de Electrificación, Panama's government-owned electric utility company. I was poring over a sheet of statistics when a man knocked gently on the frame of my open door. I invited him in, pleased with any excuse to take my attention off the numbers. He announced himself as the general's chauffeur and said he had come to take me to one of the general's bungalows.

An hour later, I was sitting across the table from General Omar Torrijos. He was dressed casually, in typical Panamanian style: khaki slacks and a short-sleeved shirt buttoned down the front, light blue with a delicate green pattern. He was tall, fit, and handsome. He seemed amazingly relaxed for a man with his responsibilities. A lock of dark hair fell over his prominent forehead.

He asked about my recent travels to Indonesia, Guatemala, and Iran. The three countries fascinated him, but he seemed especially intrigued with Iran's king, Mohammad Reza Shah Pahlavi. The shah had come to power in 1941, after the British and Soviets overthrew his father, whom they accused of collaborating with Hitler.[1]

"Can you imagine," Torrijos asked, "being part of a plot to dethrone your own father?"

Panama's head of state knew a good deal about the history of this far-off land. We talked about how the tables were turned on the shah in 1951, and how his own premier Mohammad Mossadegh, forced him into exile. Torrijos knew, as did most of the world, that it had been the CIA that labeled the premier a Communist and stepped in to restore the shah to power. However, he did not know — or at least did not mention — the parts Claudine had shared with me, about Kermit Roosevelt's brilliant maneuvers and the fact that this had been the beginning of a new era in imperialism, the match that had ignited the global empire conflagration.

"After the shah was reinstated," Torrijos continued, "he launched a series of revolutionary programs aimed at developing the industrial sector and bringing Iran into the modern era."

I asked him how he happened to know so much about Iran.

"I make it my point," he said. "I don't think too highly of the shah's politics — his willingness to overthrow his own father and become a CIA puppet — but it looks as though he's doing good things for his country. Perhaps I can learn something from him. If he survives."

"You think he won't?"

"He has powerful enemies."

"And some of the world's best bodyguards."

Torrijos gave me a sardonic look. "His secret police, SAVAK, have the reputation of being ruthless thugs. That doesn't win many friends. He won't last much longer." He paused, then rolled his eyes. "Bodyguards? I have a few myself." He waved at the door. "You think they'll save my life if your country decides to get rid of me?"

I asked whether he truly saw that as a possibility.

He raised his eyebrows in a manner that made me feel foolish for asking such a question. "We have the Canal. That's a lot bigger than Arbenz and United Fruit."

I had researched Guatemala, and I understood Torrijos's meaning. United Fruit Company had been that country's political equivalent of Panama's canal. Founded in the late 1800s, United Fruit soon grew into one of the most powerful forces in Central America. During the early 1950s, reform candidate Jacobo Arbenz was elected president of Guatemala in an election hailed all over the hemisphere as a model of the democratic process. At the time, less than 3 percent of Guatemalans owned 70 percent of the land. Arbenz promised to help the poor dig their way out of starvation, and after his election, he implemented a comprehensive land reform program.

"The poor and middle classes throughout Latin America applauded Arbenz," Torrijos said. "He was one of my personal heroes. But we also held our breath. We knew that United Fruit opposed these measures, since they were one of the largest and most oppressive landholders in Guatemala. They also owned big plantations in Colombia, Costa Rica, Cuba, Jamaica, Nicaragua, Santo Domingo, and here in Panama. They couldn't afford to let Arbenz give the rest of us ideas."

I knew what followed: United Fruit had launched a major public relations campaign in the United States, aimed at convincing the American public and Congress that Arbenz was part of a Russian plot and that Guatemala was a Soviet satellite. In 1954, the CIA orchestrated a coup. American pilots bombed Guatemala City, and the democratically elected Arbenz was overthrown, replaced by Colonel Carlos Castillo Armas, a ruthless right-wing dictator.

The new government owed everything to United Fruit. By way of thanks, the government reversed the land reform process, abolished taxes on the interest and dividends paid to foreign investors, eliminated the secret ballot, and jailed thousands of its critics. Anyone who dared to speak out against Castillo was persecuted. Historians trace the violence and terrorism that plagued Guatemala for most of the rest of the century to the not-so-secret alliance between United Fruit, the CIA, and the Guatemalan army under its colonel dictator.

"Arbenz was assassinated," Torrijos continued. "Political and character assassination." He paused and frowned. "How could your people swallow that CIA rubbish? I won't go so easily. The military here are my people. Political assassination won't do." He smiled. "The CIA itself will have to kill me!"

We sat in silence for a few moments, each lost in his own thoughts. Torrijos was the first to speak.

"Do you know who owns United Fruit?" he asked.

"Zapata Oil, George Bush's company — our UN ambassador," I said.[2]

"A man with ambitions." He leaned forward and lowered his voice. "And now I'm up against his cronies at Bechtel."

This startled me. Bechtel was the world's most powerful engineering firm and a frequent collaborator on projects with MAIN. In the case of Panama's master plan, I had assumed that they were one of our major competitors.

"What do you mean?"

"We've been considering building a new canal, a sea-level one, without locks. It can handle bigger ships. The Japanese may be interested in financing it."

"They're the Canal's biggest clients."

"Exactly. Of course, if they provide the money, they will do the construction."

It struck me. "Bechtel will be out in the cold."

"The biggest construction job in recent history." He paused. "Bechtel's loaded with Nixon, Ford, and Bush cronies." Bush, as US ambassador to the UN, and Ford, as House minority leader and chairman of the Republican National Convention, were well known to Torrijos as Republican powerbrokers. "I've been told that the Bechtel family pulls the strings of the Republican Party."

This conversation left me feeling very uncomfortable. I was one of the people who perpetuated the system he so despised, and I was certain he knew it. My job of convincing him to accept international loans in exchange for hiring US engineering and construction firms appeared to have hit a mammoth wall. I decided to confront him head-on.

"General," I asked, "why did you invite me here?"

He glanced at his watch and smiled. "Yes, time now to get down to our own business. Panama needs your help. I need your help."

I was stunned. "My help? What can I do for you?"

"We will take back the Canal. But that's not enough." He relaxed into his chair. "We must also serve as a model. We must show that we care about our poor, and we must demonstrate beyond any doubt that our determination to win our independence is not dictated by Russia, China, or Cuba. We must prove to the world that Panama is a reasonable country, that we stand not *against* the United States but *for* the rights of the poor."

He crossed one leg over the other. "In order to do that, we need to build up an economic base that is like none in this hemisphere. Electricity, yes — but electricity that reaches the poorest of our poor and is subsidized. The same for transportation and communications. And especially for agriculture. Doing that will take money — your money, the World Bank, and the Inter-American Development Bank."

Once again, he leaned forward. His eyes held mine. "I understand that your company wants more work and usually gets it by inflating the size of projects — wider highways, bigger power plants, deeper harbors. This time is different, though. Give me what's best for my people, and I'll give you all the work you want."

What he proposed was totally unexpected, and it both shocked and excited me. It certainly defied all I had learned at MAIN. Surely he knew that the foreign aid game was a sham — he had to know. It existed to make him rich and to shackle his country with debt. It was there so Panama would be forever obligated to the United States and the corporatocracy. It was there to keep Latin America on the path of Manifest Destiny and forever subservient to Washington and Wall Street. I was certain that he knew that the system was based on the assumption that all men in power are corruptible, and that his decision not to use it for his personal benefit would be seen as a threat, a new form of domino that might start a chain reaction and eventually topple the entire system.

I looked across the coffee table at this man who certainly understood that because of the Canal he enjoyed a very special and unique power, and that it placed him in a particularly precarious position. He had to be careful. He already had established himself as a leader among the leaders of economically developing countries. If he, like his hero Arbenz, was determined to take a stand, the world would be watching. How would the system react? More specifically, how would the US government react? Latin American history was littered with dead heroes.

I also knew I was looking at a man who challenged all the justifications I had formulated for my own actions. This man certainly had his share of personal flaws, but he was no pirate, no Henry Morgan or Francis Drake — those swashbuckling adventurers who used letters of marque from English kings as a cloak to legitimatize piracy. The picture on the billboard had not been your typical political deception. "Omar's ideal is freedom; the missile is not invented that can kill an ideal!" Hadn't Tom Paine penned something similar?

It made me wonder, though. Perhaps ideals do not die, but what about the men behind them? Che, Arbenz, Allende; the latter was the only one still alive, but for how long? And it raised another question: How would I respond if Torrijos were thrust into the role of martyr?

By the time I left him, we both understood that MAIN would get the contract for the master plan and that I would see to it that we did Torrijos's bidding.

CHAPTER 14

Entering a New and Sinister
Period in Economic History

As chief economist, I not only was in charge of a department at MAIN and responsible for the studies we carried out around the globe, but I also was expected to be conversant with current economic trends and theories. The early 1970s were a time of major shifts in international economics.

During the 1960s, a group of countries had formed OPEC, the cartel of oil-producing nations, largely in response to the power of the big refining companies. Iran was also a major factor. Even though the shah owed his position and possibly his life to the United States' clandestine intervention during the Mossadegh struggle — or perhaps because of that fact — the shah was acutely aware that the tables could be turned on him at any time. The heads of state of other petroleum-rich nations shared this awareness and the paranoia that accompanied it. They also knew that the major international oil companies, known as the Seven Sisters, were collaborating to hold down petroleum prices — and thus the revenues they paid to the producing countries — as a means of reaping their own windfall profits. OPEC was organized in order to strike back.

This all came to a head in the early 1970s, when OPEC brought the industrial giants to their knees. A series of concerted actions, ending with a 1973 oil embargo symbolized by long lines at US gas stations, threatened to bring on an economic catastrophe rivaling the Great Depression. It was a systemic shock to the developed-world economy and of a magnitude that few people could begin to comprehend.

The oil crisis could not have come at a worse time for the United States. It was a confused nation, full of fear and self-doubt, reeling from a humiliating war in Vietnam and a president who was about to resign. Nixon's problems were not limited to Southeast

Asia and Watergate. He had stepped up to the plate during an era that, in retrospect, would be understood as the threshold of a new epoch in world politics and economics. In those days, it seemed that the "little guys," including the OPEC countries, were getting the upper hand.

I was fascinated by world events. My bread was buttered by the corporatocracy, yet some secret side of me enjoyed watching my masters being put in their places. I suppose it assuaged my guilt a bit.

None of us could have been aware of the full impact of the embargo at the time it was happening. We certainly had our theories, but we could not understand what has since become clear. In hindsight, we know that economic growth rates after the oil crisis were about half those prevailing in the 1950s and 1960s, and that they have taken place against much greater inflationary pressure. The growth that did occur was structurally different and did not create nearly as many jobs, so unemployment soared. To top it all off, the international monetary system took a blow; the network of fixed exchange rates, which had prevailed since the end of World War II, essentially collapsed.

During that time, I frequently got together with friends to discuss these matters over lunch or over beers after work. Some of these people worked for me — my staff included very smart men and women (I had taken a lead in hiring women professionals to my staff), mostly young, who for the most part were freethinkers, at least by conventional standards. Others were executives at Boston think tanks or professors at local colleges, and one was an assistant to a state congressman. These were informal meetings, sometimes attended by as few as two of us, while others might include a dozen participants. The sessions were always lively and raucous.

When I look back at those discussions, I am embarrassed by the sense of superiority I often felt. I knew things I could not share. My friends sometimes flaunted their credentials — connections on Beacon Hill or in Washington, professorships and PhDs — and I would answer this in my role as chief economist of a major consulting firm, who traveled around the world first class. Yet, I could not discuss my private meetings with men like Torrijos or the things I knew about the ways we were manipulating countries on every continent. It was both a source of inner arrogance and a frustration.

When we talked about the power of the little guys, I had to exercise a great deal of restraint. I knew what none of my colleagues could possibly know, that the corporatocracy, its band of EHMs, and the jackals waiting in the background would never allow the little guys to gain control. I only had to draw upon the examples of Arbenz and Mossadegh — and more recently, the 1973 CIA overthrow of Chile's democratically elected president, Salvador Allende. In fact, I understood that the stranglehold of global empire was growing stronger, despite OPEC — or, as I suspected at the time but did not confirm until later, with OPEC's help.

Our conversations often focused on the similarities between the early 1970s and the 1930s. The latter represented a major watershed in the international economy and in the way it was studied, analyzed, and perceived. That decade opened the door to Keynesian economics and to the idea that government should play a major role in managing markets and providing services such as health care, unemployment compensation, and other forms of welfare. We were moving away from old assumptions that markets were self-regulating and that the state's intervention should be minimal.

The Depression resulted in the New Deal and in policies that promoted economic regulation, government financial manipulation, and the extensive application of fiscal policy. In addition, both the Depression and World War II led to the creation of organizations like the World Bank, the International Monetary Fund, and the General Agreement on Tariffs and Trade. The 1960s was a pivotal decade in this period and in the shift from neoclassic to Keynesian economics. It happened under the Kennedy and Johnson administrations, and perhaps the most important single influence was one man, Robert McNamara.

McNamara was a frequent visitor to our discussion groups — in absentia, of course. We all knew about his meteoric rise to fame, from manager of planning and financial analysis at Ford Motor Company in 1949 to Ford's president in 1960, the first company head selected from outside the Ford family. Shortly after that, Kennedy appointed him secretary of defense.

McNamara became a strong advocate of a Keynesian approach to government, using mathematical models and statistical approaches to determine troop levels, allocation of funds, and other strategies in Vietnam. His advocacy of "aggressive leadership" became a hallmark not only of government managers but also of corporate executives. It formed the basis of a new philosophical approach to teaching management at the nation's top business schools, and it ultimately led to a new breed of CEOs who would spearhead the rush to global empire.[1]

As we sat around the table discussing world events, we were especially fascinated by McNamara's role as president of the World Bank, a job he accepted soon after leaving his post as secretary of defense. Most of my friends focused on the fact that he symbolized what was popularly known as the military-industrial complex. He had held the top position in a major corporation, in a government cabinet, and now at the most powerful bank in the world. Such an apparent breach in the separation of powers horrified many of them; I may have been the only one among us who was not in the least surprised.

I see now that Robert McNamara's greatest and most sinister contributions to history were to jockey the World Bank into becoming an agent of global empire on a scale never before witnessed and to set a dangerous precedent. His ability to bridge the gaps between the primary components of the corporatocracy would be fine-tuned by his successors.

This happened during my time as an EHM and it continues today. For instance, George Shultz was secretary of the Treasury and chairman of the Council on Economic Policy under Nixon, served as Bechtel president, and then became secretary of state under Reagan. Caspar Weinberger was a Bechtel vice president and general counsel, and later secretary of defense under Reagan. Richard Helms was Johnson's CIA director and then became ambassador to Iran under Nixon. Richard Cheney served as secretary of defense under George H. W. Bush, as Halliburton president, and as US vice president to George W. Bush. Condoleezza Rice was a member of Chevron's board of directors before she became Bush's secretary of state. Bill Clinton's Treasury secretary, Robert Rubin, had been cochairman at Goldman Sachs. Even a president of the United States, George H. W. Bush, began as a founder of Zapata Petroleum, served as US ambassador to the United Nations under presidents Nixon and Ford, and was Ford's CIA director. Barack Obama named members of big business and Wall Street to key posts, including tapping a former Federal Reserve Bank of New York president, Timothy Geithner, as Treasury secretary, and a real estate magnate and one of America's four hundred wealthiest people, Penny Pritzker, as commerce secretary.

Looking back, I am struck by the innocence of the days when I was an EHM and McNamara ran the World Bank. In many respects, we were still caught up in the old approaches to empire building. Kermit Roosevelt had shown us a better way when he overthrew an Iranian democrat and replaced him with a despotic king. We EHMs were accomplishing many of our objectives in places like Indonesia and Ecuador, and yet Vietnam was a stunning example of how easily we could slip back into old patterns.

It would take the leading member of OPEC, Saudi Arabia, to change that.

CHAPTER 15

The Saudi Arabian
Money-Laundering Affair

In 1974, a diplomat from Saudi Arabia showed me photos of Riyadh, the capital of his country. Included in these photos was a herd of goats rummaging among piles of refuse outside a government building. When I asked the diplomat about them, his response shocked me. He told me that they were the city's main garbage disposal system.

"No self-respecting Saudi would ever collect trash," he said. "We leave it to the beasts."

Goats! In the capital of the world's greatest oil kingdom. It seemed unbelievable.

At the time, I was one of a group of consultants just beginning to try to piece together a solution to the oil crisis. Those goats led me to an understanding of how that solution might evolve, especially given the country's pattern of development over the previous three centuries.

In the eighteenth century, Muhammad ibn Saud, a local warlord, joined forces with fundamentalists from the ultraconservative Wahhabi sect. It was a powerful union, and during the next two hundred years the Saud family and their Wahhabi allies conquered most of the Arabian Peninsula, including Islam's holiest sites, Mecca and Medina.

Saudi society reflected the puritanical idealism of its founders, and a strict interpretation of Koranic beliefs was enforced. Religious police ensured adherence to the mandate to pray five times a day. Women were required to cover themselves from head to toe. Punishment for criminals was severe; public executions and stonings were common. During my first visit to Riyadh, I was amazed when my driver told me I could leave my camera, my briefcase, and even my wallet in plain sight inside our car, parked near the open market, without locking it.

"No one," he said, "would think of stealing here. Thieves have their hands cut off."

Later that day, he asked me if I would like to visit so-called Chop Chop Square and watch a beheading. Wahhabism's adherence to what we would consider extreme puritanism made the streets safe from thieves — and demanded the harshest form of corporal punishment for those who violated the laws. I declined the invitation.

The Saudi view of religion as an important element of politics and economics contributed to the oil embargo that shook the Western world. On October 6, 1973 (Yom Kippur, the holiest of Jewish holidays), Egypt and Syria launched simultaneous attacks on Israel. It was the beginning of the October War — the fourth and most destructive of the Arab–Israeli wars, and the one that would have the greatest impact on the world. Egypt's President Sadat pressured Saudi Arabia's King Faisal to retaliate against the United States' complicity with Israel by employing what Sadat referred to as "the oil weapon." On October 16, Iran and the five Arab Gulf states, including Saudi Arabia, announced a 70 percent increase in the posted price of oil.

Meeting in Kuwait City, Arab oil ministers pondered further options. The Iraqi representative was vehemently in favor of targeting the United States. He called on the other delegates to nationalize American businesses in the Arab world, to impose a total oil embargo on the United States and on all other nations friendly to Israel, and to withdraw Arab funds from every American bank. He pointed out that Arab bank accounts were substantial and that this action could result in a panic not unlike that of 1929.

Other Arab ministers were reluctant to agree to such a radical plan, but on October 17 they did decide to move forward with a more limited embargo, which would begin with a 5 percent cut in production and then impose an additional 5 percent reduction every month until their political objectives were met. They agreed that the United States should be punished for its pro-Israel stance and should therefore have the most severe embargo levied against it. Several of the countries attending the meeting announced that they would implement cutbacks of 10 percent, rather than 5 percent.

On October 19, President Nixon asked Congress for $2.2 billion in aid to Israel. The next day, Saudi Arabia and other Arab producers imposed a total embargo on oil shipments to the United States.[1]

The oil embargo ended on March 18, 1974. Its duration was short, its impact immense. The selling price of Saudi oil leaped from $1.39 a barrel on January 1, 1970, to $8.32 on January 1, 1974.[2] Politicians and future administrations would never forget the lessons learned during the early to mid-1970s. In the long run, the trauma of those few months served to strengthen the corporatocracy; its three sectors — big corporations, international banks, and government — bonded as never before. That bond would endure.

The embargo also resulted in significant attitude and policy changes. It convinced Wall Street and Washington that such an embargo could never again be tolerated. Protecting our oil supplies had always been a priority; after 1973, it became an obsession. The embargo elevated Saudi Arabia's status as a player in world politics and forced Washington to recognize the kingdom's strategic importance to our own economy. Furthermore, it encouraged US corporatocracy leaders to search desperately for methods to funnel petrodollars back to America, and to ponder the fact that the Saudi government lacked the administrative and institutional frameworks to properly manage its mushrooming wealth.

For Saudi Arabia, the additional oil income resulting from the price hikes was a mixed blessing. It filled the national coffers with billions of dollars; however, it also served to undermine some of the strict religious beliefs of the Wahhabis. Wealthy Saudis traveled around the world. They attended schools and universities in Europe and the United States. They bought fancy cars and furnished their houses with Western-style goods. Conservative religious beliefs were replaced by a new form of materialism — and it was this materialism that presented a solution to fears of future oil crises.

Almost immediately after the embargo ended, Washington began negotiating with the Saudis, offering them technical support, military hardware and training, and an opportunity to bring their nation into the twentieth century, in exchange for petrodollars and, most important, assurances that there would never again be another oil embargo. The negotiations resulted in the creation of a most extraordinary organization, the United States–Saudi Arabian Joint Commission on Economic Cooperation. Known as JECOR, it embodied an innovative concept that was the opposite of traditional foreign aid programs: it relied on Saudi money to hire American firms to build up Saudi Arabia.

Although overall management and fiscal responsibility were delegated to the US Department of the Treasury, this commission was independent to the extreme. Ultimately, it would spend billions of dollars over a period of more than twenty-five years, with virtually no congressional oversight. Because no US funding was involved, Congress had no authority in the matter, despite Treasury's role. After studying JECOR extensively, David Holden and Richard Johns state, "It was the most far-reaching agreement of its kind ever concluded by the US with a developing country. It had the potential to entrench the US deeply in the Kingdom, fortifying the concept of mutual interdependence."[3]

The Department of the Treasury brought MAIN in at an early stage to serve as an adviser. I was summoned and told that my job would be critical, and that everything I did and learned should be considered highly confidential. From my vantage point, it seemed like a clandestine operation. At the time, I was led to believe that MAIN was the lead consultant in that process; I subsequently came to realize that we were one of several consultants whose expertise was sought.

Because everything was done in the greatest secrecy, I was not privy to Treasury's discussions with other consultants, and I therefore cannot be certain about the importance of my role in this precedent-setting deal. I do know that the arrangement established new standards for EHMs and that it launched innovative alternatives to the traditional approaches for advancing the interests of empire. I also know that most of the scenarios that evolved from my studies were ultimately implemented, that MAIN was rewarded with one of the first major — and extremely profitable — contracts in Saudi Arabia, and that I received a large bonus that year.

My job was to develop forecasts of what might happen in Saudi Arabia if vast amounts of money were invested in its infrastructure, and to map out scenarios for spending that money. In short,

I was asked to apply as much creativity as I could to justifying the infusion of hundreds of millions of dollars into the Saudi Arabian economy, under conditions that would include US engineering and construction companies. I was told to do this on my own, not to rely on my staff, and I was sequestered in a small conference room several floors above the one where my department was located. I was warned that my job was both a matter of national security and potentially very lucrative for MAIN.

I understood, of course, that the primary objective here was not the usual — to burden this country with debts it could never repay — but rather to find ways that would assure that a large portion of petrodollars found their way back to the United States. In the process, Saudi Arabia would be drawn in, its economy would become increasingly intertwined with and dependent upon ours, and presumably it would grow more Westernized and therefore more sympathetic to and integrated with our system.

Once I got started, I realized that the goats wandering the streets of Riyadh were the symbolic key; they were a sore point among Saudis jet-setting around the world. Those goats begged to be replaced by something more appropriate for this desert kingdom that craved entry into the modern world. I also knew that OPEC economists were stressing the need for oil-rich countries to obtain more value-added products from their petroleum. Rather than simply exporting crude oil, the economists were urging these countries to develop industries of their own, to use this oil to produce petroleum-based products they could sell to the rest of the world at a higher price than that brought by the crude itself.

This twin realization opened the door to a strategy I felt certain would be a win-win situation for everyone. The goats, of course, were merely an entry point. Oil revenues could be employed to hire US companies to replace the goats with the world's most modern garbage collection and disposal system, and the Saudis could take great pride in this state-of-the-art technology.

I came to think of the goats as one side of an equation that could be applied to most of the kingdom's economic sectors, a formula for success in the eyes of the royal family, the US Department of the Treasury, and my bosses at MAIN. Under this formula, money would be earmarked to create an industrial sector focused on transforming raw petroleum into finished products for export. Large petrochemical complexes would rise from the desert, and around them, huge industrial parks. Naturally, such a plan would also require the construction of thousands of megawatts of electrical generating capacity, transmission and distribution lines, highways, pipelines, communications networks, and transportation systems, including new airports, improved seaports, a vast array of service industries, and the infrastructure essential to keep all these cogs turning.

We all had high expectations that this plan would evolve into a model of how things should be done in the rest of the world. Globetrotting Saudis would sing our praises; they would invite leaders from many countries to come to Saudi Arabia and witness the miracles we had accomplished; those leaders would then call on us to help them devise similar plans for their countries and — in most cases, for countries outside the ring of OPEC — would arrange World Bank or other debt-ridden methods for financing them. The global empire would be well served.

As I worked through these ideas, I thought of the goats, and the words of my driver often echoed in my ears: "No self-respecting Saudi would ever collect trash." I had heard that refrain repeatedly, in many different contexts. It was obvious that the Saudis had no intention of putting their own people to work at menial tasks, whether as laborers in industrial facilities or in the actual construction of any of the projects. In the first place, there were too few of them. In addition, the royal House of Saud had indicated a commitment to providing its citizens with a level of education and a lifestyle that were inconsistent with those of manual laborers. The Saudis might manage others, but they had no desire or motivation to become factory and construction workers. Therefore, it would be necessary to import a labor force from other countries — countries where labor was cheap and where people needed work. If possible, the labor should come from other Middle Eastern or Islamic countries, such as Egypt, Palestine, Pakistan, or Yemen.

This prospect created an even greater new stratagem for development opportunities. Mammoth housing complexes would have to be constructed for these laborers, as would shopping malls, hospitals, fire and police department facilities, water and sewage treatment

plants, electrical, communications, and transportation networks —
in fact, the end result would be to create modern cities where
once only deserts had existed. Here, too, was the opportunity
to explore emerging technologies in, for example, desalinization
plants, microwave systems, health care complexes, and computer
technologies.

Saudi Arabia was a planner's dream come true, and also a
fantasy realized, for anyone associated with the engineering and
construction business. It presented an economic opportunity unri-
valed by any in history: an economically developing country with
virtually unlimited financial resources and a desire to enter the
modern age in a big way, very quickly.

I must admit that I enjoyed this job immensely. There was no
solid data available in Saudi Arabia, in the Boston Public Library,
or anywhere else that justified the use of econometric models in
this context. In fact, the magnitude of the job — the total and immediate transformation of an entire nation on a scale never before
witnessed — meant that even had historical data existed, it would
have been irrelevant.

Nor was anyone expecting this type of quantitative analysis, at
least not at this stage of the game. I simply put my imagination to
work and wrote reports that envisioned a glorious future for the
kingdom. I had rule-of-thumb numbers I could use to estimate
such things as the approximate cost to produce a megawatt of electricity, a mile of road, or adequate water, sewage, housing, food,
and public services for one laborer. I was not supposed to refine
these estimates or draw final conclusions. My job was simply to
describe a series of plans (more accurately, perhaps, "visions") of
what might be possible, and to arrive at rough estimates of the costs
associated with them.

I always kept in mind the true objectives: maximizing payouts
to US firms and making Saudi Arabia increasingly dependent on
the United States. It did not take long to realize how closely the
two went together. Almost all the newly developed projects would
require continual upgrading and servicing, and they were so highly
technical as to assure that the companies that originally developed
them would have to maintain and modernize them. In fact, as I

moved forward with my work, I began to assemble two lists for each of the projects I envisioned: one for the types of design-and-construction contracts we could expect, and another for long-term service and management agreements. MAIN, Bechtel, Brown & Root, Halliburton, Stone & Webster, and many other US engineers and contractors would profit handsomely for decades to come.

Beyond the purely economic, there was another twist that would render Saudi Arabia dependent on us, though in a very different way. The modernization of this oil-rich kingdom would trigger adverse reactions. For instance, conservative Muslims would be furious; Israel and other neighboring countries would feel threatened. The economic development of this nation was likely to spawn the growth of another industry: protecting the Arabian Peninsula. Private companies specializing in such activities, as well as the US military and defense industry, could expect generous contracts — and, once again, long-term service and management agreements. Their presence would require another phase of engineering and construction projects, including airports, missile sites, personnel bases, and all of the infrastructure associated with such facilities.

I sent my reports in sealed envelopes through interoffice mail, addressed to "Treasury Department Project Manager." I occasionally met with a couple of other members of our team — vice presidents at MAIN and my superiors. Because we had no official name for this project, which was still in the research and development phase and was not yet part of JECOR, we referred to it only — and with hushed voices — as SAMA. Ostensibly, this stood for Saudi Arabian Money-Laundering Affair, but it was also a tongue-in-cheek play on words; the kingdom's central bank was called the Saudi Arabian Monetary Agency, or SAMA.

Sometimes a Treasury representative would join us. I asked few questions during these meetings. Mainly, I just described my work, responded to their comments, and agreed to try to do whatever was asked of me. The vice presidents and Treasury representatives were especially impressed with my ideas about the long-term service and management agreements. It prodded one of the vice presidents to coin a phrase we often used after that, referring to the kingdom as "the cow we can milk until the sun sets on our retirement." For me, that phrase always conjured images of goats rather than cows.

It was during those meetings that I came to realize that several of our competitors were involved in similar tasks, and that in the end we all expected to be awarded lucrative contracts as a result of our efforts. I assumed that MAIN and the other firms were footing the bill for this preliminary work, taking a short-term risk in order to throw our hats into the ring. This assumption was reinforced by the fact that the number I charged my time to on our daily personal time sheets appeared to be a general and administrative overhead account. Such an approach was typical of the research and development/proposal preparation phase of most projects. In this case, the initial investment certainly far exceeded the norm, but those vice presidents seemed extremely confident about the payback.

Despite the knowledge that our competitors were also involved, we all assumed that there was enough work to go around. I also had been in the business long enough to believe that the rewards bestowed would reflect the level of Treasury's acceptance of the work we had done, and that those consultants who came up with the approaches that were finally implemented would receive the choicest contracts. I took it as a personal challenge to create scenarios that would make it to the design-and-construct stage. My star was already rising rapidly at MAIN. Being a key player in SAMA would guarantee its acceleration, if we were successful.

During our meetings, we also openly discussed the likelihood that SAMA and the entire JECOR operation would set new precedents. It represented an innovative approach to creating lucrative work in countries that did not need to incur debts through the international banks. Iran and Iraq came immediately to mind as two additional examples of such countries. Moreover, given human nature, we felt that the leaders of such countries would likely be motivated to try to emulate Saudi Arabia. There seemed little doubt that the 1973 oil embargo — which had initially appeared to be so negative — would end up offering many unexpected gifts to the engineering and construction business, and would help to further pave the road to global empire.

I worked on that visionary phase for about eight months —

although never for more than several intense days at a time — sequestered in my private conference room or in my apartment overlooking Boston Common. My staff all had other assignments and pretty much took care of themselves, although I checked in on them periodically. Over time, the secrecy around our work declined. More people became aware that something big involving Saudi Arabia was going on. Excitement swelled, rumors swirled. The vice presidents and Treasury representatives grew more open — in part, I believe, because they themselves became privy to more information as details about the ingenious scheme emerged.

Under this evolving plan, Washington wanted the Saudis to guarantee to maintain oil supplies and prices at levels that could fluctuate but that would always remain acceptable to the United States and our allies. If other countries, such as Iran, Iraq, Indonesia, or Venezuela, threatened embargoes, Saudi Arabia, with its vast petroleum supplies, would step in to fill the gap; simply the knowledge that they might do so would, in the long run, discourage other countries from even considering an embargo. In exchange for this guarantee, Washington would offer the House of Saud an amazingly attractive deal: a commitment to provide total and unequivocal US political and — if necessary — military support, thereby ensuring their continued existence as the rulers of their country.

It was a deal the House of Saud could hardly refuse, given its geographic location, lack of military might, and general vulnerability to neighbors like Iran, Syria, Iraq, and Israel. Naturally, therefore, Washington used its advantage to impose one other critical condition, a condition that redefined the role of EHMs in the world and served as a model we would later attempt to apply in other countries, most notably in Iraq. In retrospect, I sometimes find it difficult to understand how Saudi Arabia could have accepted this condition. Certainly, most of the rest of the Arab world, OPEC, and other Islamic countries were appalled when they discovered the terms of the deal and the manner in which the royal house capitulated to Washington's demands.

The condition was that Saudi Arabia would use its petrodollars to purchase US government securities; in turn, the interest earned by these securities would be spent by the US Department of the Treasury in ways that enabled Saudi Arabia to emerge from a medieval society into the modern, industrialized world. In other words, the interest compounding on billions of dollars of the kingdom's oil income would be used to pay US companies to fulfill the vision I (and presumably some of my competitors) had come up with, to convert Saudi Arabia into a modern industrial power. Our own US Department of the Treasury would hire us, at Saudi expense, to build infrastructure projects and even entire cities throughout the Arabian Peninsula.

Although the Saudis reserved the right to provide input regarding the general nature of these projects, the reality was that an elite corps of foreigners (mostly infidels, in the eyes of Muslims) would determine the future appearance and economic makeup of the Arabian Peninsula. And this would occur in a kingdom that had been founded on conservative Wahhabi principles and run according to those principles for several centuries. It seemed a huge leap of faith on their part, yet under the circumstances, and due to the political and military pressures undoubtedly brought to bear by Washington, I suspected that the Saud family felt they had few alternatives.

From our perspective, the prospects for immense profits seemed limitless. It was a sweetheart deal with potential to set an amazing precedent. And to make the deal even sweeter, no one had to obtain congressional approval — a process loathed by corporations, particularly privately owned ones like Bechtel and MAIN, which prefer not to open their books or share their secrets with anyone. Thomas W. Lippman, an adjunct scholar at the Middle East Institute and a former journalist, eloquently summarizes the salient points of this deal:

> The Saudis, rolling in cash, would deliver hundreds of millions of dollars to Treasury, which held on to the funds until they were needed to pay vendors or employees. This system assured that the Saudi money would be recycled back into the American economy.... It also ensured that the commission's managers could undertake whatever projects they and the Saudis agreed were useful without having to justify them to Congress.[4]

Establishing the parameters for this historic undertaking took less time than anyone could have imagined. After that, however, we had to figure out a way to implement it. To set the process in motion, someone at the highest level of government was dispatched to Saudi Arabia — an extremely confidential mission. I never knew for sure, but I believe the envoy was Henry Kissinger.

Whoever the envoy was, his first job was to remind the royal family about what had happened in neighboring Iran when Mossadegh tried to oust British petroleum interests. Next, he would outline a plan that would be too attractive for them to turn down, in effect conveying to the Saudis that they had few alternatives. I have no doubt that they were left with the distinct impression that either they could accept our offer and thus gain assurances that we would support and protect them as rulers, or they could refuse — and go the way of Mossadegh. When the envoy returned to Washington, he brought with him the message that the Saudis would like to comply.

There was just one slight obstacle. We would have to convince key players in the Saudi government. This, we were informed, was a family matter. Saudi Arabia was not a democracy, and yet it seemed that within the House of Saud there was a need for consensus.

In 1975, I was assigned to one of those key players. I always thought of him as Prince W., although I never determined that he was actually a crown prince. My job was to persuade him that the Saudi Arabian Money-Laundering Affair would benefit his country as well as him personally.

This was not as easy as it appeared at first. Prince W. professed himself a good Wahhabi and insisted that he did not want to see his country follow in the footsteps of Western commercialism. He also claimed that he understood the insidious nature of what we were proposing. We had, he said, the same objectives as the crusaders a millennium earlier: the Christianization of the Arab world. In fact, he was partially right about this. In my opinion, the difference between the crusaders and us was a matter of degree. Europe's medieval Catholics claimed their goal was to save Muslims from purgatory; we claimed that we wanted to help the Saudis modernize. In truth, I believe the crusaders, like the corporatocracy, were primarily seeking to expand their empire.

Religious beliefs aside, Prince W. had one weakness — for beautiful blonds. It seems almost ludicrous to mention what has now become an unfair stereotype, and I should mention that Prince W. was the only man among many Saudis I have known who had this proclivity, or at least the only one who was willing to let me see it. Yet, it played a role in structuring this historic deal, and it demonstrates how far I would go to complete my mission.

CHAPTER 16

Pimping, and Financing Osama bin Laden

From the start, Prince W. let me know that whenever he came to visit me in Boston, he expected to be entertained by a woman of his liking, and that he expected her to perform more functions than those of a simple escort. But he most definitely did not want a professional call girl, someone he or his family members might bump into on the street or at a cocktail party. My meetings with Prince W. were held in secret, which made it easier for me to comply with his wishes.

"Sally" lived in the Boston area. I knew the prince would be attracted to her blond hair and blue eyes. Her husband, a United Airlines pilot who traveled a great deal both on and off the job, made little attempt to hide his infidelities. It seemed to me that Sally had a cavalier attitude about her husband's activities. She appreciated his salary, the plush Boston condo, and the benefits a pilot's spouse enjoyed in those days. She agreed to meet Prince W. on one condition: she insisted that the future of their relationship depended entirely upon his behavior and attitude toward her.

Fortunately for me, each met the other's criteria.

The Prince W.-Sally Affair, a subchapter of the Saudi Arabian Money-Laundering Affair, created its own set of problems for me. MAIN strictly prohibited its partners from doing anything illicit. From a legal standpoint, I was procuring sex — pimping — an illegal activity in Massachusetts, so I needed to find a way to pay for Sally's services. Luckily, the accounting department allowed me great liberties with my expense account. I was a good tipper, and I managed to persuade waiters in some of the most posh restaurants in Boston to provide me with blank receipts; it was an era when people, not computers, filled out receipts.

Prince W. grew bolder as time went by. Eventually, he wanted me to arrange for Sally to come and live in his private cottage in

Saudi Arabia. This was not an unheard-of request in those days; there was an active trade in young women between certain European countries and the Middle East. These women were given contracts for some specified period of time, and when the contract expired, they went home to very substantial bank accounts. Robert Baer, a case officer in the CIA's directorate of operations for twenty years, and a specialist in the Middle East, sums it up: "In the early 1970s, when the petrodollars started flooding in, enterprising Lebanese began smuggling hookers into the kingdom for the princes.... Since no one in the royal family knows how to balance a checkbook, the Lebanese became fabulously wealthy."[1]

I was familiar with this situation and even knew people who could arrange such contracts. However, for me, there were three major obstacles: Sally, the payment, and the fact I was doing something illegal and morally reprehensible. I was certain that Sally was not about to leave Boston and move to a desert mansion in the Middle East. It was also pretty obvious that no collection of blank restaurant receipts would cover this expense.

Prince W. took care of my financial concerns by assuring me that he expected to pay for his new mistress himself; I was only required to make the arrangements. It also gave me great relief when he went on to confide that the Saudi Arabian Sally did not have to be the exact same person as the one who had kept him company in the United States. I made calls to several friends who had Lebanese contacts in London and Amsterdam. Within a couple of weeks, a surrogate Sally signed a contract. My worries around the legal issues were eased by brokering the deal through people in England and the Netherlands. I tried to assuage my conscience by telling myself that everyone involved was a mature adult, making his or her own decision. Who was I to judge?

Prince W. was a complex person. Sally satisfied a corporeal desire, and my ability to help the prince in this regard earned me his trust. However, it by no means convinced him that SAMA was a strategy he wanted to recommend for his country. I had to work very hard to win my case. I spent many hours showing him statistics and helping him analyze studies we had undertaken for other countries, including the econometric models I had developed for Kuwait while training with Claudine, during those first few months before heading to Indonesia. Eventually he relented.

I am not familiar with the details of what went on between my fellow EHMs and the other key Saudi players. All I know is that the entire package was finally approved by the royal family. MAIN was rewarded for its part with one of the first highly lucrative contracts, administered by the US Department of the Treasury. We were commissioned to make a complete survey of the country's disorganized and outmoded electrical system and to design a new one that would meet standards equivalent to those in the United States.

As usual, it was my job to send in the first team, to develop economic and electric load forecasts for each region of the country. Three of the men who worked for me — all experienced in international projects — were preparing to leave for Riyadh when word came down from our legal department that under the terms of the contract, we were obligated to have a fully equipped office up and running in Riyadh within the next few weeks. This clause had apparently gone unnoticed for more than a month. Our agreement with Treasury further stipulated that all equipment had to be manufactured either in the United States or in Saudi Arabia. Because Saudi Arabia did not have factories for producing such items, everything had to be sent from the States. To our chagrin, we discovered that long lines of tankers were queued up, waiting to get into ports on the Arabian Peninsula. It could take many months to get a shipment of supplies into the kingdom.

MAIN was not about to lose such a valuable contract over a couple of rooms of office furniture. At a conference of all the partners involved, we brainstormed for several hours. The solution we settled on was to charter a Boeing 747, fill it with supplies from Boston-area stores, and send it off to Saudi Arabia. I remember thinking that it would be fitting if the plane were owned by United Airlines and commanded by a certain pilot whose wife had played such a critical role in bringing the House of Saud around.

The deal between the United States and Saudi Arabia transformed the kingdom practically overnight. The goats were replaced by two hundred bright yellow American trash compactor trucks, provided under a $200 million contract with Waste Management

Inc.[2] In similar fashion, every sector of the Saudi economy was modernized, from agriculture and energy to education and communications. As Thomas Lippman observed in 2004:

> Americans have reshaped a vast, bleak landscape of nomads' tents and farmers' mud huts in their own image, right down to Starbucks on the corner and the wheelchair-accessible ramps in the newest public buildings. Saudi Arabia today is a country of expressways, computers, air-conditioned malls filled with the same glossy shops found in prosperous American suburbs, elegant hotels, fast-food restaurants, satellite television, up-to-date hospitals, high-rise office towers, and amusement parks featuring whirling rides.[3]

The plans we conceived in 1974 set a standard for future negotiations with oil-rich countries. In a way, SAMA/JECOR was the next plateau after the one Kermit Roosevelt had established in Iran. It introduced an innovative level of sophistication to the arsenal of political-economic weapons used by a new breed of soldiers for global empire.

The Saudi Arabian Money-Laundering Affair and the Joint Commission also set new precedents for international jurisprudence. This was very evident in the case of Idi Amin. When the notorious Ugandan dictator went into exile in 1979, he eventually was given asylum in Saudi Arabia. Although he was considered a murderous despot responsible for the deaths of between one hundred thousand and three hundred thousand people, he retired to a life of luxury, complete with cars and domestic servants provided by the House of Saud. The United States quietly objected but refused to press the issue for fear of undermining its arrangement with the Saudis. Amin whiled away his last years fishing and taking strolls on the beach. In 2003, he died in Jeddah, succumbing to kidney failure.[4]

More subtle and ultimately much more damaging was the role Saudi Arabia was allowed to play in financing international terrorism. The United States made no secret of its desire to have the House of Saud bankroll Osama bin Laden's Afghan war against the Soviet Union during the 1980s, and Riyadh and Washington together contributed an estimated $3.5 billion to the mujahideen.[5] However, US and Saudi participation went far beyond this.

In late 2003, *US News & World Report* conducted an exhaustive study titled "The Saudi Connection." The magazine reviewed thousands of pages of court records, US and foreign intelligence reports, and other documents, and interviewed dozens of government officials and experts on terrorism and the Middle East. Its findings include the following:

> The evidence was indisputable: Saudi Arabia, America's longtime ally and the world's largest oil producer, had somehow become, as a senior Treasury Department official put it, "the epicenter" of terrorist financing....
>
> Starting in the late 1980s — after the dual shocks of the Iranian revolution and the Soviet war in Afghanistan — Saudi Arabia's quasi-official charities became the primary source of funds for the fast-growing jihad movement. In some 20 countries the money was used to run paramilitary training camps, purchase weapons, and recruit new members....
>
> Saudi largess encouraged US officials to look the other way, some veteran intelligence officers say. Billions of dollars in contracts, grants, and salaries have gone to a broad range of former US officials who had dealt with the Saudis: ambassadors, CIA station chiefs, even cabinet secretaries....
>
> Electronic intercepts of conversations implicated members of the royal family in backing not only Al Qaeda but also other terrorist groups.[6]

After the 2001 attacks on the World Trade Center and the Pentagon, more evidence emerged about the covert relationships between Washington and Riyadh. In October 2003, *Vanity Fair* magazine disclosed information that had not previously been made public, in an in-depth report titled "Saving the Saudis." The story that emerged about the relationship between the Bush family, the House of Saud, and the bin Laden family did not surprise me. I knew that those relationships went back at least to the time of the Saudi Arabian Money-Laundering Affair, which began in 1974, and to George H. W. Bush's terms as US ambassador to the United

Nations (from 1971 to 1973) and then as head of the CIA (from 1976 to 1977). What surprised me was the fact that the truth had finally made the press. *Vanity Fair* concluded:

> The Bush family and the House of Saud, the two most powerful dynasties in the world, have had close personal, business, and political ties for more than 20 years....
>
> In the private sector, the Saudis supported Harken Energy, a struggling oil company in which George W. Bush was an investor. Most recently, former president George H. W. Bush and his longtime ally, former Secretary of State James A. Baker III, have appeared before Saudis at fundraisers for the Carlyle Group, arguably the biggest private equity firm in the world. Today, former president Bush continues to serve as a senior adviser to the firm, whose investors allegedly include a Saudi accused of ties to terrorist support groups....
>
> Just days after 9/11, wealthy Saudi Arabians, including members of the bin Laden family, were whisked out of the US on private jets. No one will admit to clearing the flights, and the passengers weren't questioned. Did the Bush family's long relationship with the Saudis help make it happen?[7]

PART III: 1975–1981

CHAPTER 17

Panama Canal Negotiations and Graham Greene

Saudi Arabia made many careers. Mine was already well on the way, but my successes in the desert kingdom certainly opened new doors for me. By 1977, I had built a small empire that included a staff of around twenty professionals headquartered in our Boston office, and a stable of consultants from MAIN's other departments and offices scattered across the globe. I had become the youngest partner in the firm's hundred-year history. In addition to my title of Chief Economist, I was named manager of Economics and Regional Planning. I was lecturing at Harvard and other venues, and newspapers were soliciting articles from me about current events.[1] I owned a sailing yacht that was docked in Boston Harbor next to the historic battleship *Constitution*, "Old Ironsides," renowned for subduing the Barbary pirates not long after the Revolutionary War. I was being paid an excellent salary, and I had equity that promised to elevate me to the rarefied heights of millionaire well before I turned forty. True, my marriage had fallen apart, but I was spending time with women on several continents.

Bruno came up with an idea for an innovative approach to forecasting: an econometric model based on the writings of a turn-of-the-century Russian mathematician. The model involved assigning subjective probabilities to predictions that certain specific sectors of an economy would grow. It seemed an ideal tool to justify the inflated rates of increase we liked to show in order to obtain large loans, and Bruno asked me to see what I could do with the concept.

I brought a young MIT mathematician, Dr. Nadipuram Prasad, into my department and gave him a budget. Within six months he developed the Markov method for econometric modeling. Together we hammered out a series of technical papers that presented Markov as a revolutionary method for forecasting the impact of infrastructure investment on economic development.

It was exactly what we wanted: a tool that scientifically "proved"
we were doing countries a favor by helping them incur debts they
would never be able to pay off. In addition, only a highly skilled
econometrician with lots of time and money could possibly comprehend the intricacies of Markov or question its conclusions.
The papers were published by several prestigious organizations,
and we formally presented them at conferences and universities
in a number of countries. The papers — and we — became famous
throughout the industry.[2]

Omar Torrijos and I honored our secret agreement. I made sure
that our studies were honest and that our recommendations took
into account the poor. Although I heard grumbling that my forecasts in Panama were not up to their usual inflated standards, and
even that they smacked of socialism, the fact was that MAIN kept
winning contracts from the Torrijos government. These contracts
included a first: to provide innovative master plans that involved
agriculture along with the more traditional infrastructure sectors.
I also watched from the sidelines as Torrijos and Jimmy Carter set
out to renegotiate the Canal treaty.

The Canal negotiations generated great interest and great passions around the world. People everywhere waited to see whether
the United States would do what most of the rest of the world
believed was the right thing — allow the Panamanians to take control — or would instead try to reestablish our global version of Manifest Destiny, which had been shaken by our Vietnam debacle. For
many, it appeared that a reasonable and compassionate man had
been elected to the US presidency at just the right time. However,
the conservative bastions of Washington and the pulpits of the
religious right rang with indignation. How could we give up this
bulwark of national defense, this symbol of US ingenuity, this rib-
bon of water that tied South America's fortunes to the whims of
US commercial interests?

During my trips to Panama, I became accustomed to staying at
the Hotel Continental. However, on my fifth visit I moved across
the street to the Hotel Panama because the Continental was undergoing renovations and the construction was very noisy. At first, I
resented the inconvenience — the Continental had been my home

away from home. But the expansive lobby where I sat in the Hotel Panama, with its rattan chairs and paddle-bladed wooden ceiling fans, was growing on me. It could have been the set of *Casablanca*, and I fantasized that Humphrey Bogart might stroll in at any moment. I set down the copy of the *New York Review of Books* in which I had just finished reading a Graham Greene article about Panama and stared up at those fans, recalling an evening almost two years earlier.

"Ford is a weak president who won't be reelected," Omar Torrijos had predicted during that evening in 1975 at a private club in Panama City. He was speaking to a group of influential Panamanians. I was one of the few foreigners who had been invited to the elegant old club. "That's the reason I decided to accelerate this Canal issue. It's a good time to launch an all-out political battle to win it back."

The speech inspired me. I returned to my hotel room and scratched out a letter that I eventually mailed to the *Boston Globe*. Back in Boston, an editor responded by calling me at my office to request that I write an op-ed piece. I knew that it was a risky thing to do, but I felt strongly about the Canal issue, and, looking back, I see that it helped me deal with a growing sense of frustration over my job. Furthermore, I told myself that Torrijos would appreciate it, and I might use it to help MAIN get more business in Panama.

"Colonialism in Panama Has No Place in 1975" took up nearly half the page opposite the editorials in the September 19, 1975, edition.

The article cited three specific reasons for transferring the Canal to Panama. First, "the present situation is unjust — a good reason for any decision." Second, "the existing treaty creates far graver security risks than would result from turning more control over to the Panamanians." I referenced a study conducted by the Interoceanic Canal Commission, which concluded that "traffic could be halted for two years by a bomb planted — conceivably by one man — in the side of Gatun Dam," a point General Torrijos himself had publicly emphasized. And third, "the present situation is creating serious problems for already-troubled United States–Latin American relations." I ended with the following:

The best way of assuring the continued and efficient operation of the Canal is to help Panamanians gain control over
and responsibility for it. In so doing, we could take pride in
initiating an action that would reaffirm commitments to the
cause of self-determination to which we pledged ourselves
200 years ago....

Colonialism was in vogue at the turn of the century (early
1900s) as it had been in 1775. Perhaps ratification of such a
treaty can be understood in the context of those times. Today
it is without justification. Colonialism has no place in 1975.
We, celebrating our bicentennial, should realize this, and act
accordingly.[3]

Writing that piece was a bold move on my part, especially
since I had recently been made a partner at MAIN. Partners were
expected to avoid the press, and certainly to refrain from publishing political diatribes on the editorial pages of New England's most
prestigious newspaper. I received through interoffice mail a pile
of nasty, mostly anonymous notes stapled to copies of the article.
I was certain that I recognized the handwriting on one as that of
Charlie Illingworth. My first project manager had been at MAIN
for over ten years (compared to less than five for me) and was not
yet a partner. A fierce skull and crossbones figured prominently
on the note, and its message was simple: "Is this Commie really a
partner in our firm?"

Bruno summoned me to his office and said, "You'll get loads of
grief over this. MAIN's a pretty conservative place. But I want you
to know I think you're smart. Torrijos will love it; I do hope you're
sending him a copy. Good. Well, these jokers here in this office, the
ones who think Torrijos is a Socialist, really won't give a damn as
long as the work flows in."

Bruno had been right — as usual. Now it was 1977, Carter was in
the White House, and serious Canal negotiations were under way.
Many of MAIN's competitors had taken the wrong side and had
been turned out of Panama, but our work had multiplied. And I
was sitting in the lobby of the Hotel Panama, having just finished
reading an article by Graham Greene in the *New York Review of
Books*.

The article, "The Country with Five Frontiers," was a gutsy piece that included a discussion of corruption among senior officers in Panama's National Guard. The author pointed out that the general himself admitted to giving many of his staff special privileges, such as superior housing, because "if I don't pay them, the CIA will." The clear implication was that the US intelligence community was determined to undermine the wishes of President Carter and, if necessary, would bribe Panama's military chiefs into sabotaging the treaty negotiations.[4] I could not help but wonder if the jackals had begun to circle Torrijos.

I had seen, in the "People" section of *Time* or *Newsweek*, a photograph of Torrijos and Greene sitting together; the caption indicated that the writer was a special guest who had become a good friend. I wondered how the general felt about this novelist, whom he apparently trusted, writing such a critique.

Graham Greene's article raised another question, one that related to that day in 1972 when I had sat across a coffee table from Torrijos. At the time, I had assumed that Torrijos knew the foreign aid game was there to make him rich while shackling his country with debt. I had been sure he knew that the process was based on the assumption that men in power are corruptible, and that his decision not to seek personal benefit — but rather to use foreign aid to truly help his people — would be seen as a threat that might eventually topple the entire system. The world was watching this man; his actions had ramifications that reached far beyond Panama and would therefore not be taken lightly.

I had wondered how the corporatocracy would react if loans made to Panama helped the poor without contributing to impossible debts. Now I wondered whether Torrijos regretted the deal he and I had struck that day — and I wasn't quite sure how I felt about those deals myself. I had stepped back from my EHM role. I had played his game instead of mine, accepting his insistence on honesty in exchange for more contracts. In purely economic terms, it had been a wise business decision for MAIN. Nonetheless, it had been inconsistent with what Claudine had instilled in me; it was not advancing the global empire. Had it now unleashed the jackals?

I recalled thinking, when I left Torrijos's bungalow that day, that Latin American history is littered with dead heroes. A system based on corrupting public figures does not take kindly to public figures who refuse to be corrupted.

Then I thought my eyes were playing tricks. A familiar figure was walking slowly across the lobby. At first, I was so confused that I believed it was Humphrey Bogart, but Bogart was long deceased. Then I recognized the man ambling past me as one of the great figures in modern English literature, author of *The Power and the Glory, The Comedians, Our Man in Havana*, and the article I had just set down on the table next to me. Graham Greene hesitated a moment, peered around, and headed for the coffee shop.

I was tempted to call out or to run after him, but I stopped myself. An inner voice said he needed his privacy; another warned that he would shun me. I picked up the *New York Review of Books* and was surprised a moment later to discover that I was standing in the doorway to the coffee shop.

I had breakfasted earlier that morning, and the maitre d' gave me an odd look. I glanced around. Greene sat alone at a table near the wall. I pointed to the table beside him.

"Over there," I told the maitre d.' "Can I sit there for another breakfast?"

I was always a good tipper; the maitre d' smiled knowingly and led me to the table.

The novelist was absorbed in his newspaper. I ordered coffee and a croissant with honey. I wanted to discover Greene's thoughts about Panama, Torrijos, and the Canal affair but had no idea how to initiate such a conversation. Then he looked up to take a sip from his glass.

"Excuse me," I said.

He glared at me — or so it seemed. "Yes?"

"I hate to intrude. But you are Graham Greene, aren't you?"

"Why, yes indeed." He smiled warmly. "Most people in Panama don't recognize me."

I gushed that he was my favorite novelist and then gave him a brief life history, including my work at MAIN and my meetings with Torrijos. He asked if I was the consultant who had written an article about the United States getting out of Panama. "In the *Boston Globe*, if I recall correctly."

I was flabbergasted.

"A courageous thing to do, given your position," he said. "Won't you join me?"

I moved to his table and sat there with him for what must have been an hour and a half. I realized as we chatted how very close to Torrijos he had grown. He spoke of the general at times like a father speaking about his son.

"The general," he said, "invited me to write a book about his country. I'm doing just that. This one will be nonfiction — something a bit off the line for me."

I asked him why he usually wrote novels instead of nonfiction.

"Fiction is safer," he said. "Most of my subject matter is controversial. Vietnam. Haiti. The Mexican Revolution. A lot of publishers would be afraid to publish nonfiction about these matters." He pointed at the *New York Review of Books*, where it lay on the table I had vacated. "Words like those can cause a great deal of damage." Then he smiled. "Besides, I like to write fiction. It gives me much greater freedom." He looked at me intensely. "The important thing is to write about things that matter. Like your *Globe* article about the Canal."

His admiration for Torrijos was obvious. It seemed that Panama's head of state could impress a novelist every bit as much as he impressed the poor and dispossessed. Equally obvious was Greene's concern for his friend's life.

"It's a huge endeavor," he exclaimed, "taking on the Giant of the North." He shook his head sadly. "I fear for his safety."

Then it was time for him to leave.

"Must catch a flight to France," he said, rising slowly and shaking my hand. He peered into my eyes. "Why don't you write a book?" He gave me an encouraging nod. "It's in you. But remember, make it about things that matter." He turned and walked away. Then he stopped and came back a few steps into the restaurant.

"Don't worry," he said. "The general will prevail. He'll get the Canal back."

Torrijos did get it back. In that same year, 1977, he successfully negotiated new treaties with President Carter that transferred the Canal Zone and the Canal itself over to Panamanian control. Then the White House had to convince the US Congress to ratify it. A long and arduous battle ensued. In the final tally, the Canal treaty was ratified by a single vote. Conservatives swore revenge.

When Graham Greene's nonfiction book *Getting to Know the General* came out many years later, it was dedicated "To the friends of my friend, Omar Torrijos, in Nicaragua, El Salvador, and Panama."[5]

⊕ CHAPTER 18

Iran's King of Kings

Between 1975 and 1978, I frequently visited Iran. Sometimes I commuted between Latin America or Indonesia and Tehran. The Shah of Shahs (literally, "King of Kings," his official title) presented a completely different situation from that in the other countries where we worked.

Iran was oil rich, and like Saudi Arabia, it did not need to incur debt in order to finance its ambitious list of projects. However, Iran differed significantly from Saudi Arabia in that its large population, though predominantly Middle Eastern and Muslim, was not Arabic. The people were also Shiite, not Sunni; most Iranian women did not wear veils — in fact, some even sported miniskirts. In addition, the country had a history of political turmoil — both internally and in its relationships with its neighbors. Therefore, we took a different approach: Washington and the business community joined forces to turn the shah into a symbol of progress.

We launched an immense effort to show the world what a strong, democratic friend of US corporate and political interests could accomplish. Never mind his obviously undemocratic title or the less obvious fact of the CIA-orchestrated coup against the democratically elected premier who preceded him; Washington and its European partners were determined to present the shah's government as an alternative to those in Iraq, Libya, China, Korea, and other nations where a powerful undercurrent of anti-Americanism was surfacing.

To all appearances, the shah was a progressive friend of the underprivileged. In 1962, he ordered large private landholdings broken up and turned over to peasant owners. The following year, he inaugurated his White Revolution, which involved an extensive agenda for socioeconomic reforms. The power of OPEC grew during the 1970s, and the shah became an increasingly influential world leader. At the same time, Iran developed one of the most powerful military forces in the Muslim Middle East.[1]

MAIN was involved in projects that covered most of the country, from tourist areas along the Caspian Sea in the north to secret military installations overlooking the Strait of Hormuz in the south. Once again, the focus of our work was to forecast regional development potentials and then to design electrical generating, transmission, and distribution systems that would provide the all-important energy required to fuel the military, industrial, and commercial growth that would realize these forecasts.

I visited most of the major regions of Iran at one time or another. I followed the old caravan trail through the desert mountains, from Kirman to Bandar 'Abbas, and I roamed the ruins of Persepolis, the legendary palace of ancient kings and one of the wonders of the classical world. I toured the country's most famous and spectacular sites: Shiraz, Isfahan, and the magnificent tent city near Persepolis where the shah had been crowned. In the process, I developed a genuine love for this land and its complex people.

On the surface, Iran seemed to be a model example of Christian–Muslim cooperation. However, I soon learned that tranquil appearances may mask deep resentment.

Late one evening in 1977, I returned to my hotel room to find a note shoved under my door. I was shocked to discover that it was signed by a man named Yamin. I had never met him, but he had been described to me during a government briefing as a famous and most subversive radical. In beautifully crafted English script, the note invited me to meet him at a designated restaurant. However, there was a warning: I was to come only if I was interested in exploring a side of Iran that most people "in [my] position" never saw. I wondered whether Yamin knew what my true position was. I realized that I was taking a big risk; however, I could not resist the temptation to meet this enigmatic figure.

My taxi dropped me off in front of a tiny gate in a high wall – so high that I could not see the building behind it. An Iranian woman ushered me in and led me down a corridor illuminated by ornate oil lamps hanging from a low ceiling. At the end of this corridor, we entered a room that dazzled like the interior of a diamond, blinding me with its radiance. When my eyes finally adjusted, I saw that the walls were inlaid with semiprecious stones and mother-of-pearl. The restaurant was lighted by tall white candles protruding from intricately sculpted bronze chandeliers.

A tall man with long black hair, wearing a tailored navy blue suit, approached and shook my hand. He introduced himself as Yamin, in an accent that suggested he was an Iranian who had been educated in the British school system, and I was immediately struck by how little he looked like a subversive radical. He directed me past several tables where couples sat quietly eating, to a very private alcove; he assured me that we could talk in complete confidentiality. I had the distinct impression that this restaurant catered to secret rendezvous. Ours, quite possibly, was the only non-amorous one that night.

Yamin was very cordial. During our discussion, it became obvious that he thought of me merely as an economic consultant, not as someone with ulterior motives. He explained that he had singled me out because he knew I had been a Peace Corps volunteer and because he had been told that I took every possible opportunity to get to know his country and to mix with its people.

"You are very young compared to most in your profession," he said. "You have a genuine interest in our history and our current problems. You represent our hope."

His attitude, as well as the elegant setting, his Western clothes, and the presence of so many others in the restaurant, gave me a certain degree of comfort. I had become accustomed to people befriending me, like Rasy in Java and Fidel in Panama, and I accepted it as a compliment and an opportunity. I knew that I stood out from other Americans because I was in fact infatuated with the places I visited. I have found that people warm to you very quickly if you open your eyes, ears, and heart to their culture.

Yamin asked if I knew about the Flowering Desert project.[2] "The shah believes that our deserts were once fertile plains and lush forests. At least, that's what he claims. During Alexander the Great's reign, according to this theory, vast armies swept across these lands, traveling with millions of goats and sheep. The animals ate all the grass and other vegetation. The disappearance of these plants caused a drought, and eventually the entire region became a desert. Now all we have to do, or so the shah says, is plant millions upon millions of trees. After that — presto! — the rains will return and the desert will bloom again. Of course, in the process we will have to spend hundreds of millions of dollars." He smiled condescendingly. "Companies like yours will reap huge profits."

"I take it you don't believe in this theory."

"The desert is a symbol. Turning it green is about much more than agriculture."

Several waiters descended upon us with trays of beautifully presented Iranian food. Asking my permission first, Yamin proceeded to select an assortment from the various trays. Then he turned back to me.

"A question for you, Mr. Perkins, if I might be so bold. What destroyed the cultures of your own native peoples, the Indians?"

I responded that I felt there had been many factors, including greed and superior weapons.

"Yes. True. All of that. But more than anything else, did it not come down to a destruction of the environment?" He went on to explain how, once forests and animals such as the buffalo are destroyed, and once people are moved onto reservations, the very foundations of cultures collapse.

"You see, it is the same here," he said. "The desert is our environment. The Flowering Desert project threatens nothing less than the destruction of our entire fabric. How can we allow this to happen?"

I told him that it was my understanding that the whole idea behind the project came from his people. He responded with a cynical laugh, saying that the idea was planted in the shah's mind by my own US government and that the shah was just a puppet of that government.

"A true Persian would never permit such a thing," Yamin said. Then he launched into a long dissertation about the relationship between his people — the Bedouin — and the desert. He emphasized that many urbanized Iranians take their vacations in the desert. They set up tents large enough for the entire family and spend a week or more living in them.

"We — my people — are part of the desert. The people the shah claims to rule with that iron hand of his are not just *of* the desert. We *are* the desert."

After that, he told me stories about his personal experiences in the desert. When the evening was over, he escorted me back to the tiny door in the large wall. My taxi was waiting in the street outside. Yamin shook my hand and expressed his appreciation for the time I had spent with him. He again mentioned my young age and my openness, and the fact that my occupying such a position gave him hope for the future.

"I am so glad to have had this time with a man like you." He continued to hold my hand in his. "I would request of you only one more favor. I do not ask this lightly. I do it only because, after our time together tonight, I know it will be meaningful to you. You'll gain a great deal from it."

"What is it I can do for you?"

"I would like to introduce you to a dear friend of mine, a man who can tell you a great deal about our King of Kings. He may shock you, but I assure you that meeting him will be well worth your time."

CHAPTER 19

Confessions of a Tortured Man

Several days later, Yamin drove me out of Tehran, through a dusty and impoverished shantytown, along an old camel trail, and out to the edge of the desert. With the sun setting behind the city, he stopped his car at a cluster of tiny mud shacks surrounded by palm trees.

"A very old oasis," he explained, "dating back centuries before Marco Polo." He preceded me to one of the shacks. "The man inside has a PhD from one of your most prestigious universities. For reasons that will soon be clear, he must remain nameless. You can call him Doc."

He knocked on the wooden door, and there was a muffled response. Yamin pushed the door open and led me inside. The tiny room was windowless and lit only by an oil lamp on a low table in one corner. As my eyes adjusted, I saw that the dirt floor was covered with Persian carpets. Then the shadowy outline of a man began to emerge. He was seated in front of the lamp in a way that kept his features hidden. I could tell only that he was bundled in blankets and was wearing something around his head. He sat in a wheelchair, and other than the table, this was the only piece of furniture in the room. Yamin motioned for me to sit on a carpet. He approached and gently embraced the man, speaking a few words in his ear, then returned and sat at my side.

"I've told you about Mr. Perkins," he said. "We're both honored to have this opportunity to visit with you, sir."

"Mr. Perkins. You are welcome." The voice, with barely any detectable accent, was low and hoarse. I found myself leaning forward into the small space between us as he said, "You see before you a broken man. I have not always been so. Once I was strong like you. I was a close and trusted adviser to the shah." There was a long pause. "The Shah of Shahs, King of Kings." His tone of voice sounded, I thought, more sad than angry.

"I personally knew many of the world's leaders. Eisenhower, Nixon, de Gaulle. They trusted me to help lead this country into the capitalist camp. The shah trusted me, and," he made a sound that could have been a cough, but which I took for a laugh, "I trusted the shah. I believed his rhetoric. I was convinced that Iran would lead the Muslim world into a new epoch, that Persia would fulfill its promise. It seemed our destiny — the shah's, mine, all of ours who carried out the mission we thought we had been born to fulfill."

The lump of blankets moved; the wheelchair made a wheezing noise and turned slightly. I could see the outline of the man's face in profile, his shaggy beard, and — then it grabbed me — the flatness. He had no nose! I shuddered and stifled a gasp.

"Not a pretty sight, would you say, ah, Mr. Perkins? Too bad you can't see it in full light. It is truly grotesque." Again there was the sound of choking laughter. "But as I'm sure you can appreciate, I must remain anonymous. Certainly, you could learn my identity if you tried, although you might find that I am dead. Officially, I no longer exist. Yet I trust you won't try. You and your family are better off not knowing who I am. The arm of the shah and SAVAK reaches far."

The chair wheezed and returned to its original position. I felt a sense of relief, as though not seeing the profile somehow obliterated the violence that had been done. At the time, I did not know of this custom among some Islamic cultures. Individuals deemed to have brought dishonor or disgrace upon society or its leaders are punished by having their noses cut off. In this way, they are marked for life — as this man's face clearly demonstrated.[1]

"I'm sure, Mr. Perkins, you're wondering why we invited you here." Without waiting for my response, the man in the wheelchair continued, "You see, this man who calls himself the King of Kings is in reality satanic. His father was deposed by your CIA with — I hate to say it — my help, because he was said to be a Nazi collaborator. And then there was the Mossadegh calamity.[2] Today, our shah is on the route to surpassing Hitler in the realms of evil. He does this with the full knowledge and support of your government."

"Why is that?" I asked.

"Quite simple. He is your only real ally in the Middle East, and the industrial world rotates on the axle of oil that is the Middle East. Oh, you have Israel, of course, but that's actually a liability to you, not an asset. And no oil there. Your politicians must placate the Jewish vote, must get their money to finance campaigns. So you're stuck with Israel, I'm afraid. However, Iran is the key. Your oil companies — which carry even more power than the Jews — need us. You need our shah — or you think you do, just as you thought you needed South Vietnam's corrupt leaders."

"Are you suggesting otherwise? Is Iran the equivalent to Vietnam?"

"Potentially much worse. You see, this shah won't last much longer. The Muslim world hates him. Not just the Arabs, but Muslims everywhere — Indonesia, the United States, but mostly right here, his own Persian people." There was a thumping sound and I realized that he had struck the side of his chair. "He is evil! We Persians hate him." Then silence. I could hear only his heavy breathing, as though the exertion had exhausted him.

"Doc is very close to the mullahs," Yamin said to me, his voice low and calm. "There is a huge undercurrent among the religious factions here, and it pervades most of our country, except for a handful of people in the commercial classes who benefit from the shah's capitalism."

"I don't doubt you," I said. "But I must say that, during four visits here, I've seen nothing of it. Everyone I talk with seems to love the shah, to appreciate the economic upsurge."

"You don't speak Farsi," Yamin observed. "You hear only what is told to you by those men who benefit the most. The ones who have been educated in the States or in England end up working for the shah. Doc here is an exception — now."

He paused, seeming to ponder his next words. "It's the same with your press. They only talk with the few who are his kin, his circle. Of course, for the most part, your press is also controlled by oil. So they hear what they want to hear and write what their advertisers want to read."

"Why are we telling you all this, Mr. Perkins?" Doc's voice was even more hoarse than before, as if the effort of speaking and the emotions were draining what little energy the man had mustered for this meeting. "Because we'd like to convince you to get out and to persuade your company to stay away from our country. We want to warn you that although you may think you'll make a great deal of money here, it's an illusion. This government will not last." Again, I heard the sound of his hand thudding against the chair. "And when it goes, the one that replaces it will have no sympathy for you and your kind."

"You're saying we won't be paid?"

Doc broke down in a fit of coughing. Yamin went to him and rubbed his back. When the coughing ended, he spoke to Doc in Farsi and then came back to his seat.

"We must end this conversation," Yamin said to me. "In answer to your question: Yes, you will not be paid. You'll do all that work, and when it comes time to collect your fees, the shah will be gone."

During the drive back, I asked Yamin why he and Doc wanted to spare MAIN the financial disaster he had predicted.

"We'd be happy to see your company go bankrupt. However, we'd rather see you leave Iran. Just one company like yours, walking away, could start a trend. That's what we're hoping. You see, we don't want a bloodbath here, but the shah must go, and we'll try anything that will make that easier. So we pray to Allah that you'll convince your Mr. Zambotti to get out while there is still time."

"Why me?"

"I knew during our dinner together, when we spoke of the Flowering Desert project, that you were open to the truth. I knew that our information about you was correct — you are a man between two worlds, a man in the middle."

It made me wonder just how much he did know about me.

The Fall of a King

One evening in 1978, while I was sitting alone at the luxurious bar off the lobby of the Hotel InterContinental in Tehran, I felt a tap on my shoulder. I turned to see a heavyset Iranian in a business suit.

"John Perkins! You don't remember me?"

The former soccer player had gained a lot of weight, but the voice was unmistakable. It was my old Middlebury friend Farhad, whom I had not seen in more than a decade. We embraced and sat down together. It quickly became obvious that he knew all about me and my work. It was equally obvious that he did not intend to share much about his own work. He told me that something "dangerous" was about to happen and that it was his responsibility to see to it that I left the country. At that point, I figured Farhad worked for the CIA or some other US agency.

"Let's get right to the point," he said. "I'm flying to Rome tomorrow. My parents live there. I have a ticket for you on my flight." He handed me an airline ticket. I did not doubt him for a moment. I had a job to do, but by now I figured part of that meant staying out of trouble — and staying alive.

In Rome, we dined with Farhad's parents. His father, the retired Iranian general who once stepped in front of a would-be assassin's bullet to save the shah's life, expressed disillusionment with his former boss. He said that during the past few years the shah had shown his true colors, his arrogance and greed. The general blamed US policy — particularly its backing of Israel, of corrupt leaders, and of despotic governments — for the hatred sweeping the Middle East, and he predicted that the shah would be gone within months.

"You know," he said, "you sowed the seeds of this rebellion in the early fifties, when you overthrew Mossadegh. You thought it very clever back then — as did I. But now it returns to haunt you — us."[1]

I was astounded by his pronouncements. I had heard something similar from Yamin and Doc, but coming from this man, it took on new significance. By this time, everyone knew of the existence of a fundamentalist Islamic underground, but we had convinced ourselves that the shah was immensely popular among the majority of his people and was therefore politically invincible. The general, however, was adamant.

"Mark my words," he said solemnly, "the shah's fall will be only the beginning. It's a preview of where the Muslim world is headed. Our rage has smoldered beneath the sands too long. Soon it will erupt."

Over dinner, I heard a great deal about Ayatollah Ruhollah Khomeini. Farhad and his father made it clear that they did not support his fanatical Shiism, but they were obviously impressed by the inroads he had made against the shah. They told me that this cleric, whose given name translated to "inspired of God," was born into a family of dedicated Shiite scholars in a village near Tehran, in 1902.

Khomeini had made it a point not to become involved in the Mossadegh–shah struggles of the early 1950s, but he actively opposed the shah in the 1960s, criticizing the ruler so adamantly that Khomeini was banished to Turkey, then to the Shiite holy city of An Najaf in Iraq, where he became the acknowledged leader of the opposition. He sent out letters, articles, and tape-recorded messages urging Iranians to rise up, overthrow the shah, and create a clerical state.

Two days after that dinner with Farhad and his parents, news came out of Iran of bombings and riots. Ayatollah Khomeini and the mullahs had begun the offensive that would soon give them control. After that, things happened fast. The rage that Farhad's father had described exploded in a violent Islamic uprising. The shah fled his country for Egypt in January 1979, and then, diagnosed with cancer, headed for a New York hospital.

Followers of the Ayatollah Khomeini demanded his return. In November 1979, a militant Islamic mob seized the US Embassy in Tehran and held fifty-two American hostages for the next 444 days.[2] President Carter attempted to negotiate the release of the hostages. When this failed, he authorized a military rescue mission, launched in April 1980. It was a disaster, and it turned out to be the hammer that would drive the final nail into Carter's presidential coffin.

Tremendous pressure, exerted by US commercial and political groups, forced the cancer-ridden shah to leave the United States. From the day he fled Tehran he had a difficult time finding sanctuary; all his former friends shunned him. However, General Torrijos exhibited his customary compassion and offered the shah asylum in Panama, despite a personal dislike of the shah's politics. The shah arrived and received sanctuary at the same resort where the new Panama Canal Treaty had so recently been negotiated.

The mullahs demanded the shah's return in exchange for the hostages held in the US Embassy. Those in Washington who had opposed the Canal treaty accused Torrijos of corruption and collusion with the shah, and of endangering the lives of US citizens. They, too, demanded that the shah be turned over to Ayatollah Khomeini. Ironically, until only a few weeks earlier, many of these same people had been the shah's staunchest supporters. The once-proud King of Kings eventually returned to Egypt, where he died of cancer.

Doc's prediction came true. MAIN lost millions of dollars in Iran, as did many of our competitors. Carter lost his bid for reelection. The Reagan-Bush administration marched into Washington with promises to free the hostages, to bring down the mullahs, to return democracy to Iran, and to set straight the Panama Canal situation.

For me, the lessons were irrefutable. Iran illustrated beyond any doubt that the United States was a nation laboring to deny the truth of its role in the world. It seemed incomprehensible that we could have been so misinformed about the shah and the tide of hatred that had surged against him. Even those of us in companies like MAIN, which had offices and personnel in the country, had not known. I felt certain that the NSA and the CIA must have seen what had been so obvious to Torrijos even as far back as my meeting with him in 1972, but that our own intelligence community had intentionally encouraged us all to close our eyes.

CHAPTER 21

Colombia: Keystone of Latin America

Although Saudi Arabia, Iran, and Panama offered fascinating and disturbing studies, they also stood out as exceptions to the rule. Due to vast oil deposits in the first two and the Canal in the third, they did not fit the norm. Colombia's situation was more typical, and MAIN was the designer and lead engineering firm on a huge hydroelectric project there.

A Colombian college professor writing a book on the history of Pan-American relations once told me that Teddy Roosevelt had appreciated the significance of his country. Pointing at a map, the US president and former Rough Rider reportedly described Colombia as "the keystone to the arch of South America." I have never verified that story; however, it is certainly true that on a map Colombia, poised at the top of the continent, appears to hold the rest of the continent together. It connects all the southern countries to the Isthmus of Panama and therefore to both Central and North America.

Whether Roosevelt actually described Colombia in those terms or not, he was only one of many presidents who understood its pivotal position. For nearly two centuries, the United States has viewed Colombia as a keystone—or, perhaps more accurately, as a portal into the Southern Hemisphere for both business and politics.

The country also is endowed with great natural beauty: spectacular palm-lined beaches on both the Atlantic and Pacific coasts, majestic mountains, pampas that rival the Great Plains of the North American Midwest, and vast rain forests rich in biodiversity. The people, too, have a special quality, combining the physical, cultural, and artistic traits of diverse ethnic backgrounds, ranging from the local Tairona to imports from Africa, Asia, Europe, and the Middle East.

Historically, Colombia has played a crucial role in Latin American history and culture. During the colonial period, Colombia was the seat of the viceroy for all Spanish territories north of Peru and south of Costa Rica. The great fleets of gold galleons set sail from its coastal city of Cartagena to transport priceless treasures from as far south as Chile and Argentina to ports in Spain. Many of the critical actions in the wars for independence occurred in Colombia; for example, forces under Simón Bolívar were victorious over Spanish royalists at the pivotal Battle of Boyacá, in 1819.

In modern times, Colombia has had a reputation for producing some of Latin America's most brilliant writers, artists, philosophers, and other intellectuals, as well as fiscally responsible and relatively democratic governments. It became the model for President Kennedy's nation-building programs throughout Latin America. Unlike Guatemala's, its government was not tarnished with the reputation of being a CIA creation, and unlike Nicaragua's, the government was an elected one, which presented an alternative to both right-wing dictators and Communists. Finally, unlike so many other countries, including powerful Brazil and Argentina, Colombia did not mistrust the United States. The image of Colombia as a reliable ally has continued, despite the blemish of its drug cartels.[1]

The glories of Colombia's history, however, are counterbalanced by hatred and violence. The seat of the Spanish viceroy was also home to the Inquisition. Magnificent forts, haciendas, and cities were constructed over the bones of Indian and African slaves. The treasures carried on the gold galleons, sacred objects and masterpieces of art that had been melted down for easy transport, were ripped from the hearts of ancient peoples. The proud cultures themselves were laid to waste by conquistador swords and diseases. More recently, a controversial presidential election in 1945 resulted in a deep division between political parties and led to "La Violencia" (1948-1957), during which more than two hundred thousand people died.

Despite the conflicts and ironies, both Washington and Wall Street historically have viewed Colombia as an essential factor in promoting Pan-American political and commercial interests. This is due to several factors, in addition to Colombia's critical geographic location, including the perception that leaders throughout the hemisphere look to Bogotá for inspiration and guidance, and the fact that the country is both a source of many products purchased in the United States — coffee, bananas, textiles, emeralds, flowers, oil, and cocaine — and a market for our goods and services.

One of the most important services we sold to Colombia during the late twentieth century was engineering and construction expertise. Colombia was typical of many places where I worked. It was relatively easy to demonstrate that the country could assume vast amounts of debt and then repay these debts from the benefits realized from the projects themselves and from the country's natural resources. Thus, huge investments in electrical power grids, highways, and telecommunications would help Colombia open up its vast gas and oil resources and its largely undeveloped Amazonian territories; these projects, in turn, would generate the income necessary to pay off the loans, plus interest.

That was the theory. However, the reality, consistent with our true intent around the world, was to subjugate Bogotá, to further the global empire. My job, as it had been in so many places, was to present the case for exceedingly large loans. Colombia did not have the benefit of a Torrijos; therefore, I felt I had no choice but to develop inflated economic and electric load forecasts.

With the exception of the occasional bouts of guilt over my job, Colombia became a personal refuge for me. Ann and I had spent a couple of months there in the early 1970s and had even made a down payment on a small coffee farm located in the mountains along the Caribbean coast. I think our time together during that period came as close as anything could to healing the wounds I had inflicted on her over the preceding years. Ultimately, however, the wounds went too deep, and it was not until after our marriage fell apart that I became truly acquainted with the country.

During the 1970s, MAIN had been awarded a number of contracts to develop various infrastructure projects, including a network of hydroelectric facilities and the distribution systems to transport the electricity from deep in the jungle to cities high in the mountains. I was given an office in the coastal city of Barranquilla, and it was there, in 1977, that I met a beautiful Colombian woman who would become a powerful agent of change in my life.

Paula was a political activist with long blond hair and striking green eyes — not what most foreigners expect in a Colombian. Her mother and father had emigrated from northern Italy, and in keeping with her heritage, she became a fashion designer. She went a step further, however, and built a small factory where her creations were transformed into clothes, which she then sold at upscale boutiques throughout the country, as well as in Panama and Venezuela. She was a deeply compassionate person who helped me get through some of the personal trauma of my broken marriage and begin dealing with some of my attitudes toward women, which had affected me so negatively. She also taught me a great deal about the consequences of the actions I took in my job.

As I have said before, life is composed of a series of coincidences over which we have no control. For me, those included being raised as the son of a teacher at an all-male prep school in rural New Hampshire, meeting Ann and her Uncle Frank, the Vietnam War, and meeting Einar Greve. However, once we are presented with such coincidences, we face choices. How we respond, the actions we take in the face of coincidences, makes all the difference. For example, excelling at that school, marrying Ann, entering the Peace Corps, and choosing to become an economic hit man — all these decisions had brought me to my current place in life.

Paula was another coincidence, and her influence would lead me to take actions that changed the course of my life. Until I met her, I had pretty much gone along with the system. I often found myself questioning what I was doing, sometimes feeling guilty about it, yet I always discovered a way to rationalize staying in the system. Perhaps Paula just happened along at the right time. It is possible that I would have taken the plunge anyway, that my experiences in Saudi Arabia, Iran, and Panama would have nudged me into action. But I am certain that even as one woman, Claudine, had been instrumental in persuading me to join the ranks of EHMs, another, Paula, was the catalyst I needed at that time. She convinced me to go deep inside myself and see that I would never be happy as long as I continued in that role.

CHAPTER 22

American Republic vs. Global Empire

"**I**'ll be frank," Paula said one day, while we were sitting in a coffee shop. "The Indians and all the farmers who live along the river you're damming hate you. Even people in the cities, who aren't directly affected, sympathize with the guerrillas who've been attacking your construction camp. Your government calls these people Communists, terrorists, and narcotics traffickers, but the truth is they're just people with families who live on lands your company is destroying."

I had just told her about Manuel Torres. He was an engineer employed by MAIN and one of the men recently attacked by guerrillas at our hydroelectric dam construction site. Manuel was a Colombian citizen who had a job because of a US Department of State rule prohibiting us from sending US citizens to that site. We referred to it as the Colombians Are Expendable doctrine, and it symbolized an attitude I had grown to hate. My feelings toward such policies were making it increasingly difficult for me to live with myself.

"According to Manuel, they fired AK-47s into the air and at his feet," I told Paula. "He sounded calm when he told me about it, but I know he was almost hysterical. They didn't shoot anyone. Just gave them that letter and sent them downriver in their boats."

"My God!" Paula exclaimed. "The poor man must have been terrified."

"Of course he was." I told her that I had asked Manuel whether he thought they were FARC or M-19, referring to two of the most infamous Colombian guerrilla groups.

"And?"

"He said neither. But he told me that he believes what they said in that letter."

Paula picked up the newspaper I had brought and read the letter aloud.

"'We, who work every day just to survive, swear on the blood of our ancestors that we will never allow dams across our rivers. We are simple Indians and mestizos, but we would rather die than stand by as our land is flooded. We warn our Colombian brothers: stop working for the construction companies.'" She set the paper down. "What did you say to him?"

I hesitated, but only for a moment. "I had no choice. I had to toe the company line. I asked him if he thought that sounds like a letter a farmer would write."

She sat watching me patiently.

"He just shrugged." Our eyes met. "Oh, Paula, I detest myself for playing this role."

"What did you do next?" she pressed.

"I slammed my fist on the desk. I intimidated him. I asked him whether farmers with AK-47s made any sense to him. Then I asked if he knew who invented the AK-47."

"Did he?"

"Yes, but I could hardly hear his answer. 'A Russian,' he said. Of course, I assured him that he was right, that the inventor had been a Communist named Kalashnikov, a highly decorated officer in the Red Army. I brought him around to understand that the people who wrote that note were Communists."

"Do you believe that?" she asked.

Her question stopped me. How could I answer honestly? I recalled Iran and the time Yamin described me as a man caught between two worlds, a man in the middle. In some ways, I wished I had been in that camp when the guerrillas attacked, or that I was one of the guerrillas. An odd feeling crept over me, a sort of jealousy for Yamin and Doc and the Colombian rebels. These were men with convictions. They had chosen real worlds, not a no-man's-territory somewhere between.

"I have a job to do," I said at last.

She smiled gently.

"I hate it," I continued. I thought about the men whose images had come to me so often over the years, Tom Paine and other Revolutionary War heroes, pirates and frontiersmen. They stood at the edges, not in the middle. They took stands and lived with the consequences. "Every day I come to hate my job a little more."

She took my hand. "Your job?"

Our eyes met and held. I understood the implication. "Myself."

She squeezed my hand and nodded slowly. I felt an immediate sense of relief, just admitting it.

"What will you do, John?"

I had no answer. The relief turned into defensiveness. I stammered out the standard justifications: that I was trying to do good, that I was exploring ways to change the system from within, and — the old standby — that if I quit, someone even worse would fill my shoes. But I could see from the way she watched me that she was not buying it. Even worse, I knew that I was not buying it, either. She had forced me to understand the essential truth: it was not my job, but me, that was to blame.

"What about you?" I asked at last. "What do you believe?"

She gave a little sigh and released my hand, asking, "You trying to change the subject?"

I nodded.

"Okay," she agreed. "Under one condition. That we'll return to it another day." She picked up a spoon and appeared to examine it. "I know that some of the guerrillas have trained in Russia and China." She lowered the spoon into her *café con leche*, stirred, and then slowly licked the spoon. "What else can they do? They need to learn about modern weapons and how to fight the soldiers who've gone through your schools. Sometimes they sell cocaine in order to raise money for supplies. How else can they buy guns? They're up against terrible odds. Your World Bank doesn't help them defend themselves. In fact, it forces them into this position." She took a sip of coffee. "I believe their cause is just. The electricity will help only a few, the wealthiest Colombians, and thousands will die because the fish and water are poisoned, after you build that dam of yours."

Hearing her speak so compassionately about the people who opposed us — me — caused my flesh to crawl. I found myself clawing at my forearms.

"How do you know so much about the guerrillas?" Even as I asked it, I had a sinking feeling, a premonition that I did not want to know the answer.

"I went to school with some of them," she said. She hesitated, pushed her cup away. "My brother joined the movement."

There it was. I felt absolutely deflated. I thought I knew all about her, but this... I had the fleeting image of a man coming home to find his wife in bed with another man.

"How come you never told me?"

"Seemed irrelevant. Why would I? It isn't something I brag about." She paused. "I haven't seen him for two years. He has to be very careful."

"How do you know he's alive?"

"I don't, except recently the government put him on a wanted list. That's a good sign."

I was fighting the urge to be judgmental or defensive. I hoped she could not discern my jealousy. "How did he become one of them?" I asked.

Fortunately, she kept her eyes on the coffee cup. "Demonstrating outside the offices of an oil company — Occidental, I think. He was protesting drilling on indigenous lands, in the forests of a tribe facing extinction — him and a couple dozen of his friends. They were attacked by the army, beaten, and thrown into prison — for doing nothing illegal, mind you, just standing outside that building waving placards and singing." She glanced out a nearby window. "They kept him in jail for nearly six months. He never did tell us what happened there, but when he came out, he was a different person."

It was the first of many similar conversations with Paula, and I now know that these discussions set the stage for what was to follow. My soul was torn apart, yet I was still ruled by my wallet and by those other weaknesses the NSA had identified when they profiled me a decade earlier, in 1968. By forcing me to see this and to confront the deeper feelings behind my fascination with pirates and other rebels, Paula helped me along the trail toward salvation.

Beyond my own personal dilemmas, my times in Colombia also helped me comprehend the distinction between the ideals behind the old American republic and those of the new global empire.

The republic offered hope to the world. Its foundation was moral and philosophical rather than materialistic. It was based on concepts of equality and justice for all. But it also could be pragmatic — not merely a utopian dream but also a living, breathing entity. It could make big mistakes, like denying nonlandowners, women, and minorities the right to vote for more than a century. It could open its arms to shelter the downtrodden, then force their children to work under slave-like conditions in its factories. It could be an inspiration and at the same time a force to reckon with; if needed, it could swing into action, as it had during World War II, to defend the principles for which it stood. The very institutions — the big corporations, banks, and government bureaucracies — that have threatened those ideals could instead be redirected to institute fundamental changes in the world. At least in theory. Such institutions possess the communications networks and transportation systems necessary to end disease, starvation, and even wars — if only they could be convinced to take that course.

The global empire, on the other hand, is the republic's nemesis. It is self-centered, self-serving, greedy, and materialistic, a system based on mercantilism. Like earlier empires, it opens its arms only to accumulate resources, to grab everything in sight and stuff its insatiable maw. It will do whatever is needed to help its rulers gain more power and riches.

Of course, in learning to understand this distinction, I also developed a clearer sense of my own role. Claudine had warned me; she had honestly outlined what would be expected of me if I accepted the job MAIN offered. Yet, it took the experience of working in countries like Indonesia, Panama, Iran, and Colombia in order for me to face the deeper implications. And it took the patience, love, and personal stories of a person like Paula.

I was loyal to the American republic, but what we were perpetrating through this new, highly subtle form of imperialism was the financial equivalent of what we had attempted to accomplish militarily in Vietnam. If Southeast Asia had taught us that armies have limitations, the economists had responded by devising a better plan, and the foreign aid agencies and the private contractors who served them (or, more appropriately, were served by them) had become proficient at executing that plan.

In countries on every continent, I saw how men and women working for US corporations — though not officially part of the EHM network — participated in something far more pernicious than anything envisioned in conspiracy theories. They would do whatever they thought it would take — or were told it would take — to perpetuate the system we EHMs advocated. Like many of MAIN's engineers, these workers were blind to the consequences of their actions, convinced that the sweatshops and factories that made shoes and automotive parts for their companies were help-ing the poor climb out of poverty, instead of simply burying them deeper in a type of slavery reminiscent of medieval manors and Southern plantations.[1] As in those earlier manifestations of exploi-tation, modern serfs or slaves were socialized into believing they were better off than the unfortunate souls who lived on the mar-gins, in the dark hollows of Europe, in the jungles of Africa, or in the wilds of the American frontier.

The struggle over whether I should continue at MAIN or should quit had become an open battlefield. There was no doubt that my conscience wanted out, but that other side, what I liked to think of as my business-school persona, was not so sure. My own empire kept expanding; I added employees, countries, and shares of stock to my various portfolios and to my ego. In addition to the seduc-tion of the money and lifestyle, and the adrenaline high of power, I often recalled Claudine warning me that once I was in, I could never get out.

Claudine had been right about a great many things.

"That was a long time ago," Paula said. "Lives change. Any-way, what difference does it make? You're not happy with yourself. What can anyone do to make things worse than that?"

It was a refrain Paula often came back to, and I eventually agreed. I admitted to her and to myself that it was growing more difficult to use the money, adventure, and glamour to justify the turmoil, guilt, and stress. As a MAIN partner, I was becoming wealthy, and I knew that if I stayed longer, I would be perma-nently trapped.

One day, while we were strolling along the beach near the old Spanish fort at Cartagena, a place that had endured countless pirate attacks, Paula hit upon an approach that had not occurred to me. "What if you never say anything about the things you know?" she asked.

"You mean... just keep quiet?"

"Exactly. Don't give them an excuse to come after you. In fact, give them every reason to leave you alone, to not muddy the water."

It made a great deal of sense—I wondered why it had never occurred to me before. I would not write books or do anything else to expose the truth as I had come to see it. I would not be a crusader; instead, I would just be a person, concentrate on enjoying life, travel for pleasure, perhaps even start a family with someone like Paula. I had had enough; I simply wanted out.

"Everything you've learned is a lie," Paula said. "Your life is a lie." She added, "Have you looked at your own résumé recently?"

I admitted that I had not.

"Do," she advised. "I read the Spanish version the other day. If it's anything like the English one, I think you'll find it very interesting."

CHAPTER 23

The Deceptive Résumé

While I was in Colombia, word arrived that Jake Dauber had retired as MAIN's president. As expected, chairman and CEO Mac Hall appointed Bruno as Dauber's replacement. The phone lines between Boston and Barranquilla went crazy. Everyone predicted that I, too, would soon be promoted; after all, I was one of Bruno's most trusted protégés.

These changes and rumors were an added incentive for me to review my own position. While still in Colombia, I followed Paula's advice and read the Spanish version of my résumé. It shocked me. Back in Boston, I pulled out both the English original and a November 1978 copy of *Mainlines*, the corporate magazine; that edition featured me in an article titled "Specialists Offer MAIN's Clients New Services" (figure 1 and figure 2).

I once had taken great pride in that résumé and that article, and yet now, seeing them as Paula did, I felt a growing sense of anger. The material in these documents represented intentional deceptions. The basic facts were correct, but the important stories behind the facts were omitted. And these documents carried a deeper significance, a reality that reflected our times and reached to the core of our current march to global empire: they epitomized a strategy calculated to convey appearances, to shield an underlying reality. In a strange way, they symbolized the story of my life up to that point, a glossy veneer covering synthetic surfaces.

Of course, it did not give me any great comfort to know that I had to take much of the responsibility for what was included in my résumé. According to standard operating procedures, I was required to constantly update both a basic résumé and a file with pertinent backup information about clients served and the type of work done. If a marketing person or project manager wanted to include me in a proposal or to use my credentials in some other way, he could massage this basic data in a manner that emphasized his particular needs.

For instance, he might choose to highlight my experience in the Middle East, or in making presentations before the World Bank and other multinational forums. Whenever this was done, that person was supposed to get my approval before actually publishing the revised résumé. However, since like many other MAIN employees I traveled a great deal, exceptions were frequently made. Thus, the résumé that Paula suggested I look at, and its English counterpart, were completely new to me, although the information certainly was included in my file.

At first glance, my résumé seemed innocent enough. Under "Experience," it stated that I had been in charge of major projects in the United States, Asia, Latin America, and the Middle East, and it provided a laundry list of the types of projects: development planning, economic forecasting, energy demand forecasting, and so on. This section ended by describing my Peace Corps work in Ecuador; however, it omitted any reference to the Peace Corps itself, leaving the impression that I had been the professional manager of a construction materials company instead of a volunteer assisting a small cooperative comprising illiterate Andean peasant brick makers.

Following that was a long list of clients. This list included the International Bank for Reconstruction and Development (the official name of the World Bank), the Asian Development Bank, the government of Kuwait, the Iranian Ministry of Energy, the Arabian-American Oil Company of Saudi Arabia, Instituto de Recursos Hidráulicos y de Electrificación, Perusahaan Umum Listrik Negara; and many others. But the one that caught my attention was the final entry: US Treasury Department, Kingdom of Saudi Arabia. Of course it was true, but I was amazed that such a listing had ever made it to print, even though it was obviously part of my file.

Setting aside the résumé for a moment, I turned to the *Mainlines* article. I clearly recalled my interview with its author, a very talented and well-intentioned reporter. She had given it to me for my approval before publishing it. I remembered feeling gratified that she had painted such a flattering portrait of me, and I immediately

EXPERIENCE

John M. Perkins is Manager of the Economics Department of the Power and Environmental Systems Division.

Since joining MAIN, Mr. Perkins has been in charge of major projects in the United States, Asia, Latin America and the Middle East. This work has included development planning, economic forecasting, energy demand forecasting, marketing studies, plant siting, fuel allocation analysis, economic feasibility studies, environmental and economic impact studies, investment planning and management consulting. In addition, many projects have involved training clients in the use of techniques developed by Mr. Perkins and his staff.

Recently Mr. Perkins has been in charge of a project to design computer program packages for 1) projecting energy demand and quantifying the relationships between economic development and energy production, 2) evaluating environmental and socio-economic impacts of projects, and 3) applying Markov and econometric models to national and regional economic planning.

Prior to joining MAIN, Mr. Perkins spent three years in Ecuador conducting marketing studies and organizing and managing a construction materials company. He also conducted studies of the feasibility of organizing credit and savings cooperatives throughout Ecuador.

EDUCATION

Bachelor of Arts in Business Administration
Boston University
Post Graduate Studies:
Model Building, Engineering Economics,
Econometrics, Probability Methods

LANGUAGES

English, Spanish

PROFESSIONAL AFFILIATIONS

American Economic Association
Society for International Development

PUBLICATIONS

"A Markov Process Applied to Forecasting
the Demand for Electricity"
"A Macro Approach to Energy Forecasting"
"A Model for Describing the Direct and
Indirect Interrelationships between the
Economy and the Environment"
"Electric Energy from Interconnected Systems"
"Markov Method Applied to Planning"

JOHN M. PERKINS

CREDENTIALS

Forecasting Studies
Marketing Studies
Feasibility Studies
Site Selection Studies
Economic Impact Studies
Investment Planning
Fuel Supply Studies
Economic Development Planning
Training Programs
Project Management
Allocation Planning
Management Consulting

Clients served:

o Arabian-American Oil Company, Saudi Arabia
o Asian Development Bank
o Boise Cascade Corporation
o City Service Corporation
o Dayton Power & Light Company
o General Electric Company
o Government of Kuwait
o Instituto de Recursos Hidraulicos y Electrificacion, Panama
o Inter-American Development Bank
o International Bank for Reconstruction and Development
o Ministry of Energy, Iran
o New York Times
o Power Authority of the State of New York
o Perusahaan Umum Listrik Negara, Indonesia
o South Carolina Electric and Gas Company
o Technical Association of the Pulp and Paper Industry
o Union Camp Corporation
o U.S. Treasury Dept., Kingdom of Saudi Arabia

MAIN

Figure 1: *Mainlines* résumé.

approved it. Once again, the responsibility fell on my shoulders. The article began:

> Looking over the faces behind the desks, it's easy to tell that Economics and Regional Planning is one of the most recently formed and rapidly growing disciplines at MAIN....
>
> While several people were influential in getting the economics group started, it basically came about through the efforts of one man, John Perkins, who is now head of the group.
>
> Hired as an assistant to the head load forecaster in January, 1971, John was one of the few economists working for MAIN at the time. For his first assignment, he was sent as part of an 11-man team to do an electricity demand study in Indonesia.

The article briefly summarized my previous work history, described how I had "spent three years in Ecuador," and then continued with the following:

> It was during this time that John Perkins met Einar Greve (a former employee) [he had since left MAIN to become president of the Tucson Gas & Electric Company] who was working in the town of Paute, Ecuador, on a hydroelectric project for MAIN. The two became friendly and, through continual correspondence, John was offered a position with MAIN.
>
> About a year later, John became the head load forecaster and, as the demands from clients and institutions such as the World Bank grew, he realized that more economists were needed at MAIN.

None of the statements in either document were outright lies — the backup for both documents was on the record, in my file; however, they conveyed a perception that I now found to be twisted and sanitized. And in a culture that worships official documents, they perpetrated something that was even more sinister. Outright lies can be refuted. Documents like those two were impossible to refute because they were based on glimmers of truth, not open deceptions, and because they were produced by a corporation that

Specialists offer MAIN's clients new services

by Pauline Ouellette

Perkins

Looking over the faces behind the desks, it's easy to tell that Economics and Regional Planning is one of the most recently formed and rapidly growing disciplines at MAIN. To date, there are about 20 specialists in this group, gathered over a seven-year period. These specialists include not only economists, but city planners, demographers, market specialists and MAIN's first sociologist.

While several people were influential in getting the economics group started, it basically came about through the efforts of one man, **John Perkins**, who is now head of the group.

Hired as an assistant to the head load forecaster in January, 1971, John was one of the few economists working for MAIN at the time. For his first assignment, he was sent as part of an 11-man team to do an electricity demand study in Indonesia.

"They wanted to see if I could survive there for three months," he said laughing reminiscently. But with his background, John had no trouble "surviving." He had just spent three years in Ecuador with a Construction Materials Co-op helping the Quechua Indians, direct descendants of the Incas. The Indians, John said, were being exploited in their work as brick makers so he was asked by an Ecuadorian agency to form a co-op. He then rented a truck to help them sell their bricks directly to the consumers. As a result, profits rapidly increased by 60%. The profits were divided among the members of the co-op which, after 2½ years, included 200 families.

It was during this time that John Perkins met **Einar Greve** (a former employee) who was working in the town of Paute, Ecuador, on a hydroelectric project for MAIN. The two became friendly and, through continual correspondence, John was offered a position with MAIN.

About a year later, John became the head load forecaster and, as the demands from clients and institutions such as the World Bank grew, he realized that more economists were needed at MAIN. "While MAIN is an engineering firm," he said, "the clients were telling us we had to be more than that." He hired more economists in 1973 to meet the clients' needs and, as a result, formed the discipline which brought him the title of Chief Economist.

John's latest project involves agricultural development in Panama from where he recently returned after a month's stay. It was in Panama that MAIN conducted its first sociological study through **Martha Hayes**, MAIN's first sociologist. Marti spent 1½ months in Panama to determine the impact of the project on people's lives and cultures. Specialists in agriculture and other related fields were also hired in conjunction with this study.

The expansion of Economics and Regional Planning has been fast paced, yet John feels he has been lucky in that each individual hired has been a hard working professional. As he spoke to me from across his desk, the interest and support he holds for his staff was evident and admirable.

Frank Fullerton participant in MIT program for executives

Frank M. Fullerton, Vice President and Division Manager of the Power Systems Division, is attending the MIT Sloan School of Management Program for Senior Executives.

The program is designed for senior level management and it seeks to develop in them a broad understanding of the major forces which will influence the future of a firm. Areas of study such as policy formulation, management information and decision systems, organization behavior and the business environment form the basic content of the program. Also included are specific seminars in marketing, finance, human resources management, system dynamics and corporate strategy.

The program is attended by 28 participants selected from applications received from all over the world. The group is staying at the MIT Endicott House in Dedham, Mass., and, except for one four-day weekend break, participants are expected to remain in residence.

During Mr. Fullerton's nine-week absence (Sept. 17 — Nov. 17), **Edward J. Fitzsimmons**, Chief Discipline Engineer of the Structural Department, in the Pulp and Paper Division, is Acting Division Manager of the Power Systems Division.

Figure 2: *Mainlines* article.

had earned the trust of other corporations, international banks, and governments.

This was especially true of the résumé, because it was an official document, as opposed to the article, which was a bylined interview in a magazine. The MAIN logo, appearing on the bottom of the résumé and on the covers of all the proposals and reports that résumé was likely to grace, carried a lot of weight in the world of international business; it was a seal of authenticity that elicited the same level of confidence as those stamped on diplomas and framed certificates hanging in doctors' and lawyers' offices.

These documents portrayed me as a very competent economist, head of a department at a prestigious consulting firm, who was traveling around the globe conducting a broad range of studies that would make the world a more civilized and prosperous place. The deception was not in what was stated but in what was omitted. If I put on an outsider's hat — took a purely objective look — I had to admit that those omissions raised many questions.

For example, there was no mention of my recruitment by the NSA or of Einar Greve's connection with the army and his role as an NSA liaison. There obviously was no discussion of the fact that I had been under tremendous pressure to produce highly inflated economic forecasts, or that much of my job revolved around arranging huge loans that countries like Indonesia and Panama could never repay. There was no praise for the integrity of my predecessor, Howard Parker, or any acknowledgment that I became the head load forecaster because I was willing to provide the biased studies my bosses wanted, rather than — like Howard — saying what I believed was true and getting fired as a result. Most puzzling was that final entry, under the list of my clients: US Treasury Department, Kingdom of Saudi Arabia.

I kept returning to that line, and I wondered how people would interpret it. They might well ask what the connection is between the US Department of the Treasury and Saudi Arabia. Perhaps some would take it as a typo, two separate lines erroneously compressed into one. Most readers, though, would never guess the truth, that it had been included for a specific reason. It was there so that those in the inner circle of the world where I operated would understand that I had been part of the team that crafted the deal of the century, the deal that changed the course of world history but never reached the newspapers. I helped create a covenant that guaranteed continued oil for America, safeguarded the rule of the House of Saud, and assisted in the financing of Osama bin Laden and the protection of international criminals like Uganda's Idi Amin. That single line in my résumé spoke to those in the know. It said that MAIN's chief economist was a man who could deliver.

The final paragraph of the *Mainlines* article was a personal observation by the author, and it struck a raw nerve:

> The expansion of Economics and Regional Planning has been fast paced, yet John feels he has been lucky in that each individual hired has been a hard-working professional. As he spoke to me from across his desk, the interest and support he holds for his staff was evident and admirable.

The fact was that I had never thought of myself as a bona fide economist. I had graduated with a bachelor of science in business administration from Boston University, emphasis on marketing. I had always been lousy in mathematics and statistics. At Middlebury College, I had majored in American literature; writing had come easily to me. My status as chief economist and as manager of Economics and Regional Planning could not be attributed to my capabilities in either economics or planning; rather, it was a function of my willingness to provide the types of studies and conclusions my bosses and clients wanted, combined with a natural talent for persuading others through the written and spoken word. In addition, I was clever enough to hire very competent people, many with master's degrees and a couple with PhDs, acquiring a staff who knew a whole lot more about the technicalities of my business than I did. Small wonder that the author of that article concluded that "the interest and support he holds for his staff was evident and admirable."

I kept these two documents and several other similar ones in the top drawer of my desk, and I returned to them frequently. Afterward, I sometimes found myself outside my office, wandering among the desks of my staff, looking at those men and women who worked for me and feeling guilty about what I had done to them, and about the role we all played in widening the gap between rich and poor. I thought about the people who starved each day while my staff and I slept in first-class hotels, ate at the finest restaurants, and built up our financial portfolios.

I thought about the fact that people I trained had now joined the ranks of EHMs. I had brought them in. I had recruited them and trained them. But it had not been the same as when I joined. The world had shifted, and what I'd later come to understand as the corporatocracy had progressed. We had gotten better or more pernicious. The people who worked for me were a different breed from me. There had been no NSA polygraphs or Claudines in their lives. No one had spelled it out for them, what they were expected to do to carry on the mission of global empire. They had never heard the term "economic hit man" or even "EHM," nor had they been told they were in for life. They simply had learned from my example and from my system of rewards and punishments. They knew that they were expected to produce the types of studies and results I wanted. Their salaries, their Christmas bonuses, indeed their very jobs, depended on pleasing me.

I, of course, had done everything I could imagine to lighten their burden. I had written papers, given lectures, and taken every possible opportunity to convince them of the importance of optimistic forecasts, of huge loans, of infusions of capital that would spur gross national product growth and make the rich much richer. It had required less than a decade to arrive at this point, where the seduction, the coercion, had taken a much more subtle form, a sort of gentle style of brainwashing. Now these men and women who sat at desks outside my office overlooking Boston's Back Bay were going out into the world to advance the cause of global empire. In a very real sense, I had created them, even as Claudine had created me. But unlike me, they had been kept in the dark.

Many nights I lay awake, thinking, fretting about these things. Paula's reference to my résumé had opened a Pandora's box, and I often felt jealous of my employees for their naiveté. I had intentionally deceived them, and in so doing, I had protected them from their own consciences. They did not have to struggle with the moral issues that haunted me.

I also thought a great deal about the idea of integrity in business, about appearances versus reality. Certainly, I told myself, people have deceived each other since the beginning of history. Legend and folklore are full of tales about distorted truths and fraudulent deals: cheating rug merchants, usurious moneylenders, and tailors willing to convince the emperor that his clothes are invisible only to him.

However, much as I wanted to conclude that things were the same as they always had been, that the facade of my MAIN résumé and the reality behind it were merely reflections of human nature, I knew in my heart this was not the case. Things had changed. I now understood that we have reached a new level of deception, one that convinces us to do whatever it takes to promote a corrupt system that widens the rich-poor gap through fear, debt, and policies that constantly expand materialist consumption and advocate dividing and conquering anyone who appears to oppose us. These deceptions will lead to our own destruction — not only morally but also physically, as a culture — unless we make significant changes soon.

The example of organized crime seemed to offer a metaphor. Mafia bosses often start out as street thugs. But over time, the ones who make it to the top transform their appearance. They take to wearing impeccably tailored suits, owning legitimate businesses, and wrapping themselves in the cloak of upstanding society. They support local charities and are respected by their communities. They are quick to lend money to those in desperate straits. Like the John Perkins in the MAIN résumé, these men appear to be model citizens. However, beneath this patina is a trail of blood. When the debtors cannot pay, hit men move in to demand their pound of flesh. If this is not granted, the jackals close in with baseball bats. Finally, as a last resort, out come the guns.

I realized that my gloss as chief economist, head of Economics and Regional Planning, was not the simple deception of a rug dealer, not something of which a buyer can beware. It was part of a sinister system aimed not at outfoxing an unsuspecting customer but, rather, at promoting the most subtle and effective form of imperialism the world has ever known. Every one of the people on my staff also held a title — financial analyst, sociologist, economist, lead economist, econometrician, shadow pricing expert, and so forth — and yet none of those titles indicated that every one of them was, in his or her own unsuspecting way, an EHM, that every one of them was serving the interests of global empire.

Nor did the fact of those titles among my staff suggest that we were just the tip of the iceberg. Every major international company — from ones that marketed shoes and sporting goods to those that manufactured heavy equipment — had its own EHM equivalents. The march had begun and it was rapidly encircling the planet. The hoods had discarded their leather jackets, dressed up in business suits, and taken on an air of respectability. Men and women were descending from corporate headquarters in New York, Chicago, San Francisco, London, Beijing, and Tokyo, streaming across every continent to convince corrupt politicians to allow their countries to be ensnared by the global corporate network, and to induce desperate people to sell their bodies to sweatshops and assembly lines.

It was disturbing to understand that the unspoken details behind the written words of my résumé and of that article defined a world of smoke and mirrors intended to keep us all trapped in a system that is morally repugnant and ultimately self-destructive. By getting me to read between the lines, Paula had nudged me to take one more step along a path that would ultimately transform my life.

CHAPTER 24

Ecuador's President Battles Big Oil

My work in Colombia and Panama gave me many opportunities to stay in touch with and to visit the first country to be my home away from home. Ecuador had suffered under a long line of dictators and right-wing oligarchies manipulated by US political and commercial interests. In a way, the country was the quintessential banana republic, and corporate giants such as Dole Food Company had made major inroads there.

The serious exploitation of oil in the Ecuadorian Amazon basin began in the late 1960s, and it resulted in a buying spree in which the small club of families who ran Ecuador played into the hands of the international banks. They saddled their country with huge amounts of debt, backed by the promise of oil revenues.[1] Roads and industrial parks, hydroelectric dams, transmission and distribution systems, and other power projects sprang up all over the country. International engineering and construction companies struck it rich — once again.

One man whose star was rising over this Andean country was the exception to the rule of political corruption and complicity with the corporatocracy. Jaime Roldós was a university professor and attorney in his late thirties, whom I had met on several occasions. He was charismatic and charming. Once, I impetuously offered to fly to Quito and provide free consulting services any time he asked. I said it partially in jest, but also because I would gladly have done it on my own vacation time — I liked him and, as I was quick to tell him, was always looking for a good excuse to visit his country. He laughed and offered me a similar deal, saying that whenever I needed to negotiate my oil bill, I could call on him.

He had established a reputation as a populist and a nationalist, a person who believed strongly in the rights of the poor and in the responsibility of politicians to use a country's natural resources prudently. When he began campaigning for the presidency in 1978, he captured the attention of his countrymen and of citizens in every nation where foreign interests exploited oil – or where people desired independence from the influences of powerful outside forces. Roldós was the rare modern politician who was not afraid to oppose the status quo. He went after the oil companies and the not-so-subtle system that supported them.

For instance, I heard that he accused the Summer Institute of Linguistics (SIL), an evangelical missionary group from the United States, of sinister collusion with the oil companies. I was familiar with SIL missionaries from my Peace Corps days. The organization had entered Ecuador, as it had so many other countries, with the professed goal of studying, recording, and translating indigenous languages.

SIL had been working extensively with the Huaorani people in the Amazon basin area, during the early years of oil exploration, when a disturbing pattern appeared to emerge. Although it might have been a coincidence (and no link was ever proved), stories were told in many Amazonian communities that when seismologists reported to corporate headquarters that a certain region had characteristics indicating a high probability of oil beneath the surface, some SIL members went in and encouraged the indigenous people to move from that land, onto missionary reservations; there they would receive free food, shelter, clothes, medical treatment, and missionary-style education. The condition, according to these stories, was that the people had to deed their lands to the oil companies.

Rumors abounded that SIL missionaries used an assortment of underhanded techniques to persuade the people to abandon their homes and move to the missions. A frequently repeated story was that they had donated food heavily laced with laxatives – then offered medicines to cure the diarrhea epidemic. Throughout Huaorani territory, it was said, SIL airdropped false-bottomed food baskets containing tiny radio transmitters; the rumor was that receivers at highly sophisticated communications stations, manned by US military personnel at the army base in the town named after the oil company Shell, tuned in to these transmitters. When a member of the community was bitten by a poisonous snake or became seriously ill, an SIL representative arrived with antivenom or the proper medicines — often in oil company helicopters.

During the early days of oil exploration, five missionaries were found dead with Huaorani spears protruding from their bodies. Later, the Huaorani claimed they did this to send a message to keep missionaries out. The message went unheeded. In fact, it ultimately had the opposite effect. Rachel Saint, the sister of one of the murdered men, toured the United States, appearing on national television in order to raise money and support for SIL and the oil companies, who she claimed were helping the "savages" become civilized and educated. According to some sources, SIL received funding from the Rockefeller charities. Family scion John D. Rockefeller had founded Standard Oil — which later divested into the majors, including Chevron, Exxon, and Mobil.[2]

Roldós struck me as a man who walked the path blazed by Torrijos. Both stood up to the world's strongest superpower. Torrijos wanted to take back the Canal, while Roldós's strongly nationalistic position on oil threatened the world's most influential companies. Like Torrijos, Roldós was not a Communist but instead stood for the right of his country to determine its own destiny. And as they had with Torrijos, pundits predicted that big business and Washington would never tolerate Roldós as president — that if elected, he would meet a fate similar to that of Guatemala's Arbenz or Chile's Allende.

It seemed to me that the two men together might spearhead a new movement in Latin American politics and that this movement might form the foundation of changes that could affect every nation on the planet. These men were not Castros or Gadhafis. They were not associated with Russia or China or, as in Allende's case, the international Socialist movement. They were popular, intelligent, charismatic leaders who were pragmatic rather than dogmatic. They were nationalistic but not anti-American. If corporatocracy was built by three sectors — major corporations, international banks, and colluding governments — Roldós and Torrijos held out the possibility of removing the element of government collusion.

A major part of the Roldós platform was what came to be known as the Hydrocarbons Policy. This policy was based on the premise that Ecuador's greatest potential resource was petroleum and that all future exploitation of that resource should be done in a manner that would bring the greatest benefit to the largest percentage of the population. Roldós was a firm believer in the state's obligation to assist the poor and disenfranchised. He expressed hope that the Hydrocarbons Policy could in fact be used as a vehicle for social reform. He had to walk a fine line, however, because he knew that in Ecuador, as in so many other countries, he could not be elected without the support of at least some of the most influential families, and that even if he should manage to win without them, he would never see his programs implemented without their support.

I was personally relieved that Carter was in the White House during this crucial time. Despite pressures from Texaco and other oil interests, Washington stayed pretty much out of the picture. I knew this would not have been the case under most other administrations — Republican or Democrat.

More than any other issue, I believe it was the Hydrocarbons Policy that convinced Ecuadorians to send Jaime Roldós to the Presidential Palace in Quito — their first democratically elected president after a long line of dictators. He outlined the basis of this policy in his August 10, 1979, inaugural address:

> We must take effective measures to defend the energy resources of the nation. The State [must] maintain the diversification of its exports and not lose its economic independence.... Our decisions will be inspired solely by national interests and in the unrestricted defense of our sovereign rights.[3]

Once in office, Roldós had to focus on Texaco, because by that time it had become the main player in the oil game. It was an extremely rocky relationship. The oil giant did not trust the new president and did not want to be part of any policy that would set new precedents. It was very aware that such policies might serve as models in other countries.

A speech delivered by a key adviser to Roldós, José Carvajal, summed up the new administration's attitude:

If a partner [Texaco] does not want to take risks, to make
investments for exploration, or to exploit the areas of an oil
concession, the other partner has the right to make those
investments and then to take over as the owner....

We believe our relations with foreign companies have to
be just; we have to be tough in the struggle; we have to be
prepared for all kinds of pressures, but we should not
display fear or an inferiority complex in negotiating with
those foreigners.[4]

On New Year's Day 1980 I made a resolution. It was the beginning of a new decade. In twenty-eight days, I would turn thirty-five.
I resolved that during the next year I would make a major change
in my life and that in the future I would try to model myself after
modern heroes like Jaime Roldós and Omar Torrijos.

In addition, something shocking had happened months earlier.
From a profitability standpoint, Bruno had been the most successful president in MAIN's history. Nonetheless, suddenly and without warning, Mac Hall had fired him.

CHAPTER 25

I Quit

Mac Hall's firing of Bruno hit MAIN like an earthquake. It caused turmoil and dissension throughout the company. Bruno had his share of enemies, but even some of them were dismayed. To many employees it was obvious that the motive had been jealousy. During discussions across the lunch table or around the coffee wagon, people often confided that they thought Hall felt threatened by this man who was more than fifteen years his junior and who had taken the firm to new levels of profitability.

"Hall couldn't allow Bruno to go on looking so good," one man said. "Hall had to know that it was just a matter of time before Bruno would take over and the old man would be put out to pasture."

As if to prove such theories, Hall appointed Paul Priddy as the new president. Paul had been a vice president at MAIN for years and was an amiable, nuts-and-bolts engineer. In my opinion, he was also lackluster, a yes-man who would bow to the chairman's whims and would never threaten him with stellar profits. My opinion was shared by many others.

For me, Bruno's departure was devastating. He had been a personal mentor and a key factor in our international work. Priddy, on the other hand, had focused on domestic jobs and knew little if anything about the true nature of our overseas roles. I had to question where the company would go from here. I called Bruno at his home and found him philosophical.

"Well, John, he knew he had no cause," he said of Hall, "so I demanded a very good severance package, and I got it. Mac controls a huge block of voting stock, and once he made his move, there was nothing I could do." Bruno indicated that he was considering several offers of high-level positions at multinational banks that had been our clients.

I asked him what he thought I should do.

"Keep your eyes open," he advised. "Mac Hall has lost touch with reality, but no one will tell him so — especially not now, after what he did to me."

In late March 1980, still smarting from the firing, I took a sailing vacation in the Virgin Islands. Although I did not think about it when I chose the location, I now know that the region's history was a factor in helping me make a decision that would start to fulfill my New Year's resolution.

As I sailed up Sir Frances Drake Channel, tacking back and forth into the wind, a wooden boat with a rainbow flag sailed toward me, its sails billowing out on both sides, downwinding through the channel. A half dozen young men and women shouted and waved, hippies in brightly colored sarongs. It was obvious from the boat itself and the look about them that they lived aboard, a communal society, modern pirates, free, uninhibited.

I felt a surge of jealousy. I wanted that sort of freedom. And then I understood. My resentment, my anger, was not about my parents. I realized in that moment that my life was a gift from those parents I had so often disparaged. I owed Mom and Dad a great deal for all they'd done to prepare and inspire me to wend my way down the path that had taken me to this moment. I also had to accept personal responsibility for all the mistakes I'd made. Blaming them, as I'd done so many times, was not just foolish and unfair; it was self-defeating.

Soon after that I entered Leinster Bay, nestled into Saint John Island, a cove where pirate ships had lain in wait for the gold fleet when it passed through this very body of water. I nudged the anchor over the side; the chain rattled down into the crystal clear water and the boat drifted to a stop.

After settling in, I rowed the dinghy ashore and beached it just below the ruins of an old sugar plantation. I sat there next to the water for a long time, trying not to think, concentrating on emptying myself of all emotion. But it did not work.

Late in the afternoon, I struggled up the steep hill and found myself standing on the crumbling walls of this ancient plantation, looking down at my anchored sloop. I watched the sun sink toward the Caribbean. It all seemed very idyllic, yet I knew that the plantation surrounding me had been the scene of untold misery; hundreds of African slaves had died here — forced at gunpoint to build the stately mansion, to plant and harvest the cane, and to operate the equipment that turned raw sugar into the basic ingredient of rum. The tranquility of the place masked its history of brutality.

The sun disappeared behind a mountain-ridged island. A vast magenta arch spread across the sky. The sea began to darken, and I came face-to-face with the shocking fact that I too had been a slaver, that my job at MAIN had not been just about using debt to draw poor countries into the global empire. My inflated forecasts were not merely vehicles for assuring that when my country needed oil we could call in our pound of flesh, and my position as a partner was not simply about enhancing the firm's profitability. My job was also about people and their families, people akin to the ones who had died to construct the wall I sat on, people I had exploited.

For ten years, I had been the heir of those earlier slavers. Mine had been a more modern approach, subtler — I never had to see the dying bodies, smell the rotting flesh, or hear the screams of agony. But I too had committed sin, and because I could remove myself from it, because I could cut myself off from the personal aspects, the bodies, the flesh, and the screams, perhaps in the final analysis I was the greater sinner.

I turned away from the sea and the bay and the magenta sky. I closed my eyes to the walls that had been built by slaves torn from their African homes. I tried to shut it all out. When I opened my eyes, I was staring at a large gnarled stick, as thick as a baseball bat and twice as long. I leaped up, grabbed the stick, and began slamming it against the stone walls. I beat on those walls until I collapsed from exhaustion. I lay in the grass after that, watching the clouds drift over me.

Eventually I made my way back down to the dinghy. I stood there on the beach, looking out at my sailboat anchored in the azure waters, and I knew what I had to do. I had to take responsibility. I knew that if I ever went back to my former life, to MAIN and all it represented, I would be lost forever. The raises, the pensions, the insurance and perks, the equity... The longer I stayed, the more difficult it was to get out. I could continue to beat myself up as I had beat on those stone walls, or I could escape.

Two days later I returned to Boston. On April 1, 1980, I walked into Paul Priddy's office and resigned.

PART IV: 1981–2004

CHAPTER 26

Ecuador's Presidential Death

Leaving MAIN was no easy matter; Paul Priddy refused to believe me. "April Fool's," he winked.

I assured him that I was serious. Recalling Paula's advice that I should do nothing to antagonize anyone or to give cause for suspicion that I might expose my EHM work, I emphasized that I appreciated everything MAIN had done for me but that I needed to move on. I had always wanted to write about the people that MAIN had introduced me to around the world, but nothing political. I said I wanted to freelance for *National Geographic* and other magazines, and to continue to travel. I declared my loyalty to MAIN and swore that I would sing its praises at every opportunity. At the time, I believed everything I said. I simply wanted out. I wanted to stop being a slaver. Finally, Paul gave in.

After that, everyone else tried to talk me out of resigning. I was reminded frequently about how good I had it, and I was even accused of insanity. I came to understand that no one wanted to accept the fact that I was leaving voluntarily, at least in part because it forced them to look at themselves. If I were not crazy for leaving, then they might have to consider their own sanity in staying. It was easier to see me as a person who had departed from his senses.

Particularly disturbing were the reactions of my staff. In their eyes, I was deserting them, and there was no strong heir apparent. However, I had made up my mind. After all those years of vacillation, I now was determined to make a clean sweep.

Unfortunately, it did not quite work out that way. True, I no longer had a job, but since I had been far from a fully vested partner, the cash-out of my stock was not sufficient for retirement. Had I stayed at MAIN another few years, I might have become the forty-year-old millionaire I had once envisioned; however, at thirty-five

I had a long way to go to accomplish that objective. It was a cold and dreary April in Boston.

Then one day Paul Priddy called and pleaded with me to come to his office. "One of our clients is threatening to drop us," he said. "They hired us because they wanted you to represent them on the expert witness stand."

I thought a lot about it. By the time I sat across the desk from Paul, I had made my decision. I named my price, a retainer that was more than three times what my MAIN salary had been. To my surprise, he agreed, and that started me on a new career.

For the next several years, I was employed as a highly paid expert witness — primarily for US electric utility companies seeking to have new power plants approved for construction by public utilities commissions. One of my clients was the Public Service Company of New Hampshire. My job was to justify, under oath, the economic feasibility of the highly controversial Seabrook nuclear power plant.

Although I was no longer directly involved with Latin America, I continued to follow events there. As an expert witness, I had lots of time between appearances on the stand. I kept in touch with Paula and renewed old friendships from my Peace Corps days in Ecuador — a country that had suddenly jumped to center stage in the world of international oil politics.

Jaime Roldós was moving forward. He took his campaign promises seriously, and he was launching an all-out attack on the oil companies. He seemed to see clearly the things that many others on both sides of the Panama Canal either missed or chose to ignore. He understood the underlying currents that threatened to turn the world into a global empire and to relegate the citizens of his country to a very minor role, bordering on servitude. As I read the newspaper articles about him, I was impressed not only by his commitment but also by his ability to perceive the deeper issues. And the deeper issues pointed to the fact that we were entering a new epoch of world politics.

In November 1980, Carter lost the US presidential election to Ronald Reagan. The Panama Canal Treaty he had negotiated with Torrijos and the situation in Iran, especially the hostages held at the US Embassy and the failed rescue attempt, were major factors. However, something subtler was also happening. A president whose greatest goal was world peace and who was dedicated to reducing US dependence on oil was replaced by a man who believed that the United States' rightful place was at the top of a world pyramid held up by military muscle, and that controlling oil fields wherever they existed was part of our Manifest Destiny. A president who installed solar panels on White House roofs was replaced by one who, immediately upon occupying the Oval Office, had them removed.

Carter may have been an ineffective politician, but he had a vision for America that was consistent with the one defined in our Declaration of Independence. In retrospect, he now seems naively archaic, a throwback to the ideals that molded this nation and drew so many of our grandparents to her shores. When we compare him to his immediate predecessors and successors, he is an anomaly. His worldview was inconsistent with that of the EHMs.

Reagan, on the other hand, was most definitely a global empire builder and a servant of the corporatocracy. At the time of his election, I found it fitting that he was a Hollywood actor, a man who had followed orders passed down from moguls, who knew how to take direction. That would be his signature. He would cater to the men who shuttled back and forth from corporate CEO offices to bank boards and into the halls of government. He would serve the men who appeared to serve him but who in fact ran the government — men like Vice President George H. W. Bush, Secretary of State George Shultz, Secretary of Defense Caspar Weinberger, Richard Cheney, Richard Helms, and Robert McNamara. He would advocate what those men wanted: an America that controlled the world and all its resources, a world that answered to the commands of that America, a US military that would enforce the rules as they were written by America, and an international trade and banking system that supported America as CEO of the global empire.

As I looked into the future, it seemed we were entering a period that would be very good to the EHMs. It was another twist of fate that I had chosen this moment in history to drop out. The more I reflected on it, however, the better I felt about it. I knew that my timing was right.

As for what this meant in the long term, I had no crystal ball;
however, I knew from history that empires do not endure and that
the pendulum always swings in both directions. From my perspective, men like Roldós offered hope. I was certain that Ecuador's
new president understood many of the subtleties of the current
situation. I knew that he had been a Torrijos admirer and had
applauded Carter for his courageous stand on the Panama Canal
issue. I felt certain that Roldós would not falter. I could only hope
that his fortitude would light a candle for the leaders of other countries, who needed the type of inspiration he and Torrijos could
provide.

Early in 1981, the Roldós administration formally presented
his new hydrocarbons law to the Ecuadorian congress. If implemented, it would reform the country's relationship to oil companies. By many standards, it was considered revolutionary and
even radical. It certainly aimed to change the way business was
conducted. Its influence would stretch far beyond Ecuador, into
much of Latin America and throughout the world.[1]

The oil companies reacted predictably — they pulled out all the
stops. Their public relations people went to work to vilify Jaime
Roldós, and their lobbyists swept into Quito and Washington,
briefcases full of threats and payoffs. They tried to paint the first
democratically elected president of Ecuador in modern times as
another Castro. But Roldós would not cave in to intimidation. He
responded by denouncing the conspiracy between politics and
oil — and religion. Although he offered no tangible proof, he openly
accused the Summer Institute of Linguistics of colluding with the
oil companies, and then, in an extremely bold move, he ordered
SIL out of the country.[2]

Only weeks after sending his legislative package to congress,
and a couple of days after expelling the SIL missionaries, Roldós
warned all foreign interests, including but not limited to oil companies, that unless they implemented plans that would help
Ecuador's people, they would be forced to leave his country. He
delivered a major speech at the Atahualpa Olympic Stadium in
Quito and then headed off to a small community in southern
Ecuador.

He died there in a fiery airplane crash, on May 24, 1981.[3]

The world was shocked. Latin Americans were outraged. Newspapers throughout the hemisphere blazed, "CIA Assassination!" In addition to the fact that Washington and the oil companies hated him, many circumstances appeared to support these allegations, and such suspicions were heightened as more facts became known. Nothing was ever proven, but eyewitnesses claimed that Roldós, forewarned about an attempt on his life, had taken precautions, including traveling in two airplanes. At the last moment, it was said, one of his security officers had convinced him to board the decoy airplane. It had blown up.

Despite world reaction, the news hardly made the US press.

Osvaldo Hurtado took over as Ecuador's president. Under his administration, the Summer Institute of Linguistics continued working in Ecuador, and SIL members were granted special visas. By the end of the year, he had launched an ambitious program to increase oil drilling by Texaco and other foreign companies in the Gulf of Guayaquil and the Amazon basin.[4]

Omar Torrijos, in eulogizing Roldós, referred to him as "brother." He also confessed to having nightmares about his own assassination; he saw himself dropping from the sky in a gigantic fireball. It was prophetic.

⊕ CHAPTER 27

Panama: Another Presidential Death

I was stunned by Roldós's death, but perhaps I should not have been. I was anything but naive. I knew about Arbenz, Mossadegh, Allende — and about many other people whose names never made the newspapers or history books but whose lives were destroyed and sometimes cut short because they stood up to the corporatocracy. Nevertheless, I was shocked. It was just so very blatant.

I had concluded, after our phenomenal success in Saudi Arabia, that such wantonly overt actions were a thing of the past. I thought the jackals had been relegated to zoos. Now I saw that I was wrong. I had no doubt that Roldós's death had not been an accident. It had all the markings of a CIA-orchestrated assassination. I also understood that it had been executed so blatantly in order to send a message. The new Reagan administration, complete with its fast-draw Hollywood cowboy image, was the ideal vehicle for delivering such a message. The jackals were back, and they wanted Omar Torrijos and everyone else who might consider joining an anti-corporatocracy crusade to know it.

But Torrijos was not buckling. Like Roldós, he refused to be intimidated. He, too, expelled the Summer Institute of Linguistics, and he adamantly refused to give in to the Reagan administration's demands to renegotiate the Canal treaty.

Two months after Roldós's death, Omar Torrijos's nightmare came true; he died in a plane crash. It was July 31, 1981.

Latin America and the world reeled. Torrijos was known across the globe; he was respected as the man who had forced the United States to relinquish the Panama Canal to its rightful owners, and who continued to stand up to Ronald Reagan. He was a champion of human rights, the head of state who had opened his arms to refugees across the political spectrum, including the shah of Iran. He was a charismatic voice for social justice who, many believed, would be nominated for the Nobel Peace Prize. Now he was dead.

166

"CIA Assassination!" once again headlined articles and editorials. Graham Greene began his book *Getting to Know the General*, the one that grew out of the trip when I met him at the Hotel Panama, with the following paragraph:

> In August 1981 my bag was packed for my fifth visit to Panama when the news came to me over the telephone of the death of General Omar Torrijos Herrera, my friend and host. The small plane in which he was flying to a house which he owned at Coclesito in the mountains of Panama had crashed, and there were no survivors. A few days later the voice of his security guard, Sergeant Chuchu, alias José de Jesús Martínez, ex-professor of Marxist philosophy at Panama University, professor of mathematics and a poet, told me, "There was a bomb in that plane. *I know* there was a bomb in the plane, but I can't tell you why over the telephone."[1]

People everywhere mourned the death of this man who had earned a reputation as defender of the poor and defenseless, and they clamored for Washington to open investigations into CIA activities. However, this was not about to happen. There were men who hated Torrijos, and the list included people with immense power. Before his death, he was openly loathed by President Reagan, Vice President Bush, Secretary of Defense Weinberger, and the Joint Chiefs of Staff, as well as by the CEOs of many powerful corporations.

The military chiefs were especially incensed by provisions in the Torrijos–Carter treaty that forced them to close the School of the Americas and the US Southern Command's tropical warfare center. The chiefs thus had a serious problem. Either they had to figure out some way to get around the new treaty, or they needed to find another country that would be willing to harbor these facilities — an unlikely prospect in the closing decades of the twentieth century. Of course, there was also another option: dispose of Torrijos and renegotiate the treaty with his successor.

Among Torrijos's corporate enemies were the huge multinationals. Most had close ties to US politicians and were involved in exploiting Latin American labor forces and natural resources — oil, lumber, tin, copper, bauxite, and agricultural lands. They included manufacturing firms, communications companies, shipping and transportation conglomerates, and engineering and other technologically oriented corporations.

The Bechtel Group was a prime example of the cozy relationship between private companies and the US government. I knew Bechtel well; we at MAIN often worked closely with the company, and its chief architect became a close personal friend. Bechtel was the United States' most influential engineering and construction company. Its president and senior officers included George Shultz and Caspar Weinberger, who despised Torrijos because he brazenly courted a Japanese plan to replace Panama's existing canal with a new, more efficient one.[2] Such a move not only would transfer ownership from the United States to Panama but also would exclude Bechtel from participating in the most exciting and potentially lucrative engineering project of the century.

Torrijos stood up to these men, and he did so with grace, charm, and a wonderful sense of humor. Now he was dead, and he had been replaced by a dictator who referred to himself as the Maximum Leader of National Liberation, Manuel Noriega, a man who lacked Torrijos's wit, charisma, and intelligence, and a man who many suspected had no chance against the Reagans, Bushes, and Bechtels of the world.

I was personally devastated by the tragedy. I spent many hours reflecting on my conversations with Torrijos. Late one night, I sat for a long time staring at his photo in a magazine and recalling my first night in Panama, riding in a cab through the rain, stopping before his gigantic billboard picture. "Omar's ideal is freedom; the missile is not invented that can kill an ideal!" The memory of that inscription sent a shudder through me, even as it had on that stormy night.

I could not have known, back then, that Torrijos would collaborate with Carter to return the Panama Canal to the people who rightfully deserved to own it, or that this victory, along with his attempts to reconcile differences between Latin American Socialists and the dictators, would so infuriate the Reagan–Bush administration that it would seek to assassinate him.[3] I could not have known that on another dark night he would be killed during a routine flight in his Twin Otter, or that most of the world outside the

United States would have no doubt that Torrijos's death at the age of fifty-two was just one more in a series of CIA assassinations.

Had Torrijos lived, he undoubtedly would have sought to quell the growing violence that has plagued so many Central and South American nations. Based on his record, we can assume that he would have tried to work out an arrangement to mitigate international oil company destruction of the Amazon regions of Ecuador, Brazil, Colombia, and Peru. One result of such action would have been the alleviation of the terrible conflicts that Washington refers to as terrorist and drug wars, but which Torrijos would have seen as actions taken by desperate people to protect their families and homes. Most important, I feel certain that he would have been served as a role model for a new generation of leaders in the Americas, Africa, and Asia — something the CIA, the NSA, and the EHMs could not allow.

CHAPTER 28

My Energy Company, Enron, and George W. Bush

At the time of Torrijos's death, I had not seen Paula for several months. I was dating other women, including Winifred Grant, a young environmental planner I had met at MAIN, whose father happened to be chief architect at Bechtel. Paula was dating a Colombian journalist, but we remained friends.

I struggled with my job as an expert witness, particularly in justifying the Seabrook nuclear power plant. It often seemed as though I had sold out again, slipping back into an old role simply for the sake of money. Winifred was an immense support to me during this period. She was an avowed environmentalist, yet she understood the practical necessities of providing ever-increasing amounts of electricity. She had grown up in the Berkeley area of San Francisco's East Bay and had graduated from UC Berkeley. She was a freethinker whose views on life contrasted with those of my puritanical parents and of Ann.

Our relationship developed. Winifred took a leave of absence from MAIN, and together we sailed my boat down the Atlantic coast toward Florida. We took our time, frequently leaving the boat in different ports so I could fly off to provide expert witness testimony. Eventually, we sailed into West Palm Beach, Florida, and rented an apartment. We married, and our daughter, Jessica, was born on May 17, 1982. I was thirty-six, considerably older than all the other men who hung out in Lamaze class.

Part of my job on the Seabrook case was to convince the New Hampshire Public Utilities Commission that nuclear power was the best and most economical choice for generating electricity in the state. Ironically, the longer I studied the issue, the more I began to doubt the validity of my own arguments. The literature was constantly changing at that time, reflecting a growth in research, and the evidence increasingly indicated that many alternative forms of energy were technically superior and more economical than nuclear power.

The balance also was beginning to shift away from the old theory that nuclear power was safe. Serious questions were being raised about the integrity of backup systems, the training of operators, the human tendency to make mistakes, equipment fatigue, and the inadequacy of nuclear waste disposal. I personally became uncomfortable with the position I was expected to take — was paid to take — under oath in what amounted to a court of law. At the same time, I was becoming convinced that some of the emerging technologies offered electricity-generating methods that could actually help the environment. This was particularly true in the area of generating electricity from substances previously considered waste products.

One day I informed my bosses at the New Hampshire utility company that I could no longer testify on their behalf. I gave up this very lucrative career and decided to create a company that would move some of the new technologies off the drawing boards and put the theories into practice. Winifred supported me one hundred percent, despite the uncertainties of the venture and the fact that, for the first time in her life, she was starting a family.

Several months after Jessica's birth in 1982, I founded Independent Power Systems (IPS), a company whose mission included developing environmentally beneficial power plants and establishing models to inspire others to do likewise. It was a high-risk business, and most of our competitors eventually failed. However, "coincidences" came to our rescue. In fact, I was certain that many times someone stepped in to help, that I was being rewarded for my past service and for my commitment to silence.

Bruno Zambotti had accepted a high-level position at the Inter-American Development Bank. He agreed to serve on the IPS board and to help finance the fledgling company. We received backing from Bankers Trust, ESI Energy, Prudential Insurance Company, Chadbourne and Parke (a major Wall Street law firm, in which former US senator, presidential candidate, and secretary of state Ed Muskie was a partner), and Riley Stoker Corporation (an engineering firm, owned by Ashland Oil and Refinery Company, which designed and built highly sophisticated and innovative power plant boilers). We even had backing from the US Congress, which singled out IPS for exemption from a specific tax, and in the process gave us a distinct advantage over our competitors.

In 1986, IPS and Bechtel simultaneously — but independently of each other — began construction of power plants that used highly innovative, state-of-the-art technologies for burning waste coal without producing acid rain. At that time, people were much more concerned about acid rain (sulfur dioxide, nitrogen oxides, and particulate matter) than about carbon emissions. By the end of the decade, these two plants had revolutionized the utility industry, directly contributing to new national antipollution laws by proving once and for all that many so-called waste products actually can be converted into electricity, and that coal can be burned without creating acid rain, thereby dispelling long-standing utility company claims to the contrary. Our plant also established that such unproven, state-of-the-art technologies could be financed by a small independent company, through Wall Street and other conventional means.[1] As an added benefit, the IPS power plant sent vented heat to a three-and-a-half-acre hydroponic greenhouse, rather than into cooling ponds or cooling towers.

My role as IPS president gave me an inside track on the energy industry. I dealt with some of the most influential people in the business: lawyers, lobbyists, investment bankers, and high-level executives at the major firms. I also had the advantage of a father-in-law who had spent more than thirty years at Bechtel, had risen to the position of chief architect, and now was in charge of building a city in Saudi Arabia — a direct result of the work I had done in the early 1970s, during the Saudi Arabian Money-Laundering Affair. Winifred grew up near Bechtel's San Francisco world headquarters and also was a member of the corporate family; her first job after graduating from UC Berkeley was at Bechtel.

The energy industry was undergoing major restructuring. The big engineering firms were jockeying to take over — or at least to compete with — the utility companies that previously had enjoyed the privileges of local monopolies. Deregulation was the watchword of the day, and rules changed overnight. Opportunities abounded for ambitious people to take advantage of a situation that baffled the courts and Congress. Industry pundits dubbed it the "Wild West of Energy" era.

One casualty of this process was MAIN. As Bruno predicted, Mac Hall had lost touch with reality and no one dared tell him so. Paul Priddy never asserted control, and MAIN's management not only failed to take advantage of the changes sweeping the industry but also made a series of fatal mistakes. Only a few years after Bruno delivered record profits, MAIN dropped its EHM role and was in dire financial straits. The partners sold MAIN to one of the large engineering and construction firms that had played its cards right.

While I had received almost thirty dollars a share for my stock in 1980, the remaining partners settled for less than half that amount, approximately four years later. Thus did one hundred years of proud service end in humiliation. I was sad to see the company fold, but I felt vindicated that I had gotten out when I did. The MAIN name continued under the new ownership for a while, but then it was dropped. The logo that had once carried such weight in countries around the globe fell into oblivion.

MAIN was one example of a company that did not cope well in the changing atmosphere of the energy industry. At the opposite end of the spectrum was a company we insiders found fascinating: Enron. One of the fastest-growing organizations in the business, it seemed to come out of nowhere and immediately began putting together mammoth deals. Most business meetings open with a few moments of idle chatter while the participants settle into their seats, pour themselves cups of coffee, and arrange their papers; in those days the idle chatter often centered on Enron. No one outside the company could fathom how Enron was able to accomplish such miracles. Those on the inside simply smiled at the rest of us and kept quiet. Occasionally, when pressed, they talked about new approaches to management, about "creative financing," and about their commitment to hiring executives who knew their way through the corridors of power in capitals across the globe.

To me, this all sounded like a new version of old EHM techniques. The global empire was marching forward at a rapid pace.

For those of us interested in oil and the international scene, there was another frequently discussed topic: the vice president's son, George W. Bush. His first energy company, Arbusto (Spanish for *bush*), was a failure that ultimately was rescued through a 1984 merger with Spectrum 7. Then, Spectrum 7 found itself poised at the brink of bankruptcy and was purchased, in 1986, by Harken Energy Corporation; G. W. Bush was retained as a board member and consultant with an annual salary of $120,000 (in 1986 dollars).[2]

We all assumed that having a father who was the US vice president factored into this hiring decision, since the younger Bush's record of accomplishment as an oil executive certainly did not warrant it. It also seemed no coincidence that Harken took this opportunity to branch out into the international field for the first time in its corporate history, and to begin actively searching for oil investments in the Middle East. *Vanity Fair* reported, "Once Bush took his seat on the board, wonderful things started to happen to Harken — new investments, unexpected sources of financing, serendipitous drilling rights."[3]

In 1989, Amoco was negotiating with the government of Bahrain for offshore drilling rights. Then newly elected President George H. W. Bush took office. Shortly thereafter, Michael Ameen — a State Department consultant assigned to brief the newly confirmed US ambassador to Bahrain, Charles Hostler — arranged for meetings between the Bahraini government and Harken Energy. Suddenly, Amoco was replaced by Harken. Although Harken had not previously drilled outside the southeastern United States, and never offshore, it won exclusive drilling rights in Bahrain, something previously unheard of in the Arab world. Within a few weeks, the price of Harken Energy stock increased by more than 20 percent, from $4.50 to $5.50 per share.[4]

Even seasoned energy people were shocked by what had happened in Bahrain. "I hope G. W. isn't up to something his father will pay for," said a lawyer friend of mine who specialized in the energy industry and was a major supporter of the Republican Party. We were enjoying cocktails at a bar around the corner from Wall Street, high atop the World Trade Center. He expressed dismay. "I wonder if it's really worth it," he continued, shaking his head sadly. "Is the son's career worth risking the presidency?"

I was less surprised than my peers, but I suppose I had a unique perspective. I had worked for the governments of Kuwait, Saudi

Arabia, Egypt, and Iran; I was familiar with Middle Eastern politics; and I knew that the Bush family, just like the Enron executives, was part of the network that I and my EHM colleagues had created; they were the feudal lords and plantation masters.[5]

⊕ CHAPTER 29

I Take a Bribe

During this time in my life, I came to realize that we truly had entered a new era in world economics. Events set in motion while Robert McNamara — the man who had served as one of my models — reigned as secretary of defense and president of the World Bank had escalated beyond my gravest fears. McNamara's Keynesian-inspired approach to economics, and his advocacy of aggressive leadership, had become pervasive. The EHM concept had expanded to include all manner of executives in a wide variety of businesses. They may not have been recruited or profiled by the NSA, but they were performing similar functions.

The only difference now was that the corporate executive EHMs did not necessarily involve themselves with the use of funds from the international banking community. While the old branch, my branch, continued to thrive, the new version took on aspects that were even more sinister. During the 1980s, young men and women rose up through the ranks of middle management believing that any means was justified by the end: an enhanced bottom line. Global empire was simply a pathway to increased profits.

The new trends were typified by the energy industry, in which I worked. The Public Utility Regulatory Policy Act (PURPA) was passed by Congress in 1978, went through a series of legal challenges, and finally became law in 1982. Congress originally envisioned the law as a way to encourage small, independent companies like mine to develop alternative fuels and other innovative approaches to producing electricity. Under this law, the major utility companies were required to purchase energy generated by the smaller companies, at fair and reasonable prices (calculated using the "avoided cost" method). This policy was a result of Carter's desire to reduce US dependence on oil — all oil, not just imported oil. The intent of the law was clearly to encourage both alternative energy sources and the development of independent companies that reflected

America's entrepreneurial spirit. However, the reality turned out
to be something very different.

During the 1980s and into the 1990s, the emphasis switched
from entrepreneurship to deregulation. Milton Friedman, a member of the Chicago school of economics, had won the Nobel Prize
in Economics by maintaining that the only goal of business should
be to maximize profits, regardless of the social and environmental
costs, and that government oversight, in general, was unnecessary
and counterproductive. Combined with McNamara's emphasis on
aggressive leadership, this doctrine inspired CEOs to muscle their
companies into focusing totally on the bottom line. The wealthiest
companies in the energy industry interpreted these ideas as license
to do whatever it would take to gain more control and market share
and to increase profits, rather than honoring the intent of PURPA
to develop innovative approaches and new sources of energy.

I watched in horror as most of the other small independents
were swallowed up by the large engineering and construction
firms, and by the public utility companies themselves. The latter
found legal loopholes that allowed them to create holding companies, which could own both the regulated utility companies and the
unregulated independent energy-producing corporations. Many of
them launched aggressive programs to drive the independents into
bankruptcy and then purchase them. Others simply started from
scratch and developed their own equivalent of the independents.

The idea of reducing our oil dependence fell by the wayside.
Reagan was deeply indebted to the oil companies; George H. W.
Bush had made his own fortune as an oilman. And most of the key
players and cabinet members in these two administrations were
either part of the oil industry or part of the engineering and construction companies so closely tied to it. Moreover, in the final analysis, oil and construction were not partisan; many Democrats also
had profited from and were beholden to them.

IPS continued to maintain a vision of environmentally beneficial energy. We were committed to the original PURPA goals, and
we seemed to lead a charmed life. We were one of the few independents that not only survived but also thrived. I have no doubt
that the reason for this was because of my past services to the
corporatocracy.

What was going on in the energy field was symbolic of a trend that was affecting the whole world. Friedman's "maximize profits" credo was promoted by government and business leaders on every continent. Concerns about social welfare, the environment, and other quality-of-life issues took a backseat to greed. In the process, an overwhelming emphasis was placed on promoting private businesses. At first, this was justified on theoretical bases, including the idea that capitalism was superior to and would deter communism. Eventually, however, such justification was unneeded. It was simply accepted a priori that there was something inherently better about projects owned by wealthy investors rather than by governments. International organizations such as the World Bank bought into this notion, advocating deregulation and privatization of water and sewer systems, communications networks, utility grids, and other facilities that up until then had been managed by governments.

As a result, it was easy to expand the EHM concept into the larger community, to send executives from a broad spectrum of businesses on missions previously reserved for the few of us recruited into an exclusive club. These executives fanned out across the planet. They sought the cheapest labor pools, the most accessible resources, and the largest markets. They were ruthless in their approach. Like the EHMs who had gone before them — like me, in Indonesia, in Panama, and in Colombia — they found ways to rationalize their misdeeds. And like us, they ensnared communities and countries. They promised affluence, a way for countries to use the private sector to dig themselves out of debt. They built schools and highways; they donated telephones, televisions, and medical services. In the end, however, if they found cheaper workers or more accessible resources elsewhere, they left. When they abandoned a community whose hopes they had raised, the consequences were often devastating, but they apparently did this without a moment's hesitation or a nod to their own consciences.

I had to wonder, though, what all this was doing to their psyches, whether they had their moments of doubt, as I had had mine. Did they ever stand next to a befouled canal and watch a young woman try to bathe while an old man defecated upriver? Were there no Howard Parkers left to ask the tough questions?

Although I enjoyed my IPS successes and my life as a family man, I could not fight my moments of severe disillusionment. I was now the father of a young girl, and I feared for the future she would inherit. I was weighed down with guilt for the part I had played.

I also could look back and see a very disturbing historical trend. The modern international financial system was created near the end of World War II, at a meeting of leaders from many countries, held in Bretton Woods, New Hampshire—my home state. The World Bank and the International Monetary Fund were formed in order to reconstruct a devastated Europe, and they achieved remarkable success. The system expanded rapidly, and it was soon sanctioned by every major US ally and hailed as a panacea for oppression. It would, we were assured, save us all from the evil clutches of communism.

But I could not help wondering where all this would lead us. By the late 1980s, with the collapse of the Soviet Union and the world Communist movement, it became apparent that deterring communism was not the goal; it was equally obvious that the global empire, which was rooted in capitalism, would have free rein. As Jim Garrison, president of the State of the World forum, observes:

> Taken cumulatively, the integration of the world as a whole, particularly in terms of economic globalization and the mythic qualities of "free market" capitalism, represents a veritable "empire" in its own right.... No nation on earth has been able to resist the compelling magnetism of globalization. Few have been able to escape the "structural adjustments" and "conditionalities" of the World Bank, the International Monetary Fund, or the arbitrations of the World Trade Organization, those international financial institutions that, however inadequate, still determine what economic globalization means, what the rules are, and who is rewarded for submission and punished for infractions. Such is the power of globalization that within our lifetime we are likely to see the integration, even if unevenly, of all national economies in the world into a single global, free market system.[1]

As I mulled over these issues, in 1987, I decided it was time to

write a tell-all book, *Conscience of an Economic Hit Man*, but I made
no attempt to keep the work quiet. Even today, I am not the sort
of writer who writes in isolation. I find it necessary to discuss
the work I am doing. I receive inspiration from other people, and
I call upon them to help me remember and put into perspective
events of the past. In this particular case, I wanted to include the
stories of other EHMs and jackals, and I began to contact people
I had known.

Then I received an anonymous phone call threatening my life
and that of my young daughter, Jessica. And another. I was terrified. I'd seen what the jackals could do. However, I was at a loss.
Claudine's warning about being in for life echoed through my consciousness. What were my options?

The day after the second phone call, another former MAIN
partner contacted me and offered me an extremely lucrative consulting contract with Stone & Webster Engineering Corporation
(SWEC). At that time, SWEC was one of the world's premier engineering and construction companies, and it was trying to forge a
place for itself in the changing environment of the energy industry.
My contact explained that I would report to their new subsidiary,
an independent energy-development branch modeled after companies like my own IPS. I was relieved to learn that I would not be
asked to get involved in any international or EHM-type projects.

In fact, he told me, I would not be expected to do very much at
all. I was one of the few people who had founded and managed a
successful independent energy company, and I had an excellent
reputation in the industry. SWEC's primary interest was to use my
résumé and to include me on its list of advisers, which was legal
and was consistent with standard industry practices. The offer
was especially attractive to me because, due to a number of circumstances, I was considering selling IPS. The idea of joining the
SWEC stable and receiving a spectacular retainer was welcome.

The day he hired me, the CEO of SWEC took me out to a private lunch. We chatted informally for some time, and as we did
so, I realized that a side of me was eager to get back into the consulting business, to leave behind the responsibilities of running a
complicated energy company, of being responsible for more than a

hundred people when we were constructing a facility, and of dealing with all the liabilities associated with building and operating
power plants. I had already envisioned how I would spend the substantial retainer I knew he was about to offer me. I had decided to
use it, among other things, to support my desire to write and to
create a nonprofit organization.

Over dessert, my host and I discussed my interest in writing.
He looked me squarely in the eye. "Do you intend to write books
about our profession?" he asked.

My stomach tightened. Suddenly I understood what this was
all about. I recalled the threats. I did not hesitate. "No," I said.
"I've been writing a book about the way indigenous people manage stress, but I don't intend to try to publish any books about this
business."

"I'm glad to hear that," he said. "We value our privacy at this
company. Just like at MAIN."

"I understand that."

He sat back and, smiling, seemed to relax. "Of course, books
about dealing with stress and such things are perfectly acceptable.
Sometimes they can even further a man's career. As a consultant
to SWEC, you are perfectly free to publish that sort of thing." He
looked at me as though expecting a response.

"That's good to know."

"Yes, perfectly acceptable. However, it goes without saying that
you'll never mention the name of this company in your books, and
that you will not write about anything that touches on the nature
of our business here, or the work you did at MAIN. You will not
mention political subjects or any dealings with international banks
and development projects." He peered at me. "Simply a matter of
confidentiality."

"It goes without saying," I assured him. For an instant, my
heart seemed to stop beating. An old feeling returned, similar
to ones I had experienced around Howard Parker in Indonesia,
while driving through Panama City beside Fidel, and while sitting
in a Colombian coffee shop with Paula. I was selling out — again.
This was not a bribe in the legal sense — it was perfectly above-
board and legitimate for this company to pay to include my name

on its roster, to call upon me for advice, or to ask me to show up at a meeting from time to time, but I understood the real reason I was being hired.

He offered me a consultant's retainer that was equivalent to a top executive's annual salary.

Later that afternoon I sat in an airport, stunned, waiting for my flight back to Florida. I felt like a prostitute. Worse than that, I felt I had betrayed my daughter, my family, and my country. And yet, I told myself, I had little choice. I knew that if I had not accepted this bribe, the jackals would not hesitate to kill my daughter, me, and anyone else who threatened to expose the stories behind the "facts" that the EHM system presented to the world.

CHAPTER 30

The United States Invades Panama

Torrijos was dead, but Panama continued to hold a special place in my heart. Living in South Florida, I had access to many sources of information about current events in Central America. Torrijos's legacy lived on, even if it was filtered through people who were not graced with his compassionate personality and strength of character. Attempts to settle differences throughout the hemisphere continued after his death, as did Panama's determination to force the United States to live up to the terms of the Canal treaty.

Manuel Noriega became Torrijos's de facto successor, and at first he appeared committed to following in his mentor's footsteps. I never met Noriega personally, but by all accounts, he initially endeavored to further the cause of Latin America's poor and oppressed. One of his most important projects was the continued exploration of prospects for building a new canal, to be financed and constructed by the Japanese. Predictably, he encountered a great deal of resistance from Washington and from private US companies. As Noriega himself writes:

> Secretary of State George Shultz was a former executive of the multinational construction company Bechtel; Defense Secretary Caspar Weinberger had been a Bechtel vice president. Bechtel would have liked nothing better than to earn the billions of dollars in revenue that canal construction would generate. . . . The Reagan and Bush administrations feared the possibility that Japan might dominate an eventual canal construction project; not only was there a misplaced concern about security, there was also the question of commercial rivalry. US construction firms stood to lose billions of dollars.[1]

But Noriega was no Torrijos. He did not have his former boss's charisma or integrity. Over time, he developed an unsavory reputation for corruption and drug dealing and was even suspected of participating, along with the CIA, in Torrijos's assassination, and of arranging the assassination of a political rival, Hugo Spadafora.

Noriega began building his reputation as a colonel, heading up the Panamanian Defense Forces' G-2 unit, the military intelligence command that was the national liaison with the CIA. In this capacity, he developed a close relationship with CIA Director William J. Casey. The CIA used this connection to further its agenda throughout the Caribbean and Central and South America. For example, when the Reagan administration wanted to give Castro advance warning of the 1983 US invasion of Grenada, Casey turned to Noriega, asking him to serve as messenger. The colonel also helped the CIA infiltrate Colombian and other drug cartels.

By 1984, Noriega had been promoted to general and commander in chief of the Panamanian Defense Forces. It is reported that when Casey arrived in Panama City that year and was met at the airport by the local CIA chief, he asked, "Where's my boy? Where's Noriega?" When the general visited Washington, the two men met privately at Casey's house. Many years later, Noriega would admit that his close bond with Casey made him feel invincible. He believed that the CIA, like G-2, was the strongest branch of its country's government. He was convinced that Casey would protect him, despite Noriega's stance on the Panama Canal Treaty and US Canal Zone military bases.[2]

Thus, whereas Torrijos had been an international icon for justice and equality, Noriega became a symbol of corruption and decadence. His notoriety in this regard was assured when, on June 12, 1986, the *New York Times* ran a front-page article with the headline "Panama Strongman Said to Trade in Drugs and Illicit Money." The exposé, written by a Pulitzer Prize–winning reporter, alleged that the general was a secret and illegal partner in several Latin American businesses; that he had spied on and for both the United States and Cuba, acting as a sort of double agent; that G-2, under his orders, had in fact beheaded Hugo Spadafora; and that Noriega had personally directed "the most significant drug running in Panama." The article was accompanied by an unflattering portrait of the general, and a follow-up the next day included more details.[3]

Compounding his other problems, Noriega also was saddled with a US president who suffered from an image problem, what journalists referred to as George H. W. Bush's "wimp factor."[4] This took on special significance when Noriega adamantly refused to consider a fifteen-year extension for the School of the Americas. The general's memoirs provide an interesting insight:

> As determined and proud as we were to follow through with Torrijos's legacy, the United States didn't want any of this to happen. They wanted an extension or a renegotiation for the installation [School of the Americas], saying that with their growing war preparations in Central America, they still needed it. But that School of the Americas was an embarrassment to us. We didn't want a training ground for death squads and repressive right-wing militaries on our soil.[5]

Perhaps, therefore, the world should have anticipated it, but in fact the world was stunned when, on December 20, 1989, the United States attacked Panama City with what was reported to be the largest airborne assault on a city since World War II.[6] It was an unprovoked attack on a civilian population. Panama and her people posed absolutely no threat to the United States or to any other country. Politicians, governments, and press around the world denounced the unilateral US action as a clear violation of international law.

Had this military operation been directed against a country that had committed mass murder or other human rights crimes – Pinochet's Chile, Stroessner's Paraguay, Somoza's Nicaragua, D'Aubuisson's El Salvador, or Saddam's Iraq, for example – the world might have understood. But Panama had done nothing of the sort; it had merely dared to defy the wishes of a handful of powerful politicians and corporate executives. It had insisted that the Canal treaty be honored, it had held discussions with social reformers, and it had explored the possibility of building a new canal with Japanese financing and construction companies. As a result, it suffered devastating consequences. As Noriega puts it:

> I want to make it very clear: the destabilization campaign launched by the United States in 1986, ending with the 1989

> Panama invasion, was a result of the US rejection of any
> scenario in which future control of the Panama Canal might
> be in the hands of an independent, sovereign Panama — sup-
> ported by Japan.... Shultz and Weinberger, meanwhile,
> masquerading as officials operating in the public interest and
> basking in popular ignorance about the powerful economic
> interests they represented, were building a propaganda
> campaign to shoot me down.[7]

Washington's stated justification for the attack was based on
one man. The United States' sole rationale for sending its young
men and women to risk their lives and consciences in killing innocent people, including untold numbers of children, and setting fire
to huge sections of Panama City, was Noriega. He was character-
ized as evil, as the enemy of the people, as a drug-trafficking monster, and as such he provided the administration with an excuse
for the massive invasion of a country with two million inhabit-
ants — which coincidentally happened to sit on one of the most
valuable pieces of real estate in the world.

I found the invasion deeply disturbing. I knew that Noriega had
bodyguards, yet I could not help believing that the jackals could
have taken him out, as they had Roldós and Torrijos. Most of his
bodyguards, I suspected, had been trained by US military personnel and probably could have been paid either to look the other way
or to carry out an assassination themselves.

The more I thought and read about the invasion, therefore, the
more convinced I became that it signaled a US policy turn back
toward the old methods of empire building, that the Bush administration was determined to go one better than Reagan and to demonstrate to the world that it would not hesitate to use massive force
in order to achieve its ends. It also seemed that the goal in Panama,
in addition to replacing the Torrijos legacy with a puppet administration favorable to the United States, was to frighten countries
like Iraq into submission.

David Harris, a contributing editor at the *New York Times Magazine* and the author of many books, has an interesting observation.
In his 2001 book *Shooting the Moon*, he states:

Of all the thousands of rulers, potentates, strongmen, juntas, and warlords the Americans have dealt with in all corners of the world, General Manuel Antonio Noriega is the only one the Americans came after like this. Just once in its 225 years of formal national existence has the United States ever invaded another country and carried its ruler back to the United States to face trial and imprisonment for violations of American law committed on that ruler's own native foreign turf.[8]

Following the bombardment, the United States suddenly found itself in a delicate situation. For a while, it seemed as though the whole thing would backfire. The Bush administration might have quashed the wimp rumors, but now it faced the problem of legitimacy, of appearing to be a bully caught in an act of terrorism. It was disclosed that the US Army had prohibited the press, the Red Cross, and other outside observers from entering the heavily bombed areas for three days, while soldiers incinerated and buried the casualties. The press asked questions about how much evidence of criminal and other inappropriate behavior was destroyed, and about how many died because they were denied timely medical attention, but such questions were never answered.

We shall never know many of the facts about the invasion, nor shall we know the true extent of the massacre. Richard Cheney, defense secretary at the time, claimed the death toll was between five hundred and six hundred, but human rights observers estimated it at three thousand to five thousand, with another twenty-five thousand left homeless.[9] Noriega was arrested, flown to Miami, and sentenced to forty years' imprisonment; at that time, he was the only person in the United States officially classified as a prisoner of war.[10]

The world was outraged by this breach of international law and by the needless destruction of a defenseless people at the hands of the most powerful military force on the planet, but few in the United States were aware of either the outrage or the crimes Washington had committed. Press coverage was very limited. A number of factors contributed to this, including government policy,

White House phone calls to publishers and television executives, congresspeople who dared not object lest the wimp factor become their problem, and journalists who thought the public needed heroes rather than objectivity.

One exception was Peter Eisner, a *Newsday* editor and Associated Press reporter who covered the Panama invasion and continued to analyze it for many years. In *America's Prisoner: The Memoirs of Manuel Noriega*, published in 1997, Eisner writes:

> The death, destruction and injustice wrought in the name of fighting Noriega — and the lies surrounding that event — were threats to the basic American principles of democracy.... Soldiers were ordered to kill in Panama and they did so after being told they had to rescue a country from the clamp of a cruel, depraved dictator; once they acted, the people of their country [the US] marched lockstep behind them.[11]

After lengthy research, including interviews with Noriega in his Miami prison cell, Eisner states:

> On the key points, I do not think the evidence shows Noriega was guilty of the charges against him. I do not think his actions as a foreign military leader or a sovereign head of state justify the invasion of Panama or that he represented a threat to US national security.[12]

He concludes:

> My analysis of the political situation and my reporting in Panama before, during, and after the invasion brought me to the conclusion that the US invasion of Panama was an abominable abuse of power. The invasion principally served the goals of arrogant American politicians and their Panamanian allies, at the expense of unconscionable bloodshed.[13]

The Arias family and the pre-Torrijos oligarchy, which had served as US puppets from the time when Panama was torn from Colombia until Torrijos took over, were reinstated. The new Canal treaty became a moot point. In essence, Washington once again controlled the waterway, despite anything the official documents said.

As I reflected on those incidents and all that I had experienced while working for MAIN, I found myself asking the same questions over and over: How many decisions — including ones of great historical significance that impact millions of people — are made by men and women who are driven by personal motives rather than by a desire to do the right thing? How many of our top government officials are driven by personal greed instead of national loyalty? How many wars are fought because a president does not want his constituents to perceive him as a wimp?

Despite my promises to SWEC's president, my frustration and feelings of impotence about the Panama invasion prodded me into resuming work on my book, except now I decided to focus on Torrijos. I saw his story as a way to expose many of the injustices that infect our world and as a way to rid myself of my guilt. This time, however, I was determined to keep silent about what I was doing, rather than seeking advice from friends and peers.

As I worked on the book, I was stunned by the magnitude of what we EHMs had accomplished, in so many places. I tried to concentrate on a few countries that stood out, but the list of places where I had worked and which were worse off afterward was astounding. I also was horrified by the extent of my own corruption. I had done a great deal of soul searching, yet I realized that while I was in the midst of it, I had been so focused on my daily activities that I had not seen the larger perspective. Thus, when I was in Indonesia, I fretted over the things Howard Parker and I discussed or the issues raised by Rasy's young Indonesian friends. While I was working in Panama, I was deeply affected by the implications of what I had seen during Fidel's introduction of the slums, the Canal Zone, and the discotheque. In Iran, my conversations with Yamin and Doc troubled me immensely. Now, the act of writing this book gave me an overview. I understood how easy it had been not to see the larger picture and therefore to miss the true significance of my actions.

How simple this sounds, and how self-evident; yet, how insidious the nature of these experiences. For me it conjures the image of soldiers. In the beginning, they are naive. They may question the morality of killing other people, but mostly they have to deal with their own fears, have to focus on survival. After they kill their first enemies, they are overwhelmed with emotions. They may wonder about the families of the dead men and feel a sense of remorse. But as time goes on and they participate in more battles, kill more people, they become hardened. They are transformed into professional soldiers.

In some sense, I had become a professional soldier. Admitting that fact opened the door for a better understanding of the process by which crimes are committed and empires are built. I could now comprehend why so many people have committed atrocious acts — how, for example, good, family-loving Iranians could work for the shah's brutal secret police, how good Germans could follow the orders of Hitler, how good American men and women could bomb Panama City.

As an EHM, I never drew a penny directly from the NSA or any other government agency; MAIN paid my salary. I was a private citizen, employed by a private corporation. Understanding this helped me see more clearly the emerging role of the corporate executive-as-EHM. A whole new class of soldier was emerging on the world scene, and these people were becoming desensitized to their own actions. I wrote:

> Today, men and women are going into Thailand, the Philippines, Botswana, Bolivia, and every other country where they hope to find people desperate for work. They go to these places with the express purpose of exploiting wretched people — people whose children are severely malnourished, even starving, people who live in shantytowns and have lost all hope of a better life, people who have ceased to even dream of another day. These men and women leave their plush offices in Manhattan or San Francisco or Chicago, streak across continents and oceans in luxurious jetliners, check into first-class hotels, and dine at the finest restaurants the country has to offer. Then they go searching for desperate people.

Today, we still have slave traders. They no longer find it necessary to march into the forests of Africa looking for people who will bring top dollar on the auction blocks in Charleston, Cartagena, and Havana. They simply recruit desperate people and build a factory to produce the jackets, blue jeans, tennis shoes, automobile parts, computer components, and thousands of other items they can sell in the markets of their choosing. Or they may elect not even to own the factory themselves; instead, they hire a local businessman to do all their dirty work for them.

These men and women think of themselves as upright. They return to their homes with photographs of quaint sites and ancient ruins, to show to their children. They attend seminars where they pat each other on the back and exchange tidbits of advice about dealing with the eccentricities of customs in far-off lands. Their bosses hire lawyers who assure them that what they are doing is perfectly legal. They have a cadre of psychotherapists and other human resource experts at their disposal to convince them that they are helping those desperate people.

The old-fashioned slave trader told himself that he was dealing with a species that was not entirely human, and that he was offering them the opportunity to become Christianized. He also understood that slaves were fundamental to the survival of his own society, that they were the foundation of his economy. The modern slave trader assures himself (or herself) that the desperate people are better off earning one dollar a day than no dollars at all, and that they are receiving the opportunity to become integrated into the larger world community. He or she also understands that these desperate people are fundamental to the survival of the company, that they are the foundation for his or her own lifestyle. He or she never stops to think about the larger implications, the economic system behind this process — or how it will ultimately impact the future of the world's children.

CHAPTER 31

An EHM Failure in Iraq

My role as president of IPS in the 1980s, and as a consultant to SWEC in the late 1980s and throughout much of the 1990s, gave me access to information about Iraq that was not available to most people. Indeed, during the 1980s the majority of Americans knew little about the country. It simply was not on their radar screen. However, I was fascinated by what was going on there.

I kept in touch with old friends who worked for the World Bank, USAID, the IMF, or one of the other international financial organizations, and with people at Bechtel, Halliburton, and the other major engineering and construction companies, including my own father-in-law. Many of the engineers employed by IPS subcontractors and other independent power companies were also involved in projects in the Middle East. I was very aware that the EHMs were hard at work in Iraq.

The Reagan and Bush administrations were determined to turn Iraq into another Saudi Arabia. There were many compelling reasons for Saddam Hussein to follow the example of the House of Saud. He had only to observe the benefits they had reaped from the Saudi Arabian Money-Laundering Affair. Since that deal was struck, modern cities had risen from the Saudi desert, Riyadh's garbage-collecting goats had been transformed into sleek trucks, and now the Saudis enjoyed the fruits of some of the most advanced technologies in the world: state-of-the-art desalinization plants, sewage treatment systems, communications networks, and electric utility grids.

Saddam Hussein undoubtedly was aware that the Saudis also enjoyed special treatment when it came to matters of international law. Their good friends in Washington turned a blind eye to many Saudi activities, including the financing of fanatical groups — many of which were considered by most of the world to be radicals bordering on terrorism — and the harboring of international fugitives.

In fact, the United States actively sought and received Saudi Arabian financial support for Osama bin Laden's Afghan war against the Soviet Union. The Reagan and Bush administrations not only encouraged the Saudis in this regard but also pressured many other countries to do the same — or at least to look the other way.

The EHM presence in Baghdad was very strong during the 1980s. They believed that Saddam eventually would see the light, and I had to agree with this assumption. After all, if Iraq reached an accord with Washington similar to that of the Saudis, Saddam could basically write his own ticket in ruling his country and might even expand his circle of influence throughout that part of the world.

It hardly mattered that he was a pathological tyrant, that he had the blood of mass murders on his hands, or that his mannerisms and brutal actions conjured images of Adolf Hitler. The United States had tolerated and even supported such men many times before. We would be happy to offer him US government securities in exchange for petrodollars, for the promise of continued oil supplies, and for a deal whereby the interest on those securities was used to hire US companies to improve infrastructure systems throughout Iraq, to create new cities, and to turn the deserts into oases. We would be willing to sell him tanks and fighter planes and to build him chemical and nuclear power plants, as we had done in so many other countries, even if these technologies could conceivably be used to produce advanced weaponry.

Iraq was extremely important to us, much more important than was obvious on the surface. Contrary to common public opinion, Iraq is not simply about oil. It is also about water and geopolitics. Both the Tigris and the Euphrates rivers flow through Iraq; thus, among all the countries in that part of the world, Iraq controls much of the increasingly critically important water resources. During the 1980s the importance of water — politically as well as economically — was becoming obvious to those of us in the energy and engineering fields. In the rush toward privatization, many of the major companies that had set their sights on taking over the small independent power companies now looked toward privatizing water systems in Africa, Latin America, and the Middle East.

In addition to having abundant oil and water, Iraq is situated in a very strategic location. It borders Iran, Kuwait, Saudi Arabia, Jordan, Syria, and Turkey, and it has a coastline on the Persian Gulf. It is within easy missile-striking distance of both Israel and the former Soviet Union. Military strategists equate modern Iraq to the Hudson River valley during the French and Indian War and the American Revolution. In the eighteenth century, the French, British, and Americans knew that whoever controlled the Hudson River valley controlled the continent. Today, it is common knowledge that whoever controls Iraq holds a trump card in the Middle East.

Above all else, Iraq presented a vast market for American technology and engineering expertise. The fact that it sits atop one of the world's most extensive oil fields (by some estimates, even greater than Saudi Arabia's) ensured that it was in a position to finance huge infrastructure and industrialization programs. All the major players — engineering and construction companies; computer systems suppliers; aircraft, missile, and tank manufacturers; and pharmaceutical and chemical companies — were focused on Iraq.

However, by the late 1980s it was apparent that Saddam was not buying into the EHM scenario. This was a major frustration and a great embarrassment to the first Bush administration. Like Panama, Iraq contributed to George H. W. Bush's wimp image. As Bush searched for a way out, Saddam played into his hands. In August 1990, he invaded the oil-rich sheikhdom of Kuwait. Bush responded with a denunciation of Saddam for violating international law, even though it had been less than a year since Bush himself had staged the illegal and unilateral invasion of Panama.

It was no surprise when the president finally ordered an all-out military attack. Five hundred thousand US troops were sent in as part of an international force. During the early months of 1991, an aerial assault was launched against Iraqi military and civilian targets. It was followed by a one hundred–hour land assault that routed the outgunned and desperately inferior Iraqi army. Kuwait was safe. A true despot had been chastised, though not brought to justice. Bush's popularity ratings soared to 90 percent among the American people.

I was in Boston attending meetings at the time of the Iraq

invasion – one of the few occasions when I was actually asked to do something for SWEC. I vividly recall the enthusiasm that greeted Bush's decision. Naturally, people throughout the Stone & Webster organization were excited, though not only because we had taken a stand against a murderous dictator. For them, a US victory in Iraq offered possibilities for huge profits, promotions, and raises.

The excitement was not limited to those of us in businesses that would directly benefit from war. People across the nation seemed almost desperate to see our country reassert itself militarily. I believe there were many reasons for this attitude, including the philosophical change that occurred when Reagan defeated Carter, the Iranian hostages were released, and Reagan announced his intention to renegotiate the Panama Canal Treaty. Bush's invasion of Panama stirred the already smoldering flames.

Beneath the patriotic rhetoric and the calls for action, however, I believe a much more subtle transformation was occurring in the way US commercial interests – and therefore most of the people who worked for American corporations – viewed the world. The march toward global empire had become a reality in which much of the country participated. The dual ideas of globalization and privatization were making significant inroads into our psyches.

In the final analysis, this was not solely about the United States. The global empire had become just that; it reached across all borders. What we had previously considered US corporations were now truly international, even from a legal standpoint. Many of them were incorporated in a multitude of countries; they could pick and choose from an assortment of rules and regulations under which to conduct their activities, and a multitude of globalizing trade agreements and organizations made this even easier. Words like *democracy*, *socialism*, and *capitalism* were becoming almost obsolete. Corporatocracy had become a fact, and it increasingly exerted itself as the single major influence on world economies and politics. Its members would do whatever it took to consolidate the powers of this global empire.

In a strange turn of events, I succumbed to the corporatocracy when I sold IPS in November 1990. It was a lucrative deal for my partners and me, but we sold out mainly because Ashland Oil put tremendous pressure on us. I knew from experience that fighting them would be extremely costly in many ways, whereas selling would make us wealthy. However, it did strike me as ironic that an oil company would become the new owners of my alternative energy company; part of me felt like a traitor.

SWEC continued to demand very little of my time. Occasionally, I was asked to fly to Boston for meetings or to help prepare a proposal. I was sometimes sent to places like Rio de Janeiro, to hobnob with the movers and shakers there. Once, I flew to Guatemala on a private jet. I frequently called project managers to remind them that I was on the payroll and available. Receiving all that money for doing so very little rubbed at my conscience. I knew the business well and wanted to contribute something useful. But it simply was not on the agenda.

The image of being a man in the middle haunted me. I wanted to take some action that would justify my existence and that might turn all the negatives of my past into something positive. I continued to work surreptitiously – and very irregularly – on *Conscience of an Economic Hit Man*, and yet I did not deceive myself into believing that it would ever be published.

In 1991, I formed a nonprofit organization, Dream Change, based on the Shuar philosophy that "your life, the world, is as you dream it," that whatever you believe you can do, you can in fact do. I began guiding small groups of people into the Amazon to spend time with and learn from the Shuar, who were eager to share their knowledge about environmental stewardship and indigenous healing techniques. During the next few years, the demand for these trips increased rapidly, as did Dream Change. Dedicated to changing the way people from industrialized countries see the earth and our relationship to it, Dream Change developed a following around the world and empowered people to create organizations with similar missions in many countries.

Two people were particularly instrumental in Dream Change's success. Llyn Roberts holds a master's degree in Buddhist psychology and, in addition to teaching powerful workshops about shamanism and transformation, was the nonprofit's executive director for many years. She led trips to the Andes, the Amazon, and the Asian Steppe. Dr. Eve Bruce was a pioneer in demonstrating to the medical profession the importance of applying aspects of shamanic approaches to modern medicine. She wrote the book *Shaman M.D.*, led trips to the Amazon, the Andes, and Africa, and developed the Dream Change website. *Time* magazine selected Dream Change as one of thirteen organizations whose websites best reflected the ideals and goals of Earth Day.[1]

Throughout the 1990s, I became increasingly involved in the nonprofit world, helping to create several organizations and serving on the boards of directors of others. Many of these grew out of the work of highly dedicated people at Dream Change and involved working with indigenous people in Latin America — the Shuar and Achuar of the Amazon, the Quechua of the Andes, the Maya in Guatemala — or teaching people in the United States and Europe about these cultures. The Pachamama Alliance — cofounded by Bill and Lynne Twist and me — has been especially successful at raising funds to keep oil companies off indigenous lands and to protect the rain forests from encroaching industrialization, and in developing programs to raise consciousness about the importance of such activities in countries across the planet.

SWEC approved of this philanthropic work; it was consistent with SWEC's own commitment to the United Way. I also wrote more books, always careful to focus on indigenous teachings and to avoid references to my EHM activities. Besides alleviating my boredom, these measures helped me keep in touch with Latin America and the political issues that were dear to me.

But try as I might to convince myself that my nonprofit and writing activities provided a balance, that I was making amends for my past activities, I found this increasingly difficult to believe. In my heart, I knew I was shirking my responsibilities to my daughter. Jessica was inheriting a world where millions of children are born saddled with debts they will never be able to repay. And I had to accept responsibility for it.

My books grew in popularity, especially one titled *The World Is As You Dream It*. Its success led to increasing demands for me to give workshops and lectures. Sometimes, standing in front of an audience in Boston or New York or Milan, I was struck by the irony. If the world is as you dream it, why had I dreamed such a world? How had I managed to play such an active role in manifesting such a nightmare?

In 1997, I was commissioned to teach a weeklong Omega Institute workshop in the Caribbean, at a resort on Saint John Island. I arrived late at night. When I awoke the next morning, I walked onto a tiny balcony and found myself looking out at the very bay where, seventeen years earlier, I had made the decision to quit MAIN. I collapsed into a chair, overcome with emotion.

Throughout the week, I spent much of my free time on that balcony, looking down at Leinster Bay, trying to understand my feelings. I came to realize that although I had quit, I had not taken the next step, and that my decision to remain in the middle was exacting a devastating toll. By the end of the week, I had concluded that the world around me was not one that I wanted to dream, and that I needed to do exactly what I was instructing my students to do: to do whatever it would take to change my dreams in ways that reflected what I really wanted in my life.

When I returned home, I gave up my corporate consulting practice. The president of SWEC who had hired me was now retired. A new man had come aboard, one who was younger than me and was apparently unconcerned about me telling my story. He had initiated a cost-cutting program and was happy not to have to pay me that exorbitant retainer any longer.

I decided to complete the book I had been working on for so long, and just making the decision brought a wonderful sense of relief. I shared my ideas about writing with close friends, mostly people in the nonprofit world who were involved with indigenous cultures and rain forest preservation. To my surprise, they were dismayed. They feared that speaking out would undermine my teaching work and jeopardize the nonprofit organizations I supported. Many of us were helping Amazon nations protect their lands from oil companies; coming clean, I was told, could undermine my credibility and might set back the whole movement. Some even threatened to withdraw their support.

So, once again, I stopped writing. Instead, I focused on taking people deep into the Amazon, showing them a place that is mostly untouched by the modern world, and introducing them to people who continue to live in harmony with nature. In fact, that is where I was on September 11, 2001.

CHAPTER 32

September 11 and Its Aftermath for Me, Personally

On September 10, 2001, I was traveling down a river in the Ecuadorian Amazon with Shakaim Chumpi, the coauthor of my book *Spirit of the Shuar*. We were leading a group of sixteen North Americans to his community deep in the rain forest. The visitors had come to learn about his people and to help them preserve their precious rain forests.

Shakaim had fought as a soldier in the recent Ecuador–Peru conflict. Most people in the major oil-consuming nations have never heard about this war, yet it was fought primarily to provide them with oil. Although the border between these two countries had been disputed for many years, only recently did a resolution become urgent. The reason for the urgency was that the oil companies needed to know with which country to negotiate in order to win concessions for specific tracts of the oil-rich lands. Borders had to be defined.

The Shuar formed Ecuador's first line of defense. They proved themselves to be ferocious fighters, often overcoming superior numbers and better-equipped forces. The Shuar did not know anything about the politics behind the war or that its resolution would open the door to oil companies. They fought because they come from a long tradition of warriors and because they were not about to allow foreign soldiers onto their lands.

As we paddled down the river, watching a flock of chattering parrots fly overhead, I asked Shakaim whether the truce was still holding.

"Yes," he said, "but I'm afraid I must tell you that we are now preparing to go to war with you." He went on to explain that, of course, he did not mean me personally or the people in our group. "You are our friends," he assured me. He was, he said, referring to our oil companies and to the military forces that would come into his jungle to defend them.

"We've seen what they did to the Huaorani. They destroyed their forests, polluted the rivers, and killed many people, including children. Today, the Huaorani hardly exist as a people anymore. We won't let that happen to us. We won't allow oil companies into our territory, any more than we would the Peruvians. We have all sworn to fight to the last man."[1]

That night our group sat around a fire in the center of a beautiful Shuar longhouse built from split bamboo slats placed in the ground and covered with a thatched roof. I told them about my conversation with Shakaim. We all wondered how many other people in the world felt similarly about our oil companies and our country. How many, like the Shuar, were terrified that we would come into their lives and destroy their culture and their lands? How many hated us?

The next morning, I went down to the little office where we kept our two-way radio. I needed to arrange for pilots to fly in and pick us up in a few days. As I was talking with them, I heard a shout.

"My God!" the man on the other end of the radio exclaimed. "New York is under attack." He turned up the commercial radio that had been playing music in the background. During the next half hour, we received a minute-by-minute account of the events unfolding in the United States. Like everyone else, I shall never forget that experience.

When I returned to my home in Florida, I knew I had to visit Ground Zero, the former site of the World Trade Center towers, so I arranged to fly to New York. I checked into my uptown hotel in early afternoon. It was a sunny November day, unseasonably balmy. I strolled along Central Park, filled with enthusiasm, then headed for a part of the city where once I had spent a lot of time.

As I approached Ground Zero, my enthusiasm was replaced with a sense of horror. The sights and smells were overwhelming — the incredible destruction; the twisted and melted skeletons of those once-great buildings; the debris; the rancid odor of smoke, charred ruins, and what I took to be burnt flesh. I had seen it all on TV, but being here was different.

I had not been prepared for this — especially not for the people. They stood around, those who lived or worked nearby, those who had survived. An Egyptian man was loitering outside his small shoe repair shop, shaking his head in disbelief. "Can't get used to it," he muttered. "I lost many customers, many friends. My nephew died up there." He pointed at the blue sky. "I think I saw him jump. I don't know.... So many were jumping, holding hands and flapping their arms as though they could fly."

It came as a surprise, the way people talked with one another. In New York City. And it went beyond language. Their eyes met. Although somber, they exchanged looks of compassion, half-smiles that spoke more than a million words.

But there was something else, a sense about the place itself. At first, I couldn't figure it out; then it struck me: the light. Lower Manhattan had been a dark canyon, back in the days when I made the pilgrimage to this part of town to raise capital for IPS, when I used to plot strategy with my investment bankers over dinner at Windows on the World. You had to go that high, to the top of the World Trade Center, if you wanted to see light. Now, here it was at street level. The canyon had been split wide open, and we who stood on the street beside the ruins were warmed by the sunshine. I couldn't help wondering if the view of the sky, of the light, had helped people open their hearts. I felt guilty just thinking such thoughts.

I turned the corner at Trinity Church and headed down Wall Street. Back to the old New York, enveloped in shadow. No sky, no light. People hurried along the sidewalk, ignoring one another. A cop screamed at a stalled car.

I sat down on the first steps I came to, at number fourteen. From somewhere, the sounds of giant fans or an air blower rose above the other noises. It seemed to come from the massive stone wall of the New York Stock Exchange building. I watched the people. They hustled up and down the street, leaving their offices, hurrying home, or heading to a restaurant or bar to discuss business. A few walked in tandem and chatted with each other. Most, though, were alone and silent. I tried to make eye contact; it didn't happen.

The wail of a car alarm drew my attention down the street. A man rushed out of an office and pointed a key at the car; the alarm went silent. I sat there quietly for a few long moments. After a while, I reached into my pocket and pulled out a neatly folded piece of paper covered with statistics.

Then I saw him. He shuffled along the street, staring down at his feet. He had a scrawny gray beard and wore a grimy overcoat that looked especially out of place on this warm afternoon on Wall Street. He looked to be Afghan.

He glanced at me. Then, after only a second of hesitation, he started up the steps. He nodded politely and sat down beside me, leaving a yard or two between us. From the way he looked straight ahead, I realized it would be up to me to begin the conversation.

"Nice afternoon."

"Beautiful." His accent was thick. "Times like these, we want sunshine."

"You mean because of the World Trade Center?"

He nodded.

"You're from Afghanistan?"

He stared at me. "Is it so obvious?"

"I've traveled a lot. Recently, I visited the Himalayas, Kashmir."

"Kashmir." He pulled at his beard. "Fighting."

"Yes, India and Pakistan, Hindus and Muslims. Makes you wonder about religion, doesn't it?"

His eyes met mine. They were deep brown, nearly black. They struck me as wise and sad. He turned back toward the New York Stock Exchange building. With a long gnarled finger, he pointed at the building.

"Or maybe," I agreed, "it's about economics, not religion."

"You were a soldier?"

I couldn't help but chuckle. "No. An economic consultant." I handed him the paper with the statistics. "These were my weapons."

He reached over and took the paper. "Numbers."

"World statistics."

He studied the list, then gave a little laugh. "I can't read." He handed it back to me.

"The numbers tell us that twenty-four thousand people die every day from hunger." I didn't bother to mention that slightly fewer than three thousand had died at Ground Zero on 9/11.

He whistled softly, then took a moment to think about this, and sighed. "I was almost one of them. I had a little pomegranate farm near Kandahar. Russians arrived and mujahideen hid behind trees and in water ditches." He raised his hands and pointed them like a rifle. "Ambushing." He lowered his hands. "All my trees and ditches were destroyed."

"After that, what did you do?"

He nodded at the list I held. "Does it show beggars?"

It did not, but I thought I remembered. "About eighty million in the world, I believe."

"I was one." He shook his head, seemed lost in thought. We sat in silence for a few minutes before he spoke again. "I do not like beggaring. My child dies. So I raise poppies."

"Opium?"

He shrugged. "No trees, no water. The only way to feed our families."

I felt a lump in my throat, a depressing sense of sadness combined with guilt. "We call raising opium poppies evil, yet many of our wealthiest people owe their fortunes to the drug trade."

His eyes met mine and seemed to penetrate my soul. "You were a soldier," he stated, nodding his head to confirm this simple fact. Then he rose slowly to his feet and hobbled down the steps. I wanted him to stay, but I felt powerless to say anything. I managed to get to my feet and start after him. At the bottom of the steps I was stopped by a sign. It included a picture of the building where I had been seated. At the top, it notified passersby that the sign had been erected by Heritage Trails of New York. It said:

> The Mausoleum of Halicarnassus piled on top of the bell tower of St. Mark's in Venice, at the corner of Wall and Broad — that's the design concept behind 14 Wall Street. In its day the world's tallest bank building, the 539-foot-high skyscraper originally housed the headquarters of Bankers Trust, one of the country's wealthiest financial institutions.

I stood there in awe and looked up at this building. Shortly after the turn of the last century, 14 Wall Street had played the role that the World Trade Center would later assume; it had been the very symbol of power and economic domination. It had also housed Bankers Trust, one of the firms I had employed to finance my energy company. It was an essential part of my heritage — the heritage, as the old Afghan man had so aptly put it, of a soldier.

That I had ended up here this day, talking with him, seemed an odd coincidence. Coincidence. The word stopped me. I thought about how our reactions to coincidences mold our lives. How should I react to this one?

Continuing to walk, I scanned the heads in the crowd, but I could find no sign of the man. At the next building, there was an immense statue shrouded in blue plastic. An engraving on the building's stone face revealed that this was Federal Hall, 26 Wall Street, where on April 30, 1789, George Washington had taken the oath of office as first president of the United States. This was the exact spot where the first man given the responsibility to safeguard life, liberty, and the pursuit of happiness for all people was sworn in. So close to Ground Zero; right on Wall Street.

I went on around the block, to Pine Street. There I came face-to-face with the world headquarters of Chase, the bank that David Rockefeller built, a bank seeded with oil money and harvested by men like me. This bank, an institution that served the EHMs and that was a master at promoting global empire, was in many ways the very symbol of the corporatocracy.

I recalled reading that the World Trade Center was a project started by David Rockefeller in 1960, and that in recent years the complex had been considered an albatross. It had the reputation of being a financial misfit, unsuited to modern fiber-optic and Internet technologies, and burdened with an inefficient and costly elevator system. Those two towers once had been nicknamed David and Nelson (Rockefeller). Now the albatross was gone.

I kept walking, slowly, almost reluctantly. Despite the warmth of the afternoon, I felt a chill, and I realized that a strange anxiousness, a foreboding, had taken hold of me. I could not identify its source and I tried to brush it off, picking up my pace. I eventually found myself once again looking at that smoldering hole, the twisted metal, that great scar in the earth. I leaned against a building that had escaped the destruction and stared into the pit. I tried to imagine the people rushing out of the collapsing tower and the firefighters dashing in to help them. I tried to think about the people who had jumped, the desperation they felt. But none of these things came to me.

Instead, I saw Osama bin Laden accepting money, and weapons

worth millions of dollars, from a man employed by a consulting company under contract to the United States government. Then I saw myself sitting at a computer with a blank screen.

I looked around, away from Ground Zero, at the New York streets that had avoided the fire and now were returning to normal. I wondered what the people who walked those streets today thought about all this — not simply about the destruction of the towers but also about the ruined pomegranate farms and the twenty-four thousand who starve every single day. I wondered if they thought about such things at all, if they could tear themselves away from their jobs and gas-guzzling cars and their interest payments long enough to consider their own contribution to the world they were passing on to their children. I wondered what they knew about Afghanistan — not the Afghanistan on television, the one littered with US military tents and tanks, but the old man's Afghanistan. I wondered what those twenty-four thousand who die every day think.

And then I saw myself again, sitting before a blank computer screen.

I forced my attention back to Ground Zero. At the moment, one thing was certain: my country was thinking about revenge, and it was focusing on countries like Afghanistan and Iraq. But I was thinking about all the other places in the world where people hate our companies, our military, our policies, and our march toward global empire.

I wondered, *What about Panama, Ecuador, Indonesia, Iran, Guatemala, most of Africa?*

I pushed myself off the wall I had been leaning against and started walking away. A short, swarthy man was waving a newspaper in the air and shouting in Spanish. I stopped.

"Venezuela on the brink of revolution!" he yelled above the noise of the traffic, the honking horns, and the milling people.

I bought his paper and stood there for a moment scanning the lead article. It was about Hugo Chávez, Venezuela's democratically elected, anti-American president, and the undercurrent of hatred generated by US policies in Latin America.

What about Venezuela?

CHAPTER 33

Venezuela: Saved by Saddam

I had watched Venezuela for many years. It was a classic example of a country that rose from rags to riches as a result of oil. It was also a model of the turmoil that oil wealth foments, of the disequilibrium between rich and poor, and of a country shamelessly exploited by the corporatocracy. It had become the epitome of a place where old-style EHMs like me converged with the new-style, corporate version.

The events I read about in the newspaper that day at Ground Zero were a direct result of the 1998 elections, when the poor and disenfranchised of Venezuela elected Hugo Chávez by a landslide as their president.[1] He immediately instituted drastic measures, taking control of the courts and other institutions and dissolving the Venezuelan congress. He denounced the United States for its "shameless imperialism," spoke out forcefully against globalization, and introduced a hydrocarbons law that was reminiscent, even in name, of the one Jaime Roldós had brought to Ecuador shortly before his airplane went down. The law doubled the royalties charged to foreign oil companies. Then Chávez defied the traditional independence of the state-owned oil company, Petróleos de Venezuela, by replacing its top executives with people loyal to him.

Venezuelan oil is crucial to economies around the world. In 2002, the nation was the world's fourth-largest oil exporter and the number three supplier to the United States.[2] Petróleos de Venezuela, with forty thousand employees and $50 billion a year in sales, provided 80 percent of the country's export revenue. It was by far the most important factor in Venezuela's economy.[3] By taking over the industry, Chávez had thrust himself onto the world stage as a major player.

Many Venezuelans saw this as destiny, the completion of a process that had begun eighty years earlier. On December 14, 1922, a huge oil blowout had gushed from the earth near Maracaibo. One hundred thousand barrels of crude sprayed into the air each day for the next three days, and this single geologic event changed Venezuela forever. By 1930, the country was the world's largest oil exporter. Venezuelans looked to oil as a solution to all their problems.

Oil revenues during the next forty years enabled Venezuela to evolve from one of the most impoverished nations in the world to one of the wealthiest in Latin America. All of the country's vital statistics improved: health care, education, employment, longevity, and infant survival rates. Businesses prospered.

During the 1973 OPEC oil embargo, petroleum prices skyrocketed and Venezuela's national budget quadrupled. The EHMs went to work. The international banks flooded the country with loans that paid for vast infrastructure and industrial projects and for the highest skyscrapers on the continent. Then, during the 1980s, the corporate-style EHMs arrived. It was an ideal opportunity for them to cut their fledgling teeth. The Venezuelan middle class had become sizable and provided a ripe market for a vast array of products, yet there was still a very large poor sector available to labor in the sweatshops and factories.

Then oil prices crashed, and Venezuela could not repay its debts. In 1989, the International Monetary Fund imposed harsh austerity measures and pressured Caracas to support the corporatocracy in many other ways. Venezuelans reacted violently; riots killed more than two hundred people. The illusion of oil as a bottomless source of support was shattered. From 1978 to 2003, Venezuela's per capita income plummeted by more than 40 percent.[4]

As poverty increased, resentment intensified. Polarization resulted, with the middle class pitted against the poor. As so often occurs in countries whose economies depend on oil production, demographics shifted radically. The sinking economy took its toll on the middle class, and many fell into the ranks of the poor.

The new demographics set the stage for Chávez—and for conflict with Washington. Once in power, the new president took actions that challenged the Bush administration. Just before the September 11 attacks, Washington was considering its options. The EHMs had failed; was it time to send in the jackals?

Then, 9/11 changed all priorities. President Bush and his advisers focused on rallying the world community to support US activities in Afghanistan and an invasion of Iraq. On top of that, the US economy was in the middle of a recession. Venezuela was relegated to a back burner. However, it was obvious that at some point Bush and Chávez would come to blows. With Iraqi and other Middle Eastern oil supplies threatened, Washington could not afford to ignore Venezuela for long.

Wandering around Ground Zero and Wall Street, meeting the old Afghan man, and reading about Chávez's Venezuela brought me to a point I had avoided for many years, and it forced me to take a hard look at the consequences of the things I had done over the past three decades. I had previously recognized the effect of my EHM work, but I now considered how it might directly affect my daughter and her generation. This renewed my drive. I knew I could no longer postpone taking action to atone for what I had done. I had to come clean about my life. I had to do whatever it would take to wake people up to the fact of global injustice and help them to understand why so much of the world hates us.

I started writing once again, but as I did so, it seemed to me that my story was too old. Somehow, I needed to bring it up to date. I considered traveling to Afghanistan, Iraq, and Venezuela and writing a contemporary commentary on those three countries. They seemed to embody an irony of current world affairs: each had undergone traumatic political turmoil and ended up with leaders who left a great deal to be desired (a cruel and despotic Taliban, a psychopathic Saddam, and a diplomatically inept Chávez), yet in no case did the corporatocracy respond by attempting to solve the deeper problems of these countries. Rather, the response was simply to undermine leaders who stood in the way of our oil policies. In many respects, Venezuela was the most intriguing case because, although military intervention had already occurred in Afghanistan and appeared inevitable in Iraq, the administration's response to Chávez remained a mystery. As far as I was concerned, the issue was not about whether Chávez was a good leader; it was about Washington's reaction to a leader who stood in the way of the corporatocracy's march to global empire.

Before I had time to organize such a trip, however, circumstances once again intervened. My nonprofit work took me to South America several times in 2002. A Venezuelan family whose businesses were going bankrupt under the Chávez regime joined one of my trips to the Amazon. We became close friends, and I heard their side of the story. I also met with Latin Americans from the other end of the economic spectrum, who considered Chávez a savior. The events unfolding in Caracas were symptomatic of the world we EHMs had created.

By December 2002, the situations in both Venezuela and Iraq reached crisis points. The two countries were evolving into perfect counterpoints for each other. In Iraq, all the subtle efforts — of both the EHMs and the jackals — had failed to force Saddam to comply, and now we were preparing for the ultimate solution, invasion. In Venezuela, the Bush administration was bringing Kermit Roosevelt's Iranian model into play. As the *New York Times* reported,

> Hundreds of thousands of Venezuelans filled the streets here today to declare their commitment to a national strike, now in its 28th day, to force the ouster of President Hugo Chávez.
>
> The strike, joined by an estimated 30,000 oil workers, threatens to wreak havoc on this nation, the world's fifth-largest oil producer, for months to come....
>
> In recent days, the strike has reached a kind of stalemate. Mr. Chávez is using nonstriking workers to try to normalize operations at the state-owned oil company. His opponents, led by a coalition of business and labor leaders, contend, though, that their strike will push the company, and thus the Chávez government, to collapse.[5]

This was exactly how the CIA brought down Mossadegh and replaced him with the shah. The analogy could not have been stronger. It seemed history was uncannily repeating itself, fifty years later. Five decades, and still oil was the driving force.

Chávez's supporters continued to clash with his opponents. Several people, it was reported, were shot to death, and dozens more were wounded. The next day, I talked with an old friend who for many years had been involved with the jackals. Like me, he had never worked directly for any government, but he had led clandestine operations in many countries. He told me that a private contractor had approached him to foment strikes in Caracas and to bribe military officers — many of whom had been trained at the School of the Americas — to turn against their elected president. He had rejected the offer, but he confided, "The man who took the job knows what he's doing."[6]

Oil company executives and Wall Street feared a rise in oil prices and a decline in American inventories. Given the Middle East situation, I knew the Bush administration was doing everything in its power to overthrow Chávez. Then came the news that they had succeeded; Chávez had been ousted. The *New York Times* took this turn of events as an opportunity to provide a historical perspective — and to identify the man who appeared to play the Kermit Roosevelt role in contemporary Venezuela:

> The United States… supported authoritarian regimes throughout Central and South America during and after the Cold War in defense of its economic and political interests.
>
> In tiny Guatemala, the Central Intelligence Agency mounted a coup overthrowing the democratically elected government in 1954, and it backed subsequent right-wing governments against small leftist rebel groups for four decades. Roughly 200,000 civilians died.
>
> In Chile, a CIA-supported coup helped put Gen. Augusto Pinochet in power from 1973 to 1990. In Peru, a fragile democratic government is still unraveling the agency's role in a decade of support for the now-deposed and disgraced president, Alberto K. Fujimori, and his disreputable spy chief, Vladimiro L. Montesinos.
>
> The United States had to invade Panama in 1989 to topple its narco-dictator, Manuel A. Noriega, who, for almost 20 years, was a valued informant for American intelligence.
>
> And the struggle to mount an unarmed opposition against Nicaragua's leftists in the 1980s by any means necessary, including selling arms to Iran for cold cash, led to indictments against senior Reagan administration officials.

Among those investigated back then was Otto J. Reich, a veteran of Latin American struggles. No charges were ever filed against Mr. Reich. He later became United States Ambassador to Venezuela and now serves as assistant secretary of state for inter-American affairs by presidential appointment. The fall of Mr. Chávez is a feather in his cap.[7]

If Reich and the Bush administration were celebrating the coup against Chávez, the party was suddenly cut short. In an amazing turnabout, Chávez regained the upper hand and was back in power less than seventy-two hours later. Unlike Mossadegh in Iran, Chávez had managed to keep the military on his side, despite all attempts to turn its highest-ranking officers against him. In addition, he had the powerful state oil company on his side. Petróleos de Venezuela defied the thousands of striking workers and made a comeback.

After the dust cleared, Chávez tightened his government's grip on oil company employees, purged the military of the few disloyal officers who had been persuaded to betray him, and forced many of his key opponents out of the country. He demanded twenty-year prison terms for two prominent opposition leaders, Washington-connected operatives who had joined the jackals to direct the nationwide strike.[8]

In the final analysis, the entire sequence of events was a calamity for the Bush administration. As the *Los Angeles Times* reported,

Bush administration officials acknowledged Tuesday that they had discussed the removal of Venezuelan President Hugo Chávez for months with military and civilian leaders from Venezuela.... The administration's handling of the abortive coup has come under increasing scrutiny.[9]

It was obvious that not only had the EHMs failed, but so had the jackals. Venezuela in 2003 turned out to be very different from Iran in 1953. I wondered if this was a harbinger or simply an anomaly — and what Washington would do next.

At least for the time being, I believe a serious crisis was averted in Venezuela — and Chávez was saved — by Saddam Hussein. The Bush administration could not take on Afghanistan, Iraq, and

Venezuela all at once. At the moment, it had neither the military muscle nor the political support to do so. I knew, however, that such circumstances could change quickly and that President Chávez was likely to face fierce opposition in the near future. Nonetheless, Venezuela was a reminder that not much had changed in fifty years — except that particular outcome.

When I wrote those words, in the first edition of this book, I had no idea that Chávez would be dead within a few years. The United States would be mired in endless wars in the Middle East. Russia would reemerge on the world stage. Chinese EHMs would outsmart their Western counterparts and threaten US hegemony on every continent. The corporatocracy would reign over history's first truly global empire. In fact, the next twelve years would tell a completely different story from all the others that preceded them.

PART V: 2004–TODAY

CHAPTER 34

Conspiracy: Was I Poisoned?

The situation has gotten much worse since *Confessions of an Economic Hit Man* was first published. Twelve years ago, I expected that books like mine would wake people up and inspire them to turn things around. The facts were obvious. I and others like me had created an EHM system that supported the corporatocracy. Together, the EHMs, corporate magnates, Wall Street robber barons, governments and jackals, and all their networks around the world have created a global economy that fails everyone. It is based on war or the threat of war, debt, an extreme form of materialism that pillages the earth's resources and is consuming itself into extinction. In the end, even the very rich will fall victim to this death economy.

Most of us have bought into it in a big way; we are collaborators — often unconscious ones. Now it is time to change. I had hoped that exposing these facts, making people conscious, would inspire a movement that, by 2016, would have resulted in a new vision, a new story.

People were in fact shaken awake. Activities in so many parts of the world, including localized ones such as the Occupy movements, national ones in places as diverse as Iceland, Ecuador, and Greece, and regional ones such as the Arab Spring and Latin America's Bolivarian Alliance for the Peoples of Our America (ALBA), have demonstrated that we understand our world is collapsing.

What I had not anticipated was the flexibility in the EHM system or its absolute determination to defend and promote the death economy. I had not anticipated the rise of an entirely new class of EHMs and jackals.

I made it clear in the original book that I did not believe the EHM system was driven by some nefarious, illegal, secret plan devised by a small group of people determined to control the world; in other words, I did not believe in some unified "grand conspiracy."

Then something strange happened.

In late March 2005, less than five months after publication of the book, I flew to New York City on a Monday. I was scheduled to speak at the United Nations the next day. I was in perfect health, as far as I knew. A man who identified himself only as a freelance journalist had been hounding my publicist for an interview. Because his credentials were sketchy and I was receiving a lot of press at that time, she kept putting him off. But when he suggested picking me up at LaGuardia Airport, taking me to lunch, and driving me to the apartment where I was staying with a friend, she consulted with me and I acquiesced.

He was waiting for me when I exited the airport. He took me to a small cafe, told me how much he admired my book, asked some of what had become rather standard questions about my life as an EHM, and then drove me to my friend's apartment on the Upper West Side.

I never saw that man again, and meeting him would have been an unmemorable event — except that a couple hours later I suffered severe internal bleeding. I lost about half the blood in my body, went into shock, and was rushed to Lenox Hill Hospital. I ended up spending two weeks there and having more than 70 percent of my large intestine removed.

As I lay recovering in that hospital bed, I thought that perhaps my illness was a message to slow down, that my body was overtaxed and I needed to cut back on writing and the speaking tours.

The New York gastroenterologist told me that I'd suffered from complications due to a severe case of diverticulosis. I was shocked to hear this, because I'd recently had a colonoscopy. My Florida doctor had assured me that there were no signs of cancer, which had been my main concern. He mentioned that I had some diverticula, "like most people your age," and ended by advising me to come back in five years.

Of course, my UN speech was canceled, as were numerous other media events. Word of my operation got out very quickly, and soon I was receiving lots of e-mails. Most supported me and expressed concern for my well-being. Some e-mails came from people who accused me of being a traitor to my country. Several assured me that I'd been poisoned.

When I asked my gastroenterologist, he responded that he was "quite certain" I hadn't been poisoned, but that he'd also learned "never to say never." In any case, all of it got me to thinking and reading more about conspiracies.

I still do not believe in the grand conspiracy theory. In my experience, there is no secret club of individuals who get together to plot illegal, world-dominating strategies. However, I do know that part of the power of the EHM system is that it foments many small conspiracies. By "small," I mean that they are focused on specific objectives. Such conspiracies — secret actions to accomplish illegal goals — happened when I was just beginning school, such as the CIA coup that replaced the democratically elected Iranian prime minister, Mossadegh, with the shah, in 1953. They continued during my high school years; consider the CIA-supported Bay of Pigs invasion of Cuba, in 1963. But I became most aware of them when I was an EHM and the CIA arranged the assassinations of my two clients, Ecuador's Roldós and Panama's Torrijos, in 1981. Then, as I began writing the original of this book in 2002, there was the US-led conspiracy to overthrow Venezuela's president, Hugo Chávez. After that came the conspiratorial lie about weapons of mass destruction in Iraq. This was followed by a flurry of conspiracies against leaders and governments in the Middle East and Africa.

While I was an EHM, the goals of most conspiracies were to further US and corporate interests in the economically developing countries — to do whatever it took, including overthrowing or killing government leaders, to enable our companies to exploit resources. After my colon operation, as I lounged around my home reading various reports, it became obvious that the tools I had used in Indonesia, Panama, Egypt, Iran, Saudi Arabia, and other countries were now being applied in Europe and the United States. Fortified by the so-called threat of global terrorism after 9/11, these conspiracies have given excessive power to the very wealthy individuals who control global corporations. Among the most striking are conspiracies to implement "free" trade agreements such as NAFTA and CAFTA, and the more recent Trans-Pacific Partnership (TPP) and the Transatlantic Trade and Investment

Partnership (TTIP), which empower corporations to assume de facto sovereignty over governments in countries around the world; to convince politicians to pass laws that permit the rich to avoid paying taxes, to control the media, and to use media to influence politics; and to terrify US citizens into fighting endless wars.

These and many other conspiracies took the EHM system far beyond where it had been in the 1970s. Despite all that I had written, I had to admit that I'd missed much of what had been going on beneath the surface. The old tools had been sharpened and new ones invented. The heart of this system remained the same: an economic and political ideology based on enslavement through debt and enforced by paralyzing people with fear. In my day, it had convinced the majority of Americans and much of the rest of the world that all actions were justified if they protected us from Communist subversives; the fear had now switched to Muslim terrorists, immigrants, and anyone threatening to rein in corporations. The dogma was similar, but the impact was now much greater.

Recuperating from that operation also sent me into the dark abyss of guilt. I'd wake up in the middle of the night haunted by memories of leaders I'd bribed and threatened. I had not yet come to terms with my EHM past.

I asked myself why I'd stayed in that job for ten long years. And then I realized how difficult it had been to escape. It wasn't just the seduction of money, flying first class, staying in the best hotels, and all the other perks. Nor was it the pressure exerted by my bosses and fellow employees at MAIN. It was also the aura of the job, my title — the very story of my culture. I was doing what I'd been schooled to do, what I'd been told was the right thing to do. I was educated as an American whose job it was to sell America and to believe and convince everyone else that Communist regimes were out to destroy us.

One day, a friend e-mailed me a photograph of a poster like one that had hung on the wall of the boys' bathroom in my elementary school. It depicted a sinister-looking man who asked, "Is your washroom breeding Bolsheviks?" It was an ad for Scott paper towels, and the subtitle read, "Employees lose respect for a company that fails to provide decent facilities for their comfort." It sent a strong message that not buying American was akin to treason.

That photograph got me thinking about those most formative years in my life. After the Soviet Union launched Sputnik, the first satellite, we all became convinced that nuclear warheads were on the way. The chilling scream of sirens sent us scampering under our desks in weekly drills, to hide from imagined Soviet missiles. Movies and TV shows like *I Led Three Lives*, a gripping drama based on the memoir of an FBI agent who infiltrated a Communist cell in the United States, warned us to be vigilant; Red provocateurs, like the evil Bolshevik in the poster, lurked among us, ready to pounce.

By the time I entered the EHM ranks, it had become apparent that we were losing in Vietnam, a nation portrayed as a Sino-Soviet puppet. We were told that there would be a "domino effect" — that Indonesia would go next, then Thailand, South Korea, the Philippines, and on and on. It wouldn't be long before the Red tide would sweep Europe and then engulf the United States. Democracy and capitalism were doomed — unless we halted the onslaught. And that meant doing whatever it would take to promote companies such as Scott, which portrayed themselves as bulwarks against communism.

Delving into my feelings of guilt helped me see the ease with which I had deceived myself in those years. It opened my mind to understanding that millions of people are in positions similar to mine. They are no longer taught to fear communism, but they still fear Russia, China, and North Korea, in addition to al-Qaeda and other terrorists.[1] They may not travel to foreign lands and confront, face-to-face, the consequences of what their companies do. They may not personally stand beside oil spills in the Amazon or see the hovels where sweatshop workers sleep. Instead, they anesthetize themselves with TV. They succumb to assurances by their schools, banks, human relations experts, and government officials that they are contributing to progress. But in their hearts they know otherwise. Deep down, they — we — realize that the stories misrepresent. And now it is time to admit to our complicity.

On a trip to Boston, not long after my operation, I reconnected with my former Boston University professor and the author of *A People's History of the United States*, Howard Zinn. Now in his eighties, he was still actively campaigning to reform a system he saw as an experiment that hadn't worked. When I shared with him the guilt that so often threatened to overwhelm me, he urged me to keep opening to it.

"Don't be afraid of it," he said. "You are guilty. We're all guilty. We have to admit that although the big corporations own the propaganda machine, we allow ourselves to be duped. You can set an example. Show people that the way out, redemption, comes from changing it."

I told him that I often thought of middle-class Americans as being like the medieval bourgeoisie — the majority of the people, who lived in the bourgs outside the castle walls. "We pay our taxes so soldiers and jackals will defend us from the knights in the neighboring castles."

"Exactly," he said, with that smile of his that had enchanted and inspired so many students. "We will do anything to maintain a system that has failed us."

I came to understand, during those days following my operation and in discussions with Howard, that my most important lesson since the publication of *Confessions of an Economic Hit Man* was similar to the one I had learned as a Peace Corps volunteer working with Andean brick makers: the only reason the EHM system works is because the rest of us give it permission to work. At best, we look the other way; at worst, we actively support it. One of the things that most bothered me was having to admit to myself that I not only had looked the other way but also had convinced many people to actively support that system. I made a commitment to myself that I'd be more diligent; I'd watch more closely what was going on in my own community, my country, and the world.

Although I was determined to follow Howard's advice, I also found myself envying another man, who did not struggle with his conscience — a friend who became an immense support during my physical recuperation in Florida and who seemed to have no problem justifying his own violent actions. He was a jackal, taking a short leave of absence from the Middle East.

⊕ CHAPTER 35

A Jackal Speaks:
The Seychelles Conspiracy

I have been a martial artist for much of my adult life and, by 1999, had studied for about fifteen years under a Korean master, Chung Young Lee, near my home in South Florida. One day, just before the afternoon class, a stranger walked into our *dojang*. He was about six feet tall and moved with athletic agility. He smiled in a friendly sort of way, yet there was a certain air about him that seemed threatening. He said his name was Jack.[1] He was a black belt and would like to consider signing up with our school. Master Lee invited him to put on his uniform and join the class.

As the senior black belt, I was responsible for sizing up this stranger by sparring with him at the end of class. While he was suiting up, Master Lee approached me. "Be careful." He patted my shoulder. "Defense."

As soon as we began the standard drills, it was obvious that Jack was fast and skilled. When the time came for us to spar, we lined up opposite each other and bowed. Master Lee gave the signal. Jack immediately came at me with a roundhouse kick. I blocked it and responded with a back kick. He sidestepped and sent me sprawling to the floor with a front kick to my chest.

My intuition — and Master Lee's — had been accurate. I'd learned my lesson. Jack was not an adversary I wanted to aggravate.

After the class ended, the three of us chatted. Jack mentioned countries where he had served as a "security consultant" — all of them political hot spots. He was short on details, but Master Lee and I kept exchanging glances. He signed up to join the dojang.

Over the next months, I made a point of getting to know Jack. We sometimes met for lunch or a beer. There was little doubt in my mind that he was a jackal waiting for his next assignment. The prospect of learning more about his life excited me. We circled each other in a sort of verbal sparring. Then, one day he mentioned that

221

he had paid a short visit to Seychelles, back in the 1970s. I could hardly believe it.

In the late 1970s, Chuck Noble, a MAIN senior vice president and retired US army general, told me to prepare to go to Seychelles. This island nation in the Indian Ocean is located close to Diego Garcia, home to one of the Pentagon's most strategic military bases. Seychelles' president, France-Albert René, was threatening to expose facts about Diego Garcia that Washington wanted to keep secret, facts that could have forced the United States to close down a facility that was essential to its operations in the Middle East, Africa, and parts of Asia. My job would be to bribe and threaten René into changing his mind. Very quickly, however, things happened that altered the situation.

An undercover agent who had gotten close to René concluded that, like Roldós and Torrijos, the president would not be corrupted. I was called off the job, and in 1981, a team of jackals was sent to assassinate René. They were discovered when their chartered plane landed in Seychelles. A firefight broke out. The jackals — surrounded, outnumbered, and outgunned — hijacked an Air India 707. Six of them, who believed the plane would be shot down as soon as it took off, opted to remain behind and try to escape by blending in with the local people. The rest forced the 707 crew to fly them to South Africa.

The six who remained were caught and imprisoned. Four were sentenced to death; the other two drew long prison terms. As soon as the 707 landed, it was surrounded by South African security forces. The jackals were arrested and imprisoned.[2]

I stared at Jack, wondering...

"I almost went there in the late seventies," I said. "To work with the president."

His eyes held mine. "Albert René?"

"You've heard of him?"

"I tried to kill him." He gave me a disarming grin. "But it's not something I want to talk about."

I understood his reticence. It was enough to know that he had in fact been a member of the jackal team. Later that day I went back to my files. His name was there; as one of the 707 hijackers, he had made the newspapers during the trials in South Africa.

I never asked Jack about Seychelles. I knew that prying would merely earn his mistrust. Instead, we talked about his more distant past. He had grown up amid the violence of Beirut, the son of a corporate executive. He was a US citizen, yet his life had been far removed from that of the teenagers hanging out on the streets of US cities during the love-in years of the late 1960s and early 1970s. Instead of watching flower children dancing through fountains, Jack watched as a mother was raped in front of her son and AK-47s spewed death across city streets. Soon after his eighteenth birthday, Jack was kidnapped by the Palestine Liberation Organization, accused of spying for Israel, tortured, and threatened with execution. Eventually they released him; nevertheless, it was an experience that changed his life.

"Those bastards didn't scare me," he explained. "They pissed me off, showed me that I was meant to be a fighter."

He headed to Rhodesia (now Zimbabwe). Its army was notorious for its effectiveness and brutality, and for being the number one training ground for mercenaries. Jack excelled and was selected to join the elite South African Special Forces Brigade. Popularly known as the "Recces" (reconnaissance commandos), its fighters were considered to be the most lethal in the world. By the time he graduated from the Recces, Jack had gained a reputation that appealed to the CIA.

Jack would disappear from our dojang for extended periods. He was an avid surfer, and he brought back surfing photographs. Still, Master Lee and I commented to each other that violent things happened in countries where he went surfing – a bombing in Indonesia, riots in Lebanon, an assassination in South Africa.

Then came 9/11, and the 2003 invasion of Iraq. Jack accepted an assignment to go to the Middle East. All he would say about it was "It's my type of job. And it'll be a reunion of old friends, like the guys who went to the Seychelles with me."

I did not see him again until after my operation, in 2005, when he was back in the States for a month of vacation. He visited me just about every day and forced me to take longer and longer walks. "Got to get you back to kicking ass at Master Lee's," he would say.

He did not talk much about his job. Instead, he shared photographs he'd taken: artful ones of the Iraqi people working in their fields, children riding on camels, and beautiful sunsets; and ones that told the story of bombed-out buildings, wrecked military vehicles, and men running from exploding cars.

I gave him a copy of *Confessions of an Economic Hit Man*. Twenty-four hours later, he had read it all. "You've told the real story," he said. "I hope you'll write more, go deeper." When I expressed surprise at his desire for transparency, he responded, "We got nothing to hide."

At that point, I broached the subject I'd avoided for so long. "What did you guys intend to do after you assassinated René?"

He paused, but only for a moment. "Get the hell out of there fast, turn into ghosts — spooks." He laughed at that last word. He went on to explain that the Kenyan army had an aircraft loaded with paratroopers standing by in Nairobi. After the jackals had killed René, the Kenyans would immediately arrive to accept credit for the coup. Jack and his team would take commercial airliners to other countries.

"So," I asked, "no one was supposed to know that a bunch of white mercenaries had staged this coup?"

He nodded.

"You'd simply vanish into thin air, and the world would be told that an army of Africans had swept in from the continent, killed René, destroyed his government, and reinstated the former president?"

"That was the plan."

"The CIA, South Africa, Diego Garcia. They would all be left out of the news." I whistled softly. "What a scam!"

"Clever, huh?"

"Yeah." I didn't bother to mention that it was a direct assault on the foundations of the American political system, that democracy is a farce when voters are intentionally deceived. "Except — you got caught."

"Yes." He looked off wistfully, then brightened. "But you know what? It all worked out in the end. The South African security forces and the government were our buddies. After the Air India plane landed, we were tried and found guilty — and then a couple months later quietly released." He gave me a knowing grin. "And our so-called failure turned out to be a success. The South

African government paid René a $3 million bribe to free our six guys imprisoned there. No one was executed. No one stayed jailed for long. After that, René cooperated, never exposed the Diego Garcia secrets, and became a friend to the US."

I mentioned that the undercover agent who'd concluded that René was not corruptible — the reason I'd been pulled off the job — had been wrong.

"Or perhaps," Jack said, "René saw the light. Remember, he'd come this close to death." He held his hands up and moved them together. "Our attempted assassination convinced him the CIA was serious."

I considered his words for a moment and thought about Roldós and Torrijos. "The CIA had killed the presidents of Ecuador and Panama only a few months before you went in, because they wouldn't play our game."

"Exactly." He smiled. "Don't think for a moment those deaths didn't make a big impression on Mr. René."

"Where is he now?"

"René? He just retired as president. Two decades later! And Diego Garcia's been the launching pad for US forays into the Middle East, Africa, and Asia all these years."

The story of the jackals in Seychelles says so much. On the surface, it seemed like a failure, but in fact it ended up accomplishing everything Washington could possibly have wanted. Better than actually killing a president, it had scared and bribed him into cooperating. He became a docile servant of empire. Key operatives had been caught — but they were soon back in business. And anyone who happened to read or hear about the raid on the Seychelles airport or the hijacking of an Air India 707 believed it was the work of terrorists — Communists — out to overthrow a legitimate government. The public had no idea that it was a CIA plot gone sour.[3]

CHAPTER 36

Ecuador Rebels

I kept thinking about the possibility that I'd been poisoned, as I recuperated from that operation.

I didn't want to believe that the NSA or CIA had tried to kill me — the implications were just too terrifying. I tried to convince myself, instead, that the government was smart enough to assume that my untimely death would sell lots of books — the last thing they wanted. If I'd been poisoned, I told myself, the "journalist" who took me to lunch had done it as a personal vendetta; he felt similarly to the people who wrote e-mails accusing me of being a traitor. In any case, I knew from the e-mails that I'd done things that made people hate me. How could I live with myself?

My mounting sense of guilt took me back to an experience I'd had while living in the Ecuadorian Amazon with the Shuar.

I had become terribly sick. I couldn't eat and had lost a great deal of weight in a short period of time. The nearest road was a two-day hike through dense jungle (for a healthy person), and then it was a two-day ride in rickety buses to a medical doctor — an impossible task, given that I could barely stand. I was resigned to dying. Then, a traditional Shuar healer, a shaman named Tunduam, cured me.

On an all-night shamanic journey, I saw that I'd been brought up on bland New Hampshire foods. Now I was living with people whose diet was very different. Among other things, because the rivers were filled with organic matter, they always mixed drinking water with a type of beer fermented with the aid of human saliva.

Faced with no alternatives, I ate their foods and drank their beer. That night, I saw that each time I did so, I heard a voice telling me it would kill me. I also saw that the Shuar were incredibly strong and healthy. As the night progressed, it became clear to me that it wasn't the food and drink that were killing me; it was my mind-set. The next morning I was totally healthy.

A few days later, Tunduam told me that I owed him for the healing. I needed to become his apprentice. It was the last thing I wanted. I'd been to business school; I could see no future in shamanism. But he'd saved my life and I owed him.

Spending time with Tunduam, learning about the power of mind-sets, taught me the truth of that old adage "If you can dream it, you can make it happen."

I had taken on a mind-set of paranoia and guilt. I needed to change it.

))

One day, shortly after my operation, I walked into the woods near my home, sat with my back against a large oak tree, and closed my eyes. I conjured an image of Tunduam and felt my connection to the natural world. The Shuar, like many indigenous cultures, believe that the key to changing one's mind-set is found in the heart. I placed my hands on my heart.

I sat there in silence for a few moments, until it came to me: my salvation had to include dedicating myself to doing everything possible to create a better world. I'd fallen into the trap of believing that writing the book, confessing, was enough. Now I understood that redemption required an absolute commitment to continuing to act. I had been mistaken to think I should cut back on my work after having so much of my large intestine removed. Howard Zinn had been right. I now saw that I needed to reinvigorate myself as a writer and speaker. I needed to be an activist. It came to me that the best way to do this was to get more involved with the nonprofit organizations I'd founded or cofounded.

Dream Change had accomplished a great deal over the fifteen years of its existence. We had taken people on trips to live with and learn from indigenous shamans in the Amazon, the Andes, the Asian Steppe, Africa, and Central America; had organized workshops in the United States and Europe; and had partnered with the Omega Institute to present annual shamanic gatherings that connected indigenous teachers from around the world with hundreds of participants in the United States. However, after my operation, Dream Change director Llyn Roberts and I decided to cut back. Llyn was busy writing books that would be published as *Shamanic Reiki* and *Shapeshifting into Higher Consciousness*. I was absorbed with all the activities generated by *Confessions of an Economic Hit Man*.

The Pachamama Alliance, on the other hand, was extremely active. Its history and mine were interwoven.

In 1994, my Ecuadorian friend Daniel Koupermann had insisted that I meet with Achuar leaders deep in the Ecuadorian Amazon. The Achuar, like Tunduam and the Shuar, believe that the world is as you dream it, and they'd had a communal dream. They asked me to help them form a partnership with people from the countries whose oil and other corporations threatened to destroy Achuar lands and culture — and, they said, the entire human presence on this planet.

I had delivered that message to a person I'd recently met, who impressed me as a powerful activist, Lynne Twist. In 1995, she, her husband, Bill, and I took a small group of people into the jungle, to the Achuar. At the end of that trip, those people donated more than $100,000 to start the nonprofit that became the Pachamama Alliance.

After that, I had pretty much dropped out of the picture, but Bill and Lynne drove forward with incredible determination. Two of the most dedicated, selfless, and effective people I've ever met, they did make it happen. By the time I had my postoperative mind-set change, in 2005, the Pachamama Alliance was doing more than just helping the Achuar; its offspring, Fundación Pachamama, an Ecuadorian nonprofit, was committed to keeping oil companies off lands inhabited by many other indigenous nations. The Awakening the Dreamer symposium — a four-hour program that includes inspirational videos — was going viral and soon would reach more than eighty countries.

I called Bill and Lynne and told them I'd like to become more involved in the organization. They embraced the idea enthusiastically.

Soon I was back in Ecuador. The Fundación Pachamama office in Quito was buzzing. During the past decade, the country had suffered many political upheavals — eight presidents in ten years. Now a very different type of politician had emerged.

His name was Rafael Correa. He came from a lower-middle-class family and acknowledged that, when he was five years old, his father had served a prison sentence for drug smuggling. He said that although he did not condone such illegal activities, he understood that people like his father were "desperate to feed their families."

He won a scholarship to a Catholic university in Guayaquil, then to one in Belgium, where he earned a master's degree in economics. Afterward, he attended the University of Illinois, where he received a PhD in economics.

This new presidential candidate was very much a man of the world. Handsome, intelligent, and charismatic, he spoke English, French, and Quechua in addition to his native Spanish. His wife was Belgian, and he was very familiar with both European and American politics. He understood the dangers of the system he faced when he advocated a platform of reforms that included reining in big oil and protecting the rain forests.[1]

As I read Correa's platform, leading up to the 2006 elections, I was reminded of another Ecuadorian, my former client, President Jaime Roldós. I was stricken with deep remorse when I recalled the times I'd assured him that oil would help his country pay down the debts incurred by the military dictators who had preceded him. I'd assured him that defaulting on World Bank loans was not an option, that he needed to strike the deal Texaco wanted. He hadn't listened. Instead, he'd demanded a share of Texaco's revenues and had insisted that the company implement environmental protection measures similar to those required in the United States.

Sitting in my Quito hotel room, I watched a film of the stirring speech Roldós had given at the soccer stadium in Quito in May 1981. He had urged his people to see their country as "heroic," a world leader in the struggle for liberty and freedom from all forms of oppression. At the end of that speech, the last words he spoke in public stirred my heart: "Viva la patria!" (Long live the homeland!). I was overcome with grief and guilt, looking at the footage of his private plane after it crashed and took him to his death.

Less than three months after Roldós's death, one of my other clients, Panama's Omar Torrijos, had been assassinated in exactly the same way.

Now, here was Correa, a candidate who openly invoked the memory of Jaime Roldós. Citing *Confessions of an Economic Hit Man*, Correa said that he had been approached by EHMs and was very aware of the threat posed by jackals.

Bill, Lynne, Daniel, and I decided that together we would lead annual trips for major supporters of the Pachamama Alliance. We would take them to Kapawi, an ecotourist lodge the Achuar had built in their rain forest as part of their commitment to our partnership.

The journey to Achuar territory involves a spectacular drive from Quito to the airstrip in Shell, a steamy frontier outpost and military base hacked out of the jungle to service the oil company whose name it bears. The road is both tortuous and breathtaking. It descends nearly eight thousand feet, from the top of the Andes into the rain forest. Sheer cliffs, punctuated by cascading waterfalls and brilliant bromeliads, rise up on one side. On the other side, the earth drops abruptly into a deep abyss, where the Pastaza River snakes its way toward the Atlantic Ocean, more than three thousand miles away.

While driving this road, I often think back to the first time I arrived in this part of the world, and of how much things have changed. In 1968, Texaco had only just discovered petroleum in Ecuador's Amazon. Today, oil accounts for roughly half of the country's export earnings. A trans-Andean pipeline, built shortly after my first visit, has since leaked more than half a million barrels of oil into the fragile rain forest — more than twice the amount spilled by the *Exxon Valdez*.[2] A $1.3 billion, three-hundred-mile pipeline constructed by an EHM-organized consortium had promised to make Ecuador one of the world's top ten suppliers of oil to the United States.[3] Vast areas of rain forest had fallen, macaws and jaguars had all but vanished, three Ecuadorian indigenous cultures had been driven to the verge of collapse, and pristine rivers had been transformed into flaming cesspools.

In recent years, supported by Fundación Pachamama, the indigenous nations had begun to fight back. On May 7, 2003, American lawyers, led by my friend Steven Donziger and representing more than thirty thousand Ecuadorian people, filed a $1 billion lawsuit against ChevronTexaco. The suit asserted that between 1971 and

1992 the oil giant dumped into open holes and rivers more than four million gallons per day of toxic wastewater contaminated with oil, heavy metals, and carcinogens, and that the company left behind nearly 350 uncovered waste pits that continue to kill both people and animals.[4]

A dramatic symbol of change along the Quito–Shell road is a mammoth gray wall that rears up from the Pastaza River. Its dripping concrete seems totally out of place, completely unnatural and incompatible with the landscape. This is the Agoyan hydroelectric project, which fuels the industries that make a handful of Ecuadorian families wealthy.

Every time I drive by Agoyan, I have to face the fact that it is just one of the projects developed through my efforts. Because of the way such projects were financed, by the time Correa decided to run for president, Ecuador was devoting a large share of its national budget to paying off its debts. The International Monetary Fund had assured Ecuador that the only way to end this cycle was by selling the vast sea of petroleum beneath its rain forests to the oil companies.

Rafael Correa promised to change all that if he was elected president.

He won with nearly 60 percent of the vote.

As soon as he took office, in 2007, Correa set about fulfilling his campaign promises. He refused to pay many of Ecuador's debts, proclaiming that they had been signed by CIA-supported military dictators who had been bribed by EHMs (a fact I knew only too well was true). He closed the United States' largest military base in Latin America, withdrew support for the CIA's war on rebels in neighboring Colombia, ordered Ecuador's central bank to divert to domestic projects funds that had been invested in the United States, oversaw the rewriting of the constitution to make his country the first in the world to codify the inalienable rights of nature (a threat to the bottom lines of big business), and joined ALBA, an alternative to Washington's plan to increase US hegemony through its Free Trade Area of the Americas.

But the most courageous of Correa's actions was his renegotiation of oil contracts. He insisted that the companies could no longer base Ecuador's share of oil revenues on "profits" — an all-too-common arrangement between big oil and economically developing countries, which historically has cheated these countries through creative accounting. Instead, the oil would belong to Ecuador, and the companies could only collect a fee for each barrel they produced.

The EHMs were dispatched. They offered the president and his cronies bribes—both legal and illegal—if he'd just back off. He refused.

Then, Honduran president Manuel Zelaya fell to a jackal coup.

That coup had a huge impact on all of Latin America—and especially on President Correa.

CHAPTER 37

Honduras: The CIA Strikes

I flew to Panama in 2009, right after the democratically elected Honduran president Manuel Zelaya was overthrown in a coup. I wanted to meet with Panama's movers and shakers and with people who had hands-on experience in Latin American politics.

I talked with business, government, and nongovernmental organization (NGO) leaders from Argentina, Colombia, Guatemala, Panama, and the United States. I also talked with teachers, taxi drivers, waiters, shopkeepers, and union activists. Most were convinced that the coup happened because Zelaya had advocated a 60 percent increase in the minimum wage, which had infuriated two US companies, Chiquita Brands International (formerly United Fruit) and Dole Food Company.

As the sun set behind the ships waiting at anchor to enter the Panama Canal, I sat at an outdoor cafe with "Joel," a Panamanian businessman who agreed to talk with me anonymously. He wanted to hear about my experiences with Omar Torrijos, a hero of his, who had died when Joel was in fifth grade. The knife of guilt plunged deep that afternoon. Joel said that he and his friends, like most of Latin America, had known that the plane crash that had killed Torrijos was a CIA assassination, and they had hated the United States.

"But things changed," he said. "Just like you forgave Japan and Germany, we forgave you." Then he dropped his eyes to his beer glass. "Now, this thing in Honduras ... well, it triggers memories, old resentments." He went on to explain that a friend of his from the IMF had been dispatched to Honduras to convince Zelaya to change his policies. He described that friend as "right out of your book. He tried it all. Offered World Bank loans, to load the country with more debt and build projects that would make lots of dough for Zelaya and his friends. When that didn't work, the fear tactics…" He toyed with his glass. "Zelaya should've listened. He didn't. So what you call the 'jackals' went to work." His eyes met mine. "At least they didn't kill Zelaya. Torrijos should've had it so good." He gave me a disingenuous smile. "But this wasn't just about Honduras. American CEOs know that if Honduras's hourly wage rate rises, so will that of all the other Latin American countries. Honduras, along with Haiti, sets the minimum wage benchmark. No one will go below that benchmark."

We talked about the many liberal policies introduced in Honduras during the three and a half years of Zelaya's presidency. These included subsidies for small farmers, free education and meals for poor children, a reduction in interest rates on bank loans to homeowners and local businesses, and free electricity for people who could not afford to pay for it, as well as the increase in the minimum wage. These policies paid off; Honduras enjoyed a nearly 10 percent decline in the poverty level.

Joel looked out at the anchored ships. "Memories may be short in the United States," he said. "But not in Latin America. We haven't forgotten that your president, Teddy Roosevelt, stole" — he pointed — "those lands, back in 1903, so he could build a canal for those ships. We haven't forgotten the role your corporations and Washington have played in politics all over this continent. Your government, your former secretary of state, Henry Kissinger, finally admitted to coups and assassinations they adamantly denied for years. We always knew what is now public record, that Guatemala's democratically elected president, Jacobo Arbenz, was toppled in 1954 by the CIA because he opposed United Fruit, and that the coup that brought down Chile's democratically elected president, Salvador Allende, in 1973 was initiated by ITT [International Telephone and Telegraph, one of the most powerful global corporations at that time] and was executed by the CIA." He waved his arms toward the ships. "We haven't forgotten Grenada, or Haiti, or the Argentine and Brazilian CIA-installed dictators, or Guatemala, Nicaragua, or El Salvador. We haven't forgotten Torrijos or Roldós or the 2002 failed attempt to take out President Chávez." He peered at me. "Need I go on?"

I told him that I knew that history, adding, "It's the reason I write what I do, and why I'm here in Panama now."

"Just one more thing," he said. "You know, of course, that the Honduran coup was led by General Romeo Vásquez, another graduate from your infamous CIA school."

"The School of the Americas."

"Yes, or as Torrijos called it, the School of the Assassins." He pointed at the Canal. "It used to be located over there, in the Canal Zone. Until Torrijos kicked it out. Now it's someplace in the US."

"Fort Benning, Georgia," I said.

")))

Later that night, in my hotel room, I went online and read a number of reports in Spanish that confirmed what the Panamanian businessman had told me. A 60 percent increase in the Honduran minimum wage would have had a huge impact on every corporation that operated mines, owned hotels, stores, and restaurants, or sold goods made in factories and sweatshops anywhere on the continent. The reports reminded me of the words spoken by that seismologist I'd dined with during my first week as a Peace Corps volunteer, back in 1968, words that had stuck in my mind ever since: "We own this country."

The mainstream US press, which is owned by the corporatocracy, limited its reporting about Honduras to accusations that the coup was triggered by Zelaya's attempts to introduce constitutional changes that would allow him to run for another presidential term. He had promoted a constitutional referendum, but according to everything I read and heard in Panama and through the online Spanish-language media, the coup had little to do with constitutional reform and everything to do with the deposed president's determination to raise the minimum wage.

When I returned from Panama to the United States, I discovered that although the mainstream media ignored the real story, it was available in English. England's *Guardian* announced:

> Two of the Honduran coup government's top advisers have close ties to the US secretary of state. One is Lanny Davis, an influential lobbyist who was a personal lawyer for President Bill Clinton and also campaigned for Hillary.... The other

hired gun for the coup government that has deep Clinton ties is [lobbyist] Bennett Ratcliff.[1]

Democracy Now! reported that Chiquita was represented by the Washington law firm Covington & Burling; that President Obama's attorney general, Eric Holder, had been a Covington partner and a defender of Chiquita when the company was accused of contracting "assassination squads" in Colombia; and that, during the trial, Chiquita admitted to hiring organizations listed by the US government as terrorist groups. Chiquita was found guilty in a Colombian court and agreed to pay a $25 million fine. When *Democracy Now!*'s Amy Goodman interviewed Manuel Zelaya on May 21, 2011, the former president said (translated):

> The conspiracy began when I started to join what is ALBA, the Latin American nations with Bolivarian Alternative. So, a dirty war at the psychological level was carried out against me. Otto Reich [former US ambassador to Venezuela and assistant secretary of state for Latin American Affairs] started this. The [US] ex–Under Secretary of State Roger Noriega, Robert Carmona, and the Arcadia Foundation, created by the CIA, they associated themselves with the right wing, with military groups, and they formed a conspiracy. They argued that I was a Communist and that I was attacking the security of the hemisphere.[2]

In December 2009, I asked Howard Zinn what he thought the coup against Zelaya meant for Ecuador. "Well," he mused, "if I were Correa, I'd be worried that I'd be next."

It was prophetic.

Howard died of a heart attack on January 27, 2010, at the age of eighty-seven, and did not live to witness the attempted coup against Ecuadorian president Rafael Correa on September 30, 2010. It was led by a graduate of the School of the Americas and had all the markings of the CIA. However, unlike other Latin American coups, it was instigated by the police rather than by the military. A pitched battle in the streets of Quito pitted the police against the military. The soldiers prevailed. Correa retained power.

Many observers believe that the failed coup was a warning, not a bona fide attempt to depose the president. Whatever the truth, Correa almost immediately reversed his policies toward big oil. He announced that he would auction off huge blocks of the rain forest to the oil companies.

I thought of Howard often during those days. I would have loved to hear his opinions about the events in Ecuador. His wit and humor always made calamitous news more palpable. In losing him, the world had lost a brilliant thinker — a sage observer of history and an acute interpreter of its lessons. I'd lost a friend and mentor, a great inspiration. I renewed my commitment to follow his inspiration.

CHAPTER 38

Your Friendly Banker as EHM

Over the next year, as Ecuador prepared to auction off its precious forests to oil companies, I wrote several blogs condemning Correa's decision. Among the responses I received was one, in late 2011, from an executive at a Chase bank near where I lived in South Florida.

"You rant and rage," he wrote, "about the horrible things happening in places like Ecuador. What about here, in your own country?" His e-mail ended with an invitation to an early dinner.

I joined him on the veranda of the River House in Palm Beach Gardens. Our table had a view of the Intracoastal Waterway and the parade of multimillion-dollar yachts heading south to spend the winter in the Keys.

"I read *Confessions* and I follow your blogs," the banker said, while the waiter carefully poured wine into his glass, "and I have to wonder why you didn't expose the things we bankers do right here at home. We use the same tools as you EHMs — on our own folks." He proceeded to tell me that in recent years bankers had convinced clients to purchase houses that were beyond their means. "A young newlywed couple comes in," he said, "and asks for a mortgage on a $300,000 home. We convince them to buy a $500,000 one." He swished the wine in his glass and studied the residue. "We say, 'You may have to tighten your belt a little, but soon your house will be worth a million dollars.'" He shook his head sadly. "They've been told to trust their banker. Used to be that people in my position would try to talk prospective debtors down, not up. We were supposed to do everything to avoid foreclosures. But that all changed."

"What changed it?"

"I've asked myself that question many times. Not sure of the answer. It mostly happened in this millennium. Perhaps it had something to do with 9/11, rising oceans, melting glaciers, fear, our feelings of mortality. Make all the dough you can, as soon as you can, and screw everyone else." He raised his wineglass. "Drink, dance, consume, and be merry. For us bankers, it was money, money, money. We tried to instill in our clients the idea that there is no tomorrow. Bin Laden will kill us all. So go into debt, buy that big house, fancy car..." He took a sip of wine. "When the bottom fell out of the market, the banks foreclosed, repackaged the loans, and ended up earning huge returns, while that young couple and thousands like them filed for bankruptcy." He looked toward the Intracoastal Waterway and pointed.

A yacht was motoring past. In addition to two well-tanned blond women in minuscule bikinis and two weightlifting-sculpted men, it featured a bright red Mini Cooper on its deck.

"Kind of says it all, doesn't it?" he asked. "You can bet that the guy who owns that yacht made his money by screwing other people out of theirs. It's all built on debt." He reached inside his brief-case and pulled out a manila folder. "Here's an article about an associate of mine. I think you'll find it interesting."

He handed me a *New York Times* op-ed piece titled "A Banker Speaks, with Regret." It described a Chase Home Finance vice president named James Theckston, who was quoted as saying that he and his team had written $2 billion in home mortgages. He admitted that some of them were "no documentation" loans, adding that "on the application, you don't put down a job; you don't show income; you don't show assets.... That was crazy, but the banks put programs together to make those kinds of loans."[1]

Dinner arrived. As we ate, we talked in more general terms about the economic crisis that had recently enveloped the nation and much of the world. "You know," the banker said, "the whole system stinks. From inflated home mortgages to college loans, it's all about servitude to debt. Not that homes or a college education are bad. Of course not. The problem is that we all believe we should do anything to achieve the 'good life.' Anything for the American dream. Including burying ourselves in debt."

I mentioned a woman who had recently attended one of my workshops. She'd just finished law school and said she'd intended to use her degree to defend homeless people and abused children. But when she discovered that she'd amassed more than $200,000 in student loans, she realized that she was going to have to get a job with a corporate law firm and devote years to paying off her debts. "After that," I added, "she intends to follow her dream."

"Intends," he scoffed. "Truth is, once she's in that system, she's hooked. She'll get married, take out a home mortgage she and her husband can't quite afford, have a kid, more loans... get sucked in, sell her soul to the bank."

By the time we parted, the night had turned dark. We stood under the lights of the parking lot and he held out his hand. "Look," he said, "I sympathize with everything you write about Ecuador. I volunteered to clean up beaches hit by the BP oil spill. I've seen the damage. Please don't get me wrong. I think Correa's plan to sell the Amazon to oil companies is a huge mistake, a crime. My point is that it's part of a disease that's infected us here in America also. I just want you to include that in your writings."

That meeting left me feeling sad, distraught, and — much as I hated to admit it — discouraged. I drove to a nearby beach. The moon reflecting off the water lit a path down to the ocean. I stood looking out over the breaking surf.

The image of my great-uncle Ernest, my grandmother's brother, came to me. He had been the president of a bank in Waterbury, Vermont. During the 1950s, my mom, my dad, my grandmother, and I visited him and his wife, Mabel, every summer. Uncle Ernest would drive us around town and proudly point out the homes and businesses his bank supported through loans.

In the summer after I finished fifth grade, I read a book about the stock market. On the next visit to Waterbury, I asked Uncle Ernest about it.

"It's a casino," he snorted, "a gambling house. I want nothing to do with it. All our money comes from local people, and it all goes back into the local economy. Every single penny." He told me that he viewed everyone who took a loan from his bank as a partner. "I give them the best advice I can. If one of them has problems making payments, I view that as a reflection on me, personally. I do everything I can to help out. We work together."

I sat down on the sand and watched the moonlight ripple along the waves. For my uncle, it wasn't just a matter of not wanting to foreclose. He believed that being a driving force behind the local economy was his job, his duty. It was also his joy in life.

My uncle and the banker I'd just met at the River House were both humans, both Americans, yet they represented two very different value systems. In Uncle Ernest's view, debt was a means to an end, a partnership between creditor and debtor. For the modern banker, debt paves the road to windfall profits. It delivers people into the EHM system.

A chill ran through me as I thought about how I'd led the march of the modern banker. I could almost feel my uncle looking down at me...

Within months of that night, as if to punctuate the extent to which modern bankers are willing to go in order to profit off of everyone else, a huge scandal erupted. The 2012 revelations around the London Interbank Offered Rate, or the Libor, demonstrated that Barclays, UBS, Rabobank, the Royal Bank of Scotland, and other international banks were capable of ruthlessly betraying the public trust.

The Libor is used to calculate payments on hundreds of trillions of dollars' worth of loans and other investments. It had been accepted as an objectively and mathematically derived benchmark for establishing interest rates. However, it now was revealed that the Libor had been illegally manipulated by the banks from 1991 until 2012. As a result, the bankers accumulated immeasurable sums of illicit profits. Once found guilty, the banks were fined more than $9 billion.[2] As of this writing, only one UBS trader, and not a single bank officer, has been indicted.

⊕ CHAPTER 39

Vietnam: Lessons in a Prison

In 2012, I was asked to participate in efforts to help victims of land mines and other unexploded war ordnance in Southeast Asia. Until then, I'd turned down invitations to join boards and other such activities because I was already overextended in my work with Dream Change, the Pachamama Alliance, and speaking engagements. However, this felt like another opportunity to redeem my past.

The ordnance was the result of the Vietnam War. Had it not been for that war, I would not have spent eight years avoiding the draft and probably would not have completed college, been recruited by the NSA, joined the Peace Corps, lived in the Amazon and the Andes, or become an EHM. Vietnam was also a symbol of the places where EHMs and jackals had failed and the US military had taken over — a sort of harbinger of the current situation in the Middle East. Although it had played a very significant role in my life, I'd never been to Vietnam. I was thrilled to accept an invitation to travel to meetings there in March 2013.

Late in the afternoon of my last day in Hanoi, after all the meetings were over, I decided to visit the museum of the Hỏa Lò Prison. Once known as the "Hanoi Hilton," it was the place where many US soldiers had been held captive. A woman who had attended the meetings, "Judy," who was about my age and whose life had also been impacted by the Vietnam War, decided to join me.

When Judy and I arrived at Hỏa Lò, we were disappointed to see that it had just closed for the day; we were told, through hand gestures delivered by a non–English speaker, to return another time.

I'd twisted my knee and was using a cane. Now my knee started acting up. I sat down on a nearby bench and laid my cane across my lap.

Judy sat down next to me. "I'm sorry," she said. "I know you wanted to go inside." Then she perked up. "We can come tomorrow morning, before the Bangkok flight."

"It's Sunday," I replied. "I wonder if it's even open."

Just then, a man in a khaki uniform sauntered over to a desk under an archway near the doorway and sat down.

"I'll ask." I planted my cane in the ground, rose cautiously, and limped to him. "Excuse me," I said.

He glared at me. "No speak English."

Not willing to be deterred by his gruff manner, I smiled sweetly, gestured toward the door, and, waving my cane in the air, pointed at Judy. "Tomorrow," I said, "Sunday..."

He pushed back his chair, quickly rose to his feet, and saluted me. He pointed at my cane and at Judy, who had wandered over to stand beside me. "Missus," he said, and bowed to her. Then he grabbed his own leg, made a face as though in pain, shook his head sadly, uttered a sucking sound, released his leg, and motioned for us to follow him.

I looked at Judy. We both shrugged.

He motioned again, more vigorously, and said something in Vietnamese. We followed him through a small, sunlit courtyard to a large metal door. He unlocked it and gestured for us to go inside.

The interior was dimly lit. As my eyes adjusted, I saw that we were standing in a corridor with dark cells off to the side. He reached into his pocket and pulled out a Vietnamese bill worth about ten dollars. He pointed at it, at Judy, and then at me and held out two fingers. I had no idea what the entrance fee was, but twenty dollars for the two of us seemed reasonable.

"I'll bet he thinks you're a former inmate," Judy said, "and I'm your wife."

That struck me. "I think you're right." This was an act of compassion. He thought I wanted to show my wife a place that had robbed me of years of my life and had left me crippled.

After I paid him, he led us down the corridor and into a large room. A huge apparatus loomed out of the shadows, like some prehistoric monster. I took it for a crane of some sort. However, I

quickly realized my mistake; this dark contraption was a different sort of monster. I just stood there gawking in disbelief at what
I now realized was a guillotine.

"My God!" Judy exclaimed. She pointed at an inscription on
the wall.

In English, it explained that Hỏa Lò had originally been a
French prison, built in the late 1800s, and that the French had used
the guillotine to decapitate hundreds of Vietnamese. As I wandered around the room, I continued to read explanations posted
on the walls. This entire section of the prison had once held Vietnamese women as prisoners of the French. Hundreds had been
tortured and raped here. A cutaway in one of the walls exposed a
solitary confinement cell, about the size of a doghouse. A life-size,
shackled manikin sat hunched over on the cement floor, crammed
into the small space like a doll in a box.

I froze to that spot, staring at the manikin and wondering what
motivated human beings to do such horrible things to each other.
How could the French, who prided themselves on their art, their
literature — their humanity — have been so cruel? What had driven
them to erect a guillotine? To rape and torture Vietnamese women?
I recalled that they'd justified it with religious ideals. Spreading
Catholicism. But the real goal was a commercial one, like that of
more modern EHMs. The wealthy French upper classes had sent
the young men of the poor to the killing fields of Indochina so their
corporations could profit off opium, tea, coffee, and indigo. Those
young Frenchmen had fallen victim themselves to the deprava-
tions of war; in addition to becoming murderers, they'd turned
into torturers and rapists. I looked around. Neither the attendant
nor Judy was anywhere in sight.

I hurried out of the guillotine room as fast as my bum knee
would allow, back along the corridor, toward a glimmer of light
that defined the doorway to the courtyard. Off to my right was a
dark opening in the wall. I pulled out my iPhone, flipped on the
flashlight app, and peered inside. A cave-like cell. Although it was
totally empty, I had a vivid impression that it had been filled with
frightened women, ones who had already been raped and tortured
or were awaiting their turns. I shut off my light and looked down
the corridor toward the courtyard.

A shadow bisected the halo of doorway light. "I've seen enough." Judy's voice echoed off the walls. "This place creeps me out. I'm going back to the hotel."

"Okay. I'll stay a bit longer. See you at the dinner tonight."

Her shadow slipped away. I glanced back at that dark cell. A shudder ran through me. I turned toward the doorway, let out a long breath, and headed down the corridor, beating my cane against the floor.

Once in the sunlit courtyard, I changed my mind. I, too, had seen enough. I started for the entrance doorway, and then the uniformed attendant appeared. He solemnly beckoned me toward another corridor. I hesitated. He beckoned again, more insistent than before. Obediently, I followed him.

As we arrived at a dimly lit room, I was shocked to see that it was populated by two lines of people, sitting facing each other. Then I realized that these also were manikins – replicas of Vietnamese men whose legs were shackled to the floor. I walked between the two lines. Each manikin was different from its neighbors, and amazingly lifelike. Some, despite their shackled legs, were holding others in compassionate poses, obviously offering solace to despairing comrades. One was ministering to the wounded arm of another. All of them were emaciated; their protruding ribs told the story of famished men.

At one end of the two lines was a platform with two holes in the floor and buckets underneath – the toilets. I wondered how often each man got unlocked from his shackles and led, probably in chains, to these.

I felt despondent and alone. I glanced toward the doorway I'd entered. No sign of the attendant. I was, in fact, alone. I had a strong desire to get out of this place. However, I forced myself to take a last look at those two lines of manikins. They seemed alive. I could feel both their sense of desolation and their determination to survive. I lifted my cane in a salute to them and then slowly walked away.

The attendant was waiting for me in the courtyard, at the bottom of a metal staircase that led up the outside of the building to the floor above the guillotine. Although my injured knee throbbed, I followed him up the stairs. He opened a door at the top and flipped on a dull light. I went inside.

The room was a gallery of photographs, taken long after the French had departed. In the ghostly light, they showed US military men, mostly pilots. Some were standing in lines at attention; others performed chores around the prison. There was a particularly touching series of the men preparing a Thanksgiving dinner and sharing it with one another at a long table. This was followed by scenes from the end of the war, of the prisoners marching out to be greeted by US officials, to freedom. There was no attempt in any of the photos to gloss over the fact that the men in the prison were a somber and unhappy lot; yet the contrast between them and the guillotine and manikins in the rooms below delivered a clear message: the Vietcong had treated American prisoners far more humanely than the French had treated the Vietnamese. I had no idea whether this was true. I did know that US soldiers had been tortured into confessing that what they and their country had done was criminal.

Looking at those photographs, my mind flashed to the famous photo of a naked Vietnamese child fleeing her napalmed village, and to more recent ones of hooded men at the Abu Ghraib prison in Iraq — handcuffed, bleeding, beaten, dragged across the floor on leashes, and attacked by vicious dogs, all at the hands of US soldiers and CIA agents. I hurried on to the next room.

Its walls were adorned with pictures of the havoc US forces had wreaked on Hanoi during the days prior to the American evacuation of Saigon. Government buildings, schools, and even a Buddhist temple had been reduced to rubble. I thought I recalled Nixon, at the time, claiming that this assault was a final drive to victory, waving his hands at the TV cameras and proclaiming our intent to "bomb them back to the Stone Age." Yet, judging from all I was seeing and had come to learn, the United States had known by then that it had lost the war. These photos told a story of revenge, not of a march to triumph.

I took a second look at the rubble of the Buddhist temple and wondered what on earth our leaders were thinking when they did such things. Could they not see how such ruthless disregard for people and cultures eroded the reputation of a nation that had gained the world's respect for its role in winning World War II?

I left the room and the photos of Hanoi's devastation and headed toward the next one. It was pitch black. I stood looking into the darkness. Then I turned on my iPhone flashlight and stepped inside to glance around. It was just an empty room, probably another cell for multiple prisoners. I leaned back against the cool wall and slid to the floor. I sat there, allowing my phone to cast a small funnel of light across the floor, and focused on the emotions that swirled through me. Yes, I felt ashamed and sad and angry. But there was something else I couldn't quite identify.

I felt sorry for the people who had suffered in the wars and in this prison, the Vietnamese women and men, the American soldiers, all those who had been tortured, imprisoned, maimed, or killed — and their families. I felt compassion for the prison guards who had committed torture and for the soldiers who had to deal with the fact that they had killed others — the horror of the knowledge that they'd taken a life, made children fatherless, and inflicted the worst sort of tragedy on the parents of those they killed. I felt for the emotionally wounded, the ones who survived and ended up in mental institutions, the far too many who committed suicide.

My eyes lingered on the funnel of light that spread from my phone, through my outstretched legs, and across the hard floor toward the opposite wall, and finally I got the other piece of what I was feeling. Grateful. I felt a sense of gratitude that I'd managed to avoid being in a war. I hadn't murdered anyone. I'd not bombed cities, dropped Agent Orange, or planted land mines.

Then it struck me in the gut — a resurgence of guilt. What about the people I'd corrupted? The threats and bribes? The resources I'd plundered in the name of progress? How did this compare with the killing, maiming, and raping? How did extortion and the ravaging of rain forests measure against land mines, flattened temples, and children running naked, screaming, through flaming villages? I was mulling over these questions and the horror of it all, my guilt, when I heard a noise that set my nerves on edge.

A door slammed. The sound echoed throughout the Hanoi Hilton. A metal door. I jumped to my feet, panicked by the prospect of being shut in this place alone for the night. Then I made myself calm down. I leaned into the cold cement of the wall and assured myself that the attendant would not abandon me. After all, I was an American.

And that realization — that I was an American and therefore would not be shut up in this place — brought another jab to the gut. Why should Americans feel so privileged? We, who had tried to destroy this country, somehow had the right to feel assured that we wouldn't be abandoned for the night in a prison-turned-museum. Where was the justice in that? And I, of all people, a man who had enslaved countries through debt, who had threatened and corrupted presidents... what right did I have to feel secure anywhere?

The cold cement of the wall sent another shiver through me. How could I compare what I'd done as an EHM with the actions of soldiers and torturers? Then I realized that comparison was not the issue. The one supported the other. Economic hit men counted on their marks knowing that the military waited in the wings. In the end, the only thing that really mattered was that we had to change, that there had to be a better way. Human beings had to find another means of dealing with our fears and with our urge to possess more territory, more resources. We simply had to move out of our dysfunctional patterns of exploitation and mayhem. We had to awaken from our stupor.

I turned off my light. Sitting there in the darkness of a prison where so many people had suffered for so many years, I thought about the tools used by EHMs and jackals, and about how these had changed since the days when the Vietnam War was ending and my EHM career was beginning.

CHAPTER 40

Istanbul: Tools of Modern Empire

In the 1970s, economic hit men were executives and consultants at a few multinational corporations and consulting companies. Today's EHMs are executives and consultants at thousands of multinational corporations, consulting companies, investment funds, industry groups, and associations — as well as an army of lobbyists that represents all of these.

The similarities of the EHMs of the past to those of the present, as well as the differences between them, were on my mind in April 2013. It was less than a month after my Vietnam trip. I stood at the window of my hotel in Istanbul and looked out at the ancient buildings and minarets of this city that has been both the seat and the victim of empires for centuries. After the publication of *Confessions of an Economic Hit Man*, I had been invited to Istanbul a number of times to speak at conferences of business executives. This historic city had become a center for international conferences.

I thought about the core tools we EHMs used in my day: false economics that included distorted financial analyses, inflated projections, and rigged accounting books; secrecy, deception, threats, bribes, and extortion; false promises that we never intended to honor; and enslavement through debt and fear. These same tools are used today. Now, as then, many elements are present in each "hit," although that likely is evident only to someone willing to delve deeply into the story behind the story. Now, as then, the glue that holds all of this together is the belief that any means are justified to achieve the desired ends.

A major change is that this EHM system, today, is also at work in the United States and other economically developed countries. It is everywhere. And there are many more variations on each of these tools. There are hundreds of thousands more EHMs spread around the world. They have created a truly global empire. They are working in the open as well as in the shadows. This system has become so widely and deeply entrenched that it is the normal way of doing business and therefore is not alarming to most people.

These men and women convince government officials to give them favorable tax and regulatory treatment. They force countries to compete against one another for the opportunity to host their facilities. Their ability to locate their production plants in one country, their tax-sheltered banking in a second, their phone call centers in a third, and their headquarters in a fourth gives them immense leverage. Countries must vie with one another to offer the most lenient environmental and social regulations and the lowest wage and tax rates. In many cases, governments swamp themselves with debt so they can offer perks to subsidize corporations. In the past decade we've watched this happen to countries such as Iceland, Spain, Ireland, and Greece, in addition to the economically developing countries, where it has been going on longer. When the subtler approaches fail, government officials learn that some damaging aspect of their personal lives, which they thought was secret, will be exposed or even, in some cases, fabricated.

Another change is evident in the justification used for the EHM tactics. Then, it was protecting the world from Communist takeover, from the Vietcong and other revolutionary groups, or from threats to our affluent American way of life. Today, the justification is stopping terrorists, fighting Islamic extremists, promoting economic growth, or saving our affluent way of life.

Later that day, I left my hotel to meet with Uluç Özülker, Turkey's former ambassador to Libya, the country's representative to both the European Union and the Organisation for Economic Co-Operation and Development (OECD), and a highly regarded diplomat and scholar.

We ordered Turkish coffee on the outdoor patio of a bistro with a spectacular view of the Bosporus, the waterway that allows transportation between the Mediterranean and the Black Sea and separates Asia from Europe. We talked about the critical role the Bosporus played as an avenue of commerce for ancient Greece, Persia, and Rome.

"You spell it out in your book," Uluç said. "Economics is the key to power."

I pointed at a passing freighter. "Trade."

"Yes." He smiled. "And debt." He took a sip of the strong, dark coffee that had been delivered by a waiter while we chatted. "You emphasize that your job was to bind countries with debt." He peered over the rim of his cup. "Fear and debt. The two most powerful tools of empire." He set the cup down on the table. "Most everybody thinks military might is the driver of empire, but war's important because it — and the threat of it — instills fear. People are terrified into parting with their money. They take on more debt." He smiled. "Whether we owe money or favors, debt shackles us. That's why the economic hit man approach is so effective. More so than war."

When I asked about his experiences in Libya, he said that Muammar Gadhafi provided an excellent case study in modern empire building. "He was a harsh dictator, and yet, in my opinion, he made most of his people better off. Unlike many of the other leaders you write about — in Indonesia, Ecuador, and other places — he used Libya's oil money to improve conditions. But his Soviet leanings upset the US." Uluç went on to explain that, after the collapse of the Soviet Union, Gadhafi found himself isolated and in a very precarious position. As a consequence, Gadhafi decided to reconcile his differences with the West. "He sold out to England and the US when he acknowledged Libya's role in the bombing of the Pan Am flight over Lockerbie, Scotland. He also assured London and Washington that their companies would get his country's oil. That ended most of the economic sanctions against him."

"Why did the US and England side with the rebels who fought him, then?"

"It's complex and entangled." Uluç took another sip of coffee. "Short version: the French resented the new Anglo–American–Libyan ties and the fact that Paris lost out on oil deals." He described how President Sarkozy had offered support to disgruntled tribal leaders and factions from Egypt and other Arab countries, as well as within Libya itself, who were attempting to depose Gadhafi. Eventually, the United Kingdom and the United States saw that defending Gadhafi's regime — one they had strongly denounced in the past — was resulting in worldwide condemnation. "Besides,"

he added, "Gadhafi encouraged other Arab countries to sell oil for
Libya's gold dinar instead of dollars."

"Echoes of Saddam Hussein — and now Iran."

"Yes. As you know, Washington and Wall Street view attacks
on the dollar and the Federal Reserve practically as acts of war. So,
the US and Britain joined France and the other NATO countries in
a 'civil war' that eventually overthrew and assassinated Gadhafi. It
was a classic case of the very things you write about, Mr. Perkins.
Economic hit men, jackals, and the military, all working together
in ways that were at first subtle and then overt."

He watched a passing ship. "It happened here, too, you know.
The US played a deciding role in the 1980 coup in my country."
We talked about how President Carter had sent three thousand
troops to support the coup, and $4 billion in aid. In typical EHM
fashion, some of the money had been filtered through NATO
and the OECD. Following the coup, not surprisingly, the IMF
stepped in to support privatization and takeovers by big business. "Turkey," Uluç said, "bought into the game of what you call
the corporatocracy."

I pointed out that the globalizing corporate network had desta-
bilized the world economy, building it on wars or the threat of war,
debt, and abuse of the earth's resources — a death economy. "Less
than 5 percent of the world's population," I said, "lives in the US,
and we consume more than 25 percent of the resources, while
half the world suffers from desperate poverty. That's not a model.
It can't be replicated — not by China, India, Brazil, Turkey, or any
other country, no matter how hard they try."[1]

"Yes," he said. "Fear, debt, and another very important strategy:
divide and conquer." He talked about the schism between Sun-
nis and Shiites and about how civil wars and tribal factions create
power vacuums that open the doors to exploitation. "In such dis-
putes," he continued, "both parties take on more debt, buy more
arms, destroy resources and infrastructure, and then accept even
more debt to finance reconstruction. We're seeing it throughout the
Middle East, in Syria, Iraq, Egypt, Afghanistan... So many countries are the building blocks for billionaires."

I asked what he thought it would take to transform the death economy into a life economy. "You have to go after the business-men, the CEOs and major stockholders of the multinationals that run the world. They are the roots of the problem."

))

The next day, flying home from Istanbul, looking down on the Mediterranean, I found that, in addition to guilt, I felt a growing sense of anger. Our business and government leaders were taking the EHM system way beyond anything imaginable in my time — or in the era of the feudal emperors who, during the so-called Dark Ages, ruled the lands beneath my plane.

I couldn't help suspecting that future historians would look back on the post-9/11 era as an even darker age.

My anger mounted at the realization that we in the United States are told that we must fear scarcity, that we should buy more, work harder, keep accumulating, bury ourselves in more and more debt. This mentality goes beyond the personal to become an aspect of national patriotism — our country must amass increasing amounts of the world's resources. We are assured that the debt used to finance the military is necessary for our own good — the same argu-ment that had been used on the subjects of those feudal emperors.

It was particularly infuriating to recall that, when we point out that military spending reduces our benefits, we are told that social programs encourage indolence, whereas programs that support armies, subsidize windfall profits, and encourage corporate bar-ons to speculate with our tax dollars fuel the engines of economic growth — that top-down economics works, despite the overwhelm-ing evidence of the past decade to the contrary.

As I looked down at the English Channel, once the dividing line between archenemies Protestant England and Catholic France, I was struck by how much stronger this system has become since my EHM days, and how, after 9/11, the EHM system came home to roost. The use of debt and fear, the Patriot Act, the militarization of police forces, a vast array of new surveillance technologies, the infiltration and sabotage of the Occupy movement, and the dra-matic expansion of privatized prisons have strengthened the US government's ability to marginalize those who oppose it. Giant, corporate-funded political action committees (PACs), reinforced by Citizens United and other court decisions, and billionaires like the Koch brothers, who finance groups such as the American Legislative Exchange Council (ALEC), subvert the democratic process and win elections by flooding the media with propaganda. They hire cadres of lawyers, lobbyists, and strategists to legalize corruption and to influence every level of government.

When I arrived back in the United States, I discovered something that reinforced my anger. Although Ecuador's president, Rafael Correa, had survived the coup attempt and had announced that Ecuador would auction off oil rights in its Amazon region, he was once again under attack by one of those divide-and-conquer campaigns. He was being strangled by those "roots of the problem" that Uluç had described—the people who control the big corporations.

CHAPTER 41

A Coup against Fundación Pachamama

Although the attempted coup against Correa had failed, on another level it had succeeded. I figured the jackals had learned from that other "failed" coup in Seychelles that sometimes it is better to let a president survive. Sufficiently scared, he or she then plays the game, joins the ranks of all those other heads of state who know that to resist is futile. In any case, Correa had reversed his previous position and had posted "for sale to oil companies" signs on more than six million acres in thirteen areas of the Amazon, known as "blocks."

Yet, something had gone wrong. The opposition to the oil auction had weakened Correa's resolve — or at least forced him to change his plans. He had vacillated. He had postponed the auction twice since November 2012.

By the time I returned from Vietnam and Istanbul, the oil companies and their public relations people had swung into action. The articles I read online, in the Spanish newspapers and blogs, shook me to the core. They were reminiscent of articles that had appeared during the Roldós presidency. They were aimed at convincing the Ecuadorian people who lived in the heavily populated Andean and coastal regions that the only way their country could finance better schools and hospitals and build the infrastructure needed to develop energy, transportation, water, and sewer systems — the only way it could raise itself from poverty — was through exploitation of its Amazonian oil. The argument was made, over and over, that although Ecuador was one of the poorest and most densely populated countries in the hemisphere, roughly a third of the country was sparsely populated. That third happened to be a rain forest rich with oil.

I traveled the spectacular road from Quito to Shell and, from there, by small plane and canoe, deep into Achuar territory, in the summer of 2013. I found that the Achuar and their neighbors — the Huaorani, Kichwa, Sápara, Shiwiar, and Shuar — were frightened, incensed, and most of all, determined to protect their lands. They understood the immense value of the rain forest — not just to them but also to life on this planet. They referred to the forest as both the heart and the lungs of the earth. They pointed out that, in addition to being worth protecting for its own sake, the forest is one of the most biodiverse places on earth, a defense against carbon dioxide poisoning of the atmosphere, and a place where as-yet-unidentified plant species offer potential cures for cancer and other diseases.

Bill Twist and the staffs of the Pachamama Alliance and Fundación Pachamama were spending lots of time, energy, and money supporting the indigenous people of the region. They let those people know that many of us who are the biggest consumers of oil were on their side, that we were trying to convince Americans and Europeans to consume less and to pressure oil companies to stay out of the Amazon basin.

For me, it was another opportunity to redeem the sins of my past. I'd heard the false stories in the late 1960s about how Texaco would benefit the country. I'd been one of the EHMs who had encouraged the military dictators of the 1970s to swamp their countries with debt. I'd tried to woo Jaime Roldós into our ranks. I'd felt the horrible pangs of guilt; now I'd committed to action. One of those actions was to increase my involvement with the Pachamama Alliance.

I joined Bill, Lynne, and some of our key supporters in developing a plan to help Correa. We understood that he was in a difficult position. We hoped to organize a summit that would be hosted by the president and that would show him to be a reasonable man who wanted to find alternatives to the oil auction.

During this same period, the indigenous people launched their own campaigns. Supported by Fundación Pachamama, they marched from their rain forests over the Andes to the capital, picketed the presidential palace, and demanded that Correa cancel the oil auction. The protests were reported by media around the world. None of the efforts deterred Correa. He went ahead with the auction in November 2013.

However, something miraculous happened. Most oil companies stayed away. Not a single US-based one showed up. Bids were placed on only four of the thirteen blocks. As an oil company executive admitted to me, "It just isn't worth the risk of all the bad publicity."

Ecuadorians living on the heavily populated coast and in the Andes, those who had come to believe that oil was the catalyst for economic growth, were disappointed and outraged. So were the EHMs and the CIA. Corporate moguls everywhere took notice. What had happened in Ecuador was just one more sign that consciousness was changing and that when poor people who had been marginalized in the past united, they had power.

Correa was in a bind. His presidency and perhaps his life hung in the balance. In December 2013, needing a scapegoat, he sent his police to the offices of Fundación Pachamama. Dressed in street clothes, looking like ordinary citizens, fifteen officers suddenly appeared at the door, flashed their badges at Executive Director Belén Paez, ordered the dissolution of the organization, and drove everyone out. They locked the doors and sealed them with stickers that accused the organization of destabilizing the government. Then the police demanded that Fundación Pachamama donate its computers, its desks — all its assets — to other organizations. Although the government never arrested any of our staff, on several occasions they followed and harassed Belén and other individuals.

I traveled to Ecuador after the closing of our offices. I met with Fundación Pachamama's supporters and with representatives from other nonprofit and nongovernmental organizations. Needless to say, we all were extremely upset with Correa. Organizations and individuals that had previously supported him now publicly condemned his actions. Although I agreed with them, something else gnawed at me.

I kept thinking about the man, Rafael Correa. Who had gotten through to him? What was he facing? I knew there was more to the story than the one we were hearing and telling ourselves.

Late one afternoon, I sat alone in the place where I'd been the dinner guest of the Texaco seismologist during my first week in this country, four decades earlier — the restaurant at the top of the Hotel Quito (formerly the InterContinental). Now, once again, I was treated to a spectacular view of Pichincha, hovering over the city. As the sun cast a shadow that crept down the face of the volcano, I thought about the hope that oil had seemed to offer this country in 1968. I thought about Correa's world.

Much as I hated his change of heart and his actions against Fundación Pachamama, I understood. He knew he could not beat big oil, that he had to compromise, keep his job, and fight battles he had a chance of winning. Otherwise, he would be overthrown, like Honduran President Zelaya and so many others before him, or assassinated, like the president whose memory he so often invoked, Jaime Roldós. Correa was smart enough to realize that if he was taken out, he'd be replaced by a CIA puppet.

In fact, Correa had accomplished a great deal. He'd been in office for nearly eight years, a milestone for a country that had experienced eight presidents in the decade before him. He'd invested a lot of money in public programs. He'd created Buen Vivir, a government agency charged with ascertaining that everything done by every branch of government contributed to making a good life for all Ecuadorians.[1] He'd exhibited amazing courage when he defied Washington by closing the largest US military base in Latin America and renegotiated oil contracts to the detriment of the oil companies and for the benefit of his people. His example set new standards. During his administration, the thirty thousand Ecuadorian plaintiffs won their lawsuit against Chevron (now the owner of Texaco); the company was found guilty in an Ecuadorian court and was fined $9.5 billion (although Chevron continues to employ an army of lawyers to fight this decision).[2] A new constitution was approved — the first in the world to protect the inalienable rights of nature. According to World Bank data, the poverty rate declined from 32.8 percent in 2010 to 22.5 percent in 2014.[3]

One of the things that most impressed me was the way this PhD economist stood up to the Western magnates of debt. He appointed a debt audit commission to review the legitimacy of the loans taken on by previous heads of state — especially by the CIA-supported dictators who were in power during my early EHM days. The commission uncovered many instances of "illegality and illegitimacy" in the country's foreign obligations.[4] Correa refused to make a $30.6 million interest payment, choosing instead to send his country into default and to incur the wrath of the World Bank, the International Monetary Fund, and Wall Street.

As it turned out, the "illegality and illegitimacy" of banking operations was by no means limited to Ecuador. In fact, the United States itself — and just about every country on the planet — had once again been the victims of the criminal activities of some of the world's most respected financial institutions.

⊕ CHAPTER 42

Another EHM Banking Scandal

The financial world was shaken by another major scandal in 2014. It included a couple of the banks that had been involved in the earlier Libor scandal, and some new ones. Barclays, Citigroup, JPMorgan Chase, and the Royal Bank of Scotland pleaded guilty to rigging the price of foreign currencies and were fined more than $2.5 billion. Within a year these four banks, plus one other, UBS, would be fined an additional $1.6 billion, along with another $1.3 billion in the case of Barclays, to settle related claims.[1]

Since 2007, the banks had operated what some of their members referred to as "the Cartel." Among the e-mails and chat room conversations of individuals involved were found their own names for their group: the Bandits' Club and the Mafia.[2]

US Attorney General Loretta Lynch described the banks' foreign currency scheme as "a brazen display of collusion and foreign exchange rate market manipulation." She went on to call it a "breathtaking conspiracy."[3] The words *collusion* and *conspiracy*, spoken by the US attorney general, are especially telling, given that they were used in reference to the secret collaboration of banks that for years had been considered some of the most trusted businesses in the world. The actions of the banks demonstrate that everything — conspiracy, collusion, fraud, unfair competitive practices — is justified by the corporatocracy, so long as it earns large profits.

Articles about this scandal reignited my feelings of guilt. I couldn't erase the suspicion that by doing what I had done, four decades earlier, I had helped open the floodgates for these tidal waves of seemingly endless corruption. Reading on, however, my feelings once again changed; guilt turned to anger.

Although I had to admit that things I'd done had set the stage, I was struck by the contrasts between the ways we EHMs had operated and the ruthlessness of the modern bankers. In my day, we worked hard to justify debts. We crafted fancy econometric models to demonstrate that our projects would generate economic growth in the targeted countries. In addition to convincing the citizens of those countries, we also needed to convince ourselves. These modern EHMs did not find it necessary to justify their actions. They were blatant. They were defiant. They were utterly ruthless. They relished their roles as bandits and mafiosi, bragged about being part of a cartel. It shocked and infuriated me to see that this new breed took pride in exploiting everyone else.

Then, slowly, I realized that my anger was not limited to the bankers. It included the regulators. This conspiracy had operated with impunity for at least five years. Who was watching? The lack of oversight was testament to the "see no evil, hear no evil, speak no evil" attitude that is pervasive among government agencies. It is another aspect of the EHM system. Those in charge believe they are entitled to do whatever it takes to help the banks — and other corporations — realize the goal of maximizing profits, regardless of the social or environmental consequences.

The magnitude of the punishments also said a great deal about the cozy corporate–government relationships. Although the total fines in the combined Libor and rigged foreign currency prices conspiracies — more than $14 billion — seemed at first like a large sum, on further inspection, I saw that they were minuscule in relation to the assets of the banks. Worse still was the knowledge that not a single officer at any of the banks had been indicted for criminal activities. Not one.

I was struck by how anesthetized the American public has become to being exploited. Our willingness to wear blinders is similar to attitudes in the countries I exploited during the 1970s. In addition to the relatively secret schemes of the bankers, we are exploited by overt measures that we quietly accept as standard practice. These include the skyrocketing student debt caused by state and federal cuts in public education, the constantly increasing medical debt resulting from deficient national health care and insurance policies, predatory payday loans, tax laws that subsidize a few of the richest at the expense of the many, and the outsourcing of jobs to other countries. The mantra "We will do whatever it takes" echoes from bank boardrooms into the halls of Congress.

This was brought home during the 2015 FIFA soccer scandal. The EHM system is so pervasive that it infects all areas of society, even sports. According to charges brought by the US Justice Department against leaders of international soccer's governing body, the perpetrators employed many of the tools that had been part of my EHM kit, including bribes, fraud, and money laundering, and it was done in collaboration with the big banks. The corruption was unchecked for nearly two decades and cost the communities and taxpayers of many nations fortunes while making a small number of elites wealthy.[4]

At first, I was relieved that the Justice Department had taken action. This seemed a step in the right direction. The regulators were finally regulating. Then I saw a different aspect.

The soccer scandal was a smoke-and-mirrors diversion. Media attention focused on a nonessential aspect of life — sports — at a time when the real criminals were stealing the global economy. Individual FIFA officials were carted off in handcuffs while bank executives awarded themselves multimillion-dollar bonuses. Why were individual bank officers, whose admitted crimes affected all of us, not indicted?

The obvious answer is that the bankers are members of the corporatocracy, whereas FIFA officials are not. The story that the Justice Department had uncovered so much wrongdoing among the FIFA people and was aggressively pursuing indictments diverted attention from the bigger story. The banking lobby unduly influences the Justice Department. Banks are so wealthy and powerful that they can buy our elected officials, the regulators who serve us, and the media that is supposed to keep us informed.

I found myself once again thinking a lot about Howard Zinn. He and I had discussed the growing power of lobbyists. "We vote," he said. "But those we elect don't seem to listen to us anymore. They obey the commands of the people who finance their campaigns, corporate lobbyists." He pointed out that I'd done something similar. "You obeyed the World Bank." He paused. "Did you really think the World Bank wanted to end world poverty?"

I saw an image of myself in 1967, while I was still in business school, standing at the entrance to the World Bank and reading the motto "Working for a World Free of Poverty." I believed those seven words. But not for long. Within a few years, I discovered that the motto was symbolic of the deceptions that characterize the bank's work.

Since the publication of the original version of this book, I've participated on panels and in debates where development professionals try to defend the World Bank. They argue that the work I did, and that the bank has done since, has gone a long way toward ending poverty. The facts, however, tell a different story.[5]

A recent Oxfam report revealed that almost half of the world's wealth is now owned by just 1 percent of the population and that seven out of ten people live in countries where economic inequality has increased in the past thirty years.[6] Slum dwellers in countries where I promoted World Bank projects, such as Argentina, Colombia, Egypt, and Indonesia, might now have mobile phones, but they are by no means free of poverty. In fact, from a comparative standpoint, they are worse off than when I was an EHM. According to World Bank statistics, 2.2 billion people still lived at a poverty level of less than two dollars per day in 2011 — a huge number of people, considering the billions of dollars paid to global corporations to "free the world of poverty."[7] Although the percentage of officially "impoverished" has declined, due to population growth and standard of living changes the actual numbers have increased.

Over the past three decades, sixty of the world's poorest countries have paid $550 billion in principal and interest on loans of $540 billion, yet they still owe a whopping $523 billion on those same loans. The cost of servicing that debt is more than these countries spend on health or education and is twenty times the amount they receive annually in foreign aid.[8] In addition, World Bank projects have brought untold suffering to some of the planet's poorest people. In the past ten years alone, such projects have forced an estimated 3.4 million people out of their homes; the governments in these countries have beaten, tortured, and killed opponents of World Bank projects.[9]

My colleagues and I did whatever we thought it would take to expand the corporate, capitalist empire. That was the real goal. The World Bank motto was a subterfuge. We convinced government leaders that unless they accepted our loans and paid us to train their militaries and build up their infrastructures, their citizens would be ruled by brutal Stalin-style dictators. Corporate capitalism would boost them out of the dark ages of feudalism and into the modern era of US-driven prosperity.

It is a system that has mushroomed since *Confessions of an Economic Hit Man* was first published. Today, in addition to the World Bank, it is promoted by the private banks — by the individuals who admit to criminal activities and, instead of prison terms, receive multimillion-dollar bonuses. They and their corporate colleagues convince people around the world that success is defined by personal assets rather than by contributions to the greater community, that privatization and deregulation protect the public, that government assistance for the needy is wasteful and counterproductive, that personal debt is better than government investment in social services, and that men and women who live in mansions and travel in private jets and luxury yachts are icons to be emulated.

Howard Zinn understood why a majority of us accept these platitudes. Those in the middle class, he said, who have the material trappings of prosperity, are complacent because they possess the things they were taught to covet, and they don't want to lose them. Those who live in poverty are complacent because they have to devote their energies toward simply surviving.

All of this is expertly managed by a whole new breed of EHMs.

CHAPTER 43

Who Are Today's Economic Hit Men?

Back in the 1970s, economically developing countries were looked upon as nests of corruption. People like me plied our trade quietly, but just about everyone assumed that Latin American, African, and Asian government officials thrived on bribes. The image of the banana republic politician accepting an envelope stuffed with dollars in exchange for favors granted was ingrained in the press and in Hollywood. The United States, on the other hand, was considered to be — and for the most part was — above such massive corruption.

That has totally changed. Drastically. Activities that would have been viewed as immoral, unacceptable, and illegal in the United States in my EHM days are now standard practice. They may be covered in a patina of oblique rhetoric, but beneath that surface, the same old tools — including a combination of threats, bribes, falsified reports, extortion, sex, and sometimes violence — are applied at the highest levels of business and government. EHMs are ubiquitous. They stroll from the corridors of the White House through the US Congress, along Wall Street, and into the boardrooms of every major company. Corruption at the top has become legitimized because corporate EHMs draft the laws and finance the politicians who pass them.

The last time I saw Howard Zinn, I asked him where he'd turn to learn more about the modern EHM. "Study politicians like Daschle and Dodd," he advised.

I didn't get around to following that advice until after Howard's death, when I started writing this book. Then I discovered that, once again, he had known exactly where to look.

Tom Daschle and Chris Dodd have a lot in common. Both served as distinguished, long-term members of the US Senate — Daschle from 1987 to 2005, Dodd from 1981 to 2011. Both were rising stars in the Democratic Party. Daschle was Senate majority leader. Dodd was general chairman of the Democratic National Committee and chairman of the Senate Banking Committee, as well as a presidential candidate. Both were powerful men with access to the president of the United States and the leaders of countries and corporations around the planet.

Daschle and Dodd portrayed themselves as men of the people rather than Washington insiders. Daschle's early campaigns showed him driving a beat-up Pontiac. Dodd promised he would never succumb to the greedy opportunism of lobbyists. Eventually, however, both Daschle and Dodd betrayed their images and the promises they had made to their constituents. They represent a new, powerful, and very dangerous group of people, the contemporary club of EHMs.

After leaving the Senate, Daschle joined a law firm that nets millions of dollars through political lobbying for health-care and other corporations; his salary plus bonuses was reported to be over $2 million, in addition to income from a private equity firm. Adopting ambiguous sobriquets such as "political adviser," he tried to avoid the classification of "lobbyist," although his job was exactly that — to lobby for lucrative deals that benefited his clients.

One telling example happened after a garment factory in Bangladesh collapsed in 2013, killing more than 1,100 people. Although there is no indication that Daschle himself was involved, his law firm, DLA Piper, fought the implementation of a Bangladesh plan for legally binding safety reforms aimed at protecting low-income workers. Instead, DLA Piper lobbied for legislation that would drastically limit the liability of wealthy US retailers. Joined by retired Democratic senator George Mitchell and former Senate aide Charlie Scheeler, DLA Piper sought to protect the avaricious interests of its clients, including one of the retailers identified with the factory collapse (Gap), at the expense of the people and economy of Bangladesh.[1]

Like Daschle, Senator Dodd worked hard to project the aura of a politician with deep integrity. He insisted that he would not sell out to corporate America and would never join the club of fellow politicians who had become lobbyists. Yet, when he ran for president of the United States, his campaign accepted funding from the financial services industry—the very businesses that were regulated by the Senate Banking Committee that he chaired. This apparent conflict of interest was surpassed by what he did after he retired from the Senate, in 2010. Despite his repeated promises never to be a lobbyist, in 2011 he replaced Dan Glickman as chairman and chief lobbyist for the Motion Picture Association of America.[2]

Howard had set me on a path. As I followed it, I found that such conversions are by no means limited to Democrats. Among the better-known Republicans who've jumped from the Senate into the lobbyist club are John Ashcroft, Bob Dole, Newt Gingrich, Phil Gramm, Chuck Hagel, Trent Lott, Warren Rudman... The list of both Democrats and Republicans seems endless. And there are still more, from the US House of Representatives, who have transformed themselves into EHMs.[3]

Most of these politicians, along with thousands of other men and women who pass through the "revolving door," don't call themselves lobbyists. They work for law firms and go by euphemistic titles such as "counselor," "consultant," or "adviser in government affairs"—just as I officially was "chief economist" for a highly regarded consulting firm. However, their real job, as mine was, is to con governments and the public into submitting to policies that make the rich richer and the poor poorer. They are EHMs, paid to support the corporatocracy, expand the corporate empire, and spread the tentacles of the death economy across the planet. They hide in the shadows, yet their influence is immeasurable.

It is significant that the American League of Lobbyists—a professional association for the industry—changed its name to the Association of Government Relations Professionals, in 2013. Although the number of registered lobbyists dropped to its lowest level in more than a decade during that same year, its ranks still numbered 12,281—a whopping twenty-three lobbyists for every member of the US Senate and House of Representatives, many times the number of EHMs during my time. Yet, even this shocking number is highly understated. Research by American University professor James Thurber, an expert in lobbying for more than three decades, suggests that the true number of working lobbyists is closer to one hundred thousand. Official figures indicate that annual spending to support lobbyist campaigns was more than $3 billion in 2013, but Thurber estimates that it was closer to $9 billion.[4]

The lack of transparency, the secrecy surrounding the influence peddling of lobbyists, makes it impossible to accurately measure the full impact of such activities. However, each of the biggest companies doing business in the United States today has upward of one hundred lobbyists. These corporations and their associations spend more than thirty dollars for every dollar invested by all the labor unions and public interest groups that represent "we the people" in activities that promote workers' rights, the environment, health care, education, and other social services.[5]

Officials charged with enforcing the laws are afraid to challenge the lobbyists and the corporations they represent. This passage from Common Dreams addresses the arms industry, but the statement is representative of global corporations in general:

> Out of the top ten international arms producers, eight are American. The arms industry spends millions lobbying Congress and state legislatures, and it defends its turf with an efficiency and vigor that its products don't always emulate on the battlefield. The F-35 fighter-bomber, for example — the most expensive weapons system in US history — will cost $1.5 trillion and doesn't work. It's over budget, dangerous to fly, and riddled with defects. And yet few lawmakers dare challenge the powerful corporations who have shoved this lemon down our throats.[6]

One of these arms producers, Boeing, made big news in the state where I live. Washington's largest employer, with more than eighty thousand employees, it ranks among the three largest defense contractors in the world (the other two, Lockheed Martin and Northrop Grumman, are likewise based in the United States).[7] Boeing lobbyists worked night and day to convince Washington State officials to give the company huge tax breaks, and the company threatened to move production facilities for the 777X plane to another state if the politicians did not deliver.

I heard stories about "legal" bribes that were all too familiar: consultant retainers and jobs offered to relatives and friends of government officials; entrapment into compromising situations involving sex or drugs. Although such allegations were never proven, the mere existence of the stories had an impact. People with marital problems or who had tried an illicit drug — or felt they could be framed — bowed to the pressures of anyone they feared might expose them.

In the end, the Washington State legislature passed a law that activated the largest corporate tax break in any state's history, with an estimated lifetime value to Boeing of $8.7 billion. That law ensured the aerospace giant's position as the United States' number one corporate recipient of state and local subsidies.[8] It was a spectacular victory for Boeing's EHMs, and a huge loss for Washington State taxpayers such as me — and for democracy in general.

The way Boeing manipulated Washington State officials illustrates the methods used by a special class of EHMs known as "site location consultants." Although they technically could be classified as lobbyists, they are highly specialized. For years, they have been involved in the economically developing countries. However, today, as the Boeing case shows, they are a major factor in the United States.

Business schools and planners may claim that corporate decisions about locating their job-creating facilities are based on rational analyses of such objective factors as proximity to suppliers and customers, labor markets, existing infrastructure conditions of transportation networks, and the price of energy, but the greatest determinant in many cases has become the deal made with local governments. Site location consultants play to fears that communities will be rejected unless they offer the most lenient environmental and social regulations, the lowest tax rates, and other incentives. Although public officials are usually eager to arrange such deals, they overlook the long-term consequences — deteriorating schools, roads, recreational facilities, and natural resources — even though, ironically, such community assets benefit the entire community, including the corporation's own employees.[9]

One further aspect of site location consultants is that they often are paid by the community and, in the end, may also receive a commission as high as 30 percent on the subsidies they manage to negotiate — their payment from the corporation.

The Boeing deal was reminiscent of things I'd done in Argentina, Colombia, Ecuador, Egypt, Indonesia, and Panama. The main difference is that, instead of World Bank loans, modern EHMs in the United States use tax policy and subsidies. These stratagems are even more effective than loans. Corporations avoid the need to register the money or to sign contracts that force them to set up systems to ensure that the debtor actually pays. In this US version, no one has to put up the funds. Instead, the money is simply removed from the tax base and handed to the corporation; in essence, the money is stolen from the US taxpayer. Funds that had been earmarked for health care, education, and other social services are diverted to the coffers of greedy corporations — gifts from the lobbyist EHMs and corrupt politicians.

My research took me to Good Jobs First, a national policy center that reviews the grants, loans, and other subsidies distributed by the federal government since 2000. According to its reports, over the course of the past fifteen years, the federal government has distributed $68 billion in grants and special tax credits to businesses. Two-thirds of that money was transferred to large corporations.

Good Jobs First identified the major companies whose lobbyists have been most successful at obtaining subsidies. These include Dow Chemical, Ford Motor Company, General Electric, General Motors, Goldman Sachs, JPMorgan Chase, Lockheed Martin, United Technologies, and almost half of the one hundred most profitable federal contractors. All told, a shocking 298 corporations each received subsidies of $60 million or more.[10] These companies reap benefits from ports, airports, highways, utilities, schools, fire departments, and other services, and make billions of dollars in profits, yet they do not pay their fair share toward supporting the institutions that serve them and their employees.

I was not surprised to learn that the fossil fuels industry is highly subsidized. However, the magnitude of such subsidies is far greater than I'd anticipated. A recent investigation by the *Guardian* reveals that "coal, oil, and gas industries benefited from subsidies of $550 billion, four times [the amount] given to renewable energy." Typical were three projects that, due to the efforts of EHMs, had been granted subsidies by politicians whose campaigns received large contributions from the fossil fuels industry:

A proposed Shell petrochemical refinery in Pennsylvania will receive $1.6 billion (£1 billion) in state subsidy, according to a deal struck in 2012, when the company made an annual profit of $26.8 billion.

ExxonMobil's upgrades to its Baton Rouge refinery in Louisiana are benefiting from $119 million of state subsidy, with the support starting in 2011, when the company made a $41 billion profit.

A jobs subsidy scheme worth $78 million to Marathon Petroleum in Ohio began in 2011, when the company made $2.4 billion in profit.[11]

The EHMs of agribusiness are perhaps the most famous — or infamous — of all. Just one example was the passage of HR 1599 by the US House of Representatives in July 2015. Known officially as the Safe and Accurate Food Labeling Act of 2015, but called the Deny Americans the Right to Know (DARK) Act by its opponents, the law is intended to block states from requiring the labeling of products containing genetically modified organisms, or GMOs. The Grocery Manufacturers Association and Monsanto EHMs poured millions of dollars into making this bill happen. According to the *Guardian*:

> "Passage of this bill is an attempt by Monsanto and its agribusiness cronies to crush the democratic decision making of tens of millions of Americans. Corporate influence has won and the voice of the people has been ignored," stated Andrew Kimbrell, executive director of Center for Food Safety.
>
> Environmental Working Group (EWG) was also opposed to the bill, and cited widespread public support for labeling GMOs.
>
> "It's outrageous that some House lawmakers voted to ignore the wishes of nine out of ten Americans," said Scott Faber, senior vice president of government affairs for EWG.[12]

These steal-from-the-poor, give-to-the-rich programs are by no means restricted to arms, energy, and agriculture businesses.

They are pervasive across the economic spectrum. One example is Walmart.

A Shuar friend who recently visited the United States asked to see this "most famous store," Walmart. I told him that I don't shop there but I'd be happy to take him on a tour. Before we went, I shared with him information published by Americans for Tax Fairness. It shocked us both.

That report described the ways in which Walmart has siphoned billions of dollars from US taxpayers. Among their various tools is a vast network of overseas tax havens, with assets valued at more than $76 billion. According to the report:

> [Walmart] has established at least 78 subsidiaries in 15 offshore tax havens, none of them publicly reported before....
>
> The analysis, titled *The Walmart Web: How the World's Biggest Corporation Uses Tax Havens to Dodge Taxes*, shows that Walmart has no fewer than 22 shell companies in Luxembourg — 20 established since 2009 and five in 2015 alone. According to the study, Walmart has transferred ownership of more than $45 billion in assets to those subsidiaries since 2011, but reported paying less than 1 percent in tax to Luxembourg on $1.3 billion in profits from 2010 through 2013.[13]

As we strolled down the seemingly endless aisles of merchandise, my Shuar friend pointed out that no one was talking to anyone else. "In my country," he said, "markets are places where we learn what's going on with our friends and neighbors — and the world. Here, people ignore each other. They just shop." He was also amazed at the number of different items of essentially the same product. "How do you decide," he asked, "whether to buy soap in the blue box, the red box, or the yellow box?"

One of the most disturbing reports estimated that Walmart workers are subsidized by US taxpayers to the tune of more than $6 billion a year, in public nutrition, health care, and housing assistance programs. The owners of this mega cash cow, the members of the Walton family, are listed among the wealthiest billionaires on the planet. They, like so many of their cohorts, may criticize social programs for everyone else, but they are beneficiaries of the biggest socialized programs in history.[14]

Vulture funds are one more example of how this EHM cancer has metastasized. After a country has defaulted and fallen into a state of economic chaos, these funds purchase that country's debt for a few cents on the dollar. Then, when the country's economy begins to recover, the funds demand payment of the debt, plus interest, often tacking on additional fees. Many take this a step further by suing businesses that try to work with the target country, thus compounding the damage by scaring off potential investors.

The twenty-six largest vultures have collected $1 billion from the world's poorest countries, and still have another $1.3 billion earmarked for collection. That $1 billion is more than twice the budget of the International Committee of the Red Cross for all of Africa in 2011; it could finance the entire UN appeal for the famine in Somalia.[15]

Vulture funds have gone after Argentina, Brazil, Congo-Brazzaville, Ecuador, Greece, Iceland, and Ireland, and they have their sights set on just about every other country with debt and economic problems, including Italy and other European countries. Although there are many examples, Peru's is a typical case.

Peru was caught in a downward spiral of economic and social turmoil in 1983. This was exacerbated by terrorist activities and unmanageable external loans. After long negotiations, its debts were restructured in 1996. Elliott Associates, a hedge fund run by Paul Singer, a major supporter of political campaigns, purchased around $20 million of the defaulted Peruvian loans for about $11 million and then sued the country and its central bank for the original amount, plus interest, in a New York court. Elliott won a $58 million settlement and cleared $47 million in profit—a more than 400 percent rate of return on its investment. This windfall profit came at a huge cost to environmental and social programs in Peru.[16]

The last global recession and the ensuing crises across most of the world resulted in increased exploitation by vulture funds. In addition to countries such as Peru, or European countries with "developed" economies, more than a third of the thirty-nine countries that qualify for debt relief under the World Bank's Heavily Indebted Poor Countries programs (mostly located in Africa) have been targeted.[17]

In *Confessions of an Economic Hit Man*, I portrayed the World Bank and its affiliates as organizations that use debt to enslave nations. That certainly was and is correct. Since then, however, the vulture funds have elevated debt-as-slavery to new levels.

Like so many activities promoted by EHMs, vulture funds not only devastate their target countries but also destabilize the global economy. According to Joseph Stiglitz, a Nobel laureate in economics and former senior vice president and chief economist at the World Bank:

> In Argentina, the authorities' battles with a small number of "investors" (so-called vulture funds) jeopardised an entire debt restructuring agreed to — voluntarily — by an overwhelming majority of the country's creditors. In Greece... the country is forced into austerity policies that have contributed mightily to a 25 percent decline in GDP and have left its population worse off. In Ukraine, the potential political ramifications of sovereign-debt distress are enormous.[18]

))

As I look back over the decades and compare what was happening in the 1970s with what is happening today among EHMs and their corporatocracy bosses, perhaps the most frightening observation is that the nefarious activities today are so much more pervasive than they were then, and that they are widely accepted by the executives who manage our most powerful corporations, by educators who set the standards in our business schools, and by the general public.

A handful of robber barons and their henchmen, the modern EHMs, have conspired to convince the rest of us that they have the right to do anything they deem necessary to support the debt-and-fear dogma. Citing US Supreme Court decisions and euphemisms about the virtues of their very narrow version of capitalism, they've persuaded us to give them license to make themselves fabulously wealthy. And they've done this, with our tacit approval, at our expense. One percent of Americans received 95 percent of all the wealth created since the depression was officially pronounced as ended in 2009, while 90 percent of us became poorer. For every $1 billion of wealth created, the average US citizen gets one dollar. Globally, eighty-five individuals own more resources than half of the world's population.[19]

The examples provided here are only a few drops in the bucket of impact that today's corporate EHMs have on US and global economics, politics, environmental issues, and society. They illustrate the extent to which EHMs have transformed themselves and have taken over the world since my days in those ranks.

Something equally appalling has happened among the jackals.

Who Are Today's Jackals?

"I was walking along a street in the village where my grandparents live [in Pakistan]," said Jafar, a student I met in Istanbul, where I was speaking at a business conference. "Suddenly, the building next to me exploded. Hit by a missile from a drone. People ran out, screaming. A woman carrying her baby was on fire. I rushed to her, took her baby, and told her to roll on the ground." His eyes filled with tears. "She survived, but many people died. Many."

That drone was controlled by a new breed of jackal. As I listen to people like Jafar, and as I read reports about drone strikes, I am filled with feelings that I find hard to describe. I grew up on stories of World War II heroism — images of US GIs rescuing children from flaming buildings, storming the beaches of Normandy, and liberating Nazi concentration camps. I saw the 1950s, *I Led Three Lives* type of FBI agent, who infiltrated Communist cells, as incredibly courageous. So, too, did I view the CIA agents who penetrated secret Soviet networks, and the jackals who flew into Seychelles. Even those who did things I opposed, such as planting bombs on the planes of Roldós and Torrijos, took huge personal risks.

But drone operators! They don't risk their lives; they don't hear the screams of the wounded and dying or witness the suffering of innocent victims. They sit at computer monitors. They aren't brave. There is nothing heroic about their jobs. Nor is there anything heroic about a nation that inflicts such suffering on other people.

Certainly, I feel ashamed by what we are doing in the world today. But, perhaps more than anything, I feel a profound confusion, a sense of utter bewilderment. I keep asking myself those questions that had come to me in the Hanoi prison: What are our leaders thinking? Can't they see that such ruthless disregard for life destroys the reputation of a nation that gained the world's respect during World War II?

Although there are frequent news stories about the drone assassinations of the leaders of al-Qaeda and other terrorist groups, it
is impossible to obtain statistics about all the mistakes that are
made, what the Pentagon refers to as "collateral damage" — innocent civilians killed. The best anyone can do is estimate, and these
estimates are shocking.

"At least 6,000 people's lives have been unjustly taken by United
States drone attacks in Afghanistan, Pakistan, Yemen, Somalia,
Iraq, the Philippines, Libya, and Syria," says a June 2015 letter
released by dozens of US military veterans.[1] The letter goes on to
urge drone operators to refuse to fly missions or to support such
activities in any way. These veterans understand that indiscrim-
inate drone strikes on civilians are defined by most of the world
as acts of terror.

Many veterans have seen firsthand that the actions of drone
operators and many other modern jackals fill the pockets of corporate magnates who profit from war, destruction, reconstruction, and the oil fields and other resources that are at the heart of
so many conflicts. At the same time, these actions undermine US
credibility, are contrary to the interests of American citizens, and
foster the continuation of a fear-based economy.

President Obama's former top military intelligence official,
retired US Lieutenant General Michael Flynn, described the use
of drones as a "failed strategy" that only encourages violence and
terrorism. "When you drop a bomb from a drone ... you are going
to cause more damage than you are going to cause good," he said.
And Flynn should know; he headed up the Pentagon's Defense
Intelligence Agency until the summer of 2014.[2]

Jackals today wear many disguises and perform tasks that those
in my time would have considered inappropriate, cowardly, or even
counterproductive. Documents recently released by WikiLeaks
and Edward Snowden reveal an alarming increase in the use of
CIA torture and extraordinary rendition sites, paramilitary forces
hired by governments and global corporations, and CIA and Special Forces "high-value target" assassination programs.

Unlike the loner secret agents who depend on their wits and
physical prowess, an entirely new genre of "pack jackals" is supported by airstrikes, satellites, and other modern technologies.

Although Americans are kept in the dark about the operations of the Pentagon's specially trained military teams — primarily Navy SEAL and Army Delta Force personnel — they are no secret to the communities where they strike.

The *New York Times* lamented the veil of secrecy that surrounds such units, in an article published in June 2015, "SEAL Team 6: A Secret History of Quiet Killings and Blurred Lines":

> Around the world, they have run spying stations disguised as commercial boats, posed as civilian employees of front companies and operated undercover at embassies as male-female pairs, tracking those the United States wants to kill or capture.
>
> Those operations are part of the hidden history of the Navy's SEAL Team 6, one of the nation's most mythologized, most secretive and least scrutinized military organizations. Once a small group reserved for specialized but rare missions, the unit best known for killing Osama bin Laden has been transformed by more than a decade of combat into a global manhunting machine.

The article went on to decry the fact that so much of current US policy is conducted in secret. One of the conclusions reached by the *Times* investigative team:

> Like the CIA's campaign of drone strikes, Special Operations missions offer policy makers an alternative to costly wars of occupation. But the bulwark of secrecy around Team 6 makes it impossible to fully assess its record and the consequences of its actions, including civilian casualties or the deep resentment inside the countries where its members operate.[3]

Concern for that resentment is not limited to veterans' groups and the media. It is also expressed by students in US colleges where I speak. They refer to men and women their age who travel from Australia, the US, and Europe to the Middle East to join ISIS and other militant Islamist organizations. They speculate that resentment and desperation drive these young people to take such actions. They worry that US policies encourage terrorism.

Students often mention that most of the countries where potential terrorists are recruited have long histories of advocating violence as the solution to problems, and that even the language used by US policy makers for programs that would seem to have nothing to do with violence are couched in terms like "*fighting* poverty," "*conquering* hunger," and "the *war* on drugs." They point out that movies and TV shows eulogize guns and the tough guy approach to dealing with difficult situations.

The jackals in my day usually were assigned to foreign lands, with the exception of those involved in counterinsurgency and infiltrating Communist cells inside the United States. That, too, has changed. In the aftermath of 9/11, fear drove Americans to agree to sacrifice privacy and freedom and give the NSA, the CIA, the FBI, and other agencies unprecedented powers. Tools perfected overseas, including drones and surveillance aircraft, are now used to spy on us in the United States.

Documents released by US federal authorities in response to a Freedom of Information lawsuit reveal that at least sixty-three drone sites, located in twenty states, were active in the United States (as of 2012). Many were operated by soldiers and were deployed from stateside military installations. Others were manned by law enforcement agencies and the US Border Patrol. Some, if not all, are designed to assassinate people.[4]

In June 2015, the Associated Press reported that the FBI has a "small air force with scores of low-flying planes across the US carrying video and, at times, cellphone surveillance technology — all hidden behind fictitious companies that are fronts for the government." The article went on to say that these flights are usually conducted without a judge's approval and that "in a recent 30-day period, the agency flew above more than 30 cities in 11 states across the country."[5]

))

When I read these articles, I thought about the commitment I'd made after meeting with Howard Zinn. I'd promised to be more diligent, to watch more closely what was going on in my own community, my country, and the world. I began to see a change in the public's attitudes. September 11, 2001, had terrified the nation into giving up its freedoms, but continuing reports of torture at military bases and CIA rendition sites, attacks on whistle-blowers, police brutality, and eavesdropping on personal phone calls was turning the tide of opinion. Increasingly, the media and blogs were pointing out that such activities were inconsistent with laws intended to protect our privacy. According to the Electronic Frontier Foundation:

> News reports in December 2005 first revealed that the National Security Agency (NSA) has been intercepting Americans' phone calls and Internet communications. Those news reports, combined with a *USA Today* story in May 2006 and the statements of several members of Congress, revealed that the NSA is also receiving wholesale copies of Americans' telephone and other communications records. All of these surveillance activities are in violation of the privacy safeguards established by Congress and the US Constitution.[6]

The draconian, jackal measures revealed in the thousands of pages released by WikiLeaks and Edward Snowden tell a shocking, disturbing, and sad story. Many Americans have come to understand that the democracy their government was supposed to protect has been betrayed by that government, that the very foundations of Lincoln's "government of the people, by the people, and for the people" were buried in the ashes of Ground Zero.

I was shocked to learn that the NSA monitors about two hundred million text messages each day and has surreptitiously planted spy software in some one hundred thousand computers, allowing it access to the information in those computers.[7] Perhaps it's just ego, but I wonder if my computer is one of those...

As jaded as I've become about the immoral and criminal (even if technically legal) activities of our jackal agencies, I was outraged by revelations that the organization that had recruited me—the NSA—had eavesdropped on the phone conversations of thirty-five world leaders, including listening to confidential discussions held at the highest levels of the governments of Argentina, Brazil, France, Germany, the UK, and many of our other allies. According to the *Guardian*, "The NSA encourages senior officials in its 'customer' departments, such as the White House, State and the Pentagon, to share their 'Rolodexes' so the agency can add the phone numbers of leading foreign politicians to their surveillance systems."[8]

This struck me as unacceptable, but it also was incredibly stupid diplomacy. Among the repercussions: German chancellor Angela Merkel objected strongly, and Brazilian president Dilma Rousseff postponed a state visit to Washington.

Another tool at the disposal of the modern jackal is that of character assassination. Every president, every politician and government official, is aware that a scandal can bring him or her down. President Clinton served as a warning to all leaders, present and future. Whether Linda Tripp was hired to set up Monica Lewinsky — as many suspect — or not, Clinton was impeached (politically assassinated) because of a sex scandal. In my day, everyone knew that President Kennedy was having multiple affairs, and nobody thought it was the public's business; it took a bullet to assassinate him. Today, people in powerful positions around the world know that modern eavesdropping technology can be used to destroy them — or to plant incriminating evidence that will destroy them.

In many parts of the world, today's jackals are supported by a growing class of mercenary forces — hired guns who do not answer to the same rules and standards as military personnel. By 2012, there were almost 110,000 contracted mercenary forces in Afghanistan alone, compared with 68,000 US military personnel. To place this in perspective: in Vietnam, there were 70,000 mercenaries and 359,000 military forces.[9]

Although information is not available about the number of active mercenaries worldwide who are paid with US taxpayer money, we know it is in the millions. In a 2014 survey that ranked the thirty most powerful private security companies, the number one spot went to G4S, a firm that employs more than 620,000 people and earned more than $12 billion in 2012. In addition to supplying soldiers, G4S sells state-of-the-art spying and monitoring equipment to governments and corporations. Interestingly, Blackwater (renamed Academi), the mercenary firm best known to the general public, due to the company's alleged involvement in the killing of Iraqi civilians, came in at number thirty.[10]

The use of mercenaries allows Washington to claim that the military is winding down, that US death tolls are decreasing, and that the government is not responsible for torture and other war crimes. Mercenaries avoid the need for an unpopular draft like the one during the Vietnam War that incited the antiwar movement. They support the jackals' illegal activities without reporting to the Pentagon, the president, or Congress. They are accountable to no one.

The ability and willingness of the corporatocracy to spy on our every movement and to take action — including imprisonment without habeas corpus, or assassination — when we do anything perceived as a threat to its greed-driven power is virtually unlimited. And totally undemocratic. Its lobbyists own our elected officials. Its special operations teams conduct illegal assassinations. Its low-flying pilots and robot jackals monitor our phone and Internet conversations. All of this is part of the corporatocracy's determination to do whatever it deems it will take to maintain control.

Recently, however, the corporatocracy's actions have escalated to near-panic levels. To a large degree, this is driven by its fear of a new superpower, China.

CHAPTER 45

Lessons for China

In 2015, a top Ecuadorian official told me, "We'd rather accept loans from Beijing than Washington. After all, China has never overthrown or killed our leaders — unlike the US."

When I pointed out that China had a history of invasions in Asia, he replied, "Yes. They've seen those places as part of their ancient kingdom. But they haven't done it in Latin America, or Africa, or the Middle East. The US has."

We were discussing the debt audit commission that had reviewed the legitimacy of the loans taken on by Ecuador's CIA-supported dictators during my EHM days. The commission's findings had convinced President Correa to default on loans worth more than $3 billion. In retaliation for the president's initial refusal to pay $30.6 million that was due on $519 million of outstanding global bonds in 2012, Standard and Poor's Rating Services and Fitch Ratings slashed Ecuador's credit rating.[1]

Correa turned to Beijing. China offered Ecuador a $1 billion loan, which soon was increased to $2 billion.[2] As his government repaid that loan, Correa reestablished Ecuador's global credit standing, but he also made his country beholden to China and its version of EHMs. By April 2015, Ecuador's debts to China had risen to almost $5.4 billion — representing 28 percent of its external debt.[3]

In the summer of 2015, I returned to Ecuador. Fundación Pachamama had been legally dissolved, but there had been no attempt to inhibit the work of the US-based Pachamama Alliance. I joined Bill and Lynne Twist and Daniel Koupermann on our annual trip to lead a group of supporters to Achuar territory.

As we made that spectacular trip from Quito to the airstrip in Shell, from which planes would take us deep into the jungle, I once again stared at the massive concrete wall of the Agoyan hydroelectric dam — for me, a symbol of the legal crimes I'd committed, and one that evoked memories of the assassinated Jaime Roldós and the very recent attempted coup that had changed Correa.

I thought about how the abuses of the World Bank, the IMF, Wall Street, the credit rating services, and the rest of the US/European banking community have driven Ecuador and its oil resources into the arms of China. When I traveled past this dam in 2003, it was assumed that most of the country's oil would go to the United States. By 2015, that had totally changed; China was buying almost 55 percent of Ecuador's oil. Exports to the United States, meanwhile, had decreased from about 75 percent of Ecuador's oil to none.[4] I realized that, perhaps more than anything else, China's role — not just in Ecuador but in the entire world — offers insights into the future.

China's expansionism, like that of the United States and the other empires of history, revolves around lending money to countries, plundering their resources, and paralyzing their leaders with fear. China is playing off the fears of men like Correa and citizens of countries such as Ecuador and Honduras — and just about everywhere else.

Whereas we in the United States are taught to fear China, Russia, and terrorists, a large part of the world fears *us*. They fear the Pentagon and the military presence that Washington has established in more than one hundred countries. They fear the CIA, the NSA, and all the other US spy agencies. They fear the drones, the missiles, and the bombs. They fear our dollarized, debt-based money system.

In addition to the obvious physical fears are the more subtle ones. Economically developing countries fear their vulnerability to global corporations. Because of the trade agreements and conditionalities imposed on them through the debt agreements, their economies seem dependent on those corporations. They fear they can't survive without the corporations. They fear that the corporations will go somewhere else to locate their production facilities, but they also fear that if those facilities *are* built within their borders, the corporations will bury the country in pollution and force workers to accept unlivable wages. They fear that the corporations will eventually leave them for another country with even less stringent environmental and social regulations, dooming to extreme poverty or starvation the people who abandoned their subsistence farms to work in the now-vacated factories.

A system based on fear and debt may seem effective; yet, history has shown that empires never last. The tragedy of America's rise and fall in the modern world represents a colossal failure on the part of corporate and government leaders.

After the demise of the Soviet Union, the new corporate barons believed they had license to do whatever they deemed it would take to realize their goal of maximizing profits, including corrupting politicians and manipulating the legal system. "Aid" organizations such as the World Bank increased the interest rates on loans, made political demands, and imposed conditionalities on the debtor countries, influencing the way they governed themselves and related to the United States and the corporations.

It did not take long for people in those nations to recognize that they were being exploited. However, they had nowhere to turn, no counterbalancing power. The Soviet Union was gone. The economically developing countries had no choice but to give in and feel abused and resentful.

Then, almost overnight, China emerged as a new world power. Its meteoric rise as an economic giant and major player in international manufacturing and trade thrust it onto the world stage as that counterbalance.

China appears to have learned from mistakes made by the United States, its allies, and the corporatocracy. Chinese loans usually are not accompanied by draconian demands – the conditionalities of World Bank and IMF deals – such as voting for specific UN policies, trading only in dollars, or allowing the establishment of military bases occupied by foreign troops. China makes promises that the factories it builds will continue to operate in the long term. It remains to be seen whether such promises will be kept, but the United States promotes "free trade" agreements that do exactly the opposite.

However, despite China's apparent aptitude at doing it better than the United States and its allies, the simple fact remains that China is using debt — massive amounts of it — to further its own EHM system, to control countries and their resources.

Although it is difficult to measure the total amount of debt money flowing from China, estimates are that it committed nearly $100 billion in loans to Ecuador and its Latin American neighbors from 2005 to 2013. Its current loans to the region are perhaps twice that amount and certainly surpass the combined loans of the World Bank, USAID, the Inter-American Development Bank, and the Export-Import Bank of the United States. China is the driving force behind the new BRICS (Brazil, Russia, India, China, and South Africa) bank and the Asian Infrastructure Investment Bank (AIIB), which includes more than fifty member countries. The assets and potential power of these banks dwarf those of the World Bank and all its associated financial institutions. In less than a decade, China has catapulted itself to the position of master of global debt.[5]

A *New York Times* article I read while in Ecuador reported events that sounded like the US EHM activities of my day — except that the Chinese were taking on more projects and spending more money than we ever did.

> Where the Andean foothills dip into the Amazon jungle, nearly 1,000 Chinese engineers and workers have been pouring concrete for a dam and a 15-mile underground tunnel. The $2.2 billion project will feed river water to eight giant Chinese turbines designed to produce enough electricity to light more than a third of Ecuador.
>
> Near the port of Manta on the Pacific Ocean, Chinese banks are in talks to lend $7 billion for the construction of an oil refinery, which could make Ecuador a global player in gasoline, diesel and other petroleum products.
>
> Across the country in villages and towns, Chinese money is going to build roads, highways, bridges, hospitals, even a network of surveillance cameras stretching to the Galápagos Islands. State-owned Chinese banks have already put nearly $11 billion into the country, and the Ecuadorean government is asking for more.

Ecuador, with just 16 million people, has little presence on the global stage. But China's rapidly expanding footprint here speaks volumes about the changing world order, as Beijing surges forward and Washington gradually loses ground.[6]

))

Our Pachamama Alliance group huddled in a hangar in Shell, waiting for the torrential jungle rain to stop so we could fly into Achuar territory. When I brought up the subject of China, there seemed to be a consensus that China had performed a miracle and should be feared. The country had risen from the ashes of Mao's Cultural Revolution and, in the years since President Nixon's first visit in 1972, had enjoyed amazing — "miraculous" — economic growth, like nothing ever before experienced by any country in history. However, this had come at a terrible environmental and social cost. The nation was smothering itself in pollution, and millions of Chinese were living under substandard social conditions. People expressed fear that China was rising to world prominence and that the Chinese model would cause even graver problems than the US model had.

I'd been to China a couple of times since writing *Confessions of an Economic Hit Man*. My last visit had been as a speaker at an MBA conference in Shanghai. Many of the Chinese MBA students who attended were members of the Communist Party and had been singled out as the future leaders of their country. They emphasized that they were very concerned about the environmental and social problems affecting their country, and they were committed to fixing them. One student, Mandy Zhang, insisted that economic growth was proof that China could create an economic miracle. "Now," she said, "my generation must create a green miracle."

One of the Pachamama Alliance people in the hangar asked, "What can we do? How do we stop China?"

If we are truly honest with ourselves, we in the United States have to admit that it is not so much about stopping China as about changing our own mind-sets. We need to admit that a great deal of China's pollution is *our* pollution. The same can be said of the social conditions. We purchase the goods made in those factories. We seek out stores with the lowest prices, but the vast majority of their products are made in the polluting factories of China.

In a very real sense, China's economic miracle has been possible only because of the United States — and the global corporations. Key individuals in China have joined the corporatocracy. China is the world's largest exporter of manufactured goods. From 2001 to 2010, its reported exports increased at an average annual rate of about 20 percent. In 2004, China sold less than $200 billion worth of products to the United States; by 2014, that figure had more than doubled, to $467 billion.[7]

Instead of speculating about China, we must repent and reform. We need to take a long, hard look at what we in the United States — and our corporations, now gone global — have done. China is trying to emulate a system that is a failure. If less than 5 percent of the world's population (living in the United States) is consuming more than 25 percent of the resources, how can 19 percent of the world's population (living in China) hope to replicate our lifestyle? It's certainly not possible to also add India, Brazil, and the rest of the world to that equation. We must change.

We in the United States and across the globe must stop using "them" as scapegoats. Just as we must not fear "them," we must not blame "them" or expect "them" to solve the problem — the global problem of predatory corporate capitalism, a death economy. We need to recognize that "they" are us. We ourselves — each and every one of us — must take responsibility. We must create a new model — one that the Chinese, the Brazilians, the Indians, our own president, our corporate and government leaders, and everyone else can follow.

It isn't about changing the mechanics of economics. It is about changing the ideas, the dogmas that have driven economics for centuries: debt and fear, insufficiency, divide and conquer. It is about moving from ideas about merely being sustainable to ones that include regenerating areas devastated by agriculture, mining, and other destructive activities. It is about revolution. The transition from a death economy to a life economy is truly about a change in consciousness — a consciousness revolution.

CHAPTER 46

What You Can Do

"John Lennon said, 'All you need is love,'" Samantha Thomas told me. "What better way to honor the peace prize than through a summit that reflects his ideas?"

Yoko Ono had awarded me the Lennon Ono Grant for Peace and, along with it, a major contribution to Dream Change. The organization had been relatively quiet for several years, but now Samantha, a brilliant, dynamic, and determined person in her twenties, had come on board as its executive director. She wanted to sponsor a 2015 conference that would encourage businesses to achieve higher, more compassionate standards. She and I convinced Dan Wieden, cofounder and chairman of the board of Wieden+Kennedy, one of the most successful and highly respected advertising agencies in the world, to cohost it with me. From the beginning, Samantha had called it the Love Summit. At first, Dan and I objected. We were concerned that "love" might be inappropriate for a business conference. However, our attitudes soon changed.

Like many of the attendees, who were successful entrepreneurs and corporate executives, Dan and I came to understand that when we love ourselves, the earth, and one another, everything gets better. Several speakers pointed out that marketing is aimed at convincing consumers to love a company and its products. To change the world, all we need to do is inspire consumers to love companies and products that serve life, and to persuade businesspeople that if they want their companies and products to be loved, they must commit to doing just that.

As I listened to speaker after speaker expound upon the need for businesses to move into a new consciousness, I kept thinking about Tunduam, the Shuar shaman who had saved my life by changing my mind-set. The world is as we dream it, and we've been living a dream that combines excessive materialism with a divide-and-conquer, them-versus-us mentality.

"If I am to have more stuff," we've told ourselves, "I must take from *them*." It is time to change that mind-set. It is time to act in ways that support a new dream.

When Samantha said, at the close of the summit, "It turns out that love really is all you need," I realized that she was expressing the basis of the new dream. It is the dream that indigenous people and spiritual teachers — from Mother Teresa to the Dalai Lama, from the Buddha to Pope Francis — have always dreamed. It is a dream of love — for ourselves, for each other, for nature, and for the planet. It is a dream that tells us to replace the old dream of a death economy with a new dream of a life economy.

This new dream is of an economy that cleans up polluted waters, soil, and air; empowers hungry and starving people to feed themselves; develops transportation, communications, manufacturing, and energy systems that do not deplete resources; applies recycling and solar technologies; creates market, banking, and exchange systems that are community oriented and not based on debt currencies or war. In essence, it is a new dream, founded on courage and love rather than fear and hatred.

Since 2004, when the original of this book was published, I've spoken at conferences of business executives, at rock concerts, and at consumer summits. I've met with government leaders and lectured at universities in many countries. I've grown increasingly impressed with the messages I've heard. Entrepreneurs, lawyers, executives, farmers, and homemakers — people from all walks of life — are changing their dreams from the ones prevalent ten years ago, about wealth and power, to the ones more common today, about the desire to raise families in an environmentally sustainable and regenerative, socially just, and personally fulfilling world.

People everywhere understand the need for this revolution. We know that we must do whatever it takes to birth a life economy. We also know that each of us must do the things we love. You and I — we — are the ones to make this revolution happen. To do that, we must love who we are and what we do.

This book demonstrates that global corporations run this failed geopolitical/economic system. To change the system, we must change the dream of corporations.

Some argue that we need to rid the planet of corporations; however, the likelihood of this happening – at least in my lifetime – is extremely low. I think, instead, we need to take the shamanic approach, to transform – shapeshift – the attitudes and goals of those who own and manage the corporations.

Corporations are highly effective at channeling brilliant ideas into concrete action. But their dream of maximizing profits without regard for the environmental and social costs, their orientation toward pillaging resources and promoting debt and materialism, has been disastrous. It is time for a new dream that is based on serving the earth, the public, and future generations – not just of humans but of all beings.

We are empowered by the many ways we've changed corporations in the recent past – by boycotting ones that supported apartheid, polluted our rivers, refused to hire women or minorities, objected to same-sex marriages, rejected organic produce, opposed food labeling, and so much more.

We are encouraged by the knowledge that many executives and business owners are as concerned as anyone else. Whether they are employees of Fortune 500 corporations or proprietors of mom-and-pop stores, they are not members of the corporatocracy and therefore are exploited along with the rest of us. Even the so-called 1 percent (which are actually the 0.1 percent) are threatened. If this space station crashes, we all crash.

When I was first invited to speak at corporate conferences and MBA programs, I asked the organizers why they would want to hear from the author of a book such as mine. They answered that their people were smart enough to recognize that the current system verges on collapse. Until now, businesspeople may not have thought in terms of a death economy versus a life economy, but they understand that to be successful, they will have to embrace new models. They are searching for innovative approaches and ways to implement them.

CEOs who desire to change their corporate strategies tell me that they fear that if they lose short-term market share or profits, they will be replaced by someone who cares only about market share or profits. Feeling trapped in an archaic structure, they crave consumer movements that generate thousands of letters and e-mails saying things like "I love your product but will not buy it until you pay your workers a living wage." They can then take this information to their executive committee, key stockholders, the founder, or whoever has the ability to fire them.

For me, hearing such admissions is encouraging, because it identifies us as the ones with the real power. It tells us that the marketplace is a democracy, if we choose to use it as such; that every time we buy something, we cast a vote. It also provides a way to enlist the people on the inside of corporations. This revolution needs people on the inside. They can play major roles in creating the new economy.

We are in this together. All of us. We must do what it takes to cultivate the life economy. Now. It is time to admit that we are not fighting a war against terrorists, corporations, or any other "them." We are engaged in a course of action to end the EHM system. We all are part of a process that has failed us. We've bought into it, we've supported it, we've praised and glorified it. Now we must act to change it.

Like the Andean brick makers discussed in chapter 1, we need to face our fears, take offense at the injustices we've suffered, and stop looking for others to set things right. We must be willing to do whatever it takes to ensure that our children have a future.

When I was growing up in New Hampshire, I wished I'd been born in the 1700s so I could participate in the American Revolution. But the American Revolution was only a partial success. Although the British were defeated, many injustices continued for years — affecting women, minorities, the middle class, and the poor. Now those injustices affect us all; they threaten life as we know it on this planet.

Today's revolution is much bigger than the American Revolution. It is bigger than the agricultural or industrial revolutions. It is nothing less than a consciousness revolution. The change in consciousness includes a transition from masculine, hierarchical mind-sets and actions to ones that are more fluid, egalitarian, and feminine. It necessitates an acknowledgment that defending our home now means nurturing our home, and a recognition that our home is the entire planet.

ᵒ))

This book has described the four pillars of modern empire: fear, debt, insufficiency (the temptation to keep consuming more), and the divide-and-conquer mind-set. The idea that anything and everything is justified — coups and assassinations, drone strikes, NSA eavesdropping — as long as it props up those four pillars has shackled us to a feudal and corrupt system. It is a system that cannot be sustained.

We must do whatever it takes to change the dream behind such justifications; to convert fear into the courage to create a better world; to replace debt with generosity, anxiety over insufficiency with certainty that a life economy provides sustainable abundance. We must transform masculine aggression with feminine nurturance. We must replace divide-and-conquer mentalities with compassion and a commitment to regenerating ravaged environments. We must unite as a crew that will navigate this space station toward a truly prosperous future.

During my travels, one of the things I hear from people is that *Confessions of an Economic Hit Man* "connects the dots." In 2004, those dots led to the conclusion that people had been terribly misinformed about how the United States and its corporations deceive, abuse, and exploit economically developing countries. The post-2004 dots go much further. They lead us to the conclusion that we in the United States and in the rest of the so-called developed countries also have been hit — we have been abused and exploited by many of the tools that I and other EHMs used in Africa, Asia, the Middle East, and Latin America.

Connecting the post-2004 dots leads to the additional conclusion that we must do whatever it takes to change. We must act.

Such actions start with the recognition that we are presented with many choices throughout life. Fate. Chance. Accident. Opportunity. We can see these things as good or bad. What is important is not so much that they happen as how we react to them.

I once accepted a lot of money not to write a book. I chose to use the money to help people in countries I'd exploited. Out of that came my reconnection with Amazonian people, the formation of several nonprofits, and a new career as a writer and public speaker.

When we look at things that happen to us as bearers of messages, we open doors of opportunity for action.

The earth is offering us a strong message. The ice caps and glaciers are melting. The oceans are rising. Species are going extinct. This planet, our home, is demanding that we see her as a living Earth. She is not just a mass of rock and soil spinning around an indifferent sun. She is a biological member of a living universe. And she is sending a message: repent, reform, love her.

What will we do with that message, you and I?

We have the opportunity to dream a new dream, to explore options for exciting alternative ways of living, for turning failure into success, for building systems that, like the living Earth, are organic, are locally based, and, at the same time, interweave the fabrics of our global community.

Your gifts include your personal passions and skills. Whether you are a carpenter, a dentist, a writer, a parent, a student, or whatever else, those gifts are yours. True success comes from following your unique passions, employing your skills, and joining the growing community that is determined to create a better world.

You can start with your individual behavior (recycling, driving less, turning off lights, shopping and banking locally, and so forth), but do not fall into the trap of believing that those things alone are enough. See such actions as good, but also view them as portals into new ways of relating to the world and everything around you.

On a flight a few years ago from Leh Ledakh to Jammu, India, the group I was leading ended up on the same plane as the Dalai Lama. When he learned that the author of a book that he liked, *Shapeshifting*, about indigenous shamans, was on board, he invited me to sit next to him. We had a lively discussion about shamanism, and as the plane landed, he offered a further invitation, for my group to visit him at his house in Dharamsala.

As we chatted with him that afternoon, he told us that it is good to pray for peace. "But," he added, "if that is all you do, it's a waste of time. It may even be a distraction. You need to take appropriate daily action." He smiled that Dalai Lama smile. "You must act.

Every day."

The Dalai Lama's words are applicable to the actions necessary to create a life economy. Recycling, driving less, turning off lights, and other such commitments are good – but it is important not to let them distract us from dreaming bigger and taking "appropriate daily action" to make that bigger dream a reality.

Likewise, despite all the teachers who tell us that thinking positively is all we need to do, it is not enough. More than a billion people live on the verge of starvation. For them, driving less is not an option; thinking positively will not put food in their bellies. We need to do more. We need a revolution.

Revolutions happen because people come together and act. Although key individuals inspire and lead others, revolutions succeed because of communal actions. The rugged individual as hero is an old story; it diverts from the need for the collective actions that generate real change. The Dalai Lama knows this; the *Sangha* (community) is one of the three "jewels," or tenets, of Buddhism. Every religion, every social and political movement, honors the power of community. My uncle Ernest, the bank president, understood the importance of supporting his local community in Waterbury, Vermont.

The drive to build local communities has gained strength in recent years. Farmers' markets, the emphasis on buying locally, the reemergence of community banks, and even the commitment by large grocery chains to purchase produce from neighborhood growers all are part of an important trend. At the same time, a whole new aspect of global community is evolving.

On a trip to the Himalayas several months before the first version of this book was published, I talked to a tribal elder who lived in a tent more than fourteen thousand feet above sea level. He lamented that his people would never have telephones. "The lines can't reach this high," he told me through an interpreter. I heard something similar from an Achuar leader deep in the Amazon rain forest. Now, as I write this new version, both of these men – and their communities – have satellite phones.

For the first time in history, we are communicating instantaneously across the planet. And we all are reaching the conclusion that each of us, every living being, is threatened by the same crises of rising oceans, overwhelming pollution, melting ice caps, species extinctions, overpopulation, and the devastation of natural resources. We know that we must do whatever it takes to turn that around, to dream a life economy into reality.

When audience members ask me what, specifically, they can do, I start with, "You must follow your passions and use your talents in the most efficient, satisfying, and enjoyable way you can." Then I mention some of the appropriate daily actions we all can take.

We can join nonprofit and other nongovernmental organizations and consumer movements aimed at boycotting specific corporations. We can support reform movements aimed at such things as taxing corporations, regulating banks, getting money out of the electoral process, and stopping the causes of climate change. We can participate in demonstrations and marches; write blogs, books, or articles; make videos or movies. We can run for elected office or campaign for the place where we work to commit to public service. We can spread the good news about a life economy. We can buy magazines and watch TV programs that feature women and men who express the new dream. The choices are practically unlimited.

We each can spread this new message in our own way. The carpenter can build houses with local, sustainably produced materials, incorporate solar panels and other energy-efficient technologies — and constantly brag about it. The dentist can talk about the life economy while filling a cavity. The mother can teach her child to buy local products and save in a community bank.

Each of us can take his or her own path — as long as we all head for the same destination: an economy that works for everyone. American history offers a great lesson in this. Tom Paine did not try to lead armies; George Washington did not write pamphlets; Martha Washington did not write pamphlets or lead armies. Tom Paine had a passion for writing. George Washington had a passion for leading men. Martha Washington had a passion for organizing women to make clothes for soldiers. They took separate paths and headed for the same destination: getting out from under the yoke of British tyranny.

You must take the path that is most effective for you, the one that offers you the greatest joy.

During demonstrations to end the Vietnam War, we were

invited to feel our "bliss factor." Teach-ins, love-ins, music, dances, and festivals blossomed across the nation. The most successful ones were pro-peace rather than antiwar. People stuck flowers into the muzzles of soldiers' rifles. Folk singers wrote songs honoring the demonstrators and glorifying peace. The movement was successful because we participants came together in communities that enjoyed the process – and because we were passionate about a cause.

I've watched recent social, environmental, and peace movements burn out because passions were not honored in ways that evoked joy. The dream is not just about the destination; it must include every step along the path. Obstacles – which will be encountered – can be seen as great opportunities to learn and to gain strength.

The lists presented in the following chapter offer ideas for specific actions you can take. These are only suggestions, and the lists are by no means comprehensive. At first, I was reluctant to provide these suggestions, because I thought they might seem to trivialize this dream-changing process. Then I realized that as long as they are understood to be part of a process – beginning points, inspirations – they serve a purpose.

A friend, Tracy Apple, told me that she felt a deeper connection to the earth when she stopped using plastic bags. It led her to more actions, including becoming a key developer for the Pachamama Alliance's Awakening the Dreamer program, which as of this writing has been conducted in eighty-two countries. "I understood," she said, "that when I commit to an action, I'm contributing a part to something that is far greater than the sum of those parts." Giving up plastic bags was important by itself, but it also was a portal into a new level of consciousness.

The lists in chapter 47 are divided into six categories: (1) things we all can do; (2) things students can do; (3) things retired people can do; (4) things people between student age and retirement age can do; (5) things corporations can do (and consumers can insist they do); and (6) things entrepreneurs can do. These are suggestions, intended to inspire you to do whatever it takes to follow your passions and create the world we all know is possible.

As you read the lists, please keep in mind that perhaps the most important advice of all is to enjoy the process. Follow your bliss.

Make it fun. Don't burn out. Whenever you come up against an obstacle, see it as an opportunity that excites your creative juices and enables you to experience the joy of finding solutions. Whenever someone criticizes you or tells you the life economy is impossible, or whenever you meet a roadblock such as police officers preventing you from marching, understand it as a manifestation of the old story. Like a good martial artist, gather strength from such actions; use the energy to energize you.

It is time for you — and me, us — to do whatever it takes to bury the death economy and birth the life economy.

CHAPTER 47

Things to Do

The following lists are meant to stimulate you to come up with your own plan of action and are by no means intended to be complete. Neither should they be considered exclusive to the populations identified in the titles. In other words, if you are a student, feel free to draw from the retired people's list, and vice versa.

Be sure to choose items that fit your passions, that raise your bliss factor, that bring joy into your life. Doing whatever it takes to birth the life economy must be fun. Of course, there will be times when you encounter obstacles and setbacks. See these as challenges that stir your creativity and offer opportunities to experience the joy of creating solutions.

Understand that love really is all we need. When we love ourselves, our planet, and one another — when we do the things that increase our ability to love, and encourage others to do the same — everything works!

ELEVEN THINGS WE ALL CAN DO

1. **Keep telling a new story,** one that is based on creating an environmentally sustainable, resource regenerative, socially just world where one group of people does not make other groups of people desperate. This story is about cleaning up pollution and regarding our planet as a living being; helping starving people grow, store, and transport food more efficiently; living less materialistic and more spiritually fulfilling lives; developing new technologies for energy, transportation, communications, banking, and wholesale and retail trade; bringing diverse communities together with the understanding that we all live on a fragile space station that has no escape shuttles. In other words, tell the story of converting a

death economy to a life economy. Spread this story, every chance you get, to as many people as you can. Talk; write; make videos; offer study groups; do whatever it takes.

2. Shop and invest consciously. Replace recreational and mindless shopping tendencies with activities that truly nourish you and those you love. When you must shop, buy locally, as well as at consignment and thrift stores. Make things last. Buy goods and services from (and invest in) businesses that are committed to making a better world. No one is perfect, so seek out the ones that are doing the best in their field. E-mail them about the good things they are doing, encouraging them to get even better. Also e-mail the businesses that you avoid, telling them why you refuse to patronize them. Insist that any organizations, and pensions or other funds that you are part of, do the same.

3. Live consciously. Focus on doing things that enhance your relationship with other people, your community, and the world around you, including honoring nature in whatever form it takes in your locale. Break old patterns that revolve around materialism and buying "stuff"; downsize your house, car, and wardrobe; bicycle or take public transportation; avoid activities that use fossil fuels; give talks at local schools, libraries, and other forums.

4. Pick a cause that appeals to your deepest passions, and support it on a regular basis. This could be changing a corporation, such as Monsanto, Chevron, or Walmart; or promoting a movement, radio station, blogger, nonprofit, or nongovernmental organization. Give it your attention every day — in the form of time and energy (even if only for a few minutes) or money. Use social media to let all your friends know what you are doing. Craft e-mails and letters about your cause, and distribute them frequently to your social media contacts, ask them to distribute these to all of their social media contacts, and so on.

5. Become part of the living local community. Use local banks that invest in local projects, local merchants, locally owned restaurants; as much as possible, buy food that is locally and organically grown; use materials and goods that are local and/or environmentally and socially responsible; create community gardens and urban green spaces. Encourage everyone you know to do the same. Vote for enlightened school and other local leaders. Join or form groups that bring people together to have fun doing such things: bicycle, nature, book, "change the world" clubs — be creative. Drink tap or filtered, not bottled, water.

6. Flood media outlets, corporate executives, and government officials with information about the need to move from a death economy to a life economy. Do this locally, nationally, or internationally — or all three.

7. Support reform movements that most appeal to you. These will be country- and community-dependent activities to encourage geopolitical, economic, and social reforms. Demand such things as guaranteed living wages and/or employment, health insurance, medical care, and retirement pensions.

8. Encourage the creation of local, national, and/or international parks, wildlife preserves, and other such areas. If you live in an urban setting or a run-down area, organize people to turn vacant lots into parks and playgrounds. Spend quality time in these places and encourage everyone you know to do the same.

9. Fight for campaign finance reform and/or climate change regulations in the United States and elsewhere. Join organizations such as Move to Amend, the Community Environmental Legal Defense Fund, the Citizens' Climate Lobby, the Pachamama Alliance, or others that appeal to you.

10. Avoid debt. Take positive actions to pay off credit card charges and other debt without incurring interest payments. Make a point of using cash whenever possible.

11. Make heroes and icons of people who are working to create a better world. Honor the founders and managers of institutions and movements discussed in numbers 1 through 9 above, the visible and the behind-the-scenes people who create an environmentally sustainable, resource regenerative, socially just world, who help starving people feed themselves, and who promote better business and living models — rather than the CEOs of irresponsible corporations, overpaid athletes, or celebrities.

NINE THINGS STUDENTS CAN DO

1. Learn all you can about what's really going on in the world. Understand that the mind-sets created by the stories we are told and that we tell each other, and the distorted history of humanity that is taught to our children, are extremely powerful. Look to the alternative media for the story behind the story.

2. Question authority. Know that there are many conspiracies intent on deceiving you. Question and stand up to them every chance you get. By doing so, you will change the mind-sets and a new story will evolve.

3. Understand your passions. What do you most enjoy in life? Focus on activities that bring you joy, and on developing a deeper appreciation of and knowledge about subjects that most appeal to you. Determine to live your life according to your passions. Recognize that the most important education you can get involves self-knowledge and a commitment to living your bliss.

4. Seek out others who are looking to change the story. Join or develop communities of people who are intent on helping each other rise to new levels of understanding and living in ways that are more connected to each other and to our living Earth.

5. Speak out. Help people who do not fit the definition of number 4 above to understand the deceptions we're fed. Teach your contemporaries — and let your elders know that your generation is not going to be hoodwinked.

6. Take a stand against debt. Do not accept burdensome student loans or credit card and other debt. Join organizations that help students avoid debts and/or get out from under existing debts.

7. Work for your passion. Go to work only for organizations and businesses that are consistent with your passions and philosophies. If you can't find any such jobs, create your own. Take the route of the self-starter, the entrepreneur, and refuse to be caught in work patterns that deplete your energy and creativity.

8. Join organizations. Participate in nonprofit and other nongovernmental organizations, societies, or movements that support the things you feel most passionate about, such as Generation

Waking Up, Move to Amend, the Community Environmental Legal Defense Fund, the Citizens' Climate Lobby, the Pachamama Alliance, Dream Change, and others. Get involved. Take action. Become part of those communities. Offer them your creativity and talents, or money, to support positive change.

9. Make videos or films aimed at ending the death economy and building a life economy. These could focus on whatever most appeals to you — human, animal, or plant rights; consumer or social movements; economics, politics, or history; science-fiction stories about the future; or a limitless number of other subjects.

SIX THINGS RETIRED PEOPLE CAN DO

1. You can't be fired, so rattle the cage. Get involved in activities that might have frightened you before. Don't be afraid to express yourself, and even be "outrageous."

2. Take action. Follow your heart and get involved in causes that appeal to you. Avoid the temptation to believe that you are past your prime or are unable to offer something meaningful to the world, or to become distracted by self-absorbed activities. Enjoy leisure activities such as golf, cards, tennis, sailing, watching TV, but also understand that the greater pleasure comes from offering what you have learned in life to bigger causes and creating a better world for future generations.

3. Mentor younger people. You have a great deal to offer. Whether you were a carpenter, a teacher, a health worker, a gardener, a business executive, or whatever, recognize that your experiences are precious and can help those who follow. Elders in indigenous communities traditionally have been honored for their wisdom. Honor yourself as an elder and teach young people to make every job, every activity, about nourishing life and a life economy.

4. Demand responsible investments. Insist that your pension funds, mutual funds, and other investments be dedicated to serving the public interest and creating an environmentally sustainable, resource regenerative, socially just world. Let the funds and corporations where you own stock know that you want them to be successful, and that this means participating in the creation of a life economy.

5. Participate in or create campaigns that affect government, politics, and corporate policies. Run for office or support candidates who do, join consumer movements, or take whatever path draws you to be a full participant in the democratic process. Realize that this is not just part of being a true advocate of democracy; it also is deeply rewarding and fun.

6. Share your story. Tell others, especially younger people, about your life and the world you grew up in — how it worked, where it failed, and what needs to be done now to create societies that are resilient and that honor all life. Do this in small family or community gatherings as well as before larger bodies such as service clubs, and through writing, film, art, music, or whatever vehicles work best for you. Tap your unique gifts and talents.

NINE THINGS PEOPLE BETWEEN STUDENT AGE AND RETIREMENT AGE CAN DO

1. Be aware of what is going on in your community and around the world. Dig beneath the surface. Don't allow yourself to be duped by the media, politicians, corporations, or governments.

2. Develop communications skills to help everyone around you gain greater awareness of what is going on. Realize that being dogmatic or judgmental usually does not work. "Did you know that... ?" is more effective than "Don't you know that... ?" Also, remember to ask questions that spark people's curiosity and creativity. This can be more effective than overwhelming people with your own ideas and information. Use whatever channels are easiest for you: talking, writing, e-mailing, texting, posting on Facebook and Twitter... the list goes on.

3. Demand economic and tax reforms, such as accounting practices that internalize costs, strict oversight of Wall Street and big banks, and tax laws that force the wealthy and corporations to pay their fair share and that encourage socially and environmentally beneficial technologies. Vote only for candidates who support these, buy only from businesses that comply with and promote such reforms, and let the candidates and businesses know. Write letters to editors and blogs, post on Facebook and Twitter, and so on.

4. Form or join consumer movements, nonprofits, and nongovernmental organizations that promote businesses that serve a public interest — the 99.99 percent rather than the 0.01 percent. Call and/or send e-mails to your local and national representatives, urging them to support these movements and to vote for such reforms.

5. Help form and/or support community-based businesses such as consumer co-ops, community corporations, Certified B Corporations, local public banks, and worker-owned businesses.

6. Join demonstrations, protests, and worker/student/civil movements that fight for better social and environmental conditions. Actively participate, or give them financial and social media support.

7. Develop an awareness of your own biases around race, religion, financial status, immigration, gender, and other issues, and work toward overcoming those biases.

8. Teach younger people to be activists with soul. Help them to understand that democracy is based on being informed and educated about what is going on in the world, and taking *inspired* action.

9. If you work for a corporation or own stock, speak out. Make it known that you want the company where you work or where you own stock to be successful, and that the successful businesses of the future will be those that nourish a healthy, resilient natural environment and that contribute to the joy, harmony, and equality of their employees and of the communities they serve. See also the next section, "Eleven Things Corporations Can Do."

ELEVEN THINGS CORPORATIONS CAN DO (AND THAT CONSUMERS CAN INSIST THEY DO)

1. Include in your goals and mission statement a commitment to serving the public, the natural environment, social harmony, and justice. Of course, this must be tailored to the corporation's specific goods and services. It should be the driving force behind all activities, and an integrated and powerful aspect of all marketing programs. Let it be known that this corporation is looking out for the future as well as the present, and that those who support it as customers or investors are making the world a better place.

2. Convince your owners (stockholders), executives, employees, and other stakeholders that the mission outlined in item 1 will serve the corporation's long-term best interests. Help all stakeholders understand that we really have entered a new era in human evolution and that the companies that will survive and succeed are those that wake up to and honor the transition to a life economy.

3. Launch programs to ensure that the inputs for all goods and services are sustainably produced. Raw materials and supplies should come from sources that either are recycled or are produced in ways that enable them to regenerate and that do not violate the rights of animals or of nature. Every person in the company should be aware of where materials come from, how the source is replenished, and how the company tangibly supports and honors our living Earth.

4. Implement policies that ensure fair, living, and equitable compensation for all employees and other workers. Establish wage, bonus, and other compensation standards that minimize the gap between the lowest- and the highest-paid employees (for example, the highest-paid employee receives no more than three times the salary of the lowest-paid employee). Confirm that people working for partner, contractor, subcontractor, and supplier companies, or for offshore factories, receive fair and equitable living wages, and that the conditions in which they work meet the highest standards.

5. Recognize that to hire and retain the best and the brightest, the corporation must be dedicated to a life economy. Increasingly, employees want to work for companies that are doing good work. Research shows that members of generations X and Y desire to be part of creative endeavors that will support a living Earth for them and for future generations. Hire and nurture people who thrive on innovation and socially and environmentally responsible change, not the status quo.

6. Create management systems that encourage creativity, joy, and a sense of camaraderie and community. Make the transition from the command-and-control leadership paradigm to collaborative decision-making models. The trend toward management systems that are less hierarchical (or even nonhierarchical) has proven highly rewarding for individuals and organizations alike. Although this must be tailored to the specific company, it is important to recognize that traditional, linear management structures may not be effective in systems that are moving from a death economy to a life economy. Life thrives in diversity and community.

7. **Invest wisely** in full employment and in the community where the company operates, instead of in stock buybacks and other ventures that only help Wall Street. Invest in internal operations, such as updating data security systems to protect employee confidentiality and proprietary product information; finance companies that can contribute to your corporation's supply or marketing chain; and support recreational facilities, parks, and other projects that benefit the community.

8. **Take criticism from legitimate sources seriously.** Treat environmental and social criticisms and proposals from the media, stockholders, and other sources with respect and appreciation, and commit to taking actions that facilitate constant improvement. Encourage deep evaluation of all activities, recognizing that legitimate criticism, introspection, evaluation, and improvement benefit everyone and the company.

9. **Commit to diversity and inclusion throughout the company.** Embrace variety and diversity among employees, the board of directors, and the management team; in goods and services; and throughout the stakeholder community. Insist that all partner organizations and suppliers do the same. Recognize that monocultures seldom succeed and that diversity and inclusion will be the hallmark of future success stories.

10. **Support a culture of ethical behavior and accountability.** Encourage transparency and whistle-blowing rather than blind obedience and silence.

11. **Include in all your messaging the corporation's commitment to its mission** of serving the public interest and manifesting a life economy. This will become a powerful promotional tool. In addition to

advancing the company's self-interest, it also will inspire, encourage, and empower others to do the same.

FIVE THINGS ENTREPRENEURS CAN DO

1. Follow your heart. Choose an endeavor that fulfills your strongest passions and employs your greatest skills. Don't be swayed by the opinions of "experts," parents, teachers, or others who never tried to do what you know in your heart you want to do. Don't be afraid to offer something radically different from what you see around you, especially if it has the potential to improve current products or approaches. Dare to be great, and trust that greatness will channel through you!

2. Get started. The earlier the better. Recognize that the difference between a person who fails and one who succeeds is that the latter tried one more time. There are no mistakes, just lessons and opportunities to refine your approach, clarify your goals, and deepen your inspiration.

3. Build communities and networks that support you and a more holistic worldview (B Corps, Benefit Corps, social venture networks, for-profit/not-for-profit partnerships, and the like). Use these to inspire and encourage you and to help improve your supply chains, recruitment campaigns, and marketing. Enlist and empower other entrepreneurs. When college classmates, friends, and family see entrepreneurs thriving, it emboldens them to pursue their own passions.

4. Be the company you envision for the future. By establishing an inspirational approach to a sustainable business you manifest your own dream and set an example that will empower others. Approaches for doing this include the way you hire and retain employees, the products and services you offer, the resources you use, the commitment you make to encouraging activities which regenerate depleted resources and ravaged environments, and the contributions you make to your community.

5. Undertake the eleven actions outlined in "Eleven Things Corporations Can Do," once you find yourself running a company.

Documentation of Economic Hit Man Activity, 2004–2015

The aim of this section is to supply chronological documentation of the scope and reach of the EHM system in the years since *Confessions of an Economic Hit Man* was first published. Among the following items are reports by nonprofit organizations and government bodies, leaked documents and other confidential materials, journalistic investigations, and more. Some items focus on a single, specific instance of EHM activity; others document systematic actions by a variety of entities over long periods. This list is not meant to be comprehensive but rather to illustrate the extent to which the EHM system infiltrates every aspect of our global economy.

I either have quoted directly from articles and reports or have summarized and paraphrased their content, and I have identified key points in **boldface**. I have not attempted to verify the information provided or the conclusions reached by these sources. Thus, the analyses, opinions, and conclusions presented below are those of the authors, publications, and websites referenced, not my own. I leave it to you to arrive at your own conclusions.

2004

- A United Nations study argues that tied aid is "strangling" nations, as reported by the Inter Press Service news agency: "Donor money that comes with strings attached cuts the value of aid to recipient countries 25–40 percent, because it obliges them to purchase uncompetitively priced imports from the richer nations, says a new UN study on African economies.... **'The United States makes sure that 80 cents in every aid dollar is returned to the home country,'** says Njoki Njoroge Njehu, director of 50 Years is Enough, a coalition of over 200 grassroots non-governmental organizations."
  www.ipsnews.net/2004/07/development-tied-aid-strangling-nations-says-un

- Rights and Accountability in Development (RAID) releases a report that follows up on an earlier series of United Nations reports that

309

documented "the links between business, resource exploitation, and conflict" in the Democratic Republic of the Congo. The RAID report, titled *Unanswered Questions: Companies, Conflict and the Democratic Republic of the Congo*, includes a section examining the banking sector, which cites (among other infractions) the United Nations allegation that "MIBA [Societé Minière de Bakwanga, the state-owned diamond mining company] accounts held by Belgolaise Bank have been used to conduct financial transactions involving the purchase of armaments by the Government of the DRC."

www.raid-uk.org/sites/default/files/unanswered-qq.pdf

United Nations report:

daccess-dds-ny.un.org/doc/UNDOC/GEN/N03/567/36/IMG/
    N0356736.pdf

United Nations press release on the report:

www.un.org/apps/news/story.asp?NewsID=8706

- Global Justice Now (formerly the World Development Movement) releases a report titled *Zambia: Condemned to Debt — How the IMF and World Bank Have Undermined Development*. The report "clearly demonstrates that the IMF and World Bank's involvement in Zambia has been unsuccessful, undemocratic, and unfair. The evidence suggests that the past twenty years of IMF and World Bank intervention have exacerbated rather than ameliorated Zambia's debt crisis. Ironically, in return for debt relief, Zambia is required to do more of the same."

www.globaljustice.org.uk/sites/default/files/files/resources/
    zambia01042004.pdf

2005

- In *The Great American Jobs Scam* (San Francisco: Berrett-Koehler, 2005), Greg LeRoy exposes the "$50 billion-a-year scam in which — in the name of 'job creation' — corporations play states and cities against each other to win hefty taxpayer subsidies that routinely exceed $100,000 per job." Later, LeRoy's organization Good Jobs First releases a "Megadeals" report identifying 240 corporate subsidy awards "with a total state and local cost of $75 million or more each" — more than $64 billion cumulatively. These are subsidies designed to attract or keep industry (and jobs), but which in fact function as legal bribery, to the tune of an average of $456,000 per job. These deals are made possible by some of the most brazen EHMs working today: so-called site location consultants, people who "present themselves as indispensable middlemen between communities seeking investments and companies deciding where to locate new facilities." Site location consultants are paid as much as 30 percent of the final subsidy package, giving them a **perverse incentive to force state and local governments into offering outrageous packages that are worth far more than the corporation can return in jobs and taxes.**

www.greatamericanjobsscam.com

www.goodjobsfirst.org/megadeals

www.goodjobsfirst.org/corporate-subsidy-watch/
site-location-consultants

- Global Justice Now releases a report titled *One Size for All: A Study of IMF and World Bank Poverty Reduction Strategies.* Following widespread criticism of the "structural adjustment conditionalities" imposed by the World Bank and the IMF on economically developing countries, the World Bank announced a new approach to promote local ownership of the process: Poverty Reduction Strategy Papers. The Global Justice Now report analyzes the content of fifty such PRSPs and finds that **the policies contained within them are in fact "remarkably similar" to the harmful policies of previous structural adjustment programs.**

www.globaljustice.org.uk/sites/default/files/files/resources/
onesizeforall01092005.pdf

2006

- William Easterly, a professor of economics and former research economist at the World Bank, publishes *The White Man's Burden: Why the West's Efforts to Aid the Rest Have Done So Much Ill and So Little Good* (New York: Penguin, 2006). An American Library Association review by Bryce Christensen describes it as follows: "Though he acknowledges that such projects have succeeded in some tasks—reducing infant mortality, for example—Easterly adduces sobering evidence that **Western nations have accomplished depressingly little with the trillions they have spent on foreign aid.** That evidence suggests that in some countries—including Haiti, Zaire, and Angola—**foreign aid has actually intensified the suffering of the poor.** By examining the tortured history of several aid initiatives, he shows how blind and arrogant Western aid officers have imposed on helpless clients a **postmodern neocolonialism of political manipulation and economic dependency**, stifling democracy and local enterprise in the process."

http://williameasterly.org/books/the-white-mans-burden

■ The World Bank approves $215 million in loans and grants to support an Ethiopian health services project; in 2009, financial support is extended by an additional $540 million. According to insiders, as reported in a 2015 article by the *Huffington Post* and the International Consortium of Investigative Journalists, tens of millions of dollars are diverted from the World Bank funds to support Ethiopia's "villagization" effort — a process marked by **intimidation, violence, and rape**, according to a 2012 report by Human Rights Watch called *"Waiting Here for Death": Forced Displacement and "Villagization" in Ethiopia's Gambella Region*.

http://projects.huffingtonpost.com/worldbank-evicted-abandoned/
    new-evidence-ties-worldbank-to-human-rights-abuses-ethiopia
www.hrw.org/sites/default/files/reports/ethiopia0112webwcover_
    0.pdf

2007

■ A World Bank–funded project in Kenya's Cherangani Hills leads to the **forced eviction of thousands of indigenous Sengwer people**, according to an investigation by the *Huffington Post* and the International Consortium of Investigative Journalists, published in 2015. Advocates for the Sengwer say that "the bank's funding of the project put the Sengwer in danger because the project redrew the Cherangani Hills' protected Forest Reserve in a way that included thousands of them inside the reserve's boundaries," thereby giving the Kenyan authorities a "pretext for evicting them." Furthermore, "cash from the World Bank also provided the equipment the KFS [Kenya Forest Service] needed to launch its mass eviction campaign."

http://projects.huffingtonpost.com/worldbank-evicted-abandoned/
    worldbank-projects-leave-trail-misery-around-globe-kenya

■ **Zambia is forced to pay $15.5 million to vulture fund Donegal International** for a loan Zambia took out from Romania in 1979, which Donegal bought from Romania in 1999 for $3.2 million. Donegal had been suing for $55 million.

http://news.bbc.co.uk/2/hi/business/6589287.stm

2008

■ In *A Game As Old As Empire* (San Francisco: Berrett-Koehler, 2008), edited by Steven Hiatt, twelve distinguished authors explore the many facets of modern-day economic hit men and the devastating consequences of the corporatocracy.

www.bkconnection.com/books/title/a-game-as-old-as-empire

■ **EHMs cause a global financial crisis.** On September 16, 2008, the failures caused by large US financial institutions – experienced by the exposure of subprime loans and credit default swaps – devolve into a global economic crisis, European bank failures, and stock value reductions worldwide. These and other factors contribute to a global recession that many consider to be the worst since the Great Depression.

www.bloomberg.com/bw/stories/2008-10-10/stock-market-crash-
understanding-the-panicbusinessweek-business-news-stock-
market-and-financial-advice

www.telegraph.co.uk/finance/financialcrisis/3174151/Financial-
crisis-US-stock-markets-suffer-worst-week-on-record.html

■ The European Network on Debt and Development (Eurodad), a network of fifty-one nongovernmental organizations from sixteen European countries, releases a report titled *Critical Conditions: The IMF Maintains Its Grip on Low-Income Governments.* "This report finds that since the Conditionality Guidelines were approved, the IMF has not managed to decrease the number of structural conditions attached to their development lending. Moreover, the Fund continues to make heavy use of highly sensitive conditions, such as privatization and liberalization. Eurodad's analysis finds that **a quarter of all the conditions in Fund loans approved after 2002 still contain privatisation or liberalisation reforms.**"

www.eurodad.org/uploadedfiles/whats_new/reports/critical_
conditions.pdf

■ The Jubilee USA Network releases a briefing note titled *Are IMF and World Bank Economic Policy Conditions Undermining the Impact of Debt Cancellation?* "[Twelve] years since the inception of the Heavily Indebted Poor Countries Initiative (HIPC) in 1996, the main debt relief program at the World Bank and IMF, the initiative suffers from serious flaws. Among them are the **harmful economic policy requirements attached to both debt relief and lending from the IMF and**

World Bank. These harmful policy requirements… are undermining and sometimes even negating the benefits of debt cancellation.… These requirements often hurt the poorest and most vulnerable people and should be stopped immediately to enable debt relief to meet its life saving promise."

www.jubileeusa.org/fileadmin/user_upload/Resources/Policy_
Archive/208briefnoteconditionality.pdf

■ In an article for the *Nation*, James S. Henry, a senior adviser to the Tax Justice Network and author of *The Blood Bankers: Tales from the Global Underground Economy* (New York: Four Walls Eight Windows, 2003), recounts the staggering extent of the offshore financial industry. From the article: "In the last thirty years, fueled by the globalization of financial services, lousy lending, capital flight and mind-boggling corruption, **a relatively small number of major banks, law firms, accounting firms, asset managers, insurance companies and hedge funds have come to launder and conceal at least $10 trillion to $15 trillion of private untaxed anonymous cross-border wealth.**"

www.thenation.com/article/attack-global-pirate-bankers

2009

■ The International Policy Centre for Inclusive Growth releases a one-pager examining IMF policy prescriptions and conditionalities. Titled *Is the Washington Consensus Dead?*, the paper describes the harmful effects of conditionalities in no uncertain terms: "The simple truth is that **conditionalities are paternalistic. They are meant to alter behaviour and induce changes in economic, political and social structures. They also serve as a sort of collateral; in some cases they are a form of coercion to ensure adoption of otherwise unpalatable reforms.**"

www.ipc-undp.org/pub/IPCOnePager82.pdf

■ **More proof that economic hit men continue to manipulate economic forecasts to "sell" IMF policies.** The Center for Economic and Policy Research releases a report titled *IMF-Supported Macroeconomic Policies and the World Recession: A Look at Forty-One Borrowing Countries*, which examines Stand-By Arrangements, Poverty Reduction and Growth Facilities, and Exogenous Shocks Facilities between the IMF and forty-one countries. "The paper finds that 31 of the 41 agreements contain pro-cyclical macroeconomic policies. These are either pro-cyclical fiscal or monetary policies — or in 15 cases, both — that, in the face of a significant slowdown in growth or in a recession, would be expected to exacerbate the downturn.... **In many cases the Fund's pro-cyclical policies were based on over-optimistic assumptions about economic growth.** For example, of the 26 countries that have had at least one review, **11 IMF reports had to lower previous forecasts of real GDP growth by at least 3 percentage points, and three of those had to correct forecasts that were at least 7 percentage points overestimated.** Most likely there will be more downward revisions to come."

www.cepr.net/documents/publications/imf-2009-10.pdf

■ Jackals are alive and as active as ever. Honduran President Manuel Zelaya is ousted in what some allege is a **CIA-supported coup d'état.** Shortly after the coup, the *New York Times* reports on US administration denials of CIA involvement; two years later, the former culture minister of Honduras, Rodolfo Pastor Fasquelle, outlines US involvement on *Democracy Now!*, using cables released by WikiLeaks as evidence.

www.nytimes.com/2009/06/30/world/americas/30honduras.html

www.democracynow.org/2011/6/1/former_honduran_minister_us_
undoubtedly_played

www.democracynow.org/2015/7/28/clinton_the_coup_amid_
protests_in

■ The *Guardian* publishes leaked memos from Barclays bank that purport to reveal "a number of elaborate international tax avoidance schemes by the SCM (Structured Capital Markets) division of Barclays." According to these documents, **Barclays is alleged to have been "systematically assisting clients to avoid huge amounts of tax they should be liable for across multiple jurisdictions."** Barclays obtained a court injunction that night, forcing the *Guardian* to remove the documents from its Web archive. WikiLeaks releases the original leaked memos and describes the circumstances.

www.WikiLeaks.org/wiki/The_Guardian:_Censored_Barclays_tax_
avoidance_leaked_memos%2C_16_Mar_2009

■ Israeli billionaire Dan Gertler is alleged to have earned a 500 percent return as a middleman on a mining deal in the Democratic Republic of the Congo, and is **alleged to have cheated the DRC's government out of $60 million** (one of Gertler's many dealings in the DRC, as detailed by Bloomberg.com).

www.bloomberg.com/news/articles/2012-12-05/
gertler-earns-billions-as-mine-deals-leave-congo-poorest

■ An op-ed in the *Guardian* likens the International Monetary Fund to a cold-blooded murderer in the way it punishes developing economies. On the IMF's actions against Latvia: "Latvia missed a 200 million euro disbursement from the IMF in March for not cutting its budget enough. According to press reports, the government wants to run a budget deficit of 7 percent of GDP for this year, and the IMF wants 5 percent. Latvia is already cutting its budget by 40 percent, and is planning to close some public hospitals and schools in order to make the IMF's targets, prompting street protests."

www.theguardian.com/commentisfree/cifamerica/2009/may/13/
imf-us-congress-aid

2010

■ WikiLeaks releases vast numbers of documents and files related to the wars in Iraq and Afghanistan; the collections become known as the "war logs." As summarized on Alternet.org: "These 'Afghan War Logs,' like the Iraqi war logs after them, and much material in WikiLeaks' recent release of diplomatic cables, reveal above all that **US Executive war-making is marked by massive deception of the American people** — particularly lying about (1) the enormous civilian casualties the US is causing and (2) its claim to be pursuing a 'counter-insurgency strategy' designed to install a democratic Afghan government. The *Times* and *Guardian* stories describe how these official US documents reveal constant US Executive Branch lying to the American people."

www.alternet.org/story/149393/WikiLeaks%27_most_terrifying_
revelation%3A_just_how_much_our_government_lies_to_us

■ In the *Citizens United v. Federal Election Commission* decision, the US Supreme Court declares "the corporate expenditure ban unconstitutional, holding that **independent expenditures [can] not be constitutionally limited in federal elections**, and implicitly that corporations [can] give unlimited amounts to other groups to spend, as long as the expenditures [are] made independently from the supported candidate" — thus giving rise to the super PAC.

www.cnn.com/2012/02/15/opinion/wertheimer-super-pacs

■ Global Justice Now releases a report titled *The Great Hunger Lottery: How Banking Speculation Causes Food Crises*. The report examines the "astonishing surge in staple food prices over the course of 2007–2008, when millions went hungry and food riots swept major cities around the world," and shows how this crisis "was fueled by the behavior of financial speculators." **Continued speculation on food commodities "has led to food prices becoming unaffordable for low-income families around the world,** particularly in developing countries highly reliant on food imports."

www.globaljustice.org.uk/sites/default/files/files/resources/hunger_
lottery_report_6.10.pdf

■ ProPublica launches an investigation (ongoing through 2015) into the Wall Street "money machine," exploring how Wall Street "took advantage of complicated mortgage-based instruments to reap billions, only to exacerbate the eventual crash." One of its more recent articles (published in April 2014) examined the conviction of former investment banker Kareem Serageldin and attempted to understand "why **the largest man-made economic catastrophe since the Depression resulted in the jailing of a single investment banker** – one who happened to be several rungs from the corporate suite at a second-tier financial institution."

www.propublica.org/series/the-wall-street-money-machine

www.propublica.org/article/the-rise-of-corporate-impunity

■ *Mother Jones* documents the US government's longtime kowtowing to big oil in an article titled *US Government, Brought to You By Big Oil*. The article provides extensive evidence in support of the argument that **"the oil companies not only write their own regulations and perform their own oversight; they also set energy policy and draft laws."**

www.motherjones.com/mojo/2010/06/us-government-brought-
you-big-oil

■ **Vulture funds' debt repayment suit steals Liberian funds earmarked for much-needed postconflict development.** In the same year that Liberia is awarded $4.6 billion in debt relief from the International Monetary Fund and the World Bank, the country is forced to settle with Hamsah Investment and Wall Capital, two so-called vulture funds, which sued Liberia in 2009 for a $6.5 million loan originally taken out from US-based Chemical Bank in 1978. The amount

the vulture funds were suing for purportedly climbed to a whopping
$43 million by 2010; Liberia agreed to settle for just over 3 percent of
that amount.

www.bbc.com/news/world-africa-11819276

2011

- Eurodad releases a report titled *How to Spend It: Smart Procurement
  for More Effective Aid*, which condemns "tied aid" and estimates that,
  of $69 billion annually, "more than 50 percent of total official develop-
  ment assistance is spent on procuring goods and services for development projects from external providers.... 'Tying aid' to the condition
  that all purchases are made from firms from donor countries is the
  least effective form of procurement. It turns aid into boomerang aid:
  a financial flow that is only channelled to developing countries on
  the books. Although first agreements to untie aid were signed at the
  OECD [Organisation for Economic Co-operation and Development]
  in 2001... about 20 percent of bilateral aid is still formally tied. Development projects funded with tied aid are also 15 to 40 percent more
  expensive. Furthermore, in reality **the majority of formally untied
  aid contracts from bilateral agencies also go to donor country
  firms. Two-thirds are awarded to firms from OECD countries,
  and 60 percent 'in country,' to firms from the donor country that
  funds a project.**"

  www.theguardian.com/global-development/2011/sep/07/
    aid-benefits-donor-countries-companies

  The full report can be found on Eurodad's website:
  http://eurodad.org/files/pdf/5284d26056f24.pdf

- WikiLeaks releases the "PetroCaribe Files," documenting "how **the
  US tried — and failed — to scuttle a Venezuelan oil deal** even though
  it would bring huge benefits to Haiti's impoverished people."

  www.thenation.com/article/161056/petrocaribe-files

- A cable released by WikiLeaks "shows how **US and international
  donors pushed ahead with a rigged presidential election**" in Haiti.

  www.thenation.com/article/161216/WikiLeaks-haiti-cable-
    depicts-fraudulent-haiti-election

- A leading newspaper in Nigeria, *ThisDay*, reported that **the US State
  Department, in conjunction with Shell Oil, planted operatives**

within the government to influence domestic and foreign policy. According to *ThisDay*, "Shell's top executive in Nigeria told US diplomats that Shell had seconded employees to every relevant department and so knew 'everything that was being done in those ministries.' She also reportedly boasted that the government had 'forgotten' about the extent of Shell's infiltration and were unaware of how much the company knew about its deliberations."

http://beforeitsnews.com/african-american-news/2011/01/
after-WikiLeaks-u-s-outlines-africa-priorities-amid-revelations-
338594.html

- Khalil Nakhleh, a former development worker and consultant in Palestine, publishes a book titled *Globalized Palestine: The National Sell-Out of a Homeland* (Ewing Township, NJ: Red Sea Press, 2011). According to the Amazon.com description: "The book asserts that aid advanced to Palestine under occupation is political aid par excellence, advanced to the Palestinians specifically to acquiesce and submit to an imposed political agenda and program. **It shackles, mortgages, and holds hostage the entire current society and future generations in political and economic debt.** It is aid that focuses on consumption and mortgaging people. It is aid that is anti-production and anti-liberation."

www.amazon.com/Globalized-Palestine-National-Sell-Out-Homeland/
dp/1569023557

- Global Justice Now releases a report titled *Power to the People? How the World Bank-Financed Wind Farms Fail Communities in Mexico*. By examining the case study of the La Mata and La Ventosa wind farm in Oaxaca – the World Bank's "flagship Clean Technology Fund (CTF) project in Mexico" – the report "shows that **the CTF is a flawed model for climate financing,** with inherent biases towards funding energy utilities and the private sector in middle income countries. In dispersing loans rather than grants, **the CTF risks loading further debt onto poorer countries** contrary to the original purpose of climate financing." Regarding the La Mata and La Ventosa wind farm specifically, the report finds that all of the electricity created by the project will be "sold at a discounted rate to Walmart," that the project "**misrepresented its finances** to gain additional funding from the UN's Clean Development Mechanism," and that the project will be used to promote further private sector wind projects in the Isthmus of Tehuantepec – projects that "have met with considerable local resistance…

amidst concerns that they form part of an attempt 'to **grab indigenous lands** and convert them into resources for the market.'"

www.globaljustice.org.uk/sites/default/files/files/resources/mexico_
oaxaca_la_ventosa_-_final.pdf

■ Global Justice Now releases a report titled *Broken Markets: How Financial Market Regulations Can Help Prevent Another Global Food Crisis.* The report "shows how financial speculation has boomed, turning commodity derivatives into just another asset class for investors, distorting and undermining the effective functioning of agricultural markets. It shows how **the changes in the financial markets translate into changes in the prices of food, and the devastating impact this has had on the world's poorest people.**"

www.globaljustice.org.uk/sites/default/files/files/resources/
broken-markets.pdf

■ "Did Lobbying Cause the Financial Crisis?" asks a headline in the *Economist.* The answer — *It seems so, yes* — comes from a paper, written by three IMF economists and published in the National Bureau of Economic Research, titled *A Fistful of Dollars: Lobbying and the Financial Crisis.* The paper establishes a strong correlation between lobby activity, deregulation, riskier loans, and ultimately — after it all went wrong — bailouts. As described in the *Economist,* the paper finds that "**banks were an active participant in deregulation, pushing for weaker rules that allowed all those ill-advised mortgage loans....** The IMF economists found that lenders that lobbied the most also tended to make riskier loans. They also found that the areas of the country dominated by lenders who spent the most lobbying dollars also tended to have higher rates of default. Lastly, if you thought there was connection between Washington connections and bailouts, you would be right as well. The economists found that **the firms that lobbied the most were also the most likely to get bailout cash.**"

http://business.time.com/2011/05/26/did-lobbying-cause-the-
financial-crisis/print

www.nber.org/papers/w17076

■ **The Democratic Republic of the Congo narrowly escapes being forced to repay an illegal $100 million debt to an American vulture fund.** FG Hemisphere wins a suit in the Jersey Islands against the country, and the court awards $100 million on a debt that the fund originally purchased for a $3 million. Happily, however, in the following year, the purchase is proven to be illegal, and the UK Privy Council rules in a final judgment that the vulture fund cannot collect the $100 million award. This ruling, unfortunately, came too late to prevent the DRC from being forced to settle with another American vulture fund, Red Mountain Finance, in 2002; the DRC agreed to pay $8 million on a debt that Red Mountain reportedly bought for $800,000, and for which they then sued for $27 million.

http://cadtm.org/FG-Hemisphere-vulture-fund-s

www.bbc.com/news/business-18894874

www.jubileeusa.org/vulturefunds/vulture-fund-country-studies.html

■ A team of complex system theorists at the Swiss Federal Institute of Technology in Zurich identifies a **"super-entity" of a mere 147 gigantic transnational corporations that control 40 percent of global operating revenues.** Most of these are financial institutions, according to the research. The scientists describe the map of economic power as a "bow tie," with a strongly concentrated core.

www.newscientist.com/article/mg21228354.500-revealed-the-
    capitalist-network-that-runs-the-world.html#.VYzJhqYyFLj

http://arxiv.org/PS_cache/arxiv/pdf/1107/1107.5728v2.pdf

2012

■ Investigative journalist Greg Palast exposes the **seedy connections between the oil industry, the banking industry, and governmental agencies** in his book *Vultures' Picnic: In Pursuit of Petroleum Pigs, Power Pirates, and High-Finance Carnivores* (New York: Plume, 2012). The book reveals "how environmental disasters like the Gulf oil spill, the *Exxon Valdez*, and lesser-known tragedies such as Tatitlek and *Torrey Canyon* are caused by corporate corruption, failed legislation, and, most interestingly, veiled connections between the financial industry and energy titans." Palast condemns the International Monetary Fund, the World Bank, the World Trade Organization, and central banks as "puppets for big oil."

www.gregpalast.com/vulturespicnic

■ Following the one-year anniversary of the start of Occupy Wall Street, *Bloomberg* reports that "in 2010, **the top 1 percent of US families captured as much as 93 percent of the nation's income growth,** according to a March paper by Emmanuel Saez, a University of California at Berkeley economist who studied Internal Revenue Service data."

www.bloomberg.com/news/articles/2012-10-02/top-1-got-93-of-income-growth-as-rich-poor-gap-widened

■ Indian political activist Arundhati Roy argues that **corporate philanthropy is just another method of control and influence**, in her article "Capitalism: A Ghost Story," published in *Outlook India*. From the article: "As the IMF enforced Structural Adjustment, and arm-twisted governments into cutting back on public spending on health, education, childcare, development, the NGOs [nongovernmental organizations] moved in. The Privatisation of Everything has also meant the NGO-isation of Everything. As jobs and livelihoods disappeared, NGOs have become an important source of employment, even for those who see them for what they are.... [T]he corporate or Foundation-endowed NGOs are global finance's way of buying into resistance movements, literally like shareholders buy shares in companies, and then try to control them from within."

www.outlookindia.com/article/capitalism-a-ghost-story/280234

■ The Libor scandal reveals **"a widespread plot by multiple banks—** most notably Deutsche Bank, Barclays, UBS, Rabobank, and the Royal Bank of Scotland—**to manipulate [Libor] interest rates for profit starting as far back as 2003.** In 2015, investigations continued to implicate major institutions, exposing them to civil lawsuits and shaking trust in the global financial system." A former trader for Morgan Stanley suggests that "the misreporting of Libor rates may have been common practice since at least 1991."

www.cfr.org/united-kingdom/understanding-libor-scandal/p28729

www.informath.org/media/a72/b1.pdf

■ ProPublica launches a series of reports called *Buying Your Vote: Dark Money and Big Data*. Initial investigations focus on campaign spending during the 2012 presidential election. Ongoing investigations through 2015 include reports on the rise of super PACs, the "Kochtopus" (the purportedly vast and shadowy network of institutions financed by the Koch brothers), and loopholes in campaign finance laws. Collectively, these reports illustrate **the frightening influence of corporate lobbying on public policy.**

www.propublica.org/series/buying-your-vote

■ Global Justice Now releases a briefing that describes how **UK aid "is being used to encourage private sector involvement in developing** countries, whether this is in the form of supporting pro-market policies or directly channeling aid money through companies." The briefing includes mention of £11 billion in UK aid support for the World Bank's creation of "special economic zones" in Bangladesh, including "export processing zones," which "are essentially onshore tax havens for multinational companies." According to this report, new special economic zones would restrict trade union activities and freedom of association.

www.globaljustice.org.uk/sites/default/files/files/resources/
supporter_briefing_print.pdf

■ An internal review by the World Bank for nine of its projects shows that **the bank systematically underestimates the number of people who will be adversely affected** by its development initiatives: "The number of affected people turned out to be, on average, 32 percent higher than the figure reported by the bank before approving the initiatives, understating the number of people affected by the nine projects by 77,500." A 1994 internal review examined 192 projects and found that "the real number of affected people averaged 47 percent higher than previously estimated."

http://projects.huffingtonpost.com/worldbank-evicted-abandoned/
india-uncounted

2013

■ A *New York Times* DealBook article, "How Mandela Shifted Views on Freedom of Markets," by Andrew Ross Sorkin, reveals how, during Mandela's trip to Davos for a meeting of the World Economic Forum, **proponents of the EHM system convinced Nelson Mandela to open up South Africa's markets, fueling growing inequality in South Africa** from 1993 to the present. Mandela's decision allowed international corporations to stake major claims in South African companies, Sorkin reports. "Barclays, for example, acquired Absa, South Africa's largest consumer bank, in 2005. Iscor, the country's largest steel maker, was sold to Lakshmi Mittal's LNM in 2004. Industrial and Commercial Bank of China bought a big stake in Standard Bank, South Africa's largest financial services company, in 2008. And Massmart, a South African supermarket chain, sold a majority stake to Walmart in 2011."

http://dealbook.nytimes.com/2013/12/09/how-mandela-shifted-
views-on-freedom-of-markets/?_r=1

- JPMorgan Chase reaches a $13 billion settlement with the US Justice Department and purportedly admits that "it, along with every other large US bank, had **engaged in mortgage fraud as a routine business practice**, sowing the seeds of the mortgage meltdown."

  www.globalresearch.ca/jpmorgan-chase-engaged-in-mortgage-fraud-the-securitization-fraud-that-collapsed-the-housing-market/5371764

- **Corporations' influence in Washington:** The *New York Times* reports on a bill that was allegedly written, essentially, by Citigroup: "One bill that sailed through the House Financial Services Committee this month — over the objections of the Treasury Department — was essentially Citigroup's, according to e-mails reviewed by the *New York Times*. The bill would exempt broad swathes of trades from new regulation."

  http://dealbook.nytimes.com/2013/05/23/banks-lobbyists-help-in-drafting-financial-bills/?_r=2

- Inclusive Development International, the International Accountability Project, the Bank Information Center, and Habitat International Coalition–Housing and Land Rights Network submit a report to the World Bank Safeguards Review titled *Reforming the World Bank Policy on Involuntary Settlement*. The report states that **the price being paid by people affected by the World Bank's approach to forced evictions** "**is unconscionably high.** Large-scale resettlement has been shown — time and again — to be an exceedingly difficult activity to do in a manner that upholds human rights, and one that results in **extreme poverty and injustice for affected people.**"

  www.mediafire.com/view/yjluyteklkm7wfo/Reforming%20the%20World%20Bank%20Policy%20on%20Involuntary%20Resettlement.pdf

- Global Justice Now releases a report titled *Banking While Borneo Burns: How the UK Financial Sector Is Bankrolling Indonesia's Fossil Fuel Boom*. The report analyzes the finance behind the Indonesian fossil fuel industry, which has had devastating social, economic, and environmental effects on Indonesia's people and land. Findings draw **a direct link between "the equity issues, syndicated loans and flotations"** of the UK financial sector and the "**evictions, deforestation and climate change on the ground.**" A second report by the same organization focuses on a single project: "BHP Billiton is planning to build a series of massive coal mines that would destroy primary rain forest, deprive indigenous peoples of their customary land, and pollute water resources relied on by up to 1 million people."

www.globaljustice.org.uk/sites/default/files/files/resources/
banking_while_borneo_burns_0.pdf

www.globaljustice.org.uk/sites/default/files/files/resources/
indo-met_project_factsheet_lowrez.pdf

- Global Justice Now releases a briefing on coal exploitation in the Cerrejón mine in Colombia. Expansion of the mine has led to human rights abuses (including the destruction of villages and the exploitation of cheap labor), and the coal that is extracted "is almost exclusively for export to rich countries." The briefing calculates that the three owners of the mine (BHP Billiton, Anglo American, and Xstrata) have been **financed by British banks, investors, and pension funds** (including Barclays, HSBC, Lloyds, and the Royal Bank of Scotland) to the tune of approximately £25 billion since 2009.

www.globaljustice.org.uk/sites/default/files/files/resources/
cerrejon_media_briefing.pdf

- Global Justice Now releases a briefing titled *Web of Power: The UK Government and the Energy-Finance Complex Fuelling Climate Change*. The report reveals that "one third of ministers in the UK government are linked to the finance and energy companies driving climate change." **The size and entrenched nature of the "energy-finance complex" is driven home with staggering numbers:** £900 billion (the value of fossil fuel shares on the London Stock Exchange; higher than the GDP of all of sub-Saharan Africa) and **£170 billion** (the value of bonds and share issues underwritten by the top five UK banks from 2010 to 2012; "more than 11 times the amount the UK contributed in climate finance for developing countries").

www.globaljustice.org.uk/sites/default/files/files/resources/web_
of_power_media_briefing.pdf

- In "HRC and the Vulture Fund: Making Third World Poverty Pay for LGBT Rights," human rights activist and scholar Scott Long examines the ugly source of a $3 million donation to the Human Rights Campaign, the largest US gay organization. The donation comes from two big contributors to the Republican Party; one is Paul Singer, who runs a vulture fund that supposedly "makes profits from the debt incurred by Third World countries . . . and from the misery it causes their citizens." Long examines what could be called the insidious nature of vulture funds and their effects: "Vulture funds operate by buying up a

THE NEW CONFESSIONS OF AN ECONOMIC HIT MAN

country's distressed debt just as the original lenders are about to write
it off — usually, as the *Guardian* describes it, when the country 'is in a
state of chaos. When the country has stabilised, vulture funds return
to demand millions of dollars in interest repayments and fees on the
original debt.'" According to Jubilee USA, **"As of late 2011, 16 of 40
Heavily Indebted Poor Countries (HIPC) surveyed by the International Monetary Fund were facing litigation in 78 individual cases
brought by commercial creditors. Of these, 36 cases have resulted
in court judgments against HIPCs amounting to approximately $1
billion on original claims worth roughly $500 million."**

http://paper-bird.net/2013/11/04/hrc-and-the-vulture-fund-making-
  third-world-poverty-pay-for-lgbt-rights

www.theguardian.com/global-development/2011/nov/15/
  vulture-funds-jersey-decision

www.jubileeusa.org/ourwork/vulturefunds.html

■ ProPublica launches a series of investigative reports into Goldman
  Sachs and the Federal Reserve Bank of New York, using audio record-
  ings made secretly by then–Fed examiner Carmen Segarra. Segarra
  claims she was fired for refusing to assert the validity of Goldman
  Sachs's conflict-of-interest policy, despite facing pressure, among
  other disagreements. The "Fed tapes" investigation (ongoing through
  2015) reveals **a damning history of the Fed's "deference" to Wall
  Street**.

www.propublica.org/series/fed-tapes

■ James S. Henry, a senior adviser to the Tax Justice Network and
  author of *The Blood Bankers* (New York: Four Walls Eight Windows,
  2003), discusses how **tax havens and offshore banking cripple
  developing nations** in a TEDx-RadboudU talk.

https://www.youtube.com/watch?v=znYA0yIQMqO

■ Eurodad releases a report titled *Going Offshore: How Development
  Finance Institutions Support Companies Using the World's Most Secretive
  Financial Centres*. From the executive summary: **"Developing countries lose billions of dollars every year through tax avoidance and
  evasion.** Tax havens play a pivotal role in this by providing low or no
  taxation and by promising secrecy, allowing businesses to dodge taxes
  and remain largely unaccountable for their actions. Development
  Finance Institutions (DFIs) are government-controlled institutions

that, as this report shows, often support private sector projects that are routed through tax havens, using scarce public money. By supporting projects in this way, DFIs are helping to reinforce the offshore industry as they are providing income and legitimacy."

www.eurodad.org/goingoffshore

- Eurodad releases a report titled *Hidden Profits: The EU's Role in Supporting an Unjust Global Tax System 2014*. The report compares each country "with its fellow EU member states on four critical issues: the fairness of their tax treaties with developing countries; their willingness to put an end to anonymous shell companies and trusts; their support for increasing the transparency of economic activities and tax payments of transnational companies; and their attitude towards letting the poorest countries get a seat at the table when global tax standards are negotiated." Findings include evidence that "practices which facilitate tax dodging by transnational corporations and individuals are widely used, in some cases so governments can claim to be 'tax competitive.' This is creating a 'race to the bottom' — meaning that **many countries are driving down standards to try to attract transnational corporations to their countries.** Some of the countries that have been most successful in attracting companies — Ireland, Luxembourg and the Netherlands — are also currently under investigation by the European Commission for **making competition-distorting arrangements with transnational companies behind closed doors.**"

www.eurodad.org/hiddenprofits

- Global Justice Now releases a report titled *Carving Up a Continent: How the UK Government Is Facilitating the Corporate Takeover of African Food Systems*. The report describes how UK aid monies purported to "support improvements to agriculture and food security in Africa... are in fact geared towards helping multinational companies to access resources and bringing about policy changes to facilitate those countries' expansion in Africa." The report reveals evidence that "**the pro-corporate approach of [such] initiatives... is likely to exacerbate hunger and poverty** through increased land-grabbing, insecure and poorly paid jobs, the privatisation of seed and a focus on producing for export markets rather than to feed local populations."

www.globaljustice.org.uk/sites/default/files/files/resources/
  carving_up_a_continent_report_web.pdf

- Martin Gilens, a professor of politics at Princeton University, and Benjamin Page, a professor of decision making at Northwestern

University, publish an article in *Perspectives and Politics* demonstrating evidence that "**economic elites and organized groups representing business interests have substantial independent impacts on US government policy, while mass-based interest groups and average citizens have little or no independent influence.**"

http://scholar.princeton.edu/sites/default/files/mgilens/files/ gilens_and_page_2014_-testing_theories_of_american_politics .doc.pdf

■ WikiLeaks releases documents revealing that Australian prime minister Tony Abbott is moving forward with "**secret trade negotiations aimed at bringing about radical deregulation of Australia's banking and finance sector.**" As the *Sydney Morning Herald* reports, "Highly sensitive details of the Trade in Services Agreement (TiSA) negotiations ... show Australian trade negotiators are working on a financial services agenda that could end the Australian government's 'four pillars' banking policy and allow foreign banks much greater freedom to operate in Australia. It could also see Australians' bank account and financial data freely transferred overseas, and allow an influx of foreign financial and information technology workers."

www.theage.com.au/federal-politics/political-news/secret-deal-bank- freeforall-20140619-3ah2w.html

■ Big bank traders are exposed for **manipulating foreign exchange rates**; evidence against them includes chat groups called the Bandits' Club, the Mafia, and the Cartel, in which they apparently brag about rate fixing. As reported by CNN: "Citigroup, Barclays, JPMorgan Chase, and Royal Bank of Scotland were fined more than $2.5 billion by the US after pleading guilty to conspiring to manipulate the price of dollars and euros. The four banks, plus UBS, have also been fined $1.6 billion by the Federal Reserve, and Barclays will pay regulators another $1.3 billion to settle related claims. The first four banks operated what they described as 'The Cartel' from as early as 2007, using online chat rooms and coded language to influence the twice-daily setting of benchmarks in an effort to increase their profits."

www.forbes.com/sites/leoking/2015/05/21/forex-barclays-citi-ubs- jpmorgan-online-chat-instant-messenger

http://money.cnn.com/2015/05/20/investing/ubs-foreign-exchange

■ A report by Dr. Theodore Downing, president of the International Network on Displacement and Resettlement, finds that the Kosovo Power Project's proposed forced displacement of more than seven thousand Kosovars "to make way for an open pit lignite mine" does not comply "with the international involuntary resettlement standards... that must be met for the project to obtain international financing." Nonetheless, development of the Kosovo Power Project has been spearheaded by the World Bank, which "misdirected the Kosovo agencies and lawmakers into preparing a noncompliant legal, policy, and institutional scaffolding to guide the anticipated displacement."

http://action.sierraclub.org/site/DocServer/Final_Draft_Downing_ Involuntary_Resettlement_at_KPP_Repo.pdf?docID=15541

- A joint investigation by ProPublica and *Frontline* exposes definite evidence of an intimate relationship between American corporation Firestone and brutal Liberian warlord Charles Taylor in the early 1990s: "Firestone served as a source of food, fuel, trucks and cash used by Taylor's ragtag rebel army, according to interviews, internal corporate documents and declassified diplomatic cables. The company signed a deal in 1992 to pay taxes to Taylor's rebel government. Over the next year, the company doled out more than $2.3 million in cash, checks and food to Taylor, according to an accounting in court files," in return for protection.

https://www.propublica.org/article/firestone-and-the-warlord-intro

- The *Nation* exposes the deception and secrecy of America's lobby industry in an article titled "Where Have All the Lobbyists Gone?." Thanks to legal loopholes that allow those in the lobbying industry to remain officially unregistered as lobbyists, the industry is "going underground." While only 12,281 lobbyists were registered in 2013, experts say the "true number of working lobbyists is closer to 100,000." Additionally, although official spending on lobbyists in the US in 2013 was $3.2 billion, the article estimates the unofficial total as $9 billion. Jeffrey Sachs estimates an unofficial total of $30 billion, which he breaks down sector by sector in his book *The Price of Civilization* (New York: Random House, 2011). The primary economic impact of lobbyists is the securing of government subsidies for giant corporations, whether through tax credits, fee reductions, giveaways, or simple subsidies.

www.thenation.com/article/178460/shadow-lobbying-complex

- A New York district court rules that the Democratic Republic of the Congo must pay two vulture funds – Themis Capital and Des Moines Investments – a total of about $70 million, $50 million of which represents interest on the original debt, which was valued at roughly $18 million when the funds acquired it from Citibank and others in 2008.

www.jubileeusa.org/vulturefunds/vulture-fund-country-studies.html

2015

■ A team of more than fifty journalists associated with the *Huffington Post* and the International Consortium of Investigative Journalists launches an investigative project titled "Evicted & Abandoned." The in-depth, ongoing report, *How the World Bank Broke Its Promise to Protect the Poor*, documents the people who have been displaced by World Bank projects in Ethiopia, Honduras, India, Kenya, Nigeria, Peru, and elsewhere. The introduction of the report reveals the terrifying scope of the ramifications: **"From 2004 to 2013, the bank's projects physically or economically displaced an estimated 3.4 million people**, forcing them from their homes, taking their land or damaging their livelihoods, ICIJ's analysis of World Bank records reveals."

http://projects.huffingtonpost.com/worldbank-evicted-abandoned

■ Global Justice Now releases a briefing titled *Privatising Power: UK Aid Funds Privatization in Nigeria*. The report states, "As part of a £100 million project run by consultants Adam Smith International, **the UK is using an estimated £50 million of aid money to support energy sector privatisation in Nigeria**. Although the process is yet to be completed, the results so far have been disastrous, with Nigerian people facing higher prices, poor service and regular blackouts. The companies involved in the privatisation have made many workers redundant and had to be bailed out by the central bank in 2014."

www.globaljustice.org.uk/sites/default/files/files/resources/nigeria_
energy_privatisation_briefing_online_0.pdf

■ The *New York Times* describes how the "sale of US arms fuels the wars of Arab states": "To wage war in Yemen, Saudi Arabia is using F-15 fighter jets bought from Boeing. Pilots from the United Arab Emirates are flying Lockheed Martin's F-16 to bomb both Yemen and Syria. Soon, the Emirates are expected to complete a deal with General Atomics for a fleet of Predator drones to run spying missions in their neighborhood. As the Middle East descends into proxy wars, sectarian conflicts and battles against terrorist networks, countries in the region that have stockpiled American military hardware are now actually using it and wanting more. The result is a boom for

American defense contractors looking for foreign business in an era of shrinking Pentagon budgets — but also the prospect of a dangerous new arms race in a region where the map of alliances has been sharply redrawn."

www.nytimes.com/2015/04/19/world/middleeast/sale-of-us-arms-fuels-the-wars-of-arab-states.html

- Deutsche Bank reaches a $2.5 billion settlement in the recent Libor scandal, against charges that the international financial giant "**conspired to manipulate global interest rate benchmarks.**"

http://money.cnn.com/2015/04/23/news/deutsche-bank-libor-settlement/?iid=EL

- The Centre for Research on Multinational Corporations (SOMO), a member of Eurodad, publishes a report called *Fool's Gold: How Canadian Mining Company Eldorado Gold Destroys the Greek Environment and Dodges Tax through Dutch Mailbox Companies.* As described by Eurodad: "This report reveals that **Greece's economic recovery is being undermined by large-scale tax avoidance — enabled by the Netherlands.** At the same time, Greece endures harsh austerity measures imposed by the European Commission, European Central Bank and IMF which are supported by the Netherlands."

www.eurodad.org/Entries/view/1546374/2015/04/01/Fool-s-Gold-How-Canadian-mining-company-Eldorado-Gold-destroys-the-Greek-environment-and-dodges-tax-through-Dutch-mailbox-companies

- WikiLeaks releases a confidential draft chapter from the Trans-Pacific Partnership illustrating the United States' aims to support corporations at the expense of fair trade and locally owned businesses in foreign countries. As reported by *Yes! Magazine*: "The document substantiates claims by opponents that **the TPP is a corporate-rights agreement** designed to facilitate the export of US jobs, allow corporations to sue governments for enacting labor and environmental protections, make it illegal for governments to favor local businesses, and advance the colonization of national economies by global corporations and financiers."

www.yesmagazine.org/new-economy/trade-rule-illegal-favor-local-business-tpp-leak-WikiLeaks?utm_source=YTW&utm_medium=Email&utm_campaign=20150417

- Global Justice Now releases a briefing about the Transatlantic Trade and Investment Partnership (TTIP), calling it a "threat to local democracy, affecting the freedom local authorities have in decision making when these affect the interests of large US corporations." It further states that the deal "could threaten public services, set up shady arbitration panels capable of overruling the UK court system and undermine regulations such as health and safety standards."

www.globaljustice.org.uk/sites/default/files/files/resources/local_ authorities_briefing_0.pdf

- NBC 11 reports on the American Legislative Exchange Council's "corporate bill mill," which gives corporations heavy influence over legislation. The ALEC Exposed website offers substantial evidence about how **"global corporations and state politicians vote behind closed doors to try to rewrite state laws that govern your rights."**

  https://secure2.convio.net/comcau/site/Advocacy?pagename=
  homepage&page=UserAction&id=650&autologin=true
  www.alecexposed.org/wiki/ALEC_Exposed

- WikiLeaks releases more than **half a million US diplomatic cables from 1978.** As reported by *DemocracyNow!*: "The documents include diplomatic cables and other diplomatic communications from and to US embassies and missions in nearly every country. '1978 actually set in progress many of the geopolitical elements that are playing out today,' [WikiLeaks founder Julian] Assange said. '1978 was the beginning of the Iranian revolution... the Sandinista movement started in its popular form... the war period in Afghanistan began in 1978 and hasn't stopped since.'"

  www.democracynow.org/2015/5/28/WikiLeaks_releases_500k_
  us_cables_from

- **FIFA scandal:** In May 2015, American officials announce "a sweeping indictment against 14 soccer officials and marketing executives who they said had corrupted the sport through two decades of shadowy dealing and $150 million in bribes. Authorities described international soccer in terms normally reserved for Mafia families or drug cartels, and brought charges under racketeering laws usually applied to such criminal organizations.... Whether through convoluted financial deals or old-fashioned briefcases full of cash, people were expected to pay for access to FIFA's river of money and publicity. The federal indictment lists 47 counts, including **bribery, fraud and money laundering.**"

  www.nytimes.com/2015/05/28/sports/soccer/fifa-officials-arrested-
  on-corruption-charges-blatter-isnt-among-them.html?_r=1

- The International Accountability Project releases a report titled *Back to Development: A Call for What Development Could Be*, which examines **forced evictions and other human rights abuses connected with World Bank–funded projects** in Cambodia, Egypt, Mongolia, Myanmar, Pakistan, Panama, the Philippines, Zimbabwe, and elsewhere. Among other findings, the report calculates that "in four World Bank funded projects 71 percent of those displaced received no compensation for the losses they suffered."

  www.mediafire.com/view/zw1g9k4wr83jr5v/IAP_FOR_WEB_R013.pdf

  https://medium.com/@accountability/in-chennai-india-residents-demand-the-world-bank-respect-human-rights-43a4d121b8f2

- ProPublica publishes a scathing investigative report on the Red Cross's "development" projects in Haiti — or rather, lack thereof — in a piece titled "How the Red Cross Raised Half a Billion Dollars for Haiti and Built Six Homes." In sum: "The group has publicly celebrated its work. But in fact, the Red Cross has repeatedly failed on the ground in Haiti. Confidential memos, e-mails from worried top officers, and accounts of a dozen frustrated and disappointed insiders show **the charity has broken promises, squandered donations, and made dubious claims of success....** The Red Cross won't disclose details of how it has spent the hundreds of millions of dollars donated for Haiti. But our reporting shows that less money reached those in need than the Red Cross has said."

  https://www.propublica.org/article/how-the-red-cross-raised-half-a-billion-dollars-for-haiti-and-built-6-homes

- *Profiting from Poverty, Again: DFID's Support for Privatising Education and Health*, a report released by Global Justice Now, shows how **the UK aid budget "is being used to increasingly set up private healthcare and private education across Africa and Asia."** As described in the report: "Some of these private services are being run by UK-based businesses that have an inappropriately close relationship to those making decisions in the Department for International Development (DFID). Others are being run in conjunction with mega multinationals like Coca-Cola, which clearly perceives not only an opportunity to greenwash its brand, but a direct commercial advantage." In sum, "**aid is being used as a tool to convince, cajole, and compel the majority of the world to undertake policies which help big business, but which undermine public services emerging or thriving.**"

www.globaljustice.org.uk/sites/default/files/files/resources/
profiting_from_poverty_again_dfid_global_justice_now_1.pdf

■ A report by the International Consortium of Investigative Journalists
and published in the *Huffington Post* finds "sharp growth" in **World
Bank and International Finance Corporation investments in projects "categorized by the bankers as expected to have 'irreversible
or unprecedented' social or environmental impacts."** From the article: "From 2009 to 2013, the two lenders pumped $50 billion in 239 of
these high-risk 'Category A' projects, including dams, copper mines
and oil pipelines — more than twice as much as the previous five-year
span, records show. Much of the development is in countries like Peru,
where federal governments are weak and regulations are lax."

http://projects.huffingtonpost.com/worldbank-evicted-abandoned/
how-worldbank-finances-environmental-destruction-peru

■ Oxfam releases a briefing titled *The Suffering of Others: The Human
Cost of the International Finance Corporation's Lending through Financial
Intermediaries*. The report states that the IFC made $36 billion worth
of investments into so-called "financial intermediaries" (including
commercial banks, private equity funds, and hedge funds) between
2009 and 2013, yet "does not know where much of its money under
this new model is ending up or even whether it's helping or harm-
ing," according to the head of Oxfam International's Washington,
DC, office. The report further reveals that "of the 49 investments the
IFC made to financial intermediaries since 2012 that it did classify as
'high risk,' it has only publicly disclosed sub-projects in three of these
deals. 'That means **there is no public information about where 94
percent of the IFC's "high risk" intermediary investments have
actually ended up**,' said [report coauthor Natalie] Bugalski."

www.oxfam.org/sites/www.oxfam.org/files/file_attachments/ib-
suffering-of-others-international-finance-corporation-020415-en.pdf

www.oxfam.org/en/pressroom/pressreleases/2015-04-02/billions-
out-control-ifc-investments-third-parties-causing-human-rights-
abuses

■ As of July 2015 (with data current as of November 2014), **half of
USAID's top ten vendors are multinational corporations:** Chemon-
ics (number 3); John Snow, Incorporated (number 7); DAI Washington (number 8); Management Sciences for Health, Inc. (number 9);
and Jhpiego Corporation (number 10). And the number one vendor

for USAID, with more than $2 billion in "amounts obligated"? The World Bank.

www.usaid.gov/results-and-data/budget-spending/top-40-vendors

■ The *New Republic* reveals the incentives that financial institutions offer their employees to take influential government positions — and the institutions' attempts to hide the exact nature of those incentives — in an article titled "Wall Street Pays Bankers to Work in Government and It Doesn't Want Anyone to Know." According to the article: "Citigroup is one of three Wall Street banks attempting to keep hidden their practice of paying executives multimillion-dollar awards for entering government service.... Critics argue these 'golden parachutes' ensure more financial insiders in policy positions and favorable treatment toward Wall Street." A related report by Bloomberg shows the increase in the percentage of workers who moved from regulatory jobs to banks, and vice versa, from 1988 to 2013, thus illustrating the so-called **revolving door between regulatory bodies and the companies they are charged to oversee.** These findings are fortified by evidence revealed in a 2013 investigation by the Project on Government Oversight, which demonstrates how "major corporations... make it financially advantageous for executives to take government jobs.... Through their compensation policies, companies may be fueling the revolving door and making it easier for their alumni to gain influence over public policy." One prime example may be Billy Tauzin, a former House Republican who helped draft and pass the Medicare Modernization Act of 2003, which was favorable to pharmaceutical companies; later that year, "the same month that President Bush signed the bill, the Pharmaceutical Research and Manufacturers of America, which goes by the nickname PhRMA and represents the largest American drug and biotech companies, was pursuing Tauzin to be its president." Ten months later, Tauzin took the job, at a reported annual salary of $2 million.

www.newrepublic.com/article/120967/wall-street-pays-bankers-
   work-government-and-wants-it-secret

www.bloomberg.com/news/articles/2015-01-30/fed-s-revolving-
   door-spins-faster-as-banks-boost-hiring

www.pogo.org/our-work/reports/2013/big-businesses-offer-
   revolving-door-rewards.html

www.nbcnews.com/id/11714763/t/tauzin-aided-drug-firms-then-
   they-hired-him/#.VZ3V46YyFLg

- An investigation by the *Guardian* reveals that subsidies totaling $1.62 billion to Shell, ExxonMobil, and Marathon Petroleum "were all granted by politicians who received significant campaign contributions from the fossil fuel industry." The report also finds that in 2013, **"the coal, oil and gas industries benefited from subsidies of $550 billion, four times those given to renewable energy."**

  www.theguardian.com/environment/2015/may/12/
  us-taxpayers-subsidising-worlds-biggest-fossil-fuel-companies

- Reports continue to surface about the expanded role of US government–supported jackals. An investigation by the *New York Times* reveals the **"secret history of quiet killings and blurred lines"** of the Navy's SEAL Team 6, "one of the nation's most mythologized, most secretive and least scrutinized military organizations." In other words, the team operates as modern-day jackals but do not limit themselves to the assassination of inconvenient foreign leaders, expanding their reach to all "suspected militants." In fact, **jackals have established their own industry of private security companies.** The United States is the "world's largest consumer of private military and security services," according to the University of Denver's Sié Chéou-Kang Center's Private Security Monitor project. Many of these private security companies have become embroiled in allegations of severe misconduct and the killing of civilians. The most well-known scandal, "Blackwatergate," involved a massacre of Iraqi civilians in Nisour Square (among other atrocities), allegedly by Blackwater USA, a leading US mercenary company, and **the alleged systematic evasion of prosecution by those perpetrating the violence.**

  www.nytimes.com/2015/06/07/world/asia/the-secret-history-of-
  seal-team-6.html?_r=1

  http://psm.du.edu/articles_reports_statistics/data_and_statistics
  .html#usdata

  www.thenation.com/article/blackwatergate#

- The *New Left Review* dissects the spread of EHM attitudes and activity throughout the Eurozone in an article titled "Germany's Faltering Motor?." From the article: **"A small bloc of northern countries led by Germany enjoys current account surpluses and dictates the terms of economic reorganization to indebted countries of the south,** under the imprimatur of the Troika." The Troika comprises the European Commission, the European Central Bank, and the International Monetary Fund, which collectively monitor countries "in severe economic trouble that are receiving financial loans provided for by the EU and the IMF." As Troika Watch explains, "Essentially, **the Troika ensures that the small woman and small man in the street pays for systemic problems in the economy and mistakes made by financial institutions**, which are the real causes of the crisis. At the same time, in the past few years, European lawmakers have continuously been reducing the rules and controls on those financial institutions and big businesses." The effects of these northern-countries-as-EHMs have been disastrous for other countries in the EU that are subject to dramatic austerity measures. According to the *New Left Review*, "**In Greece**, the effects of the world economic crisis of 2008 have been compounded by this grinding austerity, resulting in **unparalleled destruction of its national economy**. The country has now suffered a depression worse than that of the 1930s, with no recovery in sight within the euro framework. Spain, Portugal and Italy, the latter a founding member of the European integration process, remain trapped in a disastrous downturn. Since 2012, each has experienced an official unemployment rate in double digits — 25 percent in the case of Spain — with youth unemployment still higher."

http://newleftreview.org/II/93/joshua-rahtz-germany-s-faltering-motor

www.troikawatch.net/what-is-the-troika

- Jubilee USA describes how Cameroon probably feels hounded "by multiple vulture funds, including Grace Church Capital (Cayman Islands), Antwerp (UK Virgin Islands), Sconset Limited (UK Virgin Islands) and Winslow Bank (Bahamas).... Grace Church Capital bought Cameroonian debt for $9.5 million and then sued for nearly $40 million, while Sconset bought its share for $15 million and sued for $67 million. **Antwerp also bought its debt for about $15 million, but is claiming an astounding $196 million from a country that ranks 150th on the United Nations' Human Development Index (HDI) and has a GDP of just $22 billion.** Winslow Bank, meanwhile, sued for nearly $50 million for just $9 million worth of debt, and attempted to seize Cameroonian assets abroad as a means of enforcing its victory in court."

  www.jubileeusa.org/vulturefunds/vulture-fund-country-studies.html

- The *Wall Street Journal* reports that **corporations avoid paying an estimated $200 billion in taxes every year by using offshore banking systems**, according to the United States Conference on Trade and Development.

www.wsj.com/articles/companies-avoid-paying-200-billion-in-tax-
1435161106

- *Truthout* dissects **the World Bank and its connections to the tiny group of elites who control the global economic system** in an article titled "The World Bank, Poverty Creation and the Banality of Evil."

    www.truth-out.org/news/item/29851-the-world-bank-poverty-
    creation-and-the-banality-of-evil

- In an article titled "The Death of International Development," London School of Economics fellow Jason Hickel reminds us of the ever-increasing wealth ratio between the richest and the poorest countries: "In 1973 the gap was around 44:1. Today it's nearly 80:1. Inequality has reached such extremes that now **the richest 67 people in the world — a number of people who could fit comfortably on a London bus — have more wealth than the poorest 3.5 billion.**"

    www.thoughtleader.co.za/jasonhickel/2014/11/24/
    the-death-of-international-development

- Eric Holder retires from his position as US attorney general to return to his former law firm Covington & Burling — whose client list includes "many of the big banks Holder failed to criminally prosecute as attorney general for their role in the financial crisis, including Bank of America, JPMorgan Chase, Wells Fargo and Citigroup." In an interview with *Democracy Now!*'s Amy Goodman, *Rolling Stone* journalist Matt Taibbi says, "I think this is probably **the single biggest example of the revolving door** that we've ever had."

    www.democracynow.org/2015/7/8/eric_holder_returns_to_
    wall_street

- **Two major debt crises — in Greece and in Puerto Rico — come to a head on the international stage.** Because these crises are rapidly evolving as of the completion of this chapter in July 2015, please refer to news outlets for current information. The *New York Times* also offers a good starting point for understanding the Greek debt crisis.

    www.nytimes.com/interactive/2015/business/international/greece-
    debt-crisis-euro.html

John Perkins Personal History

1963   Graduates prep school, enters Middlebury College.

1964   Befriends Farhad, son of an Iranian general. Drops out of Middlebury.

1965   Works for Hearst newspapers in Boston.

1966   Enters Boston University's College of Business Administration.

1967   Marries former Middlebury classmate, whose "Uncle Frank" is a top-echelon executive at the National Security Agency (NSA).

1968   Profiled by the NSA as an ideal economic hit man (EHM). With Uncle Frank's blessing, joins the Peace Corps and is assigned to the Ecuadorian Amazon, where ancient indigenous nations battle US oil companies.

1969   Lives in the rain forest and the Andes. Experiences firsthand the deceitful and destructive practices employed by oil companies and government agencies, and their negative impacts on local cultures and environments.

1970   In Ecuador, meets vice president of international consulting firm MAIN, who is also an NSA liaison officer.

1971   Joins MAIN, undergoes clandestine training in Boston as an economic hit man, and is sent as part of an eleven-man team to Java, Indonesia. Struggles with conscience over pressure to falsify economic studies.

1972   Due to willingness to "cooperate," is promoted to chief economist and is viewed as a whiz kid. Meets important leaders, including World Bank president Robert McNamara. Sent on special assignment to Panama. Befriended by Panamanian president and charismatic leader Omar Torrijos; learns about history of US imperialism and Torrijos's determination to transfer Canal ownership from the United States to Panama.

1973   Career skyrockets. Builds empire within MAIN; continues work in Panama; travels extensively and conducts studies in Asia, Latin America, and the Middle East.

1974   Instrumental in initiating a huge EHM success in Saudi
Arabia. Royal family agrees to invest billions of dollars of
oil income in US securities and to allow the US Department of the Treasury to use the interest from those investments to hire US firms to build power and water systems,
highways, ports, and cities in the kingdom. In exchange,
the United States guarantees that the royal family will
continue to rule. This will serve as a model for future
EHM deals, including one that ultimately fails in Iraq.

1975   Promoted again — to youngest partner in MAIN's hundred-year history — and named manager of Econom-
ics and Regional Planning. Publishes series of influential
papers; lectures at Harvard and other institutions.

1976   Heads major projects around the world, in Africa, Asia,
Latin America, North America, and the Middle East.
Learns from the shah of Iran a revolutionary approach to
EHM empire building.

1977   Due to personal relationships in Colombia, becomes
exposed to the plight of farmers who are branded as Communist terrorists and drug traffickers but are in fact peasants trying to protect their families and homes.

1978   Rushed out of Iran by Farhad. Together, they fly to the
Rome home of Farhad's father, an Iranian general, who
predicts the shah's imminent ouster and blames US policy, corrupt leaders, and despotic governments for the
hatred sweeping the Middle East. He warns that if the
United States does not become more compassionate,
the situation will deteriorate.

1979   Struggles with conscience as the shah flees his country
and Iranians storm the US Embassy, taking fifty-two hostages. Realizes that the United States is a nation laboring
to deny the truth about its imperialist role in the world.
After years of tension and frequent separations, divorces
first wife.

1980   Suffers from deep depression, guilt, and the realization
that money and power have trapped him at MAIN. Quits.

1981   Is deeply disturbed when Ecuador's president, Jaime
Roldós (who has campaigned on an anti-oil platform),
and Panama's Omar Torrijos (who has incurred the

wrath of powerful Washington interests, due to his positions on the Panama Canal and US military bases) die in fiery airplane crashes that have all the markings of CIA assassinations. Marries for the second time, to a woman whose father is chief architect at Bechtel and is in charge of designing and building cities in Saudi Arabia — work financed through the 1974 EHM deal.

1982   Creates Independent Power Systems (IPS), a company committed to producing environmentally friendly electricity. He and his wife Winifred father Jessica.

1983-1989   Succeeds spectacularly as IPS CEO, with much help from "coincidences" — people in high places, tax breaks, etc. As a father, frets over world crises and former EHM role. Begins writing a tell-all book but is offered a lucrative consultant's retainer on the condition that he not write the book.

1990-1991   Following the US invasion of Panama and imprisonment of Manuel Noriega, sells IPS and retires at forty-five. Contemplates book about life as an EHM but instead is persuaded to direct energies toward creating a nonprofit organization, an effort that, he is told, would be negatively affected by such a book.

1992-2000   Watches the EHM failures in Iraq that result in the first Gulf War. Three times starts to write the EHM book, but instead gives in to threats and bribes. Tries to assuage conscience by writing books about indigenous peoples, supporting nonprofit organizations, teaching at New Age forums, traveling to the Amazon and the Himalayas, meeting with the Dalai Lama, and engaging in other activities.

2001-2002   Leads a group of North Americans deep into the Amazon and is there with indigenous people on September 11, 2001. Spends a day at Ground Zero and commits to writing the book that can heal his pain and expose the truth behind economic hit men.

2003-2004   Returns to the Ecuadorian Amazon to meet with the indigenous nations who have threatened war against the oil companies; writes *Confessions of an Economic Hit Man*.

2005-2016   Following publication of the international best seller *Confessions of an Economic Hit Man*, takes his message of the need to replace the death economy with a life economy on global speaking tours to corporate summits, large groups of CEOs and other business leaders, consumer conferences, music festivals, and more than fifty universities. Writes *The Secret History of the American Empire*, *Hoodwinked*, and *The New Confessions of an Economic Hit Man*.

NOTES

Chapter 1. Dirty Business

1. For a brief look at some of the long-term results of this strategy, see "A Rainforest Chernobyl," ChevronToxico, accessed July 24, 2015, chevrontoxico.com/about/rainforest-chernobyl.

Chapter 3. "In for Life"

1. Stephen Kinzer, *All the Shah's Men: An American Coup and the Roots of Middle East Terror*, 2nd ed. (Hoboken, NJ: John Wiley & Sons, 2008).
2. Jane Mayer, "Contract Sport: What Did the Vice-President Do for Halliburton?" *New Yorker*, February 16 & 23, 2004, p. 83.

Chapter 4. Indonesia: Lessons for an EHM

1. Jean Gelman Taylor, *Indonesia: Peoples and Histories* (New Haven, CT: Yale University Press, 2003); and Theodore Friend, *Indonesian Destinies* (Cambridge, MA: Belknap Press, 2003). See also Rex Mortimer, *Indonesian Communism under Sukarno: Ideology and Politics, 1959–1965* (Sheffield, UK: Equinox Publishing, 2006).

Chapter 5. Saving a Country from Communism

1. Tim Weiner, "Robert S. McNamara, Architect of a Futile War, Dies at 93," *New York Times*, July 7, 2009, www.nytimes.com/2009/07/07/us/07mcnamara.html.

Chapter 6. Selling My Soul

1. Susan Rosegrant and David R. Lampe, *Route 128: Lessons from Boston's High-Tech Community* (New York: Basic Books, 1993).

Chapter 7. My Role as Inquisitor

1. Theodore Friend, *Indonesian Destinies* (Cambridge, MA: Belknap Press, 2003), 5.

Chapter 8. Civilization on Trial

1. Arnold Toynbee and D. C. Somervell, *Civilization on Trial and The World and the West* (New York: Meridian Books, 1958).

Chapter 10. Panama's President and Hero

1. See David McCullough, *The Path Between the Seas: The Creation of the Panama Canal, 1870–1914* (New York: Simon and Schuster, 1999); William Friar, *Portrait of the Panama Canal: From Construction to the Twenty-First Century* (New York: Graphic Arts Publishing Company, 1999); and Graham Greene, *Conversations with the General* (New York: Pocket Books, 1984).
2. See "Zapata Petroleum Corp.," *Fortune*, April 1958, p. 248; Darwin Payne, *Initiative in Energy: Dresser Industries, Inc. 1880–1978* (New York: Simon and Schuster, 1979); Stephen Pizzo, Mary Fricker, and Paul Muolo, *Inside Job: The Looting of America's Savings and Loans* (New York: McGraw-Hill, 1989); Gary Webb, *Dark Alliance: The CIA, the Contras, and the Crack Cocaine Explosion* (New York: Seven Stories Press, 1999); and Gerard Colby and Charlotte Dennett, *Thy Will Be Done: The Conquest of the Amazon — Nelson Rockefeller and Evangelism in the Age of Oil* (New York: HarperCollins, 1995).

3. Manuel Noriega and Peter Eisner, *America's Prisoner: The Memoirs of Manuel Noriega* (New York: Random House, 1997); Omar Torrijos Herrera, *Ideario* (Editorial Universitaria Centroamericano, 1983); Graham Greene, *Conversations with the General* (New York: Pocket Books, 1984).

4. Greene, *Conversations*; and Noriega and Eisner, *Memoirs*.

5. Derrick Jensen, *A Language Older Than Words* (New York: Context Books, 2000), 86–88.

6. Greene, *Conversations*; and Noriega and Eisner, *Memoirs*.

Chapter 11. Pirates in the Canal Zone

1. For further reading about the Canal Zone, see John Major, *Prize Possession: The United States Government and the Panama Canal 1903–1979* (New York: Cambridge University Press, 1993); and David McCullough, *The Path Between the Seas: The Creation of the Panama Canal, 1870–1914* (New York: Simon and Schuster, 1999).

Chapter 13. Conversations with the General

1. William Shawcross, *The Shah's Last Ride: The Fate of an Ally* (New York: Simon and Schuster, 1988); and Stephen Kinzer, *All the Shah's Men: An American Coup and the Roots of Middle East Terror*, 2nd ed. (Hoboken, NJ: John Wiley & Sons, 2008), 45.

2. A great deal has been written about Arbenz, United Fruit, and the violent history of Guatemala. See, for example, Howard Zinn, *A People's History of the United States* (New York: Harper & Row, 1980); and Diane K. Stanley, *For the Record: The United Fruit Company's Sixty-Six Years in Guatemala* (Guatemala City: Centro Impresor Piedra Santa, 1994). For quick reference, see "CIA Involved in Guatemala Coup, 1954," last modified May 31, 2007, www.english.upenn.edu/~afilreis/50s/guatemala.html. For more on the Bush family's involvement, see "Zapata Petroleum Corp.," *Fortune*, April 1958, p. 248.

Chapter 14. Entering a New and Sinister Period in Economic History

1. "Robert S. McNamara: 8th Secretary of Defense," accessed August 12, 2015, www.defense.gov/specials/secdef_histories/SecDef_08.aspx.

Chapter 15. The Saudi Arabian Money-Laundering Affair

1. For more on the events leading up to the 1973 oil embargo and the impact of the embargo, see Thomas W. Lippman, *Inside the Mirage: America's Fragile Partnership with Saudi Arabia* (Boulder, CO: Westview Press, 2004), 155–159; Daniel Yergin, *The Prize: The Epic Quest for Oil, Money & Power* (New York: Free Press, 1993); Stephen Schneider, *The Oil Price Revolution* (Baltimore: Johns Hopkins University Press, 1983); and Ian Seymour, *OPEC: Instrument of Change* (London: Macmillan, 1980).

2. Lippman, *Inside the Mirage*, 160.

3. David Holden and Richard Johns, *The House of Saud: The Rise and Rule of the Most Powerful Dynasty in the Arab World* (New York: Holt, Rinehart & Winston, 1981), 359.

4. Lippman, *Inside the Mirage*, 167.

Chapter 16. Pimping, and Financing Osama bin Laden

1. Robert Baer, *Sleeping with the Devil: How Washington Sold Our Soul for Saudi Oil* (New York: Crown Publishers, 2003), 26.
2. Thomas W. Lippman, *Inside the Mirage: America's Fragile Partnership with Saudi Arabia* (Boulder CO: Westview Press, 2004), 162.
3. Lippman, *Inside the Mirage*, 2.
4. Henry Wasswa, "Idi Amin, Murderous Ugandan Dictator, Dies," Associated Press, August 17, 2003.
5. "The Saudi Connection," *US News & World Report*, December 15, 2003, p. 21.
6. "The Saudi Connection," 19, 20, 26.
7. Craig Unger, "Saving the Saudis," *Vanity Fair*, October 2003. For more on the Bush family's involvement, Bechtel, etc., see "Zapata Petroleum Corp.," *Fortune*, April 1958, p. 248; Darwin Payne, *Initiative in Energy: Dresser Industries, Inc. 1880–1978* (New York: Simon and Schuster, 1979); Nathan Vardi, "Desert Storm: Bechtel Group Is Leading the Charge," *Forbes*, June 23, 2003, pp. 63–66; Rob Wherry, "Contacts for Contracts," *Forbes*, June 23, 2003, p. 65; Graydon Carter, "Editor's Letter: Fly the Friendly Skies...," *Vanity Fair*, October 2003; and Richard A. Oppel Jr. with Diana B. Henriques, "A Nation at War: The Contractor," *New York Times*, April 18, 2003, www.nytimes.com/2003/04/18/business/a-nation-at-war-the-contractor-company-has-ties-in-washington-and-to-iraq .html.

Chapter 17. Panama Canal Negotiations and Graham Greene

1. See, for example, John M. Perkins, "Colonialism in Panama Has No Place in 1975," letter to the editor, *Boston Evening Globe*, September 19, 1975; and John M. Perkins, "US-Brazil Pact Upsets Ecuador," letter to the editor, *Boston Globe*, May 10, 1976.
2. For examples of papers by John Perkins published in technical journals, see John M. Perkins et al., "A Markov Process Applied to Forecasting — Part 1: Economic Development," Institute of Electrical and Electronics Engineers, Conference Papers C 73 475-1 (July 1973), and "Part II: The Demand for Electricity," Conference Papers C 74 146-7 (January 1974); John M. Perkins and Nadipuram R. Prasad, "A Model for Describing Direct and Indirect Interrelationships between the Economy and the Environment," *Consulting Engineer*, April 1973; Edwin Vennard, John M. Perkins, and Robert C. Ender, "Electric Demand from Interconnected Systems," *TAPPI Journal* (Technical Association of the Pulp and Paper Industry), 28th Conference Edition, 1974; John M. Perkins et al., "Iranian Steel: Implications for the Economy and the Demand for Electricity" and "Markov Method Applied to Planning," presented at the Fourth Iranian Conference on Engineering, Pahlavi University, Shiraz, Iran, May 12–16, 1974; and John M. Perkins, foreword to *Economic Theories and Applications: A Collection of Technical Papers* (Boston: Chas. T. Main, Inc., 1975).
3. Perkins, "Colonialism in Panama."
4. Graham Greene, *Getting to Know the General* (New York: Pocket Books, 1984), 89–90.
5. Greene, *Getting to Know the General*.

Chapter 18. Iran's King of Kings

1. William Shawcross, *The Shah's Last Ride: The Fate of an Ally* (New York: Simon and Schuster, 1988). For more about the Shah's rise to power, see H. D. S. Greenway, "The Iran Conspiracy," *New York Review of Books*, September 23, 2003; and Stephen Kinzer, *All the Shah's Men: An American Coup and the Roots of Middle East Terror*, 2nd ed. (Hoboken, NJ: John Wiley & Sons, 2008).
2. For more about Yamin, the Flowering Desert project, and Iran, see John Perkins, *Shapeshifting* (Rochester, VT: Destiny Books, 1997).

Chapter 19. Confessions of a Tortured Man

1. Erich Kolig, *Conservative Islam: A Cultural Anthropology* (Lanham, MD: Rowman & Littlefield, 2012).
2. Saeed Kamali Dehghan and Richard Norton-Taylor, "CIA Admits Role in 1953 Iranian Coup," *Guardian*, August 19, 2013, www.theguardian.com/world/2013/aug/19/cia-admits-role-1953-iranian-coup.

Chapter 20. The Fall of a King

1. For more about the shah's rise to power, see H. D. S. Greenway, "The Iran Conspiracy," *New York Review of Books*, September 23, 2003; and Stephen Kinzer, *All the Shah's Men: An American Coup and the Roots of Middle East Terror*, 2nd ed. (Hoboken, NJ: John Wiley & Sons, 2008).
2. See *Time* magazine cover articles on the Ayatollah Ruhollah Khomeini, February 12, 1979, January 7, 1980, and August 17, 1987.

Chapter 21. Colombia: Keystone of Latin America

1. Gerard Colby and Charlotte Dennett, *Thy Will Be Done: The Conquest of the Amazon — Nelson Rockefeller and Evangelism in the Age of Oil* (New York: HarperCollins, 1995), 381.

Chapter 22. American Republic vs. Global Empire

1. For an expert opinion, see Dylan Matthews and Kimberly Ann Elliot, "Poor Countries Can Keep Workers Safe and Still Escape Poverty," *Washington Post*, April 25, 2013, www.washingtonpost.com/blogs/wonkblog/wp/2013/04/25/poor-countries-can-keep-workers-safe-and-still-escape-poverty. For information on sweatshops in China, in particular, see "Sweatshops in China," War on Want, accessed August 12, 2015, www.waronwant.org/sweatshops-china.

Chapter 24. Ecuador's President Battles Big Oil

1. Maria Guadalupe Moog Rodrigues, "Environmental Activism Beyond Brazil I — The Struggle against Oil Exploitation in Ecuador," in *Global Environmentalism and Local Politics: Transnational Advocacy Networks in Brazil, Ecuador, and India* (Albany: State University of New York Press, 2004), 93–114.
2. For extensive details on SIL, its history, its activities, and its association with the oil companies and the Rockefellers, see Gerard Colby and Charlotte Dennett, *Thy Will Be Done: The Conquest of the Amazon — Nelson Rockefeller and Evangelism in the Age of Oil* (New York: HarperCollins, 1995); and Joe Kane, *Savages* (New York: Alfred A. Knopf, 1995). For information on Rachel Saint, see Kane, *Savages*, 85, 156, 227.
3. John D. Martz, *Politics and Petroleum in Ecuador* (New Brunswick, NJ: Transaction Books, 1987), 272.

4. José Carvajal Candall, "Objetivos y políticas de CEPE" (Quito: Primer Seminario, 1979), 88.

Chapter 26. Ecuador's Presidential Death

1. John D. Martz, *Politics and Petroleum in Ecuador* (New Brunswick, NJ: Transaction Books, 1987), 272.
2. Gerard Colby and Charlotte Dennett, *Thy Will Be Done: The Conquest of the Amazon — Nelson Rockefeller and Evangelism in the Age of Oil* (New York: HarperCollins, 1995), 813.
3. Martz, *Politics and Petroleum*, 303.
4. Ibid., 381, 400.

Chapter 27. Panama: Another Presidential Death

1. Graham Greene, *Getting to Know the General* (New York: Pocket Books, 1984), 11.
2. George Shultz was secretary of the Treasury and chairman of the Council on Economic Policy under Nixon–Ford, 1972–1974; executive president or president of Bechtel, 1974–1982; and secretary of state under Reagan–Bush, 1982–1989. Caspar Weinberger was director of the Office of Management and Budget and secretary of health, education, and welfare under Nixon–Ford, 1973–1975; vice president and general counsel of Bechtel Group, 1975–1980; and secretary of defense under Reagan–Bush, 1980–1987.
3. During the 1973 Watergate hearings, in his testimony before the US Senate, John Dean was the first to disclose US plots to assassinate Torrijos. In 1975, at Senate inquiries into the CIA, chaired by Senator Frank Church, additional testimony and documentation of plans to kill both Torrijos and Noriega were presented. See, for example, Manuel Noriega and Peter Eisner, *America's Prisoner: The Memoirs of Manuel Noriega* (New York: Random House, 1997), 107.

Chapter 28. My Energy Company, Enron, and George W. Bush

1. For additional information on IPS, its wholly owned subsidiary Archbald Power Corporation, and former CEO John Perkins, see Jack M. Daly and Thomas J. Duffy, "Burning Coal's Waste at Archbald," *Civil Engineering*, July 1988; Vince Coveleskie, "Co-Generation Plant Attributes Cited," *Scranton Times*, October 17, 1987; Robert Curran, "Archbald Facility Dedicated," *Scranton Tribune*, October 17, 1987; "Archbald Plant Will Turn Coal Waste into Power," *Wilkes-Barre (PA) Citizens' Voice*, June 6, 1988; and "Liabilities to Assets: Culm to Light, Food," editorial, *Wilkes-Barre (PA) Citizens' Voice*, June 7, 1988.
2. Joe Conason, "The George W. Bush Success Story," *Harper's Magazine*, February 2000; and Craig Unger, "Saving the Saudis," *Vanity Fair*, October 2003, p. 165.
3. Unger, "Saving the Saudis," 178.
4. See George Lardner Jr. and Lois Romano, "The Turning Point after Coming Up Dry," *Washington Post*, July 30, 1999; Conason, "The George W. Bush Success Story"; and Sam Parry, "The Bush Family 'Oiligarchy,'" Consortiumnews.com, June 12, 2015, https://consortiumnews.com/2015/06/12/the-bush-family-oiligarchy.
5. This theory took on new significance and seemed ready to fall under the spotlight of public scrutiny when, years later, it became clear that the highly respected accounting firm of Arthur Andersen had conspired with Enron executives to cheat energy consumers, Enron employees, and the American public

out of billions of dollars. The impending 2003 Iraq War pushed the spotlight away. During the war, Bahrain played a critical role in President George W. Bush's strategy.

Chapter 29. I Take a Bribe

1. Jim Garrison, *American Empire: Global Leader or Rogue Power?* (San Francisco: Berrett-Koehler, 2004), 38.

Chapter 30. The United States Invades Panama

1. Manuel Noriega and Peter Eisner, *America's Prisoner: The Memoirs of Manuel Noriega* (New York: Random House, 1997), 56.
2. David Harris, *Shooting the Moon: The True Story of an American Manhunt Unlike Any Other, Ever* (Boston: Little, Brown and Company, 2001), 31–34.
3. Harris, *Shooting the Moon*, 43.
4. Noriega and Eisner, *America's Prisoner*, 212. See also Craig Unger, "Saving the Saudis," *Vanity Fair*, October 2003, 165.
5. Noriega and Eisner, *America's Prisoner*, 114.
6. See "George H. W. Bush," Famous Texans, accessed August 12, 2015, www .famoustexans.com/georgebush.htm.
7. Noriega and Eisner, *America's Prisoner*, 56–57.
8. Harris, *Shooting the Moon*, 6.
9. "George H. W. Bush," Famous Texans.
10. Harris, *Shooting the Moon*, 4.
11. Noriega and Eisner, *America's Prisoner*, 248.
12. Ibid., 211.
13. Ibid., xxi.

Chapter 31. An EHM Failure in Iraq

1. Morris Barrett, "The Web's Wild World," *Time*, April 26, 1999, p. 62.

Chapter 32. September 11 and Its Aftermath for Me, Personally

1. For more about the Huaorani, see Joe Kane, *Savages* (New York: Alfred A. Knopf, 1995).

Chapter 33. Venezuela: Saved by Saddam

1. "Venezuela on the Brink," editorial, *New York Times*, December 18, 2002.
2. "Venezuelan President Forced to Resign," Associated Press, April 12, 2002.
3. Simon Romero, "Tenuous Truce in Venezuela for the State and Its Oil Company," *New York Times*, April 24, 2002.
4. Bob Edwards, "What Went Wrong with the Oil Dream in Venezuela," National Public Radio, *Morning Edition*, July 8, 2003.
5. Ginger Thompson, "Venezuela Strikers Keep Pressure on Chávez and Oil Exports," *New York Times*, December 30, 2002.
6. For more on the jackals and other types of hit men, see P. W. Singer, *Corporate Warriors: The Rise of the Privatized Military Industry* (Ithaca, NY: Cornell University Press, 2003); James R. Davis, *Fortune's Warriors: Private Armies and the New World Order* (Vancouver and Toronto: Douglas & McIntyre, 2000); and Felix I. Rodriguez and John Weisman, *Shadow Warrior: The CIA Hero of 100 Unknown Battles* (New York: Simon and Schuster, 1989).

7. Tim Weiner, "A Coup by Any Other Name," *New York Times*, April 14, 2002.
8. "Venezuela Leader Urges 20 Years for Strike Chiefs," Associated Press, February 22, 2003.
9. Paul Richter, "US Had Talks on Chávez Ouster," *Los Angeles Times*, April 17, 2002.

Chapter 34. Conspiracy: Was I Poisoned?

1. American men fear China more than they fear ISIS. See "What Are Americans Most Afraid Of?," *Vanity Fair*, January 2015, www.vanityfair.com/culture/2015/01/fear-60-minutes-poll.

Chapter 35. A Jackal Speaks: The Seychelles Conspiracy

1. Although his name is on record for anyone who cares to delve, at his request, I've decided to use the alias of "Jack." He has always maintained that he did not work for the CIA, which, strictly speaking, is true.
2. "Indian Ocean Isle Repulses Raiders," *New York Times*, November 27, 1981, www.nytimes.com/1981/11/27/world/indian-ocean-isle-repulses-raiders.html.
3. For more information: "Trial Gives Peek at South African Intelligence Web," by Joseph Lelyveld, *New York Times*, May 10, 1982, http://select.nytimes.com/gst/abstract.html?res=FB0A11FA3F5C0C738DDDAC0894DA484D81&scp=1&sq=TRIAL+GIVES+PEEK+AT+SOUTH+AFRICA+INTELLIGENCE+WEB+&st=nyt, and Mike Hoare, *The Seychelles Affair* (Paladin Press, 2009).

Chapter 36. Ecuador Rebels

1. *Encyclopaedia Britannica*, s.v. "Rafael Correa," updated October 23, 2014, www.britannica.com/biography/Rafael-Correa.
2. Sandy Tolan, "Ecuador: Lost Promises," National Public Radio, *Morning Edition*, July 9, 2003, www.npr.org/programs/morning/features/2003/jul/latinoil.
3. Juan Forero, "Seeking Balance: Growth vs. Culture in Amazon," *New York Times*, December 10, 2003.
4. Abby Ellin, "Suit Says ChevronTexaco Dumped Poisons in Ecuador," *New York Times*, May 8, 2003.

Chapter 37. Honduras: The CIA Strikes

1. Mark Weisbrot, "Who's in Charge of US Foreign Policy?, *Guardian*, July 16, 2009, www.theguardian.com/commentisfree/cifamerica/2009/jul/16/honduras-coup-obama-clinton.
2. Amy Goodman, "Exclusive Interview with Manuel Zelaya on the US Role in Honduran Coup, WikiLeaks and Why He Was Ousted," *Democracy Now!*, May 31, 2011, www.democracynow.org/2011/5/31/exclusive_interview_with_manuel_zelaya_on.

Chapter 38. Your Friendly Banker as EHM

1. Nicholas Kristof, "A Banker Speaks, with Regret," *New York Times*, November 30, 2011, www.nytimes.com/2011/12/01/opinion/kristof-a-banker-speaks-with-regret.html.
2. James McBride, Christopher Alessi, and Mohammed Aly Sergie, "Understanding the Libor Scandal," Council on Foreign Relations, May 21, 2015, www.cfr.org/united-kingdom/understanding-libor-scandal/p28729.

Chapter 40. Istanbul: Tools of Modern Empire

1. "Use It and Lose It: The Outsize Effect of US Consumption on the Environment," *Scientific American*, September 14, 2012, www.scientificamerican.com/article/american-consumption-habits.

Chapter 41. A Coup against Fundación Pachamama

1. Oliver Balch, "Buen Vivir: The Social Philosophy Inspiring Movements in South America," *Guardian*, February 4, 2013, www.theguardian.com/sustainable-business/blog/buen-vivir-philosophy-south-america-eduardo-gudynas.
2. "The Hague Rules against Chevron in Ecuador Case," teleSUR, March 13, 2015, www.telesurtv.net/english/news/The-Hague-Rules-against-Chevron-in-Ecuador-Case-20150313-0009.html.
3. "Data: Ecuador," World Bank, updated September 17, 2015, http://data.worldbank.org/country/ecuador.
4. Daniel Cancel and Lester Pimentel, "Ecuador's Audit Commission Finds 'Illegality' in Debt (Update 5)," Bloomberg.com, November 20, 2008, www.bloomberg.com/apps/news?pid=newsarchive&sid=a8suBA8I.3ik.

Chapter 42. Another EHM Banking Scandal

1. Virginia Harrison and Mark Thompson, "5 Big Banks Pay $5.4 Billion for Rigging Currencies," CNN Money, May 20, 2015, http://money.cnn.com/2015/05/20/investing/ubs-foreign-exchange/index.html.
2. Leo King, "Bandits, Mafia, Cartel. Bank Traders' Astonishing Online Messages," *Forbes*, May 21, 2015, www.forbes.com/sites/leoking/2015/05/21/forex-barclays-citi-ubs-jpmorgan-online-chat-instant-messenger.
3. Harrison and Thompson, "5 Big Banks Pay $5.4 Billion."
4. Stephanie Clifford and Matt Apuzzo, "After Indicting 14 Soccer Officials, US Vows to End Graft in FIFA," *New York Times*, May 27, 2015, www.nytimes.com/2015/05/28/sports/soccer/fifa-officials-arrested-on-corruption-charges-blatter-isnt-among-them.html.
5. Laura Shin, "The 85 Richest People in the World Have as Much Wealth as the 3.5 Billion Poorest," *Forbes*, January 23, 2014, www.forbes.com/sites/laurashin/2014/01/23/the-85-richest-people-in-the-world-have-as-much-wealth-as-the-3-5-billion-poorest.
6. Ricardo Fuentes-Nieva and Nick Galasso, "Working for the Few: Political Capture and Economic Inequality," 178 Oxfam briefing paper — Summary, January 20, 2014, www.oxfam.org/sites/www.oxfam.org/files/bp-working-for-few-political-capture-economic-inequality-200114-summ-en.pdf.
7. "Poverty Overview," World Bank, updated April 6, 2015, www.worldbank.org/en/topic/poverty/overview.
8. James S. Henry, "Where the Money Went," *Across the Board*, March/April 2004, 42–45. For more information, see James S. Henry, *The Blood Bankers: Tales from the Global Underground Economy* (New York: Four Walls Eight Windows, 2003).
9. Jacob Kushner et al., "Burned Out: World Bank Projects Leave Trail of Misery Around Globe," *Huffington Post*, April 16, 2015, http://projects.huffingtonpost.com/worldbank-evicted-abandoned/worldbank-projects-leave-trail-misery- and-globe-kenya.

Chapter 43. Who Are Today's Economic Hit Men?

1. Lee Fang, "Where Have All the Lobbyists Gone?," *The Nation*, February 19, 2014, www.thenation.com/article/shadow-lobbying-complex.

2. Brooks Barnes, "MPAA and Christopher Dodd Said to Be Near Deal," *New York Times*, February 20, 2011, mediadecoder.blogs.nytimes.com/2011/02/20/m-p-a-a-and-christopher-dodd-said-to-be-near-deal.

3. Center for Responsive Politics, "Former Members," OpenSecrets.org, accessed July 24, 2015, www.opensecrets.org/revolving/top.php?display=Z.

4. Fang, "Where Have All the Lobbyists Gone?"

5. Lee Drutman, "How Corporate Lobbyists Conquered American Democracy," *Atlantic*, April 20, 2015, www.theatlantic.com/business/archive/2015/04/how-corporate-lobbyists-conquered-american-democracy/390822.

6. Conn Hallinan and Leon Wofsy, "'The American Century' Has Plunged the World into Crisis. What Happens Now?," Common Dreams, June 22, 2015, www.commondreams.org/views/2015/06/22/american-century-has-plunged-world-crisis-what-happens-now.

7. Niraj Chokshi, "The United States of Subsidies: The Biggest Corporate Winners in Each State," *Washington Post*, March 18, 2015, www.washingtonpost.com/blogs/govbeat/wp/2015/03/17/the-united-states-of-subsidies-the-biggest-corporate-winners-in-each-state.

8. See Jim Brunner, "Labor Group Disinvites Inslee over Boeing Tensions," *Seattle Times*, July 20, 2015, www.seattletimes.com/seattle-news/politics/labor-group-disinvites-inslee-over-boeing-tensions; and Mike Baker, "Boeing to Throw Party to Thank Washington Lawmakers for $8.7B," *St. Louis Post-Dispatch*, February 4, 2014, www.stltoday.com/business/local/boeing-to-throw-party-to-thank-washington-lawmakers-for-b/article_6d191691-9f07-5063-8e67-c2808ad4b302.html.

9. Greg LeRoy, "Site Location 101: How Companies Decide Where to Expand or Relocate," chap. 2 in *The Great American Jobs Scam: Corporate Tax Dodging and the Myth of Job Creation* (San Francisco: Berrett-Koehler, 2005); and Leroy, "Fantus and the Rise of the Economic War among the States," chap. 3 in *The Great American Jobs Scam*.

10. Philip Mattera and Kasia Tarczynska, with Greg LeRoy, "Megadeals: The Largest Economic Development Subsidy Packages Ever Awarded by State and Local Governments in the United States," Good Jobs First, June 2013, www.goodjobsfirst.org/sites/default/files/docs/pdf/megadeals_report.pdf.

11. Damian Carrington and Harry Davies, "US Taxpayers Subsidising World's Biggest Fossil Fuel Companies," *Guardian*, May 12, 2015, www.theguardian.com/environment/2015/may/12/us-taxpayers-subsidising-worlds-biggest-fossil-fuel-companies.

12. Andrea Germanos, "'Corporate Influence Has Won': House Passes Anti-GMO Labeling Bill," Common Dreams, July 23, 2015, www.commondreams.org/news/2015/07/23/corporate-influence-has-won-house-passes-anti-gmo-labeling-bill.

13. Deirdre Fulton, "Exposed: How Walmart Spun an 'Extensive and Secretive Web' of Overseas Tax Havens," Common Dreams, June 17, 2015, www.commondreams.org/news/2015/06/17/exposed-how-walmart-spun-extensive-and-secretive-web-overseas-tax-havens.

14. Clare O'Connor, "Report: Walmart Workers Cost Taxpayers $6.2 Billion in

Public Assistance," *Forbes*, April 15, 2014, www.forbes.com/sites/clareoconnor/2014/04/15/report-walmart-workers-cost-taxpayers-6-2-billion-in-public-assistance.

15. Greg Palast, Maggie O'Kane, and Chavala Madlena, "Vulture Funds Await Jersey Decision on Poor Countries' Debts," *Guardian*, November 15, 2011, www.theguardian.com/global-development/2011/nov/15/vulture-funds-jersey-decision.

16. "Vulture Funds Case Study," Jubilee USA Network, 2007, www.jubileeusa.org/vulturefunds/vulture-fund-country-studies.html.

17. Palast, O'Kane, and Madlena, "Vulture Funds Await Jersey Decision."

18. Joseph Stiglitz, "Sovereign Debt Needs International Supervision," *Guardian*, June 16, 2015, www.theguardian.com/business/2015/jun/16/sovereign-debt-needs-international-supervision.

19. Laura Shin, "The 85 Richest People in the World Have as Much Wealth as the 3.5 Billion Poorest," *Forbes*, January 23, 2014, www.forbes.com/sites/laurashin/2014/01/23/the-85-richest-people-in-the-world-have-as-much-wealth-as-the-3-5-billion-poorest.

Chapter 44. Who Are Today's Jackals?

1. Sarah Lazare, "'You Have a Choice': Veterans Call On Drone Operators to Refuse Orders," Common Dreams, June 19, 2015, www.commondreams.org/news/2015/06/19/you-have-choice-veterans-call-drone-operators-refuse-orders.

2. "Top US General: Drones Are 'Failed Strategy' That 'Cause More Damage,'" *Democracy Now!*, July 17, 2015, www.democracynow.org/2015/7/17/headlines/top_us_general_drones_are_failed_strategy_that_cause_more_damage.

3. Mark Mazzetti et al., "SEAL Team 6: A Secret History of Quiet Killings and Blurred Lines," *New York Times*, June 6, 2015, www.nytimes.com/2015/06/07/world/asia/the-secret-history-of-seal-team-6.html.

4. "Is There a Drone in Your Neighbourhood? Rise of Spy Planes Exposed after FAA Is Forced to Reveal 63 Launch Sites across US," *Mail Online*, April 2012, www.dailymail.co.uk/news/article-2134376/Is-drone-neighbourhood-Rise-killer-spy-planes-exposed-FAA-forced-reveal-63-launch-sites-U-S.html.

5. "AP: FBI Using Low-Flying Spy Planes over US," CBS News, June 2, 2015, www.cbsnews.com/news/ap-fbi-using-low-flying-spy-planes-over-us.

6. "NSA Spying on Americans," Electronic Frontier Foundation, accessed July 24, 2015, www.eff.org/nsa-spying.

7. "Obama Bans Spying on Leaders of US Allies, Scales Back NSA Program," Reuters, January 17, 2014, www.reuters.com/article/2014/01/18/us-usa-security-obama-idUSBREA0G0JI20140118.

8. James Ball, "NSA Monitored Calls of 35 World Leaders after US Official Handed over Contacts," *Guardian*, October 25, 2013, www.theguardian.com/world/2013/oct/24/nsa-surveillance-world-leaders-calls.

9. "Statistics on the Private Security Industry," Private Security Monitor, University of Denver, accessed August 12, 2015, psm.du.edu/articles_reports_statistics/data_and_statistics.html.

10. "30 Most Powerful Private Security Companies in the World," Security Degree Hub, January 11, 2013, www.securitydegreehub.com/30-most-powerful-private-security-companies-in-the-world.

Chapter 45. Lessons for China

1. Daniel Cancel and Lester Pimentel, "Ecuador's Audit Commission Finds 'Illegality' in Debt (Update 5)," Bloomberg.com, November 20, 2008, www.bloomberg.com/apps/news?pid=newsarchive&sid=a8suBA8I.3ik.; and Mick Riordan et al., "Daily Brief: Economics and Financial Market Commentary," *Global Economic Monitor*, December 16, 2008, www-wds.worldbank.org/external/default/WDSContentServer/WDSP/IB/2011/05/31/000356161_20110531005514/Rendered/PDF/612410NEWS0DEC0BOX0358349B00PUBLIC0.pdf.

2. Mercedes Alvaro, "China, Ecuador Sign $2 Billion Loan Deal," *Wall Street Journal*, June 28, 2011, www.wsj.com/articles/SB10001424052702304314404576412373916029508.

3. There is disagreement over Ecuadorian debt and the way Chinese financing is interpreted. Some of this is due to divergent definitions of "loans" as opposed to "investments." One interpretation is offered by Adam Zuckerman, who states, "Ecuador's President Correa was well-rewarded for his trip last week to China, but this could have grave impacts for the Amazon and the people who live there. On Wednesday, Beijing agreed to lend Ecuador $7.53 billion to help the heavily oil-dependent economy cope with the recent drop in global crude prices. This latest sum — the largest China has ever lent Ecuador — brings Chinese financing to Ecuador to nearly $25 billion, over a quarter of the nation's GDP. In 2013 Beijing provided 61 percent of Ecuador's external financing and purchased 83 percent of Ecuador's oil; this latest loan will undoubtedly bring both numbers much higher" (Zuckerman, "Eye on Ecuador: Racking Up the China Debt and Paying It Forward with Oil," Amazon Watch, January 13, 2015, http://amazonwatch.org/news/2015/0113-racking-up-the-china-debt-and-paying-it-forward-with-oil). The *Wall Street Journal* analysis states, "Currently, China's loans to Ecuador exceed $6 billion, including $1.7 billion to finance 85 percent of Coca Codo Sinclair, a hydropower plant to be built by China's Sinohydro Corp. in Ecuador, which will supply about 75 percent of the country's energy needs" (Alvaro, "China, Ecuador Sign $2 Billion Loan Deal"). I've chosen to use the official government figures for debt, as reported in Ecuador's *El Commercio*, July 29, 2015, "La prensa de EE.UU. alerta la dependencia de Ecuador a China."

4. "Ecuador: Over 50% of Oil Exports Went to China in September," *Latin American Herald Tribune*, May 23, 2015, http://laht.com/article.asp?ArticleId=434747&CategoryId=14089.

5. Andrew Ross, "Why Is Ecuador Selling Its Economic and Environmental Future to China?," *The Nation*, December 18, 2014, www.thenation.com/article/193249/why-ecuador-selling-its-economic-and-environmental-future-china.

6. Clifford Krauss and Keith Bradsher, "China's Global Ambitions, with Loans and Strings Attached," *New York Times*, July 24, 2015, www.nytimes.com/2015/07/26/business/international/chinas-global-ambitions-with-loans-and-strings-attached.html.

7. "Total Value of US Trade in Goods (Export and Import) with China from 2004 to 2014," Statista, accessed July 24, 2015, www.statista.com/statistics/277679/total-value-of-us-trade-in-goods-with-china-since-2004.

Without the many people whose lives I shared and who are described in the previous pages, this book would not have been written. I am grateful for the experiences and the lessons.

Beyond them, I thank the people who encouraged me to go out on a limb and tell my original story: Stephan Rechtschaffen, Bill and Lynne Twist, Ann Kemp, and Art Roffey; so many of the people who participated in Dream Change trips and workshops, especially my co-facilitators Eve Bruce, Lyn Roberts, and Mary Tendall; and my incredible ex-wife and partner of thirty years, Winifred, and our daughter, Jessica.

I am grateful to the many men and women who provided personal insights and information about the multinational banks, international corporations, and political innuendos of various countries, with special thanks to Michael Ben-Eli, Sabrina Bologni, Juan Gabriel Carrasco, Jamie Grant, Paul Shaw, and several others, who wish to remain anonymous but who know who they are.

Once the manuscript for the first edition was written, Berrett-Koehler founder Steve Piersanti not only had the courage to take me in but also devoted endless hours as a brilliant editor, helping me to frame and reframe the book. My deepest thanks go to Steve; to Richard Perl, who introduced me to him; to Nova Brown, Randi Fiat, Allen Jones, Chris Lee, Jennifer Liss, Laurie Pellouchoud, and Jenny Williams, who read and critiqued the manuscript; to David Korten, who not only read and critiqued it but also made me jump through hoops to satisfy his high and excellent standards; to Paul Fedorko, my agent; to Valerie Brewster for crafting the book design; and to Todd Manza, a wordsmith and philosopher extraordinaire.

For this *New Confessions of an Economic Hit Man*, I want to thank Kiman Lucas, who encouraged me to keep going, organized and accompanied me on trips to countries she knows so well that played instrumental roles in the writing of this book, and whose fearless willingness to challenge my opinions, helped me immeasurably; my ex-wife, Winifred, who continues to support me in so many ways, whose generosity of heart seems limitless, and who is the wisest advisor any person could ever hope for; our daughter, Jessica, and grandson, Grant, who continue to empower me to do my best; Ali Yurtsever and Umut Tasa Yurtsever, Alper and Filiz Utku, and Berna Baykal, who facilitated my trips to Istanbul and are doing so much to change business and government leaders; Daniel Koupermann, who first connected me with the Achuar, made the Pachamama Alliance possible, and has been my friend and traveling partner on so many adventures; the people and leaders of the Achuar nation; once again, my literary agent Paul Fedorko, without whose ideas, editing skills, patience, and perseverance this book would not have been written; my publicists Peg Booth and Jessica Muto, who arranged so many of my speaking tours and media events; Becky Robinson and the team at Weaving Influence for working their magic on my website and social networking platforms, and Cathy Lewis and the team at C.S. Lewis & Co. Publicists, for their public relations expertise; my dear friend and the brilliant businessman Dan Wieden; my confidant and the genius entrepreneur Scott James; Dream Change's inspirational guiding light and executive director, Samantha Thomas, and Llyn Roberts, who stepped back into my life at a time when her help was needed.

At Berrett-Koehler, I once again owe so very much to Steve Piersanti for his amazing and brilliant talent as an editorial coach and cheerleader and for sculpting and shaping this book; Jenny Williams, for researching and preparing the extensive "Documentation" section; Alana Price, for contributing many entries to the "Documentation" section as well as much other research; Anita Simha and Claire Pershan, BK editorial interns and manuscript reviewers; Charlotte Ashlock, Anna Leinberger, Jeevan Sivasubramaniam, David Marshall, Neal Maillet, and Steve Piersanti (members of BK's Editorial Department); Kristen Frantz, Katie Sheehan, Michael Crowley, Shabnam Banerjee-McFarland, Matt Fagaly, Zoe Mackey, and Marina Cook (members of BK's Sales and Marketing Department); María Jesús Aguiló, Catherine Lengronne, Johanna Vondeling, and Leslie Crandell (members of BK's International

Sales and Subsidiary Rights Department); Lasell Whipple, Courtney Schonfeld, and Edward Wade (members of BK's Design and Production Department).

A special thanks to David Korten, Anita Simha, Lorna Garano, Mal Warwick, Maria Lewytzky-Milligan, Nic Albert, and Claire Pershan for reading the drafts of the manuscript and offering so many insightful suggestions and edits, and to radio broadcaster and author, Zohara Hieronimus, for suggesting to me the words "death economy" and "life economy."

I must thank all those men and women who worked with me at MAIN and were unaware of the roles they played in helping EHMs shape the global empire. I especially thank the ones who worked for me and with whom I traveled to distant lands and shared so many precious moments. Also Ehud Sperling and his staff at Inner Traditions International, publisher of my earlier books on indigenous cultures and shamanism, and good friends who set me on this path as an author.

I am eternally grateful to the men and women who took me into their homes in the jungles, deserts, and mountains, in the cardboard shacks along the canals of Jakarta, and in the slums of countless cities around the world, who shared their food and their lives with me, and who have been my greatest source of inspiration.

Born ± 1945

John Perkins has lived four lives: as an economic hit man (EHM); as the CEO of a successful alternative energy company, who was rewarded for not disclosing his EHM past; as an expert on indigenous cultures and shamanism, a teacher and writer who used this expertise to promote ecology and sustainability while continuing to honor his vow of silence about his life as an EHM; and now as a writer and activist who, in telling the real-life story about his extraordinary dealings as an EHM, has exposed the world of international intrigue and corruption that is turning the American republic into a global empire despised by increasing numbers of people around the planet.

As an EHM, John had the job of persuading economically developing countries to accept enormous loans for infrastructure development — loans that were much larger than needed — and to guarantee that the development projects would be contracted to US corporations such as Halliburton and Bechtel. Once these countries were saddled with huge debts, the US government and the international aid agencies allied with it were able to control these economies and to ensure that oil and other resources were channeled to serve the interests of building a global empire.

In his capacity as an EHM, John traveled all over the world and was either a direct participant in or a witness to some of the most dramatic events in modern history, including the Saudi Arabian Money-Laundering Affair, the fall of the shah of Iran, the death of Panama's head of state, the subsequent invasion of Panama, and events leading up to the 2003 invasion of Iraq.

In 1980, Perkins founded Independent Power Systems Inc., an alternative energy company. Under his leadership as CEO, IPS became an extremely successful firm in a high-risk business where most of its competitors failed. Many "coincidences" and favors from people in powerful positions helped make IPS an industry leader. John also served as a highly paid consultant to some of the corporations whose pockets he had previously helped to line — taking on this role partly in response to a series of not-so-veiled threats and lucrative payoffs.

After selling IPS in 1990, John became a champion for indigenous rights and environmental movements, working especially closely with Amazon nations to help them preserve their rain forests. He wrote five books, published in many languages, about indigenous cultures, shamanism, ecology, and sustainability; taught at universities and learning centers on four continents; and founded and served on the board of directors of several leading nonprofit organizations.

Two of the nonprofit organizations he founded or cofounded, Dream Change and the Pachamama Alliance, have become models for inspiring people to make a better world, empowering individuals to create more environmentally sustainable, resource regenerative, socially just, and balanced communities. These organizations also have played major roles in helping Amazonian people protect their lands and cultures against encroaching development.

During the 1990s and into the new millennium, John honored his vow of silence about his EHM life and continued to receive lucrative corporate consulting fees. He assuaged his guilt by applying to his nonprofit work much of the money he earned as a consultant. Arts & Entertainment television featured him in a special titled *Headhunters of the Amazon*, narrated by Leonard Nimoy. Italian *Cosmopolitan* ran a major article on his workshops in Europe that focused on inspiring participants to experience individual transformation and to take actions that create more harmonious relationships between human societies and the planet. *Time* magazine selected Dream Change as one of the thirteen organizations in the world whose websites best reflect the ideals and goals of Earth Day.

Then came September 11, 2001. The terrible events of that day led John to drop the veil of secrecy around his life as an EHM, to ignore the threats and bribes, and to write *Confessions of an Economic Hit Man*. He came to believe in his responsibility to share his insider knowledge about the role that the US government, multinational "aid" organizations, and corporations have played in bringing the world to a place where such an event could occur. He wanted to expose the fact that EHMs are more ubiquitous today than ever before. He felt that he owed this to his country, to his daughter, to all the people around the world who suffer because of the work he and his peers have done, and to himself. In this book, he outlined the dangerous path his country is taking as it moves away from the original ideals of the American republic and toward a quest for global empire.

Confessions of an Economic Hit Man became an international best seller. It spent more than seventy weeks on the *New York Times* best seller list, has sold more than 1.25 million copies, and has been published in more than thirty languages. It launched John on a global speaking tour that has continued ever since. He has taken worldwide his message of the need to replace the death economy with a life economy, speaking at corporate summits, to large groups of CEOs and other business leaders; and at consumer conferences and music festivals; and he has taught or lectured at more than fifty universities.

John has been featured on ABC, NBC, CNN, CNBC, NPR, A&E, and the History Channel; been interviewed in *Time*, the *New York Times*, the *Washington Post*, *Cosmopolitan*, *Elle*, *Der Spiegel*, and many other publications; and appeared in numerous documentaries, including *The End of Poverty?*, *Zeitgeist Addendum*, and *Apology of an Economic Hit Man*. He was awarded the Lennon Ono Grant for Peace and the Rainforest Action Network Challenging Business As Usual Award.

Since *Confessions of an Economic Hit Man*, John has written *The Secret History of the American Empire* (Penguin) and *Hoodwinked* (Random House). He also is the author of books on indigenous cultures and transformation, including *Shapeshifting*, *The World Is As You Dream It*, *Psychonavigation*, *Spirit of the Shuar*, and *The Stress-Free Habit* (all from Inner Traditions).

To learn more about John, to connect with him on his social channels, to order his books, to subscribe to his newsletter, or to contact him, please visit www.johnperkins.org.

To discover more about the work of Dream Change and Pachamama Alliance, two of his 501(c) organizations, please visit www.dreamchange.org and www.pachamama.org.

Berrett–Koehler
Publishers

Berrett-Koehler is an independent publisher dedicated to an ambitious mission: *connecting people and ideas to create a world that works for all.*

We believe that to truly create a better world, action is needed at all levels—individual, organizational, and societal. At the individual level, our publications help people align their lives with their values and with their aspirations for a better world. At the organizational level, our publications promote progressive leadership and management practices, socially responsible approaches to business, and humane and effective organizations. At the societal level, our publications advance social and economic justice, shared prosperity, sustainability, and new solutions to national and global issues.

A major theme of our publications is "Opening Up New Space." Berrett-Koehler titles challenge conventional thinking, introduce new ideas, and foster positive change. Their common quest is changing the underlying beliefs, mindsets, institutions, and structures that keep generating the same cycles of problems, no matter who our leaders are or what improvement programs we adopt.

We strive to practice what we preach—to operate our publishing company in line with the ideas in our books. At the core of our approach is stewardship, which we define as a deep sense of responsibility to administer the company for the benefit of all of our "stakeholder" groups: authors, customers, employees, investors, service providers, and the communities and environment around us.

We are grateful to the thousands of readers, authors, and other friends of the company who consider themselves to be part of the "BK Community." We hope that you, too, will join us in our mission.

A BK Currents Book

This book is part of our BK Currents series. BK Currents books advance social and economic justice by exploring the critical intersections between business and society. Offering a unique combination of thoughtful analysis and progressive alternatives, BK Currents books promote positive change at the national and global levels. To find out more, visit **www.bkconnection.com**.

Berrett–Koehler
Publishers

Connecting people and ideas
to create a world that works for all

Dear Reader,

Thank you for picking up this book and joining our worldwide community of Berrett-Koehler readers. We share ideas that bring positive change into people's lives, organizations, and society.

To welcome you, we'd like to offer you a free e-book. You can pick from among twelve of our bestselling books by entering the promotional code **BKP92E** here: http://www.bkconnection.com/welcome.

When you claim your free e-book, we'll also send you a copy of our e-newsletter, the *BK Communiqué*. Although you're free to unsubscribe, there are many benefits to sticking around. In every issue of our newsletter you'll find

- A free e-book
- Tips from famous authors
- Discounts on spotlight titles
- Hilarious insider publishing news
- A chance to win a prize for answering a riddle

Best of all, our readers tell us, "Your newsletter is the only one I actually read." So claim your gift today, and please stay in touch!

Sincerely,

Charlotte Ashlock
Steward of the BK Website

Questions? Comments? Contact me at bkcommunity@bkpub.com.

MIX
From responsible sources
FSC® C113845

Certified

Corporation
bcorporation.net

31901057082705